PENGUIN BOOKS

THE PROFESSION

Bill Bratton served as chief of the Los Angeles Police Department, chief of the New York City Transit Police, and commissioner of the Boston Police Department and the New York City Police Department (in both 1994 and 2014).

Peter Knobler cowrote Bill Bratton's autobiography, *Turnaround*. He has collaborated on books with Mary Matalin and James Carville, Sumner Redstone, Kareem Abdul-Jabbar, Ann Richards, David Dinkins, Donny Deutsch, and Tommy Hilfiger. He lives in New York City.

Praise for *THE PROFESSION*

"Succeeding as a centrist in public life these days can be an almost impossible task. But centrism in law enforcement may be the most delicate challenge of all. Bratton's ability to practice it was a startling phenomenon. Engaging . . . A remarkably candid account . . . A veritable encyclopedia of police tactics and culture . . . It may be true, as Yeats chillingly reminded us, that the center cannot hold. It doesn't seem to be holding in public life at the moment. But at certain times, in the right hands and circumstances, it does come forward." —*The New York Times Book Review*

"Bill Bratton is truly the Sir Robert Peel of American policing. In *The Profession*, he takes readers on a gripping literary ride-along and provides an intimate look into the complex world of policing. The knowledge gleaned from this book can't be found elsewhere." —Art Acevedo, chief of police, Miami Police Department

"From no matter what angle you look at the debate of how we police ourselves, this book is timely and vitally important. Half memoir, half philosophy, this is the bible on police reform and reconciliation with community. Told by a man who changed policing in three major cities, *The Profession* by Bill Bratton brings deep and new understanding to what it means to protect and serve—from both sides of the badge." —Michael Connelly, author of *The Law of Innocence*

THE
PROFESSION

A MEMOIR OF

POLICING IN AMERICA

BILL BRATTON AND PETER KNOBLER

PENGUIN BOOKS

PENGUIN BOOKS
An imprint of Penguin Random House LLC
penguinrandomhouse.com

First published in the United States of America by Penguin Press,
an imprint of Penguin Random House LLC, 2021
Published with a new epilogue in Penguin Books 2022

p. 4 (*top*) of insert: *Boston Globe* via Getty Images; p. 4 (*bottom*): Rita Barros via Getty Images;
p. 6: from *Time*. © 1996 TIME USA LLC. All rights reserved. Used under license; p. 12 (*top*):
New York Daily News via Getty Images. All other images courtesy of the author.

ISBN 9780525558217 (paperback)

THE LIBRARY OF CONGRESS HAS CATALOGED THE HARDCOVER EDITION AS FOLLOWS:

Names: Bratton, William J., author. | Knobler, Peter, author.
Title: The profession : a memoir of community, race, and the arc of
policing in America / Bill Bratton and Peter Knobler.
Description: New York : Penguin Press, [2021] | Includes index.
Identifiers: LCCN 2020045815 (print) | LCCN 2020045816 (ebook) |
ISBN 9780525558194 (hardcover) | ISBN 9780525558200 (ebook)
Subjects: LCSH: Bratton, William J. | Police—United States—Biography. |
Police administration—United States. | Police-community relations—United States. |
Crime prevention—United States. | Police misconduct—United States. |
Racism—United States. | Discrimination in law enforcement—United States.
Classification: LCC HV7911.B72 A3 2021 (print) |
LCC HV7911.B72 (ebook) | DDC 363.2092 [B]—dc23
LC record available at https://lccn.loc.gov/2020045815
LC ebook record available at https://lccn.loc.gov/2020045816

Printed in the United States of America
1st Printing

BOOK DESIGN BY LUCIA BERNARD

The Profession is dedicated to the more than twenty-two thousand law enforcement officers who have died in the line of duty and whose names are enshrined on the National Police Memorial in Washington, DC. Their ultimate sacrifice will never be forgotten. Cops Count—Police Matter.

To my extraordinary wife and partner, Rikki, for her love, support, guidance, and sacrifices over the last twenty-five years. Without her, the last twenty-five of the fifty years recounted in this memoir would have been very different.

—WJB

To Daniel

—PK

THOSE WHO DON'T STUDY HISTORY ARE DOOMED TO REPEAT IT,
AND THOSE WHO STUDY POLICING KNOW WE DON'T STUDY HISTORY.

—JOHN TIMONEY, NYPD

CONTENTS

CHAPTER I

The Assassination of Rafael Ramos and Wenjian Liu

On Saturday, December 20, 2014, Ismaaiyl Abdullah Brinsley woke up in Baltimore and thought about killing himself. He'd been arrested twenty times, his friends had robbed and pistol-whipped him, and his girlfriend had dumped him. He still had her key, so at approximately 5:30 that morning he went to her house and put a silver Taurus 9mm pistol to his head. After she talked him out of it, he shot her in the gut and ran.

Now what? Brinsley could imagine the word on the street: he was a loser who couldn't even do suicide right and didn't have the balls to kill his girlfriend; he'd only wounded her. He decided to go back to Brooklyn, where he was raised.

Counting my time as a military police officer in Vietnam, I've been in the law enforcement business for nearly fifty years, and this kind of story is less unusual than you'd imagine. In fact, it is kind of typical. Police see a lot of men and women who have put themselves in difficult positions try to change the narrative of their life stories to transform themselves into heroes. That morning, Ismaaiyl Brinsley was a bum who was going to be sought by the law for brutalizing an innocent woman. He was going to jail. So he decided he was going to kill some cops.

That July, Eric Garner had died while struggling with New York Police Department officers, and that August, Michael Brown had been killed by a police officer in Ferguson, Missouri. That November and December, grand juries had handed down "no true bills," declining to indict the officers involved in either death. In the midst of all this, the Black Lives Matter movement rose to the fore. It had first appeared as a hashtag in the social media world associated with the trial and acquittal of George Zimmerman in the 2012 shooting of Trayvon Martin and then in the physical world in 2014 with a convergence of activists in Ferguson. Now the movement was being felt nationwide, driven in part by a roiling resentment of the police in the African American and other communities throughout the country.

Throughout New York City, every day there were daunting demonstrations—large, small, medium size—at which people were yelling at the police. Demonstrators were screaming right up in cops' faces: *All police are brutal, you are murderers, you are racists!* I know from a lifetime of police work that this is not true, but the perception had taken hold.

The anger was real, though, even if the claims were not. For some demonstrators, the shouts were meant to provoke officers to prove the protesters' points. Our men and women exhibited enormous restraint, first, in taking the face-to-face verbal, personal abuse, and second, in working hard to facilitate people's protests, by following them through the streets, blocking traffic so they could maintain their groups, setting aside appropriate sites, and making sure that demonstrators were safe while demonstrating. This is, after all, America, where the right to protest is protected by our Constitution.

All assumptions to the contrary, the police work hard to make sure free-speech demonstrations happen, and happen successfully. In cities large and small, officers maintain the peace for every kind of protest imaginable. These were different: the police were the focus, not just the peacekeepers, and they were being baited at every turn. (Not until the summer of 2020 would officers see anything like this again.) The internet traffic was all about "killer cops," "cops need to pay," "cops should be killed." The rules against advocating violence had apparently gone out the window. Our Threat Assessment and Protection Unit—TAPU—was getting buried in internet incitements to harm, assault, or kill police. They were almost overwhelmed by running these threats down. Furthermore, unlike a one-day march for nuclear nonproliferation, say, these protests were nonstop and snowballed through the fall and early winter.

With this as the backdrop, Brinsley decided to make himself into an avenger. He had stolen his ex-girlfriend's cell phone. He logged into his Instagram account. Alongside a photo of that same silver Taurus 9mm handgun he posted the message: "I'm Putting Wings On Pigs Today. They Take 1 Of Ours . . . Let's Take 2 Of Theirs #ShootThePolice #RIPEriv Garner [sic] #RIPMikeBrown."

While on the bus, Brinsley called his girlfriend's mother. She recognized the number, and thinking it was her child, picked up. Brinsley apologized for shooting her daughter. She called the Baltimore County Police. "He is on Instagram, he called me and said something, I don't remember, like 'I'm sorry' or 'I didn't mean to do it' or whatever it was."

The Baltimore County Police pinged the phone. They saw it was moving slowly northward in the direction of New York. Was Brinsley on a bus? In a car? On a train? They couldn't be sure, only that he was moving. Investigators found he had a prior address in Brooklyn; maybe he was heading there. They telephoned what they thought was the Brooklyn precinct in which that address was located. "What? Where?" said the sergeant who answered. "Not us." He referred them to the right one.

"You have an alert for this guy for attempted homicide and you think he might be headed here?" said the sergeant who answered the phone at the 70th Precinct, or the 7-0, as cops call it. "Fax us what you've got."

Brinsley arrived in Brooklyn and tossed the phone in the garbage near the Barclays Center. He told some people he ran into in the street to follow him on Instagram. He said, "Watch what I'm going to do."

Baltimore had made a wanted flyer. It read, "Please use extreme caution. Threats on police." The scan arrived at the 7-0 at 2:46 p.m. At 2:47 Brinsley stood in Bedford-Stuyvesant at the passenger-side window of an NYPD cruiser. Inside were Police Officers Rafael Ramos and Wenjian Liu.

Rafael Ramos had entered the Police Academy at age thirty-seven, more than a decade older than the average starting cop. He was married, with two sons, and both at work and home Ramos was the picture of a person who cared deeply about the young. He joined the NYPD as a school safety agent and worked his way up to officer. He had been on the force only three years. Ramos was studying to be a chaplain; he was eleven days past his fortieth birthday.

Wenjian Liu left his native China when he was twelve years old. He called himself Joe and had been on the path to becoming an accountant when 9/11 changed his thinking. He first joined the NYPD as an auxiliary officer—an unpaid volunteer with no gun, just a uniform and a star-shaped shield. When two of his auxiliary brothers were murdered by a madman in Greenwich Village, he could have turned away. He could have said it wasn't worth it. Instead, four months later, he took the oath to become a New York City police officer.

Liu often cooked for his immigrant parents—he made a great vegetable soup. He was an avid fisherman. He had just gotten married that October. Liu was thirty-two years old and had been on the job seven years.

At almost the same moment the Baltimore wanted flyer came out of the 7-0 precinct's printer, Brinsley fired four shots through the cruiser's window, shattering the glass and hitting both Ramos and Liu in the head. The guy who was trying to recast himself as some kind of racial avenger had picked two officers who were part of the growing number of minority officers in the NYPD.

Two Con Ed workers who were stopped at a red light witnessed the shooting. They called 911 and followed Brinsley and tried to confront him, but he turned the weapon on them. "You want some of this?" They backed off, but after they saw him go down into the Myrtle-Willoughby Avenues G train subway station, they flagged down a patrol car and told the cops where to find him. In hot pursuit, the officers cornered Brinsley on the platform. He shot himself in the head and died. Ramos and Liu were rushed to the closest hospital, Woodhull, and into the emergency room.

My wife, Rikki Klieman, and I had gone home for the holidays to Boston, where I was born. Normally I would have had my security detail run me up there and back. But because it was Christmas and the wife of Detective Rahkim Fareaux, a member of my detail, was close to giving birth, I had opted to drive a department car myself; at least if something were to happen in the middle of the night and planes and trains weren't running, I would have the means to get back.

We were in our hotel when my BlackBerry went off. It was Mayor Bill de Blasio. "We have two cops shot in Brooklyn." I immediately called the head of my detail, Inspector Tim Trainor, who had also been trying to reach me. It was now their job to help get me back.

I rode the red light and siren from Boston and was surprised that people were yielding on the expressway. (Boston is worse than New York about people not getting out of the way of emergency vehicles.) I was working the phones, trying to get the details on the condition of the officers and find the quickest way to get to New York. At the Rhode Island state line I was greeted with a police escort to Green Airport in Warwick, where an NYPD helicopter was waiting.

The emotion and anxiety were high—one of the most terrible parts of the NYPD commissioner's job is dealing with the death of officers under one's command. But at the same time, I was trying to project a degree of calm, even over the phone, that would reassure the people of the department that they were in good hands and that we would move forward with clear purpose.

When cops get shot, as police commissioner you always have the same reaction: you're deeply concerned for their safety—How badly are they injured? Is it debilitating? Life threatening?—because often you don't know. But you have to put your emotions aside while your experience and training kick in and your brain starts to focus on a list of questions to be answered: What happened? Why did it happen? Who did it? What are we doing about it?

At that initial stage I wasn't directing anything; a set of well-designed protocols had been put into action.

We landed the chopper in Brooklyn on a ball field at Bushwick High School, and it didn't take long for my security detail to drive me to the hospital. My first priority was to offer comfort to the families and to assess the impact on other officers. There is nothing that affects cops like a line-of-duty death. The anguish felt by the families of Officers Ramos and Liu and the collective family of the NYPD was palpable.

Lieutenant Special Assignment Eugene Whyte, in the Office of the Deputy Commissioner of Public Information, had been off duty, but he was heading down the FDR Drive to get some work in at NYPD headquarters at One Police Plaza in lower Manhattan. His unmarked police car's radio, tuned to the municipal frequency Citywide 1, came alive with a woman's voice. She was shrieking.

"They're shot!"

The address was in Brooklyn. Whyte didn't have a native's intelligence of the borough—he was not, as he says, "good with Brooklyn"—but he happened to be at the Brooklyn Bridge on-ramp and flew over. A marked radio car passed, going lights and sirens, so Gene fell in behind it; the officers couldn't be going anywhere else. Gene thought there must have been a highway cop at the wheel—driving like a professional maniac, clearing parked cars by only inches on each side as they shot down one-way streets. Gene barely breathed, as if sucking in his gut would pull in his car doors.

Over the radio the sergeant on the scene was calling desperately for an ambulance—*"Get a bus, get a bus!!!"*

When Whyte arrived, Ramos was on the ground, his blood-soaked vest removed, cops pumping his chest. The sergeant stood up and Whyte ran over. "Are you okay?" The sergeant was covered in blood and Whyte thought maybe he had been shot.

"Sir, sir, I had just given them a scratch!" In the old days, in order to verify that a police officer was where he said he was, a supervisor would cruise by the patrol post and initial the cop's memo book. No one could take the time to write out his full name, and the affirmation quickly evolved into a series of check marks or quick notations. No need for penmanship. The sergeant would give his patrolmen a "scratch." Assigned to stay at their post for an hour or so, Ramos and Liu had just gotten their sarge's scratch when Brinsley had come around and shot them through the passenger-side window.

"I just walked away, and I heard the shots and I ran right back!" The sergeant was overwrought.

Whyte looked at him. "Get this guy to the hospital."

The sergeant was having none of it. "I'm good, I've gotta stay here."

Whyte stood curbside next to the hydrant at which Ramos and Liu had parked. Officer Liu was collapsed on his left side, under a blanket of shattered glass. Blood was pooled in thick clots on the seat and the floor. A McDonald's cheeseburger wrapper lay crumpled in the seat behind him.

Whyte realized the need to organize. It was not his role as a press officer to attend to procedural matters, but he said to the sergeant, "We've got to get people up on the roofs here."

"They got the guy," the sergeant said. "He's down in the train station. He's dead."

"Okay, that's good. But there's a lot of people coming here, and there's a lot of cops. I am afraid we're going to get airmail." Stuff flying down from the roofs. "This is a crime scene, we have got to get posts in there. Who is the highest-ranking guy?"

"The duty chief is on his way."

Word was out, and cops were motoring to the scene. Three-star chief

Tom Purtell arrived quickly. He had run the department's rescue and recovery operations at Ground Zero after the 9/11 attacks. Purtell grabbed Whyte for a briefing.

"What's going on?"

"That sergeant," said Whyte, "we got to get him out of here."

"Okay."

"We have to start taking control of this area, because it is a really bad scene; the cops are really upset, we need to start freezing it down, locking it, and making sure nobody else gets hurt."

Chief Purtell said, "We got to be careful. There might be other guys out here."

At this point, officers on scene knew next to nothing about the perpetrator, his background, or his motives. Was this a random act of irrational individual mayhem, or something else? Were there accomplices? We didn't know what was going on.

As the leader of the uniformed forces, Chief Purtell took control of the area. He grabbed all the bosses, brought them into a nearby church auditorium, and began laying out what they had to do.

The ambush of two cops would be a major press event. Lieutenant Whyte needed people at the hospital.

Greg Longworth, who had been my security detail number one when I was commissioner in 1994 and was now a lawyer for the Patrolmen's Benevolent Association—the police union—had spent the morning in New Jersey buying gifts for the holidays and had been about to drive back into the city through the Lincoln Tunnel. Greg could tell from the sound of the transmissions and his contacts at the hospital that this was going to be an ugly scene, and he didn't want to trivialize the situation by showing up with a Christmas tree strapped to his roof, so he pulled over and left the evergreen on the side of the road, hoping it would still be there whenever he got back to collect it.

He arrived at Woodhull Hospital to find a chaotic scene. In a big surgical operating room in the emergency room, the doctors and nurses worked frantically to prevent the worst from happening. It was pandemonium. In his years on the job, Greg thought to himself, he had never seen two cops being operated on in the same room at the same time.

The medical staff at Woodhull were magnificent. They did as good a job as any other top-performing New York City trauma center. Teams of more than six doctors and nurses each worked on both men for over an hour.

They couldn't keep enough plasma in Liu; they couldn't suture the head wound. Every time doctors put a bag of blood in his arm and pumped his heart hard in compression, his fluid shot out and hit the ceiling. They did everything they could, but they called him first. He was gone.

A young Black nurse wearing a New York Giants sweatshirt gave Ramos CPR for over an hour. She straddled him and kept pushing on his chest so hard that Longworth thought she was going to have a heart attack herself. She was covered in blood, but if she stopped, Ramos was gone; so when she asked, Greg and some others helped remove her saturated sweatshirt. It fell to the linoleum floor with a thud. Soaking wet, wearing only her bra and scrub pants, she continued applying chest compressions. But it was no good: both men had essentially been dead on arrival. (Greg and others representing the PBA returned to Woodhull weeks later and thanked the nurse for her extraordinary efforts.)

Chief of Department Jimmy O'Neill was at home in his apartment in Bronxville when he got a call from John Schell, the commanding officer of the 79th Precinct, at the scene. As Chief of Patrol, Jimmy had personally known all seventy-seven of the city's precinct, PSA, and transit district commanders. In less than two years he would be the police commissioner himself, but for now he had only been at his new job—Chief of Department, the highest uniformed officer in the NYPD—for six weeks.

"This is bad, this is really, really bad. It doesn't look like they are going to live," he was told. Jimmy jumped into his department vehicle by himself and went flying down Metropolitan Avenue to Woodhull. Upon arrival, he asked the injured officer's name and was told that it was Wenjian Liu. Jimmy knew a Joe Liu but not a Wenjian, and didn't put two and two together. Joe Liu had been borrowed from the 84th Precinct to work front-door security at the training academy on Gold Street in Brooklyn, where Jimmy worked as a chief. Jimmy had seen Liu every day as he entered the building, but for three hours he didn't know it was the same guy on the gurney, Liu was so covered in blood.

O'Neill entered the conference room, got the lowdown, and went to comfort the Ramos family. One Ramos son was away at college in Maine, but Rafael's daughter, Marissa, was at the hospital, as well as his thirteen-year-old son, Jaden. "I will just never forget the look on Jaden's face," he remembers. "The kid was absolutely lost."

He visited with the Liu family. "By my estimation," he now says, "the dad hasn't gotten one bit better since that day."

Jimmy did not know the mayor well, but in his heart he told himself, "This guy needs to go down and see these two dead cops. He needs to see the reality of it."

I was still en route when Mayor de Blasio and Public Advocate Letitia James entered the emergency room. Greg Longworth said they appeared frozen. The horror was transfixing; the mayor and Ms. James stared at Liu and seemed barely able to move.

I knew the situation was dire, but when I arrived I was still stunned to see the bodies. I had rushed so hard to get back to the city that the relief of arrival may have momentarily raised my expectations. The bodies had not yet been cleaned and prepared for removal; only the medical examiner can issue that order. Tracheotomy tubes were still in place, blood was everywhere, like a war zone. I'd served in Vietnam; I'd been in a war zone. In times of great trauma one can lose oneself. I don't remember this, but Greg Longworth tells me I was crying.

At every hospital to which a police officer is taken after a shooting, we have an established Hospital Response Plan. A room is set aside for the mayor and city government staff, the police commissioner and his executive staff, and others involved to put together the story. What do we know about what happened? What do we *not* know about what happened? And when do we *think* we are going to know? One of the guiding principles in police work is that the first story is never the last. In that room we start to piece together the puzzle. The story unfolds. Usually the middle comes together quickly. The beginning is often the hardest, because that is when the fewest people were present.

From Baltimore and Brinsley's social media entries we were starting to get a picture of the man involved in the murder. We didn't have the full portrait, but we had enough to understand what was going on. At that point we were ready to issue a statement.

Jimmy O'Neill accompanied me as I spoke to the cops from Ramos and Liu's precinct, the 8-4, before we went to the press conference. I tried to the best of my ability to comfort them as I relayed the news that both officers had passed. Emotions in that room were almost too much to bear.

As I was speaking, word began filtering up to us that, in an effort to embarrass Mayor de Blasio, who was in a protracted political battle with the Patrolmen's Benevolent Association over pay raises, there was a plan afoot to organize the crowd of grieving police officers to turn their backs on him as he addressed the city. We searched out union president Patrick Lynch, who was evidently behind the effort. "Look," we told him, "we can't tell you not to have these feelings, but this is not the time or place to express them."

Lynch denied having anything to do with it. "It's not us," he said. "They're doing this on their own." I told him, as politely as I was able, that this is not how things are done; the mayor deserves to be shown respect, particularly at a time when the city needs stability.

Jimmy O'Neill is normally a temperate man, but he was so angry, if I hadn't been there he might have punched the guy. "You are full of shit!" he told Lynch. "These guys will do whatever you tell them to! Now this is about you fuckers, instead of the two dead cops downstairs." Jimmy got hot. "For you to do this is absolutely unconscionable, it is so fucking wrong!"

Lynch insisted he had no control over his men, but that was a crock. To wage political battle when, at that moment, two cops lay nearby, dead on slabs, was beyond out of line.

The mayor and I began the walk from the temporary command center to the press conference in another part of the hospital, where we would meet the press.

When a police officer gets shot, brother and sister officers are drawn to the officer's side for support. Always. There seemed to be hundreds of police lining the corridors in Woodhull. Outside it was a cold December day, but because so many people were bundled in winter gear and crowded into such an enclosed space, the hallway filled with a strong human humidity. Everyone had a sheen, the floors were slick, and I felt a noticeable difference in climate and attitude. The overheated corridor accentuated the tension. You've heard "The air was so thick you could cut it with a knife." It felt that way.

As the mayor made his way past his police, their discontent became audible. *"Get him the fuck outta here!"* *"Fuck him, scumbag motherfucker!"* There had been grumbling earlier, but now it was so obvious that some on the mayor's staff seemed concerned about his having to walk past all these cops, for fear of somebody taking a swing at him.

My chief of staff, Chief Kevin Ward, made an attempt to order the crowd to calm down. This did not go over well. "The only thing that's gonna happen is you are going to get physically removed from here," was the prevailing sentiment. "Be careful who you think you are giving direct orders to, because these guys are not paying attention to who you are, nor do they care!"

Why did so many cops hate de Blasio? Why do they still hate him? He increased the size and scope of the NYPD by hiring two thousand new officers; he authorized and paid for new training and provided new safety equipment. But the optics were always bad. Even before he was elected, Bill de Blasio pissed off the rank and file. He ran for mayor on a platform of police reform. On the campaign trail, de Blasio talked adamantly and at great length about what he felt was the unfairness of the NYPD policy of stop-and-frisk as it was being administered by the administration of Mayor Michael Bloomberg, saying it involved the overpolicing of communities of color. One of his major campaign promises was: "I will change the police department."

Among the cops and their union there is a widespread belief that all police reformers are antipolice. This is wrongheaded: I'm a police reformer and I defy anyone to call me antipolice. But cops and the PBA see it differently. To the union, the de Blasio campaign was a direct affront to what they sincerely believed was fair and impartial policing. They heard de Blasio's words as an assault on them personally and the way they did their work on a daily basis. So from the day he was sworn in, in a ceremony that included rhetoric from an invited speaker about "the plantation called New York City," there was a widespread perception that the mayor was antipolice.

At the time de Blasio took the oath of office, the rank and file and the PBA were dealing with a significant buildup of internal resentment; they felt that the department was overdisciplining its officers for minor infractions and not rewarding them for major successes. Claiming lack of funds, the Bloomberg administration had refused to negotiate a new contract with the police union, or with any unions, for that matter. When Bloomberg left office, the entire city's union workforce was operating on expired contracts. As soon as de Blasio entered, the new mayor had to deal with 153 bargaining units. He deserves but has not received credit for negotiating with each municipal union during his first term.

The last holdout was the PBA. They wanted more. So in his relations with the cops de Blasio had to deal with the lingering hostility of his presumed antipolice sentiment, coupled with what is always first and foremost in union minds: contracts. Money is the issue unions will use as the catalyst to stir up the troops. PBA president Lynch was also up for reelection, and because of a controversial ticket-fixing scandal in the Bronx involving several PBA delegates, he had opposition. To neutralize that opposition and make the case to cops that his was their best representation, he needed a distraction, a villain to run against. De Blasio became his villain.

No mayor has had a honeymoon with the cops as far as contracts are concerned. Rudy Giuliani, in 1994–1995, refused to accede to union demands and faced the catcall "Zeros for Heroes." Bloomberg reduced the size of the department by six thousand cops, and the one contract awarded during his administration came not through successful negotiation but via an arbitration panel.

For every good reason, the police commissioner is not involved in contract negotiations, but I was sympathetic to some of the pay-raise issues. It has always driven me crazy that cops in the NYPD make the same money as sanitation workers and corrections officers. I'm sorry, but they are very different jobs. It is called parity between the uniformed unions, but nowhere in America other than New York City are sanitation workers placed on par with police or firefighters. Risking one's life every day should be recognized for the valorous and courageous job it is.

So de Blasio started his term facing a lot of pent-up anger and frustration that would only deepen during his first year. Almost immediately after he took the oath of office and was sworn in, the mayor took several actions that even worsened his relationship with the rank and file. Shortly before de Blasio was elected, federal judge Shira A. Scheindlin issued a decision in the long-running class-action lawsuit *Floyd v. City of New York*, about the police practice of stop-and-frisk. She ruled for the plaintiffs, who had sued the city and the police department alleging that the use of stop-and-frisk was racially biased, and found the NYPD's practices violated New Yorkers' Fourth Amendment rights to be free from unreasonable searches and seizures, and were also racially discriminatory in violation of the Equal Protection Clause of the Fourteenth Amendment. By increasing the number of stops in minority communities of "Blacks and Hispanics who would not have been stopped if they were white," she wrote, the NYPD's tactics amounted to a "policy of indirect racial profiling" and were therefore unconstitutional. Judge Scheindlin called for a federal monitor to oversee significant reforms, including a pilot program introducing the use of body cameras for some patrol officers, though she was "not ordering an end to the practice of stop-and-frisk." The Bloomberg administration had appealed that decision. A federal appeals court, citing previous statements by Judge Scheindlin that it said showed an appearance of partiality for the plaintiffs, removed her from the case and stayed her ruling pending resolution of the appeal. This was highly unusual, if not unprecedented.

When the new mayor came in, he immediately ordered the city's corporation counsel to withdraw the appeal, in effect enacting the remedial measures. That tore it for the cops and the union. They felt Bill de Blasio was calling them all racists, and they were offended.

The mayor and I never had a conversation about this issue. If we had, I would have lobbied very aggressively against withdrawing the appeal. First and foremost, I do not believe stop-and-frisk was racially motivated. I have many issues with my predecessor Ray Kelly's management of the department, but stop-and-frisk was not based on race. Did it have a disproportionate impact on race? It certainly did, but Judge Scheindlin's finding was about racially based intentionality, which was not present.

As Judge Scheindlin tacitly acknowledged by not demanding an end to the practice, there would be no functional policing without the ability of an officer to detain a person for questioning. The city would degenerate into chaos. I agreed that stop-and-frisk had been taken too far, but not with her conclusions and implications. For one thing, the ruling focused on cops, not the brass, and cops, who had been pressured by leadership to make these stops, were going to bear the brunt of the federal monitor. None of the restrictions percolated up to me; it was the cop in the field who was going to have to fill out all the forms. And it was the cop in the field who would be saddled with the stigma of racism.

So coming in the door, Mayor de Blasio set the wrong tone. I don't know whether he had anyone advising him on police matters prior to his appointing me as commissioner. I would have lobbied very aggressively to continue to pursue the very winnable appeal, but frankly I think I would have been overruled; I think the mayor had political interests of which he was mindful. He was, after all, elected on a platform of police reform, and the imposition of a federal monitor was a huge change. Plus, I think in his own mind he felt the ruling was appropriate.

However, in my discussions with him about the entire issue of stop-and-frisk, I found that Mayor de Blasio understood—or had come to understand—that stops are a lawful, essential policing tool. We agreed that they had been overused: every year from 2002 to 2011 there had been more stops with less impact on preventing crime and disorder, all at the expense of worsening community relations. The irony is that the unions largely agreed as well, and felt their cops had been pressured to perform stops when other, less intrusive methods of policing would have worked. That, along with the lack of contracts, had been among the points of contention they'd had with Mayor Bloomberg. But because Mayor de Blasio essentially accepted Judge Scheindlin's belief that the stops were not merely overused but were driven by bias, the unions transferred their anger and frustration at the previous administration onto the new one because they thought the new administration was potentially going to be worse, when in fact it was not. From where I sat, I saw a mayor who worked well with us, who understood and supported our policing initiatives and gave us an ample budget with which to implement them.

There were other issues. Mayor de Blasio made a series of decisions regarding the legal defense of police officers that upset many in law enforcement. He instructed the city to cease opposing the payout for the Central Park Five jogger case, in which, after confessing to the crime and spending years in prison, five young men of color had had their convictions for rape, assault, robbery, and riot vacated and then sued the city for $250 million for malicious prosecution, racial discrimination, and emotional distress.

The city's corporation counsel had analyzed the case and determined that it was very triable, but the mayor decided to settle with the young men for $41 million. DNA evidence and a confession had shown the rape to have been committed by another man, but police officers didn't and still don't believe that the investigation or interrogations were done improperly. Their feeling was that there hadn't been any impropriety on their part or on the part of the system, so why was the system going to pay out when the case had been properly tried? To a department very sensitive to the charge of systemic racism, it felt like another betrayal by the mayor.

In the investigation of the recent, highly publicized death of Eric Garner, the mayor had held a press conference at City Hall, and with several Staten Island ministers and a City Council member in attendance, made the decision to place community activist Al Sharpton directly at his side in a coequal position with the police commissioner—with me—which, according to almost every cop on the force, was unacceptable.

During my first term as NYPD commissioner, Sharpton had functioned largely as a sharp-tongued publicity-seeking political gadfly, full of sound and fury, and I had made a conscious and mostly successful effort to keep him out of the mix. In the succeeding twenty years he had come more into his own. I had met with Sharpton in Los Angeles, when I was chief of the LAPD, and had begun to get along well with him. Back in New York in 2014, I had been happy to meet with him when a prominent Black actor had been detained on suspicion of credit-card fraud—which Sharpton believed was racial profiling and was calling "shop-and-frisk"—and to discuss issues with which he and his organization were concerned. It would have been wrong not to; he had become more of a recognized and legitimized force, and was among the most prominent spokespeople for the African American community in New York, if not throughout the country. Personally, I hadn't thought about the optics of our each sitting beside the mayor at this City Hall meeting and wasn't troubled by them—it's what you *would* do—but the unions, and Rupert Murdoch's *New York Post* in particular, saw it differently. And with his comments, Sharpton did add a lot of fuel to the fire. He went on a tirade. Speaking of the mayor's son, he said, "If Dante wasn't your son, he would be a candidate for a chokehold." Speaking of the cops, he said, "You need to have people who understand that the law is what they protect and uphold—they're not above the law."

It shouldn't have been unexpected for someone in Sharpton's position to say this. The issue was that this was the mayor's meeting, and Sharpton was in effect indicting the entire department on the mayor's behalf. My natural response would have been to go across the table at him and strongly counter Sharpton's comments, but I stayed quiet so as not to embarrass the mayor. At event's end, I told the press I would "shake hands with the devil if necessary to keep this city calm, safe, and secure." This infuriated the cops and the media even more; to this day the *Post* returns to that meeting to lambaste the mayor and the department for kowtowing to Sharpton and effectively elevating his importance.

Under the Bloomberg administration, Commissioner Kelly had divested the power to prosecute civilian complaint cases from the department's attorneys and given it to the Civilian Complaint Review Board. Lower-level infractions like abuse of authority—you didn't show me your nameplate; bad memo-book entries—which might previously have occasioned a loss of three to five vacation days, were now being elevated to higher status with more dire consequences. One of the street cop's biggest fears is that of performing an assignment as ordered and not only getting disciplined, but getting sued—potentially having a personal judgment lodged and ending up living in a refrigerator box in Central Park. By extending a Bloomberg policy under which cops would no longer be represented or indemnified in lawsuits against them for actions taken when they were on the job, de Blasio stoked that fear.

So from the time de Blasio came in, the cop in the street felt: "I don't have a shot here."

Only days prior to the killing of Ramos and Liu, social justice protests had been held around the city. The *New York Post* reported on a demonstration in which participants chanted, *"What do we want? Dead cops! When do we want them? Now!"* The union and its members took tremendous exception to the fact that the mayor did not speak out immediately against an advocation of violence against the police and forcefully declare that these statements were reprehensible. Instead he chose only to acknowledge the demonstrators' right to protest, which no one was questioning. The cops felt that had the mayor not won the election in 2013, he would have been on the other side of every police barrier and in the midst of these protests. They felt that in their bones.

Then there was the statement the mayor had made less than three weeks earlier, after a grand jury had declined to indict the police officers involved in Eric Garner's death. After the decision, which was applauded by many in law enforcement but infuriated many others, the mayor, who is married to an African American woman, described having what was widely known as "the talk" with their teenage son, Dante.

"What parents have done for decades who have children of color," the mayor told ABC's George Stephanopoulos, "especially young men of color, is train them to be very careful when they have . . . an encounter with a police officer. It's different for a white child. That's just the reality in this country. And with Dante, very early on with my son, we said, look, if a police officer stops you, do everything he tells you to do, don't move suddenly, don't reach for your cell phone, because we knew, sadly, there's a greater chance it might be misinterpreted if it was a young man of color."

In another setting he said that he worried whether his son would be safe at night. "And not just from some of the painful realities of crime and violence in some of our neighborhoods, but safe from the very people they want to have faith in as their protectors.

"This is profoundly personal for me," the mayor said. "I was at the White House the other day and the president of the United States [at the time it was Barack Obama] turned to me . . . and he said that Dante reminded him of what he looked like as a teenager. He said, 'I know you see this crisis through a very personal lens.' I said to him I did, because Chirlane and I have had to talk to Dante for years about the dangers that he may face."

He called his son a "good young man, [a] law-abiding young man who never would think to do anything wrong.

"Yet, because of a history still that hangs over us, the dangers he may face, we've had to literally train him as families have all over this city for decades in how to take special care in any encounter he has with the police officers who are there to protect him."

In some communities this sounds like common sense. I didn't find those statements problematic or personally take offense. In my role as police commissioner I have had a continuing relationship with leaders of the Black community over the years, and that talk is indeed standard. You read it in books and see it in the movies: *Don't give the police any issues.* I understood that the mayor was trying to walk a thin line, respecting while not judging the approach and work of the police while at the same time speaking from the heart and making clear that the issue was personal to him and that, if he had anything to do with it, change was going to come.

Having served in Mayor Dinkins's administration (Dinkins was the city's first Black mayor) and as the city's public advocate, Mayor de Blasio was not unaware of the NYPD's history. He felt the union was right wing and had engaged in incendiary behavior, including holding a work slow-down under Mayor Lindsay and, after being egged on by mayoral candidate Rudy Giuliani, rioting in City Hall Plaza in the early 1990s. He understood that the objections were not about underlying truths but were political. He was not asked about his intent, or whether he was calling all cops racists. He would have told them, "You're not doing something wrong, I just want you to see from the eyes of these parents that their children are precious to them. I want you to see why people feel that they have to do this, and why we have to make change together."

I doubt it would have mattered if he had. All these events had added up. Everything was coming together at the same time. There was kindling, a smoldering tinder, and then all of the sudden Liu and Ramos were killed and that spark ignited everything. The cops were aflame with grief and fear and anger.

Even though de Blasio was prepared for a response he felt was fundamentally immoral but likely to happen, he still hoped that when department leadership told the union, "This is not how we honor our fallen brothers," there would be some sense of responsibility. The notion that anyone might politicize that moment or be thinking about anything but these officers and their families—de Blasio just couldn't conceive of it. Over the years I tried to help the mayor understand the union's political realities, but he had a hard time imagining that in the middle of a tragedy its leadership could be thinking of anything but the officers' families, that they could not see that this horrific scene was no place for politics.

I have lived through too many of these scenes. They are hard for police professionals, who can expect this dreadful experience sometime in their lives; they are more difficult for any elected official, any civilian, who is even less prepared. Ironically, in terms of compassion and the ability to deal with grieving families, Rudy Giuliani was the best of all of the mayors I have worked with. I used to marvel at how a man who could be so cold and distant and downright nasty would summon the compassion needed to comfort those in desperate pain.

De Blasio was still trying to find his way. This was an unimaginably difficult moment. He was there to show compassion and grief in the presence of death, while feeling the tension of being in a hostile environment. Now, together at Woodhull Hospital, fueled by emotion, he and I walked this hallway gauntlet, which had been politically constructed by the unions as part of their ongoing campaign to intimidate this mayor.

The cops' grief was palpable. They needed somewhere to put it. As more arrived and they started learning how their two brother officers had been assassinated—four shots, through a window, intentionally, by a perpetrator who said, "I'm putting wings on pigs"—the union took advantage of their emotions. As Mayor de Blasio walked down the corridors to the press conference, many cops did indeed begin to turn their backs on him.

Despite their denials, I will always believe that this whole Let's Turn Our Backs on the Mayor protest was largely orchestrated and choreographed by the union. One of the telling indicators that the fix was in was the placement of union members and trustees in key camera positions, where they could take handheld cell-phone video showing the whole scene. There was no media at the event and yet the videos made the rounds on television news and the internet.

For Patrick Lynch, these two horrific murders presented too large an opportunity to pass up. "There is blood on many hands tonight," Lynch said later that night. "Those that incited violence on the streets under the guise of protest, that tried to tear down what New York police officers did every day. That blood on the hands starts on the steps of City Hall, in the office of the mayor."

Once the press conference began, I thought Mayor de Blasio spoke well in the face of such dislike. He said, "When a police officer is murdered, it tears at the foundation of our society. It is an attack on all of us. It's an attack on everything we hold dear. We depend on our police to protect us against forces of criminality and evil. They are a foundation of our society, and when they are attacked, it is an attack on the very concept of decency. Therefore, every New Yorker should feel they, too, were attacked. Our entire city was attacked by this heinous individual."

Usually at solemn events like these the police commissioner is called upon to deliver the details—"just the facts"—while the mayor provides the sentiment. I did that. In this instance, however, I also felt the need to present my own personal feelings.

"Today," I said, "two of New York's Finest were shot and killed, with no warning, no provocation. They were, quite simply, assassinated—targeted for their uniform, and for the responsibility they embraced to keep the people of this city safe. . . .

"Tragically, too, this is not the first time this department has seen such violence. Seven times since 1972 we have seen partners murdered together, often in incidents such as this—mindless assassinations without warning.

Our officers know this, from memorial walls on our precincts and head-quarters, and from the stories they hand down. Nevertheless, they do what we expect of them. They grieve, they mourn, but then they go out on the streets of this city and work to keep it safe, every day and every night. We have never, and never will, forget that mission. We will never forget the two young men who lost their lives today."

I left the hospital and escorted the bodies to the Bellevue morgue. At many intersections stood a fire truck with its crew out saluting. At every fire station the firefighters were lined up outside. Community members lined the streets in a long procession.

The funerals of Ramos and Liu were large and wrenching affairs. It was important to me that I address their deaths, their sacrifice, in personal, institutional, and societal terms. These were men who were killed because of who they were and what they did. I turned to Assistant Commissioner Jon Murad for help.

Jon Murad was not your usual cop. He had graduated from Harvard and spent several years in Los Angeles pursuing an acting career. He had worked in the newsroom at *Newsweek* but felt uninspired, and joined the NYPD at age thirty-two. Ray Kelly had recognized his talent and pulled him from the streets into the Office of Management Analysis and Planning (OMAP), the think tank of the NYPD. He earned a second Harvard degree at the Kennedy School on a department scholarship. I gave him a six-rank promotion from sergeant to assistant commissioner, the police equivalent of jumping him from minor league A ball to the majors. When I needed words, I often looked to Murad.

Over the next few days we traveled together. We visited the Ramos and Liu families and gathered ideas to bring to the living. We found that both had been profoundly good men, murdered for wearing blue. I asked aloud, "Why do we always lose the good ones?" Jon answered, "Because it's the law of averages." Most cops are good people.

When I was chief of the Los Angeles Police Department I met an activist in the African American community named "Sweet Alice" Harris. The

LAPD had long been considered an occupying force in the Black community, but I made a great effort to include its people and leaders in our thinking. I was not fully accepted at first, but in time Sweet Alice and I got on famously. "You know why we like you, Chief?" she said. "We *see* you. You *see* us." I loved that. I thought it was the vital message that one organization, one community, one family, one individual could give to another: that no one is to be ignored, that every person needs to be acknowledged, that everyone needs to be protected and served and seen.

In my eulogy at Christ Tabernacle Church in Queens, I followed Vice President Joe Biden, who spoke about the cops he knew growing up in Scranton, and the loss he had suffered in his own life. Governor Andrew Cuomo spoke, and of course Mayor de Blasio. When my turn came, I spoke to Rafael Ramos's children:

> We're here because your dad was assassinated. That's a different word than murdered, which is awful enough.
>
> It speaks of the prominence of the person killed; it makes the crime intentional and symbolic. Your dad was assassinated because he represented something—and that's true, he did.
>
> He represented the men and women of the New York City Police Department. He was the embodiment of our motto: "fidelis ad mortem"—"faithful unto death."
>
> He represented the blue thread that holds our city together when disorder might pull it apart.
>
> He represented the public safety that is the foundation of our democracy.
>
> He represented the best of our values—as anyone can see by looking at you, and at your family. But he was also your dad.
>
> A good man, who tried hard, and sacrificed, and had a desire to serve. . . .

Rafael Ramos was assassinated because he represented all of us. Even though, beneath the uniform, he was just a good man.

And he was just your dad.

And maybe that's our challenge.

Maybe that's the reason for the struggle we're now in—as a city, as a nation.

Maybe it's because we've ALL come to see only what we represent, instead of who we are.

We don't SEE each other.

The police, the people who are angry at the police, the people who support us but want us to be better, even a madman who assassinated two men because all he could see was two uniforms, even though they were so much more.

We don't SEE each other. If we can . . .

If we can learn to SEE each other . . . to see that our cops are people like Rafael Ramos and Wenjian Liu, to see that our communities are filled with people just like them, too.

If we can learn to SEE each other, then WHEN we see each other, we'll heal. We'll heal as a Department.

We'll heal as a city.

We'll heal as a country.

What I didn't know, as I delivered these words, was that outside, among the vast crowd of some twenty thousand assembled officers, many cops had again turned their backs when Mayor de Blasio had spoken just before me. It had been an unseemly spectacle. When I found out I was furious. The idea of what was effectively a labor action being taken in the middle of a funeral where we're honoring the death of two police officers—I just don't understand it, I'm sorry—what was the need?

It certainly didn't calm tensions in the city. A minister in the Black community told one of the mayor's staff, "Do you know what people are saying in communities of color in New York City? 'If they can turn their backs on you, imagine what they can do to us!'" This was dangerous ground the union was treading. You don't do that over contract negotiations or a union election. Anyone who runs for office has to make choices about what is morally acceptable and what is not, and this went way beyond playing to the cheap seats. This was putting people's lives at risk. I found that unacceptable.

Had my predecessor as commissioner been in my position he might well have ordered the Internal Affairs Bureau to document and then punish those who had disrespected his boss, the mayor, and by implication himself. Some in my command staff were harking back to those days. "IAB needs to be out there taking photos, and every fifth guy who has turned his back gets a hammer." This was not my way. To order supervisors or executives or chiefs to take action against those cops, to go punitive, would have been counterproductive. We would have utterly lost the rank and file.

The turning of the backs developed into a weeks-long statement of antipathy for the mayor by the rank and file. The *New York Post*, a de Blasio nemesis, ran the front-page headline: TO SERVE AND REJECT. Fewer parking tickets were written, fewer summonses issued. Arrests were down, enforcement of quality-of-life laws was curtailed. Cops said out loud, "We're sitting out." There was an actual work slowdown.

Was it organized by the unions? Some chiefs felt it was. I felt the unions were responsible the night of the Ramos and Liu assassinations, and having opened that Pandora's box actually lost control of both the back turning and the slowdown. The cops were angry, and they were exhausted from dealing with all the protests, including organized street actions in which they were being confronted personally by screaming crowds calling for their murder. A protester had broken a lieutenant's nose trying to prevent him from making an arrest during a march across the Brooklyn Bridge a week before the assassinations.

New York City had been on course to see to a decrease in homicides from 2013 to 2014, but we lost the year in December—I believe because we had to pull all the citywide teams out of Brooklyn and the Bronx and insert them into Manhattan to police the marchers. There are conflicting theories as to why police presence is such a determining factor in keeping the homicide rate down, but we know that it is; that's why we do what we do. The idea that the city actually lost lives in the outer boroughs while people were in the inner borough protesting the notion of lost lives was deeply, unsettlingly ironic.

The rank and file may have wanted to prove a point. They wouldn't engage because they felt the mayor was not defending them in what they saw as a war against police officers. They felt they were back in the days of the Black Liberation Army, with cops getting ambushed and murdered in the streets. While I understood their frustrations concerning pay, any behavior that put the city at risk was unacceptable. How were we to deal with it?

I had to consider the most effective course of action, with the twin goals of keeping the city safe and reestablishing rank-and-file morale. New York needs a well-trained and highly motivated police force that earns its respect. I am aware that there is widespread skepticism these days about the honor and honesty of the men and women in police departments throughout America. But I know cops, I love cops, and I know the character that resides in the people who run toward danger, not away from it. It was my job to make them live up to their own character and fulfill their mission to prevent crime and disorder.

However, at One Police Plaza, with seventy-seven precincts and thirty-four thousand cops, it can be difficult to keep everyone on the same page. There is always the possibility of a Henry II moment—"Will no one rid me of this troublesome priest?"—in which staff, mistaking ends for means, overstep. In one precinct station, someone posted a sign saying ANYBODY WITHOUT ANY ACTIVITY FOR THIS PERIOD IS NOT GOING TO GET 28s—a 28 is the NYPD form requesting time off, so the sign said essentially that anyone who slowed down would pay for it—next to the sergeant's desk, and a photograph of it was sent to the newspapers. This caused some blow-back, but it was useful.

Let's be clear: I didn't really want the priest murdered, I just wanted somebody to go talk to him a little bit. In a nice way. Leading cops, and fighting crime for that matter, involves constant micro adjustments, like dealing with a particularly temperamental shower, where the water is constantly going from hot to cold to hot. I find it essential to gauge the city's temperature, and that of the police force, at all times. I said, "We want a velvet glove, not a hammer."

After Rafael Ramos's funeral, I issued a statement in anticipation of Wenjian Liu's. It began, "A hero's funeral is about grieving, not grievance. . . . I issue no mandates and I make no threats of discipline. But I remind you that when you don the uniform of this Department, you are bound by the tradition, honor, and decency that go with it."

Could we get it right?

The first thing to do is look at what the slowdown really was—an adjustment and a breather—and what it was not—a stoppage. Jack Maple, a Runyonesque policing genius whom I found woefully underused as a lieutenant when I was chief of the New York Transit Police, and who rose to profoundly change American policing, always used to argue that 10 percent of the cops do 50 percent of the work, while many cops are just marking time; it's not too hard to get them to stop writing tickets and summonses. If all you read was the *New York Post*, you'd think the department had ground to a halt.

But monitoring the police radio produced more nuance than the headlines would suggest. While men and women in uniform may have initiated fewer encounters, when a crime was in progress, when a description of a suspected perpetrator was distributed, when there was proactive police-work to be done—and that included stopping suspicious people, all the duties one might have thought they had stopped performing—an officer went to the scene and others fanned out to find the suspect. On the radio you could hear them out of breath, giving descriptions, chasing a guy down the street. You heard them coming from all sides to get the man who had just committed a robbery on Columbus Avenue or stolen a car up in the 2-8 precinct. You heard shots fired at them; you heard shots fired by them.

In these cops' heads they only gave up on the small stuff. The numbers were down but there was no radio backlog, felony arrests and activity response rates stayed essentially on pace, the whole place didn't just stop. Uniformed officers were choosing to say, "Hey, it's one thing for me to say 'Screw you' to my supervisor—parking summonses are about them and the numbers they report up the chain, not about me; I am not going to do this stuff that makes their job easier. But a felony, a rob run, a ten-thirty—an ongoing robbery that is happening now—I respond to that. Because that is my job."

This was the clean little secret: the cops wanted to be cops. The NYPD did not disengage from the core of police work; most officers continued to do their jobs, while for the ones who habitually underachieved, this was just another excuse to do so. Some cops stepped back from the functions they felt pleased their bosses; they wanted to show their anger but not forsake their oath. But the vital tasks that the citizens of New York City needed performed continued to be performed. Cops turned their backs on City Hall, not on the city.

There were elements of the slowdown that weren't necessarily out of keeping with my own desires for a diminishment of certain kinds of enforcement activity. The NYPD had performed 694,482 stop-and-frisks in 2011, for example. Having examined the facts and theory that went into such a huge societal disruption, we had found that my predecessor's emphasis on stops had been, in fact, counterproductive. While a large number of the almost 700,000 stops were made on the same individuals several times over—most often, people of color—almost everyone who had been pulled aside would then tell their friends and neighbors about how they were just minding their own business and had gotten rousted for no reason. And since so few of these stops resulted in arrest, the cumulative effect was that communities, particularly those of color, felt tremendous resentment, which was not only personally unpleasant for them but unproductive for us. We rely on locally sourced information in order to do our job properly. Who's going to tell a cop about a potential crime being committed in their neighborhood if that same cop has disrespected them in public? We were losing the streets. This had to stop.

During the slowdown we organized meetings with representatives of the various police unions. What could we do to bring their members back online? The discussions became intense. Louis Turco, president of the Lieutenants Benevolent Association, told us that not only his people but the sergeants and uniformed cops had transitioned from an administration under which they feared getting jammed up to one in which they were scared, not just for their livelihoods, but for their lives. This was the workforce's biggest issue: officer safety. The slowdown, he said, was almost incidental.

Most cops want to do the job as well as it can possibly be done, and appreciate when their work and life can be made more productive. In these meetings with the unions and at roll calls around the city, I told them I heard them—I heard their concerns, their complaints, their true issues. And because I was at heart a cop, I knew what this was all about. I told them, "You have four issues: pay, safety, equipment, and training. I can't work on number one; that is out of my control. But this is what I can do for you: I can advocate for you, and I can get you numbers two, three, and four."

Cops take their training seriously, but the perception among the rank and file was that previous administrations had demonstrated a distrust or lack of confidence in their capabilities. Patrol officers were not authorized to use tasers; the boss had to do it. *What are we*, officers thought, *children?* I expanded the distribution of tasers to the patrol force. I told the cop on patrol, "We are going to give you state-of-the-art equipment, train you, and we are going to trust you to use it properly."

The Liu and Ramos assassination was the catalyst for a significant number of major changes in policing, some of which we had been considering prior to the event, others that we had not discussed in any great detail. We moved toward ballistic doors and windows in our cars, which would protect officers from exactly the random close-encounter attacks that killed the two officers. Ballistic helmets and heavy-duty ballistic vests for every patrol officer in their vehicles would provide similar protection. If we expect our officers to always run toward the danger, we have an obligation, to the best of our ability, to provide for their safety.

Getting information out to the cops more quickly became imperative. Every fourteen-year-old with a smartphone and an Instagram account could move data around seamlessly. We couldn't—we were still talking about printing up flyers and passing them out to people on patrol! We weren't moving information in the snappy patter of real-time electronic communications in a new millennium; we were moving at the chatter-clatter of teletypes and machines that went back to Gutenberg. In the largest, most sophisticated, best-funded police department on planet Earth, this had to change.

With Ramos's and Liu's deaths as an accelerant, we issued every cop a custom-designed smartphone. We were one of the first police departments in America to do so. With smartphones, we could send information to cops instantaneously, no matter where they were. A major step forward in speeding our response time and the distribution of information, smartphones documented all calls and were equipped with location devices. Now even the major department accountability tool going back to the beginning of time, the memo book, could receive a sergeant's scratch electronically. At almost the exact moment a piece of paper was coming off the fax machine, a killer who had broadcast his murderous intentions had been following through on his threats. If we had broadcast the man's location and sent out his picture, perhaps Liu and Ramos would have been sufficiently forewarned to save themselves.

We also began to equip all cops with body cameras, a great advance. The vast majority of that footage, nobody watches—until something occurs, at which time it becomes vital. Some of the public may think the camera is a crucial tool because it will catch cops going beyond their lawful boundaries. We find it crucial because, in many cases, the camera documents the cop doing his job exactly as he was trained to do it.

We trust our cops. We trust our training. When I rejoined the NYPD we wanted to return to cops the ability to make enforcement decisions for themselves. So it was ironic that we were able to trust our officers, and at the same time have the ability to monitor them all the more closely. In policing, accountability and discretion are equally essential. In the twenty-first century, we had a remarkable confluence: significant growth in the means of accountability, and the expansion and support of our officers' discretion. Our emphasis on technology was awakened and continues.

During the slowdown, cops gave us a road map. Not one that they developed intentionally, because that job action was a lesson in herd decision making, but one in which they showed they were in fact capable of maintaining response and enforcement on important cases while easing up on the others. Cops were saying among themselves, "Hey, don't stop working entirely." They understood their role.

But we could not allow them to do nothing for five tours a week. If we couldn't track their effectiveness through the paperwork of arrests or summonses, how could we be certain they were addressing the conditions that those encounters were designed to address—the necessity of keeping watch on the small stuff before it became big stuff?

We needed to find better ways to get cops to do their job. Cops protect their community and engage with the people who live in it. They stem disorder and enforce the law. How could we measure their effectiveness while staying in the lane of contractual obligations, not overreaching or overextending? A cashier at Target has a manager directly watching his performance. In policing, we have two police officers on patrol who are entrusted to work in large part absent moment-to-moment supervision. How do we evaluate a police officer's conduct? Fulfilling quotas did not necessarily translate to effective police work; so how could we capture stellar and less-than-stellar behavior?

One way was through positional accountability. Automatic Vehicle Locators went into the cars. They gave us proof that Officer Jones was out there where we wanted her to be, and Officer Jones had the opportunity to write it up after the fact to prove she was doing what we wanted her to do. The cops were fully aware that the new technology, from the smartphones to the body cameras to the AVL, contained a permanent record of everything they did and every place they went. That in itself engendered a sense of accountability.

The cops came back online on their own, because they weren't tired anymore, and because we pushed ahead with projects and programs that mattered to them—including better training, better equipment, and new missions.

The murders slowed the protest movement as well. Some hard-core antipolice activists may have been happy about the killing of cops, but the vast majority of New Yorkers were horrified. As a result, I think many people who even the weekend before might have been in the streets saying, "Cops are horrible and the criminal justice system needs to be reformed," took a pause and saw these two guys for the human beings they were: a Latino pastor and an immigrant Asian, as far from the stereotypical picture of the brutal, hulking, jerk cop as you can get. Their devastating murders took the wind out of a lot of people's sails.

The NYPD found diversity even in death. There was a terrible irony in the fact that, over a short span of time—during which there was turmoil in the streets and the department was being accused of widespread racial insensitivity—the NYPD lost a white cop whose father had been a sergeant and whose every brother and cousin was a cop; a Latino who had been a school safety agent and a pastor; a Chinese immigrant who had begun as an auxiliary police officer; and a Black cop whose dad had been a cop in the Caribbean, and who had emigrated and turned into a really good police officer. That is a picture of the department that is news to some, but not to us.

The Liu family was loud with its grief at Woodhull. Liu's father dealt with that passion in a very open way that was sometimes hard to watch. He would wail. Liu and his wife, Sanny, had been trying to conceive a child. She had sadly endured a number of miscarriages and they were in the midst of trying again. When she was asked whether Liu was going to be an organ donor, to extend other people's lives after the end of his own, Mrs. Liu asked if his sperm could be preserved. Liu had passed several hours earlier, but NYPD's chief medical surgeon, Dr. Eli Kleinman, performed the procedure.

Out of death, life. Wenjian and Sanny Liu's daughter, Angelina, was born July 27, 2017.

CHAPTER 2

1970s: Boston Strong-Arm

I n 1919, looking to improve their wages and conditions, Boston police officers made an effort to unionize under the American Federation of Labor. Police Commissioner Edwin Upton Curtis denied that the men had a right to bargain collectively—trade unionization was still a radical idea at the time—and after efforts to craft an agreement with the mayor and the city administration failed, the cops went on strike.

With no law enforcement presence, the streets devolved into unrest and violence. Nine people were killed. The press called the striking officers Bolsheviks, deserters, and "agents of Lenin." The Massachusetts State Guard, bolstered by volunteers, secured the city by force. The strike lasted four days, after which the striking officers were fired and replaced by fifteen hundred new workers with higher wages. (That did it for unionization. The Boston Police Patrolmen's Association didn't get formed until forty-six years later—1965—and then only after a state law was passed giving state and municipal workers the right to organize. But even that law explicitly withholds from cops the right to strike.)

Many of the new cops were World War I veterans. "The War to End All Wars" had ended ten months earlier and these men were military, fresh from the trenches, ready and primed to obey orders and follow the chain of command. The Boston Police Department had a blunt and authoritarian history and these cops fit right in. If a policeman said "Stop!" you stopped. If you didn't, and they caught you, you'd get cuffed across the head and you'd never run again. Absolute authoritarians.

Once on the job, cops didn't leave. It was good work and the police culture was enveloping; they put in their thirty years, and because they had all come on the job together, most retired at the same time, the late 1940s, just as World War II was ending. Who got hired to replace them? World War II veterans—men who subscribed to the same kind of thinking. And twenty years later, who replaced them? Vietnam War vets. Another generation of military. Every twenty to thirty years, Boston was rolling over entire police departments.

I wanted to be a police officer since before I can remember. When I was a year and a half old, in the dead of winter, my mother brought me outside to play in the yard behind our small Cambridge, Massachusetts, basement apartment and went back inside for a moment. My mother, June, was usually extremely careful about my well-being; I had been born with a collapsed lung and had received last rites at the hospital when I was two days old. I survived, but she remained very vigilant.

Not this time.

When my mother came out, I was gone. She heard frantic honking, ran toward it, and found me—zipped into my snowsuit and cap, all eighteen inches of me—standing in the middle of Massachusetts Avenue, directing traffic. Of course I don't remember any of this, but from then on my parents joked that they knew I wanted to be a cop.

I grew up in a working-class family on the second floor of a three-decker in the Dorchester section of Boston. Dorchester was lace-curtain Irish, but we Brattons were Irish-French Canadian. My father, Big Bill—I was always Little Billy—was public high school–educated and principled. Perhaps because he came from so little, he was always conscious of abuse of authority and always resisted it. He grew up dirt poor in the all-white Boston neighborhood of Charlestown, in an environment in which the

N-word was not uncommon, and joined the Navy at age eighteen during World War II, where he encountered no Blacks. After the war, he found work as a mail sorter at the post office, the kind of job poor people crave, a civil service position secure forever. The post office was one of the federal agencies that started bringing in workers of color.

My dad worked two jobs most of his life, just to get by: nights at the post office and days at a chrome-plating company in all-Black Roxbury Crossing. Every week he'd give my mother his pay. Many afternoons at 4:00 I'd look out our window, see my father coming home for supper—which we ate at 4:30—and go running out to meet him. I didn't get much time with my dad.

He had his own code. After I got my learner's permit, my dad used to take me out for driving lessons every Sunday. One morning we were stopped at a light, and when it turned green the two cops stopped in front of us just kept sitting. "Toot your horn," he told me.

"Dad, they're cops."

"I don't care, toot your horn. The light is green."

Sure enough they pulled us over. They both ambled to our car and the lead cop cocked one arm on the roof above my head and kept the other at his gun belt. "Who the fuck do you think you are?" he said.

My dad being my dad, glared at him from the shotgun seat and told him, "The light was green." He wasn't going to let anybody push him around and he didn't let up.

Dorchester was a segregated community and I went to all-white schools. Standing on the corner, if a Black man, woman, or child walked through the neighborhood—it didn't happen often—we were acutely aware of them. I love my parents, but it wasn't until later in their lives that they stopped using occasional racial slurs, and then only because my sister, Pat, and I went after them to cut it out.

My father's best friend at the plating plant was Jack Williams, a Black man. I had the great good fortune to work beside them part time for a summer—an experience few of my street friends had the opportunity to share—which I think had something to do with my not turning out with backward racial ideas like so many of my Boston contemporaries. Jack was a great guy, not a man I would ever have run into on my own.

Yet my father occasionally tossed around the N-word. He was not particularly a bigot, but he was a product of his times. The 1950s Boston we kids grew up in was not overtly bigoted, but ruled by that subliminal northern racism that fostered redlined neighborhood boundaries into which real estate agents would guide only "appropriate" people. Not that my friends and I were consciously aware of this.

At the corner of Arcadia Street in Dorchester stood a beautiful redbrick building that housed both Boston Police District 11 and a branch of the Boston Public Library. It was one of my favorite structures, housing my two passions. I sat for hours with one young-adult Civil War novel after another, and when I was eleven years old found a 1956 picture book, *Our Police*, that changed my life forever. A child's history of the New York Police Department, *Our Police* was filled with colorful illustrations of every manner of NYPD minutiae. (Today, a copy is still one of my most prized possessions, which I intend to pass on to my grandsons.) I didn't know any cops—no one in my family was a cop—but between *Badge 714* and *Dragnet* on TV and so many fifties black-and-white movies in the theaters, policing was all I truly cared about. Here were squad cars and motorcycles, as well as all the paraphernalia every officer carried with him on the New York streets. I saw call boxes, helicopters, emergency vehicles—a full complement of real objects to fulfill a fantasy. I took that book out regularly for years. Sometimes I would just walk over and visit it.

And right in the same building were real police officers.

In October 1970, a day after my twenty-third birthday, I became one of them.

I was back from Vietnam, where I'd served in the 212th Sentry Dog Company, Eighteenth Military Police Brigade. My dog, Duchess, and I had spent the first night of the Tet Offensive under attack while guarding the Long Binh ammunition dump; the truck that picked us up was so hot from the exploding stockpiles of bombs and napalm that men burned their hands while climbing on board and our dogs howled as their feet fried on its metal bed. My post was farthest from the compound and closest to the jungle; the kid at the post next to mine was killed. In my eleven months in-country, I spent only two or three nights under fire, but that was plenty.

When I joined the Boston Police Department, what I found was not a profession. Policing may have been called a profession, but it wasn't one. There was no body of knowledge, few highly educated people were at the top, and by and large its workforce was considered laborers rather than professionals—grunts, people who had to be controlled.

In 1970, the prevailing opinion among law enforcement practitioners, city officials, academics, and the public at large was that the police's function was to respond to reports of crime that had already taken place and do our best to apprehend the people who committed them. That was our job: to hunt down criminals after they'd struck. Success was judged by the speed with which we could patch the tear in the fabric of society. Cops *chased* crime; we were not responsible for decreasing criminality, because of the overriding belief that there was nothing we could do about it. Why?

It was a time of phenomenal turmoil in the United States. In the late 1960s, rioting in Black communities had drawn attention to the conditions in what were known at the time as Negro neighborhoods, often referred to simply as ghettos. In 1965, with an executive order, President Lyndon Johnson established the President's Commission on Law Enforcement and Administration of Justice to investigate policing and "the problems of crime in our nation." During the long, hot summers of 1965 through 1967, Watts and Chicago and Detroit and Newark had all gone up in flames. In 1967 alone, America was rocked by more than 150 race riots. In response, President Johnson authorized a wide-ranging study, the National Advisory Commission on Civil Disorders—known as the Kerner Commission after its chair, Illinois governor Otto Kerner Jr.—to find out: What happened? Why did it happen? What can be done to prevent it from happening again and again? That commission spent seven months investigating, and in

February 1968 issued what became known as the Kerner Report, which along with the 1967 President's Commission report was the most exhaustive analysis of policing done to date. Its findings were societal:

"Our nation is moving toward two societies, one Black, one white—separate and unequal. . . . What white Americans have never fully understood but what the Negro can never forget—is that white society is deeply implicated in the ghetto." (The terminology is dated but the main thrust of the argument continues to be accurate to this day.) "White institutions created it, white institutions maintain it, and white society condones it."

The report's solutions were also societal. Divided among the headings Employment, Education, the Welfare System, and Housing, the Kerner Report prescribed welcome and necessary changes in the way people of color were afforded access to equal standing in the economic and social functioning of America. Well intentioned, well researched, and well stated, the report correctly defined the racial problems that were roiling America then and continue to bedevil us today. What it did not do was include law enforcement in the equation.

Essentially, the President's Commission and the Kerner Report told police that they couldn't prevent crime because the causes were so vast and cultural as to be beyond police influence or control. This was perniciously wrong. The idea that police can't have any impact on the prevention of crime—that the rates and control of crime could be affected only by changes in society—set law enforcement on the wrong course for thirty years.

The history of American policing to that point was not glorious. The role of plantation policing in the South was contain and control, to keep slaves powerless and confined to the land ruled by their owners. In the 1700s and 1800s, police were the slave catchers, hunting down runaways and keeping the system operational. In a Los Angeles slave artifact store, I was shown a badge from Green Acres Plantation that looked remarkably like today's urban badges from places like Boston and Los Angeles—a physical confirmation of the evolution of containment-suppression policing.

In the mid-nineteenth and early twentieth centuries, police often served as management enforcers in the widespread and violent strife surrounding the creation of the labor union movement. In the South, before and after World War II, cops enforced Jim Crow laws, and police were constantly the man in the middle of desegregation in the North. (Literally the *man* in the middle; female officers were almost unheard of.) Police were used in many instances to enforce laws that were oppressive, whether you were Black and asserting your rights or a college kid feeling that government was not being responsive to your concerns about the Vietnam War. Police were thought to be corrupt, unprofessional, brutal, racist. Too many were all of those things.

And yet, most officers throughout the country were drawn to duty because they wanted to serve and make their communities better places to live. For the most part, police kept our streets safe and maintained order in increasingly disorderly times. "Officer Friendly" was both myth and reality. This was the world of policing I was entering. The man in the middle. Or as one of my predecessors as NYPD commissioner, Teddy Roosevelt, might have described them, "the man in the arena." Our mission was truly uncertain.

For the first time, the President's Commission on Law Enforcement diagrammed the criminal justice system, demonstrating that its elements—policing, prosecution, corrections—were not independent, isolated activities, but came together to create a functioning whole, an institution. And within that institution, that system, the commission began to consider the role of police. The Law Enforcement Assistance Administration (LEAA), headed by three commissioners, was formed to conceive and create new initiatives to encourage the drive for professionalism in policing. Money was a key. Federal grants were established to modernize police forces around America by providing them with two elements: equipment and education. The battle for funding began almost immediately.

Equally important was the creation of the Law Enforcement Education Program (LEEP). In order to advance the profession it was decided that officers ought to get a college education. Prior generations of police officers had not been likely candidates, and it showed. Under LEEP, officers could apply for funding to pursue a college degree in criminal justice. The money didn't flow to the officers directly; it was administered by the institutions, which were thus incentivized to establish criminal justice curricula where there had been none. Federal funds facilitated the academic study and advancement of policing. A new world was being created.

The LEEP plan was laudable but not without its downside.

At Massasoit Community College in Boston, for instance, the course instructors were simply the few active police officers who held college degrees, and they presented very much the same material recruits had been learning for decades at the Police Academy. There were very few real standards and no advances. One earnest civilian professor found himself teaching a class of state police officers who were just there to get the degree and the concomitant raise in pay. As long as they stayed in the classroom, they would get certified. Learning, changing viewpoints, advancing police theory and practice were not goals. The professor, being naive about cops, expected them to do the work. His expectations were not met. The Staties didn't write the papers, didn't pass the exams, and worse, didn't seem to care. He flunked the whole lot of them. Massasoit got such pushback that they didn't invite the professor to teach the next semester.

How was the LEEP money to be spent? One of the new Department of Justice entity's three members, former Philadelphia Assistant Public Defender and Chief Assistant District Attorney Charles Rogovin became frustrated by the fact that the other commissioners were giving short shrift to education while focusing solely on providing equipment. This disagreement led him to begin discussions with the Ford Foundation, which in a visionary moment provided funding to create a new organization, the Police Foundation. Ford gave this fledgling organization $30 million, which is an estimable sum now but in 1970 was an enormous amount of money. Rogovin left the LEAA and became the Police Foundation's first president.

The new organization's goal was "to advance policing through innovation and science." Of course it had no institutional memory, and at first not a lot of operational knowledge.

I had just turned twenty-three years old. What did I know about any of this?

Numbering 157, the Boston Police Department Class of 1970 was the largest since the 1919 repopulation. The city, at that time approximately 25 percent minority, employed 2,800 cops, of which 55 were African American and only a few were Hispanic. The badge said "Patrolman." No women—they didn't come into the department until 1973. (It wasn't until 1997 that the BPD finally changed the rank and the badge to the gender-neutral "Police Officer.") I believe there were three Black officers in my class—my friend Joey Bishop was one—and one Latino.

I joined on October 7 and was immediately sent to the Police Academy, where we spent six weeks trying to learn how to be policemen, from the ground up. The Monday after Thanksgiving they outfitted us in blue police uniforms, as opposed to recruit khakis, gave us our guns and badges, and sent us out into the streets on traffic duty during the Christmas rush. During that era there were no shopping malls; everybody came into downtown Boston to shop. We had no idea what we were doing.

After about two weeks of directing traffic in uniform—looking like school guards, with white traffic straps across our chests—they put us into plain clothes, at much higher risk, searching for pickpockets and shoplifters in the various department stores and the subway system. Supervision? Two old-time detectives who basically deposited us downtown and disappeared into barrooms until late in the afternoon. Police training, as far as teaching a new generation of recruits how to be cops, was deficient to nonexistent.

When they brought us back into the Academy after Christmas we thought we were veterans. Each of us had had experiences. We had been to

Paris! The instructors had a hard time training us; in fact they couldn't wait to get rid of us because we had become unmanageable. Three months earlier we'd known nothing; now, as far as we were concerned, we knew it all. Our class was nicknamed the Wild Geese. Like young men in Ireland, we had effectively flown away beyond their control.

My first life-threatening experience as a police officer happened alongside fellow recruit Frank Corbosiero. Frankie and I were working plainclothes in the Washington Street subway station and grabbed a Black kid after he'd picked a rider's pocket. We scooped him up and threw him against the wall and immediately were surrounded by a large crowd of people who, in that particular subway stop, were on their way to the Black community of Roxbury. The young man saw the crowd and started mouthing off. So there we were, two white guys—the crowd didn't know who we were or what was going on—hassling some Black kid. The crowd was getting angry, the kid was struggling. Frank was trying to hold him against the wall and I took out my badge and folded it up for the crowd to see. *"Police!"* This didn't produce the intended effect. Then I took out my gun, which we had been taught in the Academy to do only in times of extraordinary danger. Fortunately, at that moment two uniformed transit cops, alerted by the noise and commotion, showed up on the platform and had enough policing technique to bring things under control.

I had been afraid of the crowd but had not been taught how to handle either the fear or the situation, to the point where I had endangered us all. My recognition of our lack of even the most rudimentary training stayed with me.

Some of the Academy training at the time reflected the dramatic change in policing coming out of the sixties. Rather than focus on improving the quality of life in the neighborhoods we patrolled, police were instructed to concentrate on serious crime, particularly in the Black community. (Latino communities were hardly ever mentioned.) The rules of the game were changing dramatically. Police were being told that what we had been doing for a hundred years no longer worked, that in fact it served to alienate, and that our focus would have to change.

This was not guaranteed to happen.

Policing, I found, was what I call a sensing-thinking-judging world.

Sensing: Show me what happened. I will see it, feel it, touch it.

Thinking: Is the issue black-and-white? They violated the law or they didn't. "The guy had a gun, I had to shoot—what's the problem?" "The grandfather called us because he was protecting himself from the crazy son who was trying to kill him, and now we did it for him. We killed him, yeah, but we had no choice."

Judging: We approach a case to close it, to get it done. "Give me a call, I get there, I solve it, I'm done with it, I'm moving on to the next call. Don't tell me that I have to solve the problem and keep that case open, or that I might have to get resources to work with the family or with the community; that is leaving things too open and I am not good about that."

The sensing-thinking-judging personality type is called the guardian. Guardians preserve the status quo; change is not in their vocabulary— change is what you get when you give someone five bucks for the paper and he gives back four.

Many of the bosses at that time had from twenty-eight to forty years in, and their late-1940s and '50s mentality was widespread across the policing world. It was "us versus them." In Boston, the command discipline was highly structured. Officers only spoke to their sergeant or lieutenant, never to the captain. And God forbid the captain called you into his office. Back then you never even looked at the captain; he came in, you looked the other way. You didn't want to deal with him, because if he wanted you for something, it wasn't good. He was only going to rip you a new one.

Young officers learned from the veterans.

Every street cop was issued a manifold, an 8½"-x-11" piece of paper on which, when folded in a time-honored manner, you could write just about all your reports. You would start on the top and then fold it over and start again. At roll call you would write the name of the lieutenant on duty, the sergeant, the name of the officer with whom you were partnered, and your list of assignments. Bob O'Toole, who came on the job a year earlier than I did and became a lifelong colleague and friend, noticed that he and a couple of the other new guys were the only ones writing down what the lieutenant was telling us. At some point the older cop with whom he had been assigned reached over, grabbed the manifold out of his hand, and crushed it. "Kid"—very heavy Boston accent—"write nothin' until I tell you."

"Oh, aren't we supposed to . . . ?"

"Kid, I will tell you what you need to write."

Older cops, it turned out, made arrests selectively. They booked murderers, but the bookies were flourishing.

"You can go here," the veterans told us, "but you can't go there."

"But aren't they . . . ?"

"You don't understand, kid, you can't touch that."

"Okay, thank you very much, I can't touch that."

A recruit's career often turned on whom he ended up with for a first partner. A friend of mine drew a guy from Charlestown known as Iron Head. They were stationed downtown, in the center of the city. There were no apartments in the district, only large retailers like Jordan Marsh, Macy's, Filene's, Woolworth's, DeLong Jewelry, Cartier. By nine o'clock all the stores were closed and the cops were essentially night watchmen. Like clockwork, two nights a week there would be break-ins at one of the stores, and because he was a young, hot rookie, my friend wanted to go after the robbers. "Yeah," his partner told him, "we're not going there."

"What do you mean?"

"Kid," said the partner, "here's what I'm going to tell you: Don't worry about it. There's no thief other than the guys taking the report."

"What?"

"You heard me." Two nights a week a particular car was working that shift. Those nights, the stores got hit. "We're not going there," the partner told him. "We don't go and back up that unit."

Over Christmas some guy went out partying, got drunk, and fell down. My friend heard it on the radio, drove by, and found the same two cops propping the man against the wall, shuffling through his wallet. My classmate assumed they were looking for information. Then they reached for his money.

"Hey," he called, "what's up?"

"Hey, how's it going?" And because the new kid was there, they tucked the wallet back in the man's pants, which didn't earn my friend any points back at the station house.

No one wanted to hear about this kind of abuse. You were told to simply walk away, "You don't want to make a name for yourself." Every new patrolman had to make a choice; he could fall prey, stay clean, or he could blow the whistle. And in those days, blowing the whistle wasn't going to do any good whatsoever.

I had often wondered how so many cops who started out wanting to do the right thing—to serve their community and put bad guys behind bars—sooner or later became corrupted. There is an old adage to the effect that "until the consequences and punishment outweigh the advantages, nothing is going to change." This held true in Boston, and certainly in New York in the 1970s, as the Knapp Commission uncovered departmentwide corruption.

Al Sweeney and I had known each other since kindergarten. Boston Latin School was widely considered among the best educational facilities in the United States, but I flunked out in eighth grade because I failed Latin while Al aced his way through high school. I went off to war in Vietnam, Al went to college. (I used to joke and call him the draft dodger.) Along the way we had lost touch, but there we were in October 1970, looking across the room at the largest class in the history of the Boston Police Department, and we waved to each other.

"Bill?"

"Al?"

Al's father, Dan Sweeney, with several decades on the job, gave his son a primer in police work right after Al was sworn in and beginning to learn how the department worked in practice, as opposed to theory.

"There is always going to be somebody on this job," Al's dad said, "who wants to offer you something. It could be a free meal, it could be a few extra bucks, it could be a woman if you want one, it could be a room at a hotel if you want one. They like police officers.

"But always remember, once you take that gift, they will come back for something else. Then you have no choice. So you need to make a decision up front."

The old ways didn't sit well with some of the younger officers, who arrived with the intention of actually helping the citizens of Boston. "Maybe we should work with each other," they said, "because working with the old-timers, all we are getting is how they used to do it, not how to do it. It's driving me crazy. Tommy, why don't you and I start partnering up?"

Not many bosses were at first cordial to that idea, but between the newer officers making assignment requests and the older ones wanting no part of the youngsters, they began to come around. Part of this was generational, part just old-fashioned cantankerousness.

To get a good assignment a recruit needed a "rabbi," someone who could get them through the system with divine guidance. Many new cops came from legacy families with fathers, uncles, brothers, cousins already on the job. I had none of that.

Most officers came out of the working and middle classes, and to them extra take-home pay was—and to this day still is—a big deal. In the Boston structure, cops put extra money in their pocket each month by working overtime details. The better the district, the more profitable the detail. If you were stationed near Boston Garden you got all the Celtics games, the Bruins games, the circuses and events. In District 3, out in Mattapan, where the Massachusetts Bay Transit Authority (MBTA) was still running trolleys, you got an occasional construction job and you made very little extra money. A downtown officer made literally ten times more detail pay than someone on the job in the boonies.

District 3 was the beating heart of the boonies. Most cops were assigned there because they didn't know anybody or they'd pissed somebody off. I was assigned to District 3.

In the Boston Police Department—as in many others—if a boss had trouble with an officer, he dumped the guy in a bad district. District 3 was a dumping ground. Mattapan was rapidly transitioning from a largely Jewish to a largely Black neighborhood, which I suspect in the eyes of the brass made it even less desirable.

It was also the punishment palace. Bad captains were dumped in that district; good captains and superior officers didn't get assigned there. Everybody in the place was getting punished. For instance, Dan Sweeney had been one of the founders of the Boston Police Patrolmen's Association, an endeavor that did not endear him to the brass.

The brutality of management toward cops was incredible. Officers lived at the whim of their boss. If he didn't like you, you had no recourse. There was no Civil Service Commission, the conditions were awful. The bosses had absolute power. These were the days when people took public transportation to work. Dan Sweeney didn't own a car, he shared one, and on days when he didn't have access he took the bus all the way downtown. City buses can't be counted on, and if he got to the station house five minutes late the lieutenant would say, "You're not late at all. You've got eight hours to hang around until the next shift."

There was no overtime when an officer had to appear in court. The work schedule was six days on, two off; then six on, one off; then seven on, two off. If you called in sick, the sergeant came to your house and you had to let him in to check whether you were lying. Al's father had to go to some function one night, so he called in sick. He put on his good clothes, climbed into bed, pulled the covers up over his neck, and waited. The sergeant might show up, might not. Once he checked and left, you could leave; they never doubled back.

Mr. Sweeney's punishment for forming the union had been reassignment from the best district downtown, where there was a lot of overtime money, to Mattapan, where there was none. That was the boondocks, the shithole.

Al's father was a redheaded Irishman; he would burn in November sun. When headquarters got word that he was helping form the union, he received a call to report at eight o'clock on a Monday morning. His boss said, "I understand you are a very good organizer, so here, here is a book and tickets, I want you to walk Columbus Avenue outbound to Eggleston Square"—a distance of three miles—"and back, tagging. And on the hour, check in and take another book." The message was clear: "Stop." In this case, however, the move was self-defeating; it only emboldened Mr. Sweeney to do more.

Without exception, everyone stationed in Mattapan had a transfer request pending. Everyone wanted out. Everybody. But that wasn't easy; there were rules: keep your nose clean, do as you're told, take no chances, get along.

There were also consequences. If you screwed up in Mattapan you weren't moved out, your time there was extended—you would get moved *off* the transfer list so you *couldn't* get out.

District 3 drew only five sector cars; everybody else walked. There were no radios, we used call boxes to stay in touch with the station house and carried a pocketful of dimes and a call box key. When walkie-talkies did arrive they were the size of shoeboxes; nobody wanted to carry them around all day. My beat was Mattapan Square, walking the business area of an economically challenged neighborhood. There was nothing happening.

Here's how you learned discipline:

As rookies in December 1971, Al and I ended up together in front of Carney Hospital in our old neighborhood, Dorchester, he coming from downtown (despite his union history, Al's dad still had connections), I from Mattapan. We were assigned there for the day shift, waiting for the Dorchester Day Parade to come by. It was somewhere near ten in the morning, and the parade was not even going to begin until one. There was no traffic, there were no people, so Al and I decided we were going to go inside the hospital, warm up, and get a cup of coffee. As we came back out, a police car pulled up and a white-haired captain leaned out the window. "Hi, officers," he said. "How's it going?"

"Good, sir. How are you?"

"Great," he said. "Where were you?"

"We were getting a cup of coffee, sir."

"Good," he said, friendly as could be. "Were you assigned to this post?"

"Yes, sir, we were."

"Good." He stopped. "And who gave you permission to go in and have coffee?"

Al and I looked at each other. What I saw in his eyes, and he in mine, was: "Oh crap, we're in trouble now." Al tried to finesse our way out of it.

"Well, sir, it's only ten thirty, and the parade is not here until one."

"Oh, so you make up the rules?" And then he lit into us. Up one side and down the other. We were both placed on probation, and he told us in no uncertain terms that if he came back anytime that day and we weren't on post, he would terminate us, effective immediately. Then he drove off.

Al and I looked at each other. "Who was that asshole?"

It was Deputy Superintendent James "Mickey" MacDonald, one of the best minds in Boston policing. Five years later Al and I were lieutenants under Deputy MacDonald. The lesson he taught us about respect for the job stayed with us far longer than either of us were in the BPD. He was a strong and important influence in both our lives.

In the decade before I joined the Boston Police Department, the U.S. Supreme Court, under the leadership of Chief Justice Earl Warren, changed the nature of police practice in deeply significant ways. In order to deal with the abuses of overpolicing—including the use of the third degree, inappropriate arrests, and police violence—in 1961 the Supreme Court solidified the "exclusionary rule," holding in *Mapp v. Ohio* that, pursuant to the Fourteenth Amendment, evidence gathered in violation of a suspect's constitutional rights was to be excluded from trial. In 1964 the court held in *Escobedo v. Illinois* that, under the Sixth Amendment, all criminal suspects had the right to counsel. In 1966 *Miranda v. Arizona*—the case that popularized the phrase "You have the right to remain silent"—established under the Fifth Amendment the legal requirement that an arresting officer inform all suspects of their rights to have an attorney present before and during questioning, to refrain from self-incrimination, and to understand those rights and be given the opportunity to exercise them. In 1968 the court held in *Terry v. Ohio* that without probable cause to arrest, a police officer may stop and search a suspect on the street if the officer has reasonable suspicion that the person has committed, is committing, or is about to commit a crime, and a reasonable belief that the person "may be armed and presently dangerous." So was born stop, question, and frisk.

Bob O'Toole can remember his father, who had been on the job for several decades, bemoaning *Miranda*. "He came home and said, 'That's it, we're done, we are never going to be able to make an arrest again. This is bullshit! How are we going to be able to interview anybody if we have to tell them that they have a right to remain silent?!'"

Some young cops saw things differently. Coming on in the early seventies, we simply accepted *Miranda* as the way business was done. It didn't happen overnight, but ultimately a veteran's gut feeling was folded into the new generation's verifiable reasonable suspicion, leading to probable cause and then arrest. If the suspect stuck to his story, we didn't like it, but that's how things worked. The old-timers had a harder time. "Keep talking to them," they told us. "You don't need to shut it down."

In 1972, Boston's mayor Kevin White, an ambitious young progressive, was under consideration to be Democratic candidate George McGovern's vice-presidential running mate. The Boston Police Department was widely considered corrupt, hidebound, and racist, and a police scandal on White's watch could ruin his chances. When Commissioner Ed McNamara's term expired that year, the mayor organized a national search for a reform leader to replace him.

For the preceding three decades, each incoming commissioner had been a Boston product. Mayor White wasn't looking for an insider who would maintain the department, a known quantity with allegiances to the old-boy network that had been in place for half a century and who had no desire or incentive to make drastic changes. Mayor White was a change agent intent on identifying a man who would blow it up. He found Robert di Grazia.

Bob di Grazia was one of the new breed of police thinkers starting to emerge in the early 1970s. He had started his police career at a ten-person department in California and advanced quickly. In Kansas City, he had become a protégé of future FBI director Clarence Kelley. He was police chief of St. Louis County when he took the Boston job.

Di Grazia was eager to take risks in an industry that didn't like to take risks. Six foot three, handsome as could be, Italian American, he wore his curly hair in a thick Afro and didn't look like anyone ever seen at headquarters. In a job where bosses dressed like potatoes, his three-piece suits, bell-bottom pants, and wide ties were outrageous. So you can imagine how the Irish-dominated Boston Police Department responded to this guy.

Di Grazia immediately got rid of what was called the Black Mariah, a Buick Electra limousine with the distinctive three-digit license plate, "386," in which the commissioner was driven around by a uniformed traffic officer wearing a white hat. It was replaced by a baby-blue Dodge with a dark blue vinyl roof that the commissioner drove himself.

Beyond the flash and the symbolism of change, di Grazia turned the department upside down. He started by shaking out the bad cops.

Commissioner di Grazia had heard the same rumors of corruption everyone else had, but probably couldn't prove them. His mandate was to create change, and during training had brought in David Durk, the New York detective who collaborated with Frank Serpico and testified before the Knapp Commission in an attempt to reform the NYPD. Di Grazia created the Special Investigation Unit to investigate corruption; it empowered cops to call in abuses and have some hope that they would be dealt with.

But that was a stopgap. Di Grazia, an aggressive change agent, was after more fundamental alterations. On July 5, 1975, he staged what became known as the Saturday Massacre, a changing of the guard that remains legendary in Boston police lore.

Detective sergeants were rumored to be the bagmen, the guys who interacted with the judges and the courts and dealt with the defense attorneys. They were legion. Detective sergeants were alleged to be wildly corrupt, getting payoffs from bars and from organized crime, while covering up the after-hour joints, the prostitution, and the drugs. On that Saturday morning, di Grazia transferred many of the detective sergeants in the city, either relieving them of their commands outright or moving them so far out of the way they could retain no clout.

The sudden department overhaul and run of related retirements created a phalanx of openings for promotions. But di Grazia didn't want to fill them from the established BPD pipeline. The rules as written mandated that the sergeant's exam be based on rote memorization of the Blue Book of police procedures, a manual that hadn't been updated in forever. The results were heavily weighted in favor of seniority. What this meant in the real world was, don't even think about taking the sergeant's exam until next decade. When I came on the force the average age of a sergeant was approximately fifty-five; for police officers it was around forty-three. Their thinking was older still. No matter how qualified or well informed or innovative, no one was getting promoted to sergeant until they had between ten and twelve years on the job. By that time candidates weren't likely to buck the system—they were part of it.

Di Grazia lowered seniority to 10 or 15 percent of the grade and added an oral board of experts, an assessment center, and an extensive reading list of eight books, including the Kerner Report and the American Bar Association report on race relations.

He surveyed the department and found, on the entire force, only twenty-five cops with college degrees. Previous administrations hadn't considered this a deficit, but di Grazia used federal grant money to offer four-year scholarships for officers to attend Boston State College. In theory this would plant a seed that would grow future leaders. I took the entrance exam and was accepted.

It was a great deal; the student patrolmen would work four nights a week from six to midnight, with the rest of our time free for classes and study. I had dropped out of Boston State six years earlier; now I was back.

I studied law enforcement, of course. I took an American Government course and met Governor Michael Dukakis when he was a guest lecturer. Never particularly good in science, I flunked a class in forensics training. But my two favorite classes were art appreciation and urban geography.

The college stood next to the Museum of Fine Arts on Huntington Avenue, and occasionally my art appreciation professor, Dr. Arvinites, would take his classes there. Thousands of years of history of the evolution of art were on display.

My taste in art ran and still runs to Norman Rockwell; I like the kind of illustration that showed up on *Saturday Evening Post* covers, if that reference is even understandable today. I was not an admirer of Renaissance art, I didn't respond to Picasso, but I came to really appreciate the Impressionists.

But Dr. Arvinites taught me and my classmates to see beyond the image and become aware of additional considerations involved in the creation of each painting. What was the history of its time? What was the political context in which a work was made, and what did physical articles or lighting in each picture represent? Over time I came to understand that art reflected societal changes. It reflected frustration, entanglement, enlightenment. And by extension I was taught, as I was patrolling the all-Black neighborhood of Mattapan, to look beyond the poverty and the crime to the experiences I had not encountered growing up in my white community. To take what I was looking at and see behind it.

My second favorite subject, taught by Betsy Useem, was urban geography, the study of the history and importance of cities in society. More than the rural farmlands and small towns that some considered the "real America," urban areas, I was taught, were gathering places where diverse people from diverse places would share experiences, skills, and ideas, and in the process create a richer country. Professor Useem spoke with passion about the melting pot, the great urban gumbo that blended seemingly divergent tastes into something specific and sustaining and satisfying, and particularly American.

Yet this was the 1970s; America's cities were being abandoned in droves by white people, who were fleeing to the suburbs and taking their tax revenues with them. Our country's great cities were falling into decay. And as they were deteriorating, police departments were shrinking while crime and disorder were growing. I found Professor Useem's class a real call to arms.

I, along with hundreds of Boston officers—including future Boston Police Commissioners Paul Evans, Mickey Roache, and later Kathy O'Toole—benefited from the LEEP program. Boston State College created a Bachelor of Science in Law Enforcement degree, which I pursued.

As a twenty-five-year-old freshman, I was older than most of my fellow students. I took classes and drank coffee in the cafeteria with kids who were far less experienced and had very different views of the world. Boston State was a considerably more conservative school than Harvard and the other liberal arts institutions clustered in Boston; its student body was largely comprised of kids from working- and middle-class homes like mine. But it was 1973, Richard Nixon was president, the Vietnam War was in full swing, and so was the antiwar movement. Even these blue-collar kids were beginning to question the government, and their views were well to the left of what I was thinking. Having served in Vietnam, I was more clear-eyed about it in a way than they were, but also very patriotic, and a firm believer in service to my country. Talking with them I confronted an agenda and culture a whole lot more progressive than anything I was going to find in the station house. They were growing their hair long; I kept mine at police length. They were questioning authority; I was acting on its behalf, even as I was starting to think about how to change it.

But while we disagreed on many things, we were more than just civil; we tossed our book bags on the table like we were laying down weapons and talked politics and society. No screaming, no name-calling. No placards, no handcuffs. They didn't call me a pig and I didn't call them hippies. This was exhilarating. We heard each other.

Often when on duty I was stationed in front of the John F. Kennedy Federal Building, policing antiwar demonstrations. I strapped on my riot helmet, grabbed my nightstick, and found myself on the other side of the blue barricades from the same classmates I had been debating that morning. I could literally see both sides.

Cops often get enveloped in the blue cocoon. They work with cops, drink with cops, go to cop weddings, cry at cop funerals, talk cop talk, think cop thoughts. It's an insular world and an occupational hazard. I was a young, white police officer patrolling an all-Black neighborhood and might have been well on my way. My time at Boston State sprung me. Di Grazia was right; it's good for cops to go to college.

However, after several years of frustration at the department's slow pace, incompetent leadership, and backward thinking, I'd had enough. I was considering leaving Boston and joining the force in nearby suburban Quincy. Having spent the better part of my life directing myself toward being a Boston cop, I was bitterly disappointed by what I found that world to be. I wasn't making good money, I wasn't getting good assignments, I wasn't doing good work. Boston had tradition, but maybe that tradition wasn't all it was cracked up to be.

Commissioner di Grazia liked to get out. He quickly became a darling of Boston society and media and was a fixture at an array of charitable events and society functions. He also, unlike his predecessors, made a point of attending community meetings throughout the city. His interests as commissioner were diverse. He extended that interest to his department, and drove to districts around the city to visit roll call. He wanted to be in touch with his men, to get a sense of their morale and tell them what he was planning. This was unheard of. Commissioners did not communicate directly with patrolmen; that was what the lower echelon of command staff was for. My Mattapan bosses thought the commissioner surveying their lost district was a particularly bad idea. Flushed out of their cover by his presence, they didn't want to get any more embarrassed than they already were. They didn't want us asking questions, they didn't want us slowing him down enough to take a real look around, they just wanted to get out of there with their careers intact.

So di Grazia showed up at the four o'clock roll call at District 3, the quintessential poor-relative precinct. All us cops, the rank and file and command staff alike, had no more seen a commissioner in the field than most community groups had seen one in their school basements. Pleased and a bit cowed by the attention, we stood before him as he addressed us. Over his shoulder, with hands clasped, the captain and other supervisors scowled and glared, as much as daring us to say what we knew. *Go ahead, just try it. You'll pay.*

The commissioner spoke with great seriousness, outlining his plans for the department, his vision for the future, the advances he had in store for us. He finished speaking and a silence fell. Di Grazia was not unaccustomed to this silence; people at the top of organizations encounter it consistently. How you respond to that reticence, that hesitation to engage, defines you as a leader. He said, "I need to hear from you. I want to know the things you need in order to do your job. Tell me, and I'll try to get them for you."

More silence.

"Now," he had the audacity to ask, "do you have any questions?"

Nah, no good could come from it. None of us said a word.

Except me. I didn't know it at the time, but I've since learned that a public speaker always wants that first interaction; it opens up the dialogue. I thought I was asking a tough question but apparently I was doing him a favor. I raised my hand. Di Grazia leaned forward with enthusiasm. "Yes? Who are you?"

"Patrolman Bratton, Commissioner."

"And what is your question?"

"How do I get out of here?"

"What?" I could see the bosses stiffen.

"How do I transfer out of here, sir?"

The commissioner turned to the row of brass behind him. "You put in one of those blue papers, don't you? A transfer form?"

The whole row of cops started chuckling. Everybody in District 3 knew that when you put in the blue form, it went straight into the circular file.

I didn't get any more of an answer than what was already clear; no District 3 transfer form ever saw the light of day. Commissioner di Grazia left and the bosses were steaming as they went out the door with him. In their absence, my sergeant had a few choice words, the least of which were, "Kid, what are you, nuts?" I don't know whether di Grazia thought I was busting his chops; I was just craving release from Mattapan, maybe even from the BPD entirely.

About ten days later I showed up for roll call and saluted the desk sergeant. "Officer Bratton reporting for duty."

"What the fuck are you doing here, Bratton?"

"I'm reporting for duty, Sarge."

"Get the hell outta here, you've been transferred to District Fourteen."

District 14. In the blue-collar, middle-class Brighton-Allston neighborhoods of Boston, which included Boston College and Boston University. Schools, nightclubs, paid details—a much more interesting and challenging police district! I cleaned out my locker and was gone in ten minutes.

I always thought di Grazia had noticed me and saved my career, but years later I found it was my old partner, Frank Corbosiero, who got me transferred. He had moved to the newly created anticorruption Special Investigations Unit and told his superiors, "We're going to lose a good cop." Without Frank, I was gone. I owe him and di Grazia my career.

They didn't like college guys in District 14; the old guard still reigned. My first assignment was to a "fixer," a fixed post where I was assigned to stand for six-hour tours of duty, usually from six to midnight. Most of what I was called upon to do was take up space so some rowdy kids couldn't occupy the same space. To make sure I was doing my job, my sergeants drove by regularly. Word of the department cleanup apparently hadn't reached them; they were intent on waiting di Grazia out.

I partnered with Mickey Roache, whom I had met at Boston State. Together we were eventually assigned to a sector car, breaking up New Year's fights and domestic disturbances, and learning the neighborhood. Mickey was a devout Catholic who went to church every day. Scrupulously honest, he was a living embodiment of the values the new commissioner was trying to instill in the department.

I had made it out of Mattapan but still craved what was next. For most cops in big agencies, there's a point when two roads diverge in the wood: detective or supervisor? Detectives are a breed unto themselves. The best of them have an intuitive sense of when something's wrong and a gift for finding the facts and angles they need to solve a crime. It's hard to explain, but when you're in its presence it's easy to recognize. I clearly didn't have it. I knew when something was not right in the street, but the really good detectives had a sixth sense I couldn't touch. In addition, I hated going to court. I did not like the drudgery of waiting around hour after hour to testify. I determined early on that if I was going to progress as a leader in policing it would have to be in supervision and management. I began studying for the sergeant's exam.

I had been in the department four years. Under previous regimes I still would have had a decade to wait for my opportunity. Under di Grazia, all that had changed; if I was going to advance it was up to me.

I had not yet graduated from Boston State, so I was working six-hour night shifts, going to college during the day, and studying every hour in between—and sometimes on the job. My captain caught me thumbing through 3" x 5" promotional exam flash cards during a lull while on duty. "Put 'em away," he growled. I thought he might encourage his officer's using time wisely, but the captain was going by the book, and a patrolman studying for an exam wasn't in that book.

Mickey Roache initially wasn't interested in the sergeant's exam; he felt a college degree was enough and wasn't even going to sign up. We drove around in the sector car all evening and I rode him hard enough that he agreed to take it. Al Sweeney was a college boy but was sweating because he hadn't joined the military and wasn't getting the 2-point veteran's bonus.

I placed number one on the written test and second overall. Al and Mickey and Jack Gifford, Tom Maloney, Paul Evans, Joe Saia, and a lot of the Boston State College guys made it. Three Boston police commissioners came out of that class. Di Grazia seeded the department with this fresh batch of educated sergeants.

My first assignment as a sergeant was to District 6 in South Boston, "Southie"—an insular, parochial, lower-middle-class Irish and Polish neighborhood that was policed on a wink and a nod. Neither the community nor the local cops, many of whom lived there, were particularly open to outsiders, and there were many cops in that house who had been on the job longer than I'd been alive. I was this kid—this college kid—and they eyed me silently. When I said I was going to be on the streets with them, they assumed I was just looking for blown assignments. There are so many rules, and they are so often disregarded, it's in a cop's nature to believe all supervision is punitive. "To assist as much as to supervise," I told them. *Right*, they figured.

They were right to be wary. I was there to upset their world; that's what di Grazia had in mind. But when I organized a squad into uniformed and undercover operatives to shut down a Southie nightclub that routinely degenerated into Friday night fights and stabbings—"Who's going to be inside? Who's got the back?"—they liked the radical idea of cops operating as a team. The district's captain, Morris Allen, who had previously commanded the Boston Tactical Patrol Force, encouraged this kind of fresh thinking and strong morale from his young supervisors. He became one of my first mentors.

Several months after my promotion to sergeant, I was breezing along in my standard-issue BPD AMC Matador station wagon—an unwieldy, family vacation–style, godforsaken clunker of a police vehicle—when a call came over the radio saying that a Black man in a red leisure suit was holding a white woman hostage on the streets of South Boston.

Boston in 1975 was one of the most racist cities in America. As much as we talk about the civil rights era and the South, some northern cities were deeply plagued with their own bigotry. Segregated schools, segregated housing, segregated neighborhoods—Boston had it all. Former congressperson, City Council member, and full-time anti–school busing advocate Louise Day Hicks and Alabama's governor George Wallace could have walked down the street arm in arm and nobody would have said anything. All that was missing was the white hood.

The city of Boston at the time was under federal court order to desegregate its public schools and public housing. South Boston was a white neighborhood so hostile, so smugly and proudly unwelcoming to outsiders— particularly outsiders of color—that it self-segregated. It was particularly hostile to the federal court order. Out of fear, Black people simply stayed away. White rage was not very far from the surface, and here was a Black man out on the pavement, holding a gun to a white woman's head. My radio told me the suspect had tried to rob a bank, fired a shot while inside the building, and along with the money was dragging either a teller or a customer through the streets as a hostage.

The bank was located on Dorchester Avenue, a central thoroughfare through South Boston, next to a railroad line. A four-lane bridge spanned the tracks, a hump in the road with stone-studded cement sides and municipal water pipes that served as railings, between a bus-maintenance garage on one side of the bridge and a Doughboy donut shop on the other. Traffic was dead still, bus drivers and garage workers filling the car lanes; a couple of guys had hopped off their dump truck and were striding toward the action. No one was going anywhere except to get a better view. I got out of my Matador about seventy-five yards from the bridge and moved with the surging crowd as it advanced.

The windows of an office building overlooking the bus yard were filling with workers jostling for position. On the far side sat a sandwich shop and the D Street public-housing development overflowing with poor white people—the heart and soul of South Boston—who had begun to pour out of the projects.

The crowd gave the guy and his hostage some room. No one was going to rush him: he was jerking his gun back and forth in response to the spasms of sound and movement from the growing crowd of angry white people who had him surrounded. Men and women ran up to the ring, then stopped short as the circle thickened. The man was grasping a bag of money, a gun, and the woman—where was he going to go? He backed up the bridge. The crowd climbed with him. He reached the top and stopped as if spotlit.

As the first unit on the scene, I radioed, "We've got a Black male dragging a white female onto the Broadway bridge. I'm moving up." I took out my gun.

There had been a rash of national and international hostage situations in the early-to-mid-1970s, including the standoff a few years prior at Attica Prison, where ten correctional officers and civilian employees and thirty-three inmates had been killed when the state police took control of the prison after negotiations failed. Most of the dead had been killed by police officers. One of di Grazia's recent innovations had been the creation of a new hostage negotiation training unit. After becoming a sergeant I had volunteered for and completed that five-week program. Some of its training began to kick in.

First use cover, then engage. Well, as I moved forward, the crowd moved back, heads on a swivel, as if watching a live crime show, and my cover evaporated immediately. I found myself only five steps away from the man, pointing my gun at his head. The hostage kept buckling from stress and panic, and the gunman struggled to maintain hold of the cash while keeping his human shield upright.

I had been trained to create a relationship. Use time and distance. Practice *dynamic inactivity*—slow things down. *Contain and negotiate*—isolate the attention of the hostage taker so he wouldn't get spooked by something outside your control and go off half-cocked. These were the skills I had been taught.

"Hey, look," I told him. "Calm down. You haven't hurt anyone yet. Look, you can see you can't get away, you're going to have to give it up." I took the chance that in his surveying the crowd he wouldn't make eye contact with a Southie who might set him off. Fortunately, fear and fascination had silenced everyone. "You're going to face jail time," I said, "but, you know, you hurt her or you hurt me and you're going to make this a lot worse situation."

"Stay away! Stay away!" he shouted. His first demand. Now it was a negotiation.

"Look, don't hurt her. She's got nothing to do with this. Why don't you let her go?" My counteroffer.

Dynamic inactivity works both ways. I was trying to slow the gunman, but I succeeded in losing all track of time myself. A world went by as I waited for his response. Meanwhile, the cavalry had arrived. Police on both sides of the bridge were pushing forward, getting into position. Over the man's shoulder I could see Officers Gene Kelly and Bob Dumas—beefy

Southie cops, each with forty years on the job—trying to sneak up behind this guy.

Jesus, that's all I needed. The man was all over the place. He was pointing a gun at me. He was scaring me to death. Kelly and Dumas probably thought they could lumber up, pounce, and tackle him.

But after forty years of policing, these guys could no longer pounce; if Kelly and Dumas were going into action they would careen. The gunman would shoot me, then he'd shoot her, and with cops behind him, I wouldn't be able to do anything for fear of shooting both of them. In the army and on the firing range it had been proved beyond all doubt that I was a terrible shot; if anything was certain it was that I'd end up shooting my guys.

"Stay back!" I yelled. One of the new sergeants, George Kenney, was on my walkie-talkie. "Get them back!" I shouted to him. *"Keep them back!"* Kenney finally got the pair to stand down.

Look at me, I thought. *Look at me*. I needed the gunman's total focus. Again my training took hold. I needed to de-escalate the situation, which was growing more tense by the moment.

I realized that what was causing the greatest tension was my gun; the hostage was freaking and looked anywhere except at my service revolver, but the gunman couldn't keep his eyes off it. That's the way it is with a weapon—center of attention. I stared at his gun, too, particularly when he pointed it at me. It shook me. I couldn't shoot him—I'd just hit the hostage—so my weapon was of no use to me. By this time, too, police sharpshooters who could drop him far better than I ever could, if it came to that, had arrived on the scene. I really had no choice.

"Look," I said. "I'm going to lower my weapon. I'm not going to harm you." I bent my arm and slowly dropped the weapon to my side. I could see him thinking, *What's going on here?* Then it must have all come to him: *I can't get out of here; the most immediate threat is gone for now; maybe I can live through this.*

If I was wrong, I was dead; he was pointing a gun at me.

And then he wasn't.

"Okay, it's up." He dropped his gun hand and then the money and the woman. She slumped and crawled away. Kelly and Dumas and a swarm of cops tackled the man from all directions.

It is part of the cop DNA: we are attracted to danger. Where others run from it, we—by nature and profession—run toward it. I felt no rush during the standoff, but when it was over and I had survived, I knew exhilaration to the core. I had met the cop's ultimate challenge: I had put my life at risk for another, and I'd won.

By the time I got back to the station house, word had gotten out. There was no such thing as social media back then, no viral video of me putting down my weapon and standing there in a gunsight, just talking. No shot of the gunman giving up. There was only the telephone. A witness had called and told the clerk, Charlie McLaughlin, "Jeez, this cop was amazing. He went right up and faced this guy off. He's gotta have balls as big as cannonballs!" So when I brought in my prisoner for booking, McLaughlin said, "How you doin' there, Cannonballs?"

I can't say I was sorry the name stuck.

Captain Allen nominated me for the department's highest award for valor, the Schroeder Brothers Medal, named after two brothers who had been killed in the line of duty. I received the second ever awarded and accepted it with pride.

The International Brotherhood of Police Officers honored me at their annual luncheon as their Person of the Year. Commissioner di Grazia was to make the presentation and someone from his staff asked if I would like to meet the commissioner at his office and drive over with him. I jumped at the chance.

The commissioner's office was on the sixth floor of police headquarters—hallowed ground. Oak doors held etched-glass windows, and the doorknobs were engraved with the Boston Police Department seal. I felt generations of authority as I entered. Everything I wanted to be was here. I inhaled the heritage.

The commissioner drove me to the ceremony—imagine, a police commissioner driving a sergeant!—and back to headquarters when it was over. I was a living exemplar of his new personnel strategy and he asked for my perspective as a new sergeant. I was quite in awe and told him I was enjoying the direction he was taking the department. Even in that office, that tabernacle of tradition, it was clear that new things were on the horizon. The BPD was changing, and so was the world around it.

The next time I ran into di Grazia it was Father's Day 1977, and I was backed up against South Boston High School. South Boston was the kind of place where locals who bought a home wanted to know where the church and the schools were. Then came busing. All of a sudden their kids were on a bus going somewhere else, with different people. They said, "No. No way. That's not happening."

I was at the high school trying to police an antibusing protest march that had gotten out of hand. A mob of white Bostonians who didn't like the idea of Black kids coming into their neighborhood to go to school chased us down, throwing stones and cursing us to hell. I heard the Rebel yell.

A call went out to officers all over the city: Send reinforcements! It was Sunday, we were short-staffed, and cops were getting called at home. Then di Grazia showed up. The mob hated him, the son of a bitch with those liberal ideas. The crowd surged. They trashed a police car. In our helmets and riot gear, we pushed them back. They surged again. I was ducking bottles and found myself next to the commissioner.

"Well, good afternoon, Sergeant Bratton!"

I thought that was the funniest thing. We're taking incoming and he's talking to me like we're on a buffet line.

"You know," he said, "we've been talking about a new initiative to bring some of you young sergeants into headquarters to work on my staff and get a feel for the place."

"That's great, Commissioner." I didn't want to be disrespectful but I was just trying to live through this.

"Would you be interested in coming up?"

I had been in South Boston for a year and had seen my share of cop fighters, guys who would rather do battle with a police officer than accept his authority. The rule of law was under siege and Southie had degenerated into a small-minded world of its own. At that moment, the idea of working in the commissioner's office seemed very appealing.

CHAPTER 3

Whiz Kids

B ob di Grazia referred to other American police chiefs as "pet rocks"; they just sat there, and if you turned them over nothing happened. He was a dynamic personality and a progressive thinker. After Kevin White was reelected mayor in a close race, polls showed that di Grazia was by far the most popular public figure in Boston. Successful in opening up the windows of the Boston Police Department and starting tremendous new programs, di Grazia made the fatal mistake of asking, "How do you run for mayor in this city?"

This didn't sit well with Kevin White, who was only halfway through what would turn into sixteen years in office. The newly reelected mayor prevented the commissioner from receiving a pay raise, cancelled a job di Grazia had lined up for his wife, and basically ran him out of town. Mayors, it turns out, are very concerned about popular police commissioners. Before I could get to his office, di Grazia resigned and took a job in Maryland. Boston's loss.

Superintendent-in-Chief Joe Jordan, a pipe-smoking transitional figure, was named to serve out di Grazia's term, after which he could be appointed to a full term only at Mayor White's discretion. The commissioner's position was historically a political patronage plum; the department was run on a day-to-day basis by its superintendents, who had all come up through the ranks. Jordan, a personable sort, was neither old guard nor particularly progressive. While City Hall's influence on all police matters began to increase, he nevertheless pushed forward much of di Grazia's agenda since he saw that these initiatives were highly popular with the city, if not in the department.

In 1973, in a move not guaranteed to win him any friends, di Grazia had hired nine women to the BPD. They wore pumps, skirts, blouses, and what looked like meter-maid hats. They worked like crazy and quickly were nicknamed the Dirty Dozen. Formerly, women had been hired only as pseudo police officers, dealing with some investigations and other special functions. This was the first time women were hired to be full-time officers with the same duties as their male counterparts. The selection standards were changed by di Grazia to eliminate the requirement that applicants climb a rope without using their feet to grab on with. No women had that kind of upper-body strength, and thus all previous female applicants had been eliminated from being "real" police officers.

Di Grazia also brought in a band of outsiders to help in his revitalization of the department. "There are some young people out there with smart minds," he said, "who can think of policing and never put on a uniform." Mark Furstenberg, Phil Marks, and Bob Wasserman were civilians and academics, and they became known as the "whiz kids."

The Boston Police Department, populated largely by conservative, old-line, working-class Irish Catholics, was astounded. It was like the pope ordaining Jewish prelates. The general response was, "Who the hell are these people? They don't know policing." There was great animosity directed at them from all levels of the department. "They're up in headquarters telling us what to do. What the hell do they know about being a policeman? They've never walked in our shoes! They don't even have flat feet!"

Director of Information Services Steve Dunleavy and Wasserman convinced Jordan to implement di Grazia's plan to establish a mentoring and development program for young sergeants. Jack Gifford, Al Sweeney, and I were among the chosen. Some guys wouldn't take the job; others were blackballed for jumping the line and not working their way up; still others wouldn't talk to us because we had broken the blue line and become "head-quarters people." Taking risks was not the preferred career move in the Boston Police Department of the 1970s.

Sweeney, Gifford, and I were the young guns walking around HQ, working intimately with the men who ran the place. Dunleavy and Wasserman had tagged us, and from the start we were encouraged to look at the city not as a collection of fiefdoms, but as a whole. Beat cops dealt with immediate situations; we were given the blessing of overview. Sweeney went with Wasserman in training and moved to HQ when Wasserman went up there as Assistant to the Commissioner for Operations; Dunleavy eventually became Jordan's Director of Administration, and I was assigned to his staff. He believed in systems, and research, and concentration on a specific goal.

It was a time of optimism about new ideas and new technologies. I worked on a computer program to develop the Standard Beat Plan. Thirty-inch-wide green-lined computer paper would come off the printer showing what time every car in the city logged on and logged off, and who was on call. This was the beginning of the police's ability to track the activity of the cars that were actually responding to 911 calls—how many would get there, how many would be delayed. We introduced concepts like Zero Car Availability, in which we measured how many police cars were needed at, let's say, ten o'clock on a Friday night, to ensure we could respond to Priority One emergency calls 95 percent of the time. Five percent of the time we would not have a car to respond to a call, and if we went over that 5 percent, we were failing. I helped design some of those strategies. I had a private office in the commissioner's suite, and a take-home marked car with the unit designation "Commissioner's Staff." For me, this was a big deal. I loved parking that car in front of my house; it was never vandalized.

In 1968, the Kerner Report had established a national consensus that crime was a direct result of societal circumstances and there was nothing police could do to prevent it; what we could do was chase it down. A year earlier, President Johnson's Commission on Law Enforcement and Administration of Justice had suggested that "a single number should be established" nationwide for reporting emergency situations. Thus the 911 system was created. It was first used, on a rotary phone, by Senator Rankin Fite in Haleyville, Alabama, and its appeal was universal. American technology was expanding. GPS was created in 1967, the Sony Trinitron TV in 1968. Cars were getting souped up. We were on our way to the moon! One thinks of 911 as a major advance in American law enforcement, but it had several less than beneficial consequences.

As a Boston walking cop assigned to the same beat year after year, you owned the neighborhood. You came to know everyone; block by block you knew the problems and some of the solutions. If you left your sector, for instance if my partner and I crossed the line and shot over to the other side of the street to get a pizza, that neighborhood's sector car would pull up beside us and say, "What are you doing here?"

"I was just getting a pizza."

"Okay."

They owned that beat. There was a rigorous internal integrity to this territoriality, and cops felt deeply responsible to it.

But the advent of 911 dramatically increased calls for service from the public, and more calls necessitated quicker response so cops could go from one to another without delay. The focus on response rather than prevention quickly took many officers off walking beats and put them into police cars, where they had access to radios to communicate with the 911 system and to better respond to the growing number of calls. I had started off walking a beat, and within a year I was in cars. Everybody wanted to get in cars, particularly once they became air-conditioned. The unintended consequence of this, however, was that officers quickly lost touch with the neighborhoods they were policing as they chased calls all over the district.

Across America during this period, police resources were declining. That is a constant topic of conversation in all station houses and command centers from time immemorial: Cops' jobs are being lost and what can we do about it? The thinking at the time was that with the advent of advanced technology such as 911, the increasing number of calls from the public could be expedited, and the placing of cops in cars would increase the distances they could travel and areas they could cover, as well as expedite report writing, never a favorite police officer activity. Instead of going back to the station and writing up every call, you now had codes, and the coding was used to speed up the process of dispatching and documenting calls. In Boston, "7 Paul" meant you were in service, on patrol; "14 Paul" meant you were out of service, handling a 911 call from the public.

In our haste to get to every call and handle them quickly, cops began to lose the intimacy of their relationship with the neighborhood they were policing. No longer an active physical presence there, they could not count on knowing its ins and outs as they had in the past. We couldn't do anything about preventing crime, we were told, so in order to improve our performance we expanded our ability to respond to it, and 911 sped up the way calls came in. Early computers let us develop computer-aided dispatch, or CAD, which got the calls to the cops faster. We developed resource allocation systems that used algorithms to assign manpower based on the number of calls and where they were coming from. The day-to-day workload became call logging, not to resolve problems but to manage time—how quickly you could get back into that car and go clear on a call. Police leadership, the politicians, the public—everyone was demanding rapid response. In the mid-seventies, Glen Pierce at Northeastern University analyzed 911 calls and found that 50 percent were for service at locations to which we responded twelve or more times a year. When we had beat cops, they knew that and would try to address the ongoing situation; with 911, every call was a separate incident, and treated as such.

From the Class of 1977 onward, the message was: Sector integrity doesn't count. Community ties don't count. How fast you handle a call, how quickly you respond, how fast you file the report—*that* is what is measured. It's a police truism: You can only expect what you inspect.

A Ford Motor Company executive brought in to deliver his expertise at a command training session said there are three things that everybody knows at whatever job they work: what is rewarded, what is punished, what is measured. So as quickly as you get on the call, move on it. There would be plenty of times an officer would clear a call while still on it. Otherwise the sergeant would yell at you.

"You were twenty-two minutes on that call!"

"We were dealing with them, sarge. We were talking to people."

"Our clearance time is seventeen minutes!"

There was no GPS tracking in those days; sergeants were sent to find you. The headquarters dispatch center would notify the patrol center and say, "That unit is off the air for too long." The sergeant would either call or go to the location to goose you along.

Even the terminology was ass-backward. We were deemed *out of service* when we were at a call serving the public; we were *in service* when we were in the car, just riding around. The sergeants were constantly emphasizing to the cops, get in, get the call out of the way, "Get back in service!"

When I came on in 1970—prior to the institution of 911, prior to computerization—officers working a downtown car on a Monday morning would log on via radio and the dispatcher would say, "Stand by. Are you ready?" The answer would be in the affirmative. Pen in hand, we would take down three or four calls located in our sector. If an officer was stationed in the Ten sector and four or five breaking and entering cases came in over the weekend, plus someone had called in with a car blocking their driveway, it was up to the officer to prioritize his workload and tend to each call in its proper order. If during his rounds there was an emergency—"Three-two car, we've got a holdup in progress at the diner on Blue Hill Avenue and Mattapan Square"—he would leave the call and return only after his presence at the emergency was no longer required.

When technology took over, we saw a major change. With CAD, much of that decision making and control was removed from police officers and ceded to the computer, which guided the dispatcher. Life-threatening emergencies—rape in progress; murder; robbery; major automobile accidents; fires, both natural and man-made—are always Priority One in every police department, but effectively over time the algorithms changed and the computer reigned. The idea was to get calls answered as fast as they were coming in. Officers received one call, not five, because the actual time to be spent on each individual response could vary and was not quantifiable. And because they were in proximity, these officers might be joined on that one call by a car pulled not from their neighborhood but from an adjoining sector. On a second call they might be joined by a car from a different adjoining sector. In rapid fashion we lost all concept of identification within individual neighborhoods.

Of course the 911 calls did not come in evenly. Some sectors had more crime than others, and since crime calls were always responded to, an officer might have a nice quiet sector, say the 3-1, but spend most of his time in the 3-4 because the 3-4 sector car couldn't handle the crime load. Cops were constantly at the whim of the radio, at the whim of 911, so we lost sector accountability. The businesses and individuals who had grown to know the walking cop on the beat or in the sector car covering their neighborhood who would always respond to their calls? They lost that connection. The cops lost their connectivity to the neighborhood and the community lost its intimacy with their cops. That problem continues to this day.

Even cops lost touch with each other. Rather than see each other in the street, we just waved as we drove by. Sector by sector, we lost touch with one another. A problem in a building? An officer could arrive at a crime scene outside his sector and be told by a citizen, "I reported that to you guys last week." He'd look at his partner and say, "We didn't get that report, did we?" No, because a car from another sector had taken the report.

The de-emphasis on community identification was deepened further each year when the police sectors would be redesigned, based not on neighborhood identity, but on 911 call workload. We were no longer policing communities, we were policing geographic areas that would change from year to year. It was law enforcement gerrymandering.

To meet this constantly growing need to pursue crime and improve our response time, an increasing number of cops were taken off the walking beat altogether. Fewer cops stood where people could see and feel their presence. We thought we were so smart; we were becoming very adept at amassing data that told us what had happened—we knew how long it took to get the calls, we knew how many calls it took to get the job under way, we knew our response times—but we were learning next to nothing about what to do with it. People needed the police, and we continued to show up, but the crime rate continued to rise! We were no longer focusing on prevention, it was all about response.

Eventually, by the end of the seventies, no police department in America could keep up with the 911 demand. At the same time, economic circumstances caused governments to start cutting back on resources. In the budget crisis of the seventies, the number of New York City police officers was reduced through layoffs and attrition from 27,262 in 1974 to 22,304 in 1976. The total police force, including sergeants, lieutenants, and higher-ranking commanders, went from 31,531 to 26,432. They laid off 5,000 cops. Despite our mobility, police became less visible. This idea of rapid response was something we were handcuffed to. But what we were effectively doing was de-policing the neighborhoods.

Budget considerations created deinstitutionalization. Unable or unwilling to staff and effectively and efficiently run the nation's huge mental institutions, state and federal governments made the decision to shutter them. Closing the institutions not only saved money, it addressed concerns about deplorable conditions. Horror stories abounded around such facilities as New York's state-supported Willowbrook State School for children with intellectual disabilities and Boston State Hospital in Mattapan. I can't tell you the number of people that I took to that hospital in the middle of the night. It was a place we could take certain people—not criminals, necessarily, even though sometimes they committed crimes—to get them help. In a well-intended effort to take people out of horrific conditions, the institutions were closed. But what would come next? Tremendous unintended consequences.

All across America, hundreds of thousands of poor souls, struggling with mental illness, were now going to be let out of these prisonlike entities. They were to be returned to neighborhood health centers and to monitored treatment at their homes. A laudable plan. But what happened? Many of the neighborhood health centers were never built or never funded. Treatment at home usually was self-medication. Many of the homes they came from and returned to were chaotic, so their condition didn't improve. Where did the patients go? Many ended up back on the streets. You walked out the front door here, there was a gentleman lying on the sidewalk on a piece of cardboard. The numbers of homeless skyrocketed. So what did we create? We closed the mental institutions and helped to create a part of the problem that plagues us to this day: the homeless population.

During this same period, the court system began to reevaluate America's way of looking at the law, and a sizable number of actions that would previously have taken people off the streets became decriminalized. In 1971, Congress passed the Uniform Alcoholism and Intoxication Treatment Act; in 1973, Massachusetts abolished the crime of public drunkenness. In states across the country, crimes like loitering and disorderly conduct also became much more narrowly defined. Cops suddenly had fewer enforcement powers to address problems before they got worse. Officers lost the ability to get a drunk off the street before he committed a crime or became a victim. At the same time, deinstitutionalization meant there were fewer places to take people even when enforcement was possible. And with police riding by instead of walking, and therefore less available to handle the situations that inevitably arose, American cities in the 1970s began to look and feel less safe. One result was that many would lose their middle-class residents as unsafe streets helped fuel a rush to the suburbs.

Further deterioration of the streets of America was caused by a significant increase in the sale and use of illegal drugs in public spaces. As new types of drugs were being introduced, their users expanded to include experimenting college students, returning veterans, and the ambulatory deinstitutionalized mentally ill population who needed them to deal with the world.

This was also a time of increasing racial tension throughout America, because the issues of the previous three hundred years had not been solved by the Civil Rights Acts of the 1960s. Sadly, during that period, the face of crime in America—its complexion—began to change. Look at the old prison movies of the 1930s and '40s. All the convicts are white. I do not remember seeing people of color in Edward G. Robinson movies. Because the most visible criminal contingents were increasingly on American city streets, for the police who were assigned to deal with crime, the easiest arrests were on the streets. Yet undeniably, some of the police power to control the streets was lost because it was abused. The 1970s introduced what many in minority communities reasonably felt was the beginning of the mass incarceration of African Americans.

Communities were under pressure from all sides, and police departments groped for new thinking about how best to respond. One of the most important sources of new thinking, if not *the* most important from my perspective, was the criminologist George Kelling, whose contribution is known in shorthand as the "Broken Windows" theory of policing. Kelling graduated from St. Olaf College in Minnesota in the 1960s, and while at Lutheran seminary in Minneapolis started working part time in a newly opened detention center for juveniles, which introduced him firsthand to the problems of crime and delinquency and began his interest in criminal justice. Dropping out after two years, Kelling became a probation officer in Hennepin County, which included Minneapolis. Needing a further degree to advance in the field, he enrolled at the University of Wisconsin in his hometown of Milwaukee and received his master's in social work.

While there, he developed a reputation for successfully writing grant proposals for progressive organizations, and was contacted by a militant Milwaukee group known as the Commandos to help them earn funding to work with juveniles. Through the Commandos, Kelling became involved in the civil rights movement, writing proposals behind the scenes.

Kelling worked for two years as assistant superintendent of a detention center in Milwaukee, after which he was invited to apply for a job running a psychiatric residential treatment center for aggressive and disturbed juveniles in Lino Lakes, Minnesota, outside of Minneapolis-St. Paul. He taught five years as an assistant professor at University of Wisconsin–Milwaukee, later earning a PhD in social welfare from UW–Madison.

At UW–Milwaukee, the president of the Milwaukee police union took Kelling's course and asked whether he would be willing to work for the union as well. Kelling was open about his continuing engagement with the Commandos, but the official said it didn't make much difference to him. And so, with both sides aware, Kelling had the unusual experience of working with civil rights groups and the police—"the hippies" and "the pigs"—during the height of the unrest of the sixties.

Kelling developed some interest in policing at that time, but didn't see it as a career path. In 1970, while pursuing his doctorate at UW–Madison he was mentored by one of the country's foremost criminologists, Herman Goldstein, and criminal law professor Frank Remington. Both encouraged him to take a position with the newly created Police Foundation performing evaluations.

The consulting life was not entirely easy. In Texas, a wealthy and influential right-wing police benefactor called him an eastern cultural imperialist working to take over the Dallas Police Department. Kelling kept his office blinds closed for the remainder of his tenure there. Still, Kelling grew to become a noted theorist. He never lost his focus on policing in the context of the broader community and its morale. In the 1970s, discussing his thinking, he wrote, "Permissiveness grew out of the idea of 'victimless crimes,' such as prostitution, aggressive panhandling, drug-induced and drunken behavior, creating graffiti, and squeegeeing. After all, the argument goes, who is really hurt by such crimes? Many, like prostitution, are consensual, agreed upon by and affecting only seller and buyer. Why should the state and its criminal justice apparatus be concerned when nobody is hurt? Police have enough to do just handling serious crime, let alone nonviolent deviance. This argument went further: Much behavior considered deviant is really acceptable under other cultural standards— ergo, enforcing laws against minor crimes is really imposing white middle-class standards on minorities, the poor, and later, the homeless. And the argument was extended further still: Society is enriched and ennobled by much nonviolent deviance. Graffiti is seen as a valid artistic expression by society's victims and should be appreciated as such, and aggressive panhandling is an important political message about social inequities."

But George knew that these "victimless" crimes did have a victim: the community.

"Lost in all of this," Kelling wrote, "were the enormous consequences to communities of uninterrupted disorderly conditions in neighborhoods. Johns might or might not be victims or criminals, but neighborhoods certainly lose out. Aggressive schizophrenics, drunken youths, promiscuous and scantily clad prostitutes, and all sorts of other 'nonviolent' deviants might enjoy their 'liberty interests,' but neighborhood residents who could not move were virtually imprisoned in their homes. Most tragically, such conditions affected those with the least resources to deal with it: the poor, minorities, elderly, and other inner-city residents. The idea that behaviors like public urination and defecation, drunkenness, drug dealing, aggressive panhandling, and other such forms of illegal, loutish behavior were somehow a sign of cultural pluralism was a cruel mockery; it represented condescension toward both the poor and ethnic and racial minorities, and it forestalled official efforts to restore order and reclaim neighborhood streets. Disorderly, crime-breeding conditions were allowed to exist in inner cities that simply never would have been tolerated in middle-class areas. The nurturing institutions of society—family, religion, schools, and commerce—could not function under such circumstances."

I was seeing the truth of this firsthand in Boston. The steady rise of crime that began in the seventies continued unabated, increasing every year for two decades. We knew this not least because with our increased technological professionalization we had the resources to document it fully. As we came to rely on the FBI's Uniform Crime Reporting program, which gathered data from nearly eighteen thousand city, university and college, county, state, tribal, and federal law enforcement agencies voluntarily reporting data on crimes brought to their attention, we had the facts.

In the BPD commissioner's office, Steve Dunleavy was an obsessive perfectionist almost entirely concerned with politics, technology systems, and imagery, and right across the hall, overseeing operations, Bob Wasserman was more of a philosopher. They battled for the soul of the department.

Wasserman had a degree in sociology from Antioch College and a master's in police administration from Michigan State. He looked like a scholar, with a mustached overbite and a beard that came and went, and he spoke with a stammer. Bugs Bunny jokes trailed in his path. He was a liberal, and his police philosophies were more than liberal, which put him outside the department's mainstream. He didn't care. He was curt, and didn't suffer fools gladly or at all. He had been director of the Police Academy and was roundly respected without being well liked. Al Sweeney spoke highly of him, but then Al was half cop, half maverick, so that wasn't a surprise.

Wasserman was serious about most everything. He went out of his way to identify and promote department personnel whom he thought had promise. I had Sweeney's recommendation so he took a look at me. I wasn't shaken by his gruffness; he turned out to be not only a brilliant theoretician and practitioner, but also a very good guy with a warm side all the more affecting because it was so well hidden. He became an important mentor.

Wasserman approached policing as problem solving. He believed fervently that cops should have a solid base in the communities they served, that those communities were best served by people they knew and in whom they could develop trust, that police and their neighborhoods needed to be partners against crime. He was a walking, breathing devotee of what would come to be defined as Community Policing.

Wasserman introduced me to the work of George Kelling. In 1972, Wasserman had been the primary consultant to the Kansas City Police Department under its esteemed chief Clarence M. Kelley. Kelley was disappointed in the proposals coming from his own command staff, which suggested essentially that the department do better at what they had always been doing, which was riding around in cars and responding quickly to calls for service. At a time when the KCPD was about to hire three hundred new officers, there was strong disagreement among the command staff as to where and how they would best be deployed. Chief Kelley asked, "What am I going to do with the three hundred cops?" Wasserman suggested forming a task force and studying the question: Does police omnipresence, the randomized police patrol, really have an impact on the level of crime and citizen satisfaction? He called in Kelling.

Almost everyone on the task force agreed that the new cops should go on preventative patrol. Wasserman asked, "How do you know that preventative patrol actually does anything?" The group response was, "But that's what we are supposed to be doing."

Kelling said, "We can test that." Funded by the Police Foundation, Kelling and his team developed the Kansas City Preventive Patrol Experiment.

The experiment divided the patrol routing of three different police beats in southern Kansas City into three areas: the first, termed "reactive," received no routine police car patrols, with police responding only to calls from residents; the second, termed "proactive," was assigned two to three times the normal number of patrols, while the third, termed "control," maintained its normal level. If the "reactive" area, the area without police, had a call for service, an officer from the adjoining beat would have to go answer it and then leave. He could not stay there; there was no patrol in area one. In his evaluation, Kelling would measure the impact of that assignment on the southern Kansas City community's perceptions of safety and levels of crime.

The central issue was: Did the officers riding around in cars make any difference in managing fear of serious crime in that city? The experiment was designed to answer the following questions:

> Would citizens notice changes in the level of police patrol and crime?

> Would different levels of visible police patrol affect recorded crime or the outcome of victim surveys?

> Would citizen fear of crime and attendant behavior change as a result of differing patrol levels?

> Would their degree of satisfaction with police change?

Preventive patrol—riding around in cars and responding rapidly—was simply biblical in origin for most police; there was no other way to consider policing. The Kansas City Preventive Patrol Experiment was the first empirical study into whether or not it actually worked.

Kelling's findings did not make him popular in police circles: whether it was fear of crime, noticed levels of patrol, or level of crime itself, rapid response made absolutely no difference. None whatsoever. The results also clearly showed that the demand for regular foot patrol, on the other hand, was constant; fear of crime was substantially reduced in areas where foot patrol was installed, and increased where foot patrol was withdrawn. The same results occurred regarding appreciation for officers. His summary report stated, "Analysis of the data gathered revealed that . . . while foot patrol may not have a significant effect on crime, it does affect citizens' fear of crime, the protective measures they take to avoid crime, and the perceived safety of the neighborhoods in consistent and systematic ways. In general, when foot patrol is added, citizens' fear of typical street crimes seems to go down and generalized feelings of personal safety go up."

It's hard to overstate how much these results would shake up the policing profession.

In 1977, Boston's District 4 was economically distressed and struggling. The area was home to a notable collection of museums, universities, and arts institutions, including Northeastern University, Boston University, the Museum of Fine Arts, Boston Symphony Hall, Berklee College of Music, the Boston Conservatory of Music, Fenway Park, and the First Church of Christ, Scientist. Visitors from tonier addresses like Lexington, Concord, and other suburban locations coming to see exhibits, attend performances, and take in a ball game were increasingly becoming victims of crime. The hotels in the area were having a hard time making a go of it, businesses were concerned for the well-being of their physical plants and their workers, and the lack of safety was occasioning middle-class flight. Prevalent thinking held that the cities were over and the suburbs were where you wanted to be. And since, to put it crudely, the only ones who could afford to move to the suburbs in the seventies tended to be white people, the cities were being left behind for minorities. One hundred thousand residents fled the city. Streets and houses were being abandoned; you could buy an apartment building in District 4 for $15,000 that today would go for about $1.5 million *per floor*.

In order to create a safe environment for their businesses and their visitors, a consortium of twenty-one institutions, under the leadership of writer, editor, and former Boston University vice chancellor Claire Cotton, approached Bob Wasserman to initiate a partnership among their membership, the police, and the neighborhoods that would improve public safety and address deteriorating conditions. Wasserman got the funding from the Police Foundation for the creation of what was to be called the Boston-Fenway Program. With Commissioner Jordan's blessing, he wanted me to run it. I was desperate for the chance to get back out in the field and practice what I'd been learning.

I encouraged my old college classmate and sector-car partner Mickey Roache to move up to headquarters and take my place, which worked out extremely well. Smart, moral, hardworking, unbiased, Mickey took control of a new, extraordinarily creative unit, the Community Disorders Unit, whose mandate was to investigate race crimes. He was perfectly placed and Boston was the better for it. For my part, I left the commissioner's office and was assigned to turn around District 4, working in close collaboration with Claire Cotton and the Boston-Fenway Program.

District 4 was huge and wonderful. It was home to the working-class, mixed-population South End; the upscale Back Bay, essentially Boston's Upper East Side Manhattan; and East Fenway and West Fenway, which held so many of the city's educational and cultural institutions along with beautiful Frederick Law Olmsted–designed parks, and was the home of Fenway Park and the Boston Red Sox. Kenmore Square was the heart of the city's nightclub district. Teeming with college kids, District 4 was probably Boston's most racially, culturally, and economically diverse area.

Having some hotshot young sergeant come in with the mandate to pull your shop apart might not have gone over well with any high-ranking officer. In BPD culture, a sergeant didn't go up to a captain and say, "Hey, there is another way of doing this." What he'd be likely to be told was, "That's great, kid. Shut up, just do what you were doing." Most ranking officers had tremendous pride in the history of the BPD. "We are the Boston police," they believed. "We can do everything, we don't need anyone's help." That was the mentality, going back decades: *We don't need anybody, we can do it ourselves.* If some knew di Grazia's changes were necessary—and this was not a widely held view—they really didn't want their noses rubbed in it. Even though I had been sent by the commissioner, I was working for the civilian whiz kids, and both district commander Captain James McDonald and Deputy Superintendent James "Mickey" MacDonald took their time checking me out.

Captain James McDonald was an easygoing, smart, old-school manager, definitely of the old-guard generation. His cops loved him. Mickey MacDonald—"Old Blue Eyes," a rugged, handsome, cigar-chomping Irish guy born and raised in South Boston, with a barrel chest and a constant tan; the same guy who had chewed me and Al Sweeney out in Dorchester several years earlier—had made the transition from old school to new and taken di Grazia's innovations to heart. Fortunately, he and I hit it off and he quickly became another mentor. He set me up with an office right outside his own and we rode around the district for a couple of hours each day, just so I could get a feel of the territory, patrolling together, chasing calls, observing. He gave me extraordinary access to his lifetime of experience. He understood the importance of personally observing conditions and using that knowledge to instruct or correct if necessary. Mickey MacDonald was the leader I wanted to be. He understood the importance of fighting crime, controlling disorder, and interacting with the community.

MacDonald had command presence. When he walked into a room, whether in plain clothes or his always-crisp uniform, you knew he was the guy in charge. I loved and respected Mickey, and by watching him work learned the effect a strong commander can have on an organization. Nothing went on in the district that he didn't know about. His cops respected him and they worked for him. With his collaboration and approval, Bob Wasserman and I took that district apart and put it back together.

MacDonald was a great believer in using crime statistics to target hot spots and stay on top of his detectives, but he also understood the importance of working with the community. When I arrived, the district had been divided, like all others in Boston, into sectors comprised of several federal census tracts, each with approximately the same calls-for-service workload and each assigned a police car. Seventeen sectors, seventeen sector cars, each ostensibly spending most of its time in its own area. However, a barrage of 911 calls, particularly in the more troublesome zones, could conceivably send all seventeen cars to the South End. As the system had been designed, one emergency could empty all the other sectors and leave most of the district essentially unpoliced.

Wasserman and I decided a restructuring of District 4 was crucial. He had visited London a few years earlier to examine the Metropolitan Police's methods, and had been very taken with their classifications of patrol units. London had two types of patrol cars: "Panda" cars—small, black automobiles with a white stripe around the middle, designed to remain in the neighborhoods to which they were assigned—and rapid response vehicles, Jaguars and BMWs, which zoomed to problem areas when called. The presence of Panda cars ensured that all communities would be policed all the time, while rapid response vehicles gave the police an immediate presence at every emergency. As soon as the rapid response units got things under control, they would leave and the Panda car would handle the situation, because they owned the neighborhood. This English system was the first example of a neighborhood-based policing initiative; neighborhood cops stayed in their sector, and a big part of their job was to get to know their community.

Wasserman and I developed the Neighborhood Responsive Police Plan. We divided District 4 into four quadrants—Back Bay, South End, East Fenway, West Fenway—and within them developed sixteen sectors culturally identifiable in the public's mind and assigned a car to each. We instituted a two-tiered response system consisting of two-officer rapid response cars that would respond to all Priority One calls, and two-officer neighborhood sector cars that would remain in the community at all times. A review of the previous year's dispatches told us approximately how many of each we would need.

There were 212 cops in District 4. I spent time riding with them, getting to know the men and few women individually. As a young beat cop I had always complained that we were left in the dark, not asked to contribute ideas we picked up from working our assignments, so when I got the opportunity I shared information with my officers and asked for their input. I had been excluded; I wasn't going to do that to other cops.

We had some questions about staffing. I needed approximately 50 rapid-response cops and 150 to staff up the Panda cars. How would we decide who went where? I said, "Why don't we ask them?"

I needn't have worried. We took a poll and found the idea of constant action was intriguing to younger officers, while cops with more years on the job felt "I'm too old to go running around doing all this stuff. I want to be able to work in the neighborhood." Done! The young hotshots who wanted to zoom around the district fighting crime went into rapid response, the older officers who liked the idea of staying in one area got the comforts of home. As it shaped up, the numbers worked out perfectly. I was able to get enough volunteers for each, and the two-tiered response plan rolled. I also made a conscious effort to assign the same officers to the same beats on the same shifts. I wanted the officers to be comfortable in their routines and the neighborhood to feel and be policed by their neighborhood cops.

To make a neighborhood not only be safe but *feel* safe, you've got to know what it's thinking. Police theory at that time held that major crimes were of major importance, and lesser offenses required less attention. I needed to know exactly what people in each community wanted.

District 4 was extremely large. It was unreasonable to expect that people would leave their own neighborhoods and travel great distances to meet with us, so we organized meetings in each sector—three or four a week for the entire first year I was there, at local community organizations or in schoolrooms and community halls that we set up ourselves. We leafleted, we provided refreshments, we did everything I could think of. We took the police department to the people.

We came armed with statistics, thinking this was what people wanted to hear. I was something of a computer whiz kid back in the early days of computers and I didn't want to be asked a question I couldn't answer. I had it all: major crimes broken out per FBI Uniform Crime Reporting, response times, and updates on major crime that was occurring in their sector. Instead of a deputy superintendent who would give them the party line, I brought the cops and the supervisor who patrolled their individual streets and neighborhood. Meet your police. We talked about what we were doing to keep them safe, how we were spending most of our time chasing 911 calls, and we gave them tips to help them prevent crime around them.

This was evidence-based policing, the idea being that we were able to document all of what we were doing. With my data printed out on computer sheets I could tell the gathering how many cars I had at any given time, and how many of them were in service. Once a year we would reexamine our numbers and restaff accordingly.

We explained our procedures. Measuring the numbers of calls, the amount of time our cars were in service, the time they were out of service, our development of Zero Car Accountability, the ability to respond to every Priority One call with 95 percent immediacy. We wanted the community to know we had its back.

As well as rolling out our statistics, we listened. "What are your problems?" we asked the neighbors who attended. "What is the biggest issue here?" Their answers surprised us. They wanted to talk about the quality of their lives.

Now it stands to reason. Back then we were shocked. Few people get robbed at gunpoint, fewer still know someone who has been killed in a violent confrontation. But everybody had a daughter, son, husband, wife, friend, or acquaintance who felt threatened walking by a drunk in the street. Everyone had to pass by stores that were tagged with graffiti, or was sometimes kept awake by raucous noise at night, by the gang on the corner. Nobody wanted to fight his way through a lineup of hookers to get home. The community didn't want to feel besieged.

I had hired former Amtrak policewoman Julie Rossborough and her sister, Cynthia Brown, to help identify community groups and issues and to arrange community meetings, at which they took notes. Each meeting averaged around forty questions, some of them very irate. Years of anger and frustration from not having their needs met led to some very pointed comments. Among their major complaints was that they never saw the police. *"Where are the cops?!"* We heard it consistently. Minor crime or major, they said, the only time we see you guys is after something has already occurred. The public was saying, "Where are the police? Where is the government?" Our absence created more fear. Government, in the meantime, was paying no attention. Police were being downsized and only major crime was prioritized.

Rossborough pinpointed approximately twenty key issues being raised on a regular basis. In my files I still have the old original charts of what the neighbors wanted to talk about. The lesson I took from this yearlong immersion in community awareness was that the BPD had to change its priorities. What we thought merited attention was not aligned with the community's actual overriding concerns. Cops wanted to take down felons; they were less excited about dealing with the quality-of-life issues that the community was concerned with and experienced every day. Community members wanted to feel safe in their homes and on the streets. As police managers, it was increasingly clear that our job was to satisfy both groups.

Bob Wasserman began to put systems in place to deal with this. The issues we had to face were:

- How do we motivate the cops?

- How do we get cops to respond to the identified concerns of the public?

- How do we get the cops to work with the public?

- How do we get the operational philosophy of the Boston Police Department more in sync with the needs of the district?

Our Neighborhood Responsive Police Plan took some selling. We were advocating a radical overhaul of standard BPD procedure, and there were those who were perfectly happy to choose conformity over creativity. I was to make a presentation not only to Commissioner Jordan and the brass, but also to the legendary former NYPD commissioner Patrick Murphy, who was heading up the Police Foundation. I woke up that morning with laryngitis, but croaked my way through. Murphy bought right in, and Jordon signed off on it as well. I was twenty-nine years old and running the show. I was thrilled.

For starters, I began to collect crime data. Deputy MacDonald was thrilled at this; it helped reinforce our relationship. I requisitioned giant maps of the district from City Hall, overlaid them with acetate, and covered all four walls of my office with this detailed schematic. Sergeant Bob O'Toole, a former member of the Tactical Patrol Force who would eventually serve as my adjutant, said it looked like I was planning the invasion of Normandy.

Armed with multicolored stick-on dots, I collected and collated the day's crimes—red for burglary, blue for robbery—and covered the color spectrum with the wide spread of District 4's crimes. Each dot stated crime and time, and I instructed our civilian employee, Tommy Santry, to put the dots on the map every night and pencil in the date of the crime. What emerged was a vivid, color-coded indicator of each day's specific criminal activity.

I placed these maps in my office, and then hung a duplicate in the guard room where my officers would gather for roll calls. Very soon, cops coming back from days off or about to go out in the field would come in and see the clusters that were starting to develop. It got to be a daily routine. Also in the room was a blue four-drawer file cabinet that, when opened to their sector, would provide reports that corresponded to the dots. This was visceral crime fighting. Each cop could see, in color, the hot spots in their sector; they jumped out at you. At roll call my officers would be told, "Look at it. We had ten purse snatches yesterday at the Symphony, where these old ladies are trying to go to the Wednesday matinee. Get out there and stop this!"

On Sundays I would sit in my office, look at the clusters of color, and put together directed patrol forms assigning these hot spots to each sector's officers—day tour, evening tour, morning tour. At first they laughed, called me Lord Dots. It was not an affectionate nickname. They were out there on the streets, they knew their sectors, what did they need with stick-on dots?

Cops are idealists wrapped in a shell of cynicism. The nature of the work requires self-protection: gallows humor in the face of horrible things; mistrust in the face of lies from suspects and even victims on the one side, and sometimes, they feel, from the bosses on the other. Their belief that it's possible to make a safer world—the reason they swore an oath in the first place—can get covered by something hard and wrapped in what we call the blue cocoon. Four or five years in, many feel cheated by the profession because the organization and its bureaucracy does not respond to their ideas, and the job is not what they'd hoped it would be. Alienation sets in. I had certainly felt that. Which is not to say that policing couldn't be what they hoped, but it generally isn't. It's a truism: If you want to change police culture, you don't want to make rules, you don't want to set down laws. If you want to change police culture, change the day-to-day work—change what cops *do*.

Standing in front of the maps, officers checked out their own areas and everybody else's. I made a point of being around at roll calls when they were taking all this in, just to make contact. I wasn't pushing it in their faces, I didn't order them to stand there and get lectured to—when I was a beat cop I wouldn't have stood for that any more than they would. I just made the facts available and trusted in all good cops' desire to get the job done. I watched as officers started to say, "Wait a minute, there's a pattern here. Wow, look at this." And then they got in their car and headed to that area. I understood a basic but very key concept: most cops want to do police work. I felt if I could unleash them and give them the tools they wanted and needed, they would work for me tirelessly. This was my first leadership opportunity, and I found myself seeing the work through their eyes. "What do you need?" I asked. And then, "What can I provide?"

It didn't take long for the cops to buy in. Then they went out and solved some crimes and prevented others.

One of the Boston-Fenway Program's great revelations was the undeniable benefit gained by assigning the same officer to the same neighborhood. Although 911 had changed the way we were doing business, the Boston-Fenway Program changed it back. Where 911 was incident driven, Boston-Fenway was problem driven. The businesses and people who lived in these neighborhoods began to know the officers assigned to protect them. We did not simply chase the criminals and leave, we paid attention to the tenor of the community. As opposed to simply going to the meetings and saying, as we had in the past, "This month there have been seventeen house break-ins, we've made fifteen arrests. Close your windows, lock your doors, have a great day," now officers would meet with the neighbors and say, "How can we do this better and what do you need?" And then they would listen.

Not every meeting turned out so well.

Boston's large Chinese community was very upset because there was a lot of crime in Chinatown and they felt they were being preyed on and the department was not taking it seriously. A big meeting was announced and I sent Community Service Officer John Sacco, accompanied by Cynthia Nichols, to represent us. Sacco was a personable, rough-around-the-edges lifetime cop, and despite his good intentions, things didn't go well for him. "You know," he told the sizable crowd, "you guys complain that you are victims of crime. Well, everyone knows you don't use the bank, you put the money, where do you put the money? Under the mattress? Get the money out of your mattress and put it in the bank! And another thing. When you Chinamen go to the bank, don't shuffle along and put your head down. Stand up like men and walk to the bank with some confidence. That could keep the criminals away."

At this point, as you can imagine, there was quite an uproar. People began yelling, and then a huge contingent stormed out and went to head-quarters, all screaming. This was a master class in management mistakes. Eventually, our relationship with the community healed, as we increased our presence there and crime went down.

Thanks again to Bob Wasserman, I soon had an experience that fundamentally shifted my understanding of policing.

While in London, Wasserman had become familiar with the legacy of Sir Robert Peel. Commissioner di Grazia hosted the head of London's Metropolitan Police, Sir Robert Mark, in his office, and through Wasserman's good graces I was among the small number of newly promoted young sergeants invited to meet Commissioner Mark, who discussed Peel's profound influence on British policing. I had never heard of Peel, but that was entirely my ignorance, and I made up for it as fast as I could.

Sir Robert Peel was a visionary. In 1829 he created London's first full-time professional police organization, the Metropolitan Police Force at Scotland Yard. Peel declared, "The police are the public and the public are the police," and developed the idea that the police hold and exercise their power with the implicit consent of those whom they are policing: "policing by consent." London's "bobbies" were named after Sir Robert Peel. "It should be understood, at the outset," he said, "that the object to be obtained is the prevention of crime."

Peel codified his vision in the Nine Principles of Policing, given to every new Metropolitan Police officer in 1829 and entirely applicable today:

PRINCIPLE 1: The basic mission for which the police exist is to prevent crime and disorder.

PRINCIPLE 2: The ability of the police to perform their duties is dependent upon public approval of police actions.

PRINCIPLE 3: Police must secure the willing cooperation of the public in voluntary observance of the law to be able to secure and maintain the respect of the public.

PRINCIPLE 4: The degree of cooperation of the public that can be secured diminishes, proportionately, to the necessity of the use of physical force.

PRINCIPLE 5: Police seek and preserve public favor, not by catering to the public opinion, but by constantly demonstrating absolute impartial service to the law.

PRINCIPLE 6: Police use physical force to the extent necessary to secure observance of the law or to restore order only when the exercise of persuasion, advice and warning is found to be insufficient.

PRINCIPLE 7: Police at all times should maintain a relationship with the public that gives reality to the historic tradition that the police are the public and the public are the police; the police being only members of the public who are paid to give full-time attention to duties which are incumbent on every citizen in the interests of community welfare and existence.

PRINCIPLE 8: Police should always direct their action strictly towards their functions and never appear to usurp the powers of the judiciary.

PRINCIPLE 9: The test of police efficiency is the absence of crime and disorder, not the visible evidence of police action in dealing with it.

There is so much there. The fact that police should *prevent* crime—*and disorder*. The necessity of public approval. The idea that the police are the public and the public are the police. In the United States, policing was done *to* the public. In my experience, being a cop had meant imposing the will of the law *on* the public. In Great Britain, largely because of Peel's vision, the police thought of and carried themselves as being *with* and *part of* the public. The difference in approach was profound.

This is what Wasserman was trying to instill; this was the guiding concept that di Grazia was trying to bring to life. Police needed to be *of* the people, *with* the people, rather than separate *from* the people. As much as we talked about the neighborhood cop and Officer Friendly, the guiding principle of American police organizations, from back in the 1950s and '60s and continuing into the '70s, was the idea that *We take care of business. We will take care of you, but you will keep out of our hair and leave us alone.* Wasserman is one of the underappreciated heroes of the evolution of American policing in the past fifty years; he got it long before the profession as a whole did. I took their influence to heart. With Sir Robert Peel, we felt that the basic mission for which police exist is to prevent crime and disorder. I understood very early on that if you can control disorder, you can go a long way to preventing more serious crime and addressing more effectively the concerns of the public.

The department was changing with the times in other ways, too. The Stonewall riots in New York had exploded only a few years earlier and the gay rights movement was beginning to come into its own. Complaints had been lodged that gay men would stand at urinals at the main branch of the Boston Public Library at Copley Square and solicit sex from other men. Boston PD undercover units were assigned there and many arrests were made. Barney Frank, then a member of the Massachusetts House of Representatives on his way to becoming a congressman, and not yet out of the closet, was upset at the robustness of the department's crackdown.

Wasserman told Frank, "Look, we will stop arresting, but this is a problem, and the gay community has to stop it themselves. You have to get the community organized." Wasserman assigned me to be the Boston Police Department's first liaison to the local gay community. I had had no interaction with the gay community. I told one of their representatives, David Brill, a reporter for a local gay newspaper, "You guys have got to tell your people that solicitation is out of bounds, it can't go on. We don't want to make arrests; we just want to stop illegal activity." Through a process of calm conversation rather than mutual hostility, we found common ground and both the solicitations and the arrests came to an end.

Busing, desegregation violence, and violence directed against gays had been growing in Boston, and through the influence of Bob Wasserman, a BPD unit was formed specifically designed to investigate hate crimes, the first in the country. The first federal hate crimes statute dated to 1968, but once there was an understanding that "we'll treat these crimes differently because they have different impacts," officers started to change their thinking. The aphorism again: You can only expect what you inspect. For instance, Black people moving into some white neighborhoods would have a brick thrown through their bedroom window in the middle of the night. They would call 911 and it would be classified as vandalism, a very low-priority crime that during busy weekend hours might not be responded to at all. The Community Disorders Unit was created to give such crimes the high-priority attention they deserved.

Instead of looking to keep gays and African Americans under control, we were now effectively supposed to be the instrument to help them gain their civil rights. It was an important change, though not all Boston cops were on board. Getting them there was, and is, a much longer process. Talk about a role reversal! Instead of keeping the lid on, the idea was to open the lid and help facilitate letting out some steam. At a time of turbulence, Boston was a microcosm of what was going on around the country. We established an annual cops versus gays softball game, though it wasn't until the mid-1980s that the first Boston cops felt comfortable enough to come out of the closet, and it was a lonelier journey than it should have been for years after that.

The Boston-Fenway Program showed results. When I was working in South Boston, we got hundreds of calls—always anonymous—from I and East Seventh Streets down by the beach, about gangs. Every night it was gangs. It got to be local knowledge that there were gangs in Southie. We'd take the call, run over to the corner where this gang was hanging out, break it up, and move on to the next call. Next night, same thing. More than a thousand times in the course of a year.

Nobody was happy. The callers were afraid, the young men didn't like being chased, the cops were annoyed at the constant futility of shooing away disrespectful boys. It was more nuisance than anything else; no crimes were being committed and we spent endless man-hours with nothing to show for it.

Finally, instead of just hopping in the car, we analyzed the problem. It turned out that the "gangs" were actually a bunch of ten-to-fourteen-year-old kids who lived in the neighborhood. There was a senior living complex across the street, and of course when they saw two kids bouncing a basketball, it was a gang. If the kids were out there making noise after eight o'clock at night, they were a *noisy* gang. So one of the men—the same guy every night—called it in! When we finally realized what was going on, someone was smart enough to say, "Maybe we should put the elderly and the kids together."

We sat them down in the same room. The level of hostility was high; neither the young folks nor the old ones were interested in making an accommodation. Both wanted the other gone.

"You know this kid here?" one of our officers asked a gray-haired man. Then to the kid, "What's your name, son?"

The boy answered. Might have been Billy O'Toole.

"You know any O'Tooles?" we asked the man. He gave us a couple of names.

"You know them?" we asked the boy.

"That's my dad."

"I went to school with that guy's father," said the old man.

"Sir, this is his grandchild."

They were all from Southie. All from the same community, all from the same cultural bloodline, if you will. It was just a question of getting to know each other.

It didn't take long before the kids set up a computer program to teach the elderly, and the elderly were mentoring the kids at school. All of a sudden the calls at that intersection dropped dramatically because it wasn't a gang anymore, they were neighborhood kids doing what they were doing.

I kept that in mind. I was constantly thinking, *There has to be a better way of doing this.* The Boston-Fenway Program was a step in the right direction, but it was only one district. How could we take it citywide?

In 1980, internal politics and a looming *Boston Globe* article that promised to reveal incompetence and ineffectiveness at the highest levels of the organization necessitated changes in both BPD leadership and operational structure. I had made lieutenant in March 1978 and had been getting good reviews for the District 4 neighborhood-policing initiative. The powers that be called me into headquarters to participate in the reorganization of the department. I thought, *This is incredible! Here I am in this inner circle. It's the chance of a lifetime!* Jack Gifford was moved up to deputy superintendent. I tried to get Al Sweeney considered but the "wise-ass kid" had pissed off too many powerful people. As the afternoon went on and positions were filled I didn't know where I fit in. Executive Superintendent John Doyle was being moved out laterally. Who was going to replace him?

"You are," said Commissioner Jordan.

"As superintendent?"

"Yeah. You'll be the executive superintendent."

The world had turned upside down. I had been at the bottom, now I was at the top!

I was thirty-two years old, I had been a lieutenant for a year and a half, every other superintendent was in his fifties, and almost all of them had been on the job longer than I'd been alive. Now I was number two in the department, the top uniformed officer in the BPD!

I had plans! Neighborhood Policing would bring back the beat cop. A partnership between the people and the police would bring down crime. Using District 4 as a model I intended to expand the Boston-Fenway Program to the entire city.

In my office on the legendary sixth floor of police headquarters—the same hallowed real estate where I had walked in wide-eyed to meet Commissioner di Grazia only five years earlier—we developed maps, graphs, pictures. The computer revolution was still largely in the distance, and when I arrived, pretty much all the department computer could tell me was where our patrol cars were. Not good enough. I wanted to be on top of everything.

I had a 4' x 8' piece of cobalt-blue plywood installed as a bulletin board that ran the length of one wall. From it I hung fourteen clipboards, each with a different heading: Crime Index, Clearance Rate, Response Time, Sick Time, Overtime, Personnel, Bureau Stats, District Stats, 911 Calls, Deactivated Calls, Total Calls, Homicide, Workload Analysis, and Zero Car Accountability. How many calls had we answered the day before? How many cops were out sick? How much money was left in our overtime account? I needed all the answers—timely, accurate information available to be acted upon immediately. My staff was in early each morning collating the information to put an immediate picture of what had happened the day before at my fingertips. Lord Dots gone wild! The clipboards were both functional and symbolic: I had an eye on the whole city and I wanted to show everyone who came into my office that I was staying on top of it. Al Sweeney nicknamed this the Billy Board, and ultimately I had Billy Boards installed in districts throughout the city.

But whiz-kid hard work wasn't the key to the old-boy network. At five o'clock each afternoon Commissioner Jordan would put his feet on his desk while he and his cohorts sat in his office, smoked pipes and cigars, and told cop stories, all the men and most of the stories older than I was. I'd hear them laughing, but I rarely joined in—there was work to do. But this was a mistake. Police work thrives on storytelling and community, and I wasn't smart or experienced enough to understand that sometimes you've got to both schmooze and supervise.

I chaired weekly meetings of all the superintendents, at which we reviewed command decisions and plotted out the next seven days. I'm very certain these men disliked answering to a kid who had recently jumped four ranks, but each had a direct line to Jordan if they wanted to use it. Jack Gifford gave me a sign that I displayed prominently on my bookcase for the old guard to see: YOUTH AND SKILL WILL WIN OUT EVERY TIME OVER AGE AND TREACHERY.

And then we got hit by a truck.

Boston's municipal government was funded largely by property taxes. With its abundance of colleges, universities, and religious institutions— they comprised 50 percent of the property, and as tax-exempt institutions paid zero in taxes—the city was constantly in need of revenue. When it could not convince the state legislature to implement a city sales tax, the resulting shortfall and the need to raise property taxes began to drive out both businesses and the middle class. Voter resentment around the property tax issue led to the passage of Proposition 2½, known as the Tregor Bill, which capped the growth of any city's property tax base at 2½ percent per year. Boston was devastated.

After Mayor Kevin White failed to land the vice-presidential nomination, he had made a concerted effort to regain his standing as one of America's leading mayors by encouraging expansion and growth in the city. The busing debacle had cost Boston tens of millions of dollars, but Mayor White designed a plan for citywide regeneration and development. Among his bullet points was the growth and professionalization of the police department. But when the funds vanished, he proposed cutting back on city services—which included laying off one fourth of the police department, one fourth of the fire department, and closing half the city's police stations—perhaps believing these draconian threats would move the legislature to fold under the pressure of a wounded major city. It was a game of civic chicken, and we all lost.

I was assigned to attend large public meetings and somehow explain that the cutback would improve services. It was not a task I woke up each day looking forward to. *You've closed our neighborhood station, you're going to lay off twenty-five percent of the Boston Police Department, how the hell are you going to police the city?!* Try answering that to a packed house of irate Bostonians.

My vanguard plan to bring Boston crime fighting into the modern age was dealt a death blow. Neighborhood Policing would not be implemented throughout the city. The turnaround I was absolutely certain would transform Boston was just not going to happen.

Not only were the people scared that crime would surge to their doorstep, the cops were wildly angry. The years of school-busing overtime pay associated with policing busing and other civil disorder had encouraged them to live beyond their means, and now, mortgage-saddled and cash-strapped, they suffered both financial and psychological distress, compounded by the layoffs. People with ten years in, men and women who had taken a civil-service job and believed they were secure for life, were now out of work with few prospects. It was my job to appear before the Civil Service Commission and testify at each of their layoff hearings, often attended by the cops' spouses and children, that with no money the city had to let these men and women go. To my dismay, I was the face of the layoffs.

To keep a police presence alive in the neighborhoods while still making budget cuts, support facilities were folded into the remaining station houses. This sounded like a reasonable idea; additional police personnel would be seen on the streets going to work each day rather than being invisible in disparate buildings spread across the city, and their presence would add to Boston's psychological well-being. Or so we thought. The Marine division was mothballed, the Police Museum locked up. But when the Police Academy, the very place where every cop had learned to be a cop, was closed and moved into one room of a decommissioned police station in East Boston, the decision was seen as a disgrace and an insult. The department to which I had given my heart was bleeding out.

The Boston Police Department had 2,800 officers when I joined in 1970. In 1980, as part of the defunding of the BPD, we were reduced to 1,544. Why do I remember that number? Because as executive superintendent I was exempt from removal, but I had to lay them off, including every cop who had been hired with me. All my friends and colleagues were off the job within six months. I had many over to the house for pizza and sodas to talk about what they were going through, and I tried to be completely evenhanded in what were the hardest personnel decisions of my life, but I felt terrible. A large part of a great police force was set adrift. Many of the cuts cost the department deeply in institutional memory and the goodwill of its officers. Last-in, first-out union rules meant these were the newest, best-trained, most diverse officers—the di Grazia classes. Some of our youngest and most energetic officers, almost every cop with a college degree, all of our female officers, and a significant percentage of our minority officers were let go. It would take a generation to repair the damage.

When the Tregor issue was finally resolved and we were in the process of rehiring the more than five hundred officers who had been laid off, Steve Dunleavy and George Regan of the mayor's press office arranged for *Boston* magazine to profile me. I think they were greasing the wheels for people to think of me as Commissioner Jordan's successor. I was fine with that. The writer spent considerable time with me and Sergeant Bob O'Toole, who drove every time we went out on patrol and attended the ceremony officiated by me and Jordan at District 11, welcoming back forty of the previously purged officers. At some point the journalist asked me what I saw as my future. "When Joe Jordan is ready to leave," I told him, "he'll be able to leave with his head held high and with flags flying." At the time, I felt I was being politic. "My personal goal," I said, "is to become commissioner. Be it one year or four years, that's what I want."

When the article was published, no one came out and said anything, but I could feel a seismic shift on the sixth floor.

In any organization I run, I want a second-in-command with the ambition to head up the place. I like having ambitious people around me. I couldn't care less if they want my job. Not the BPD. Not then. I was young, and in becoming executive superintendent I had stepped in front of some men who hadn't taken it well. I was in their sights. I had simply stated my desire, but Jordan's cronies heard it as a self-coronation. No one in the department says that kind of thing out loud; it's just not done.

The Boston Police Department breathes Irish-Catholic air. Irish Alzheimer's: You forget everything except the grudges. I was oblivious, too inexperienced to feel the plotting; I was going to work every day and finally beginning to enjoy my job again. I didn't know I was a dead man walking.

I got unceremoniously moved out. They named me Inspector of Bureaus, a position created for the occasion. In the BPD your car defines your status—an unmarked car was a status symbol—so they issued me a marked car, and a clunker at that. Clearly an insult. They intended to bury me. I played some of my own politics, working with Dunleavy and Regan to convince Mayor White that it wouldn't look good for the department to deep-six a young, energetic superintendent whom the press liked and supported. The mayor decided to present my demotion as a lateral transfer by letting me keep my rank and naming me liaison to the city's multiple community groups dealing with minority and gay issues.

I packed up my sign, YOUTH AND SKILL WILL WIN OUT EVERY TIME OVER AGE AND TREACHERY.

Boy, was I wrong. Rather than the heady heights of the sixth floor, I was assigned to a small corner room in Police District A. Mine was the only office on the floor; the rest of the space was taken by lockers. No secretary. Instead of being in plain clothes, I was back in uniform. Flashing message to anyone else in the organization who might have the temerity to say he's aiming for the top: Bratton's dead.

As you might expect, I was miserable. I felt my career was over. While all my friends in the department did everything they could, Bobby O'Toole, who had become my adjutant when I was promoted to executive superintendent, did the best job of softening the blow. He had been a motorcycle cop on the Tactical Patrol Force, and he got his auto-shop friends at the police garage to take my clunker and spiff it up into the best-looking car in the department. It came back looking like it just rolled off the showroom floor. No doubt the guys who had engineered my removal heard about it. It was a gesture of friendship in a time of deep pain and professional disappointment. I truly appreciated it. O'Toole, Dunleavy, Regan, and the mayor had effectively thrown me a life preserver.

CHAPTER 4

Tracks in the Wilderness

A fter four months in exile I was brought back to police headquarters. Not to put neighborhood policing into practice, mind you. I was named superintendent in charge of labor relations to be the point man arguing the case for one-officer cars, another harmful side effect of the Tregor Proposition 2½ debacle. The rank and file hated the idea of single-officer cars—partners are a staple of police culture, they become like family—and none of the other superintendents wanted to be its face. I had been the fall guy in closing police stations and firing five hundred cops, so they laid this off on me, too.

With the advent of police unions—still a relatively new development for the BPD—for the first time, cops became expensive and had aggressive union leadership lobbying on their behalf. Police unionism inevitably came in conflict with police management and professionalization. While police professionalization increasingly centered on the most efficient utilization of resources, police unionism was all about police officers' rights and working conditions. This is a constant tension that continues to this day.

Despite the assignment, I was nevertheless back in the halls of power, back on the sixth floor. Given an office next door to the commissioner's and important department symbols like an unmarked car and the opportunity to work in plain clothes, I slowly regained some authority within the organization. I turned what could have been a lasting confrontation into an effective collaboration by involving myself fully in the union world. That assignment would be an invaluable benefit to me in years to come. After several months spent successfully negotiating the new union contract involving the implementation of one-officer cars, I was then transferred to the Operations Division to straighten out the department's outdated and increasingly inefficient 911 system. I was feeling okay, but I had been burned, too. Maybe it was time to switch tracks.

Newly elected to his second term as governor, Michael Dukakis had campaigned on the promise to rebuild mass transit. As well as upgrading the infrastructure of the entire state, he and his transportation secretary, Fred Salvucci, lay the groundwork for the new Ted Williams Tunnel under Boston Harbor, reengineered the underground Central Artery that did away with the city's ugly elevated structure, and began to modernize and expand the Massachusetts Bay Transit Authority. Dukakis also decided it was time to invest in the modernization of the MBTA police department, and ordered a search for a new chief. MBTA general manager Jim O'Leary asked if I would be interested in the position. I thanked him and said I would consider it. I had been wounded by the Boston Police and here he was with a field dressing.

The MBTA was a wreck. The transit authority received nothing but negative press, including news headlines about "Terror Trains" and rising crime, and a *Globe* series focusing on police incompetence. Nobody seemed to be in charge.

I called Al Sweeney one night. I knew he'd interviewed for the job as well. "I've got some great news," I told him.

"Good. What's the news?"

"You're going to be the new deputy chief at the MBTA Transit Police."

"What do you mean, deputy chief? I applied for the chief's position. I didn't even know there was a deputy chief's position, why would there be a deputy chief's position?"

"Because I'm the new chief!"

"You son of a bitch. I have been talking to you about my interview. I poured my heart out to you!"

"Well," I told him, "I didn't want to say anything in case I didn't get it."

Governor Dukakis swore me in at the Park Street MBTA station kiosk on Boston Common. I liked the thought behind the symbolism, and the fact that the governor himself was presiding demonstrated that power and resolve were being focused on my small department.

Going from the huge resources of the BPD, even a downsized BPD, to the sixty-eight-person MBTA might have seemed like a fall, but for the first time I would actually be able to effect change on my own. When I arrived at the MBTA, its cops had terrible equipment and terrible facilities, and there were too few cops to effectively police a system that encompassed seventy-nine cities and towns. I knew if I could get our officers to feel like police officers, and upgrade their materials and equipment, they would feel better and work for me.

For instance, once MBTA cops were below ground in the subway they were out of reach; officers could not communicate with one another inside the transit system. They went down in the hole and were out of touch, with no way to relay information, call for backup, get help, or account for the safety of either the public or themselves if a problem was to occur. I lobbied for and received $4 million for the installation of a comprehensive, cutting-edge fiber-optic subway radio network. MBTA officers and the riding public were safer—and felt safer—than ever before.

Bob Wasserman, Al Sweeney, and I developed a seven-point anticrime plan, and Dukakis committed $6 million to bring it to life. I engineered a twofer: Sweeney and I would both come aboard, me as chief, he as deputy chief. Al was excellent at running day-to-day operations. He did all the hiring and handled the training side of the business. I dealt more at the policy level, creating goals and asking, "How do we get this done?" He would prepare three options, I would select one, he would make a counter-proposal, and between us we negotiated our way forward. In the two and a half years we spent together at the MBTA Police, there was never an issue I had to overrule.

I established Billy Boards specific to the MBTA. This time it was a progress chart: Here is the task, here is who is responsible, here is its current status, what's needed next, how much it's costing, and what is scheduled to be done. Every week I would gather my staff to focus on each job. We went around the table and each command staff officer would speak on the status of their project. I wanted to know where they stood, what they needed. And more important, everyone at the table had to sign off on their role in making that project succeed. I did not approve of information being shoveled into silos, where it would fight its way to the top and have to sift down before becoming accessible to anyone else in the organization. I wanted my cops to have a general understanding of the force and a great affection for it.

From 1983 to 1986, we grew the MBTA Police to 110 officers with 55 vehicles (today it has more than 350 officers). Why so many cars and trucks for a transit police force? We were a multicounty, 79-city-and-town transit system, encompassing buses, commuter trains, and subways, and while our police cops patrolled the subway, we needed the capacity to move quickly above ground.

We upgraded the equipment, changed the cars, improved the weapons, and spiffed up the uniforms. Sweeney and I hired and trained a new generation of officers, established a new set of patrol strategies, and grew the organization together for two years.

I paid intimate attention every day to the crime numbers and began comparing crime statistics week to week and month to month, showing patterns and trends as they developed. American policing somehow hadn't done that before; those comparisons were a business concept—how many sales did we make this February as compared to last? We were driving down crime and issuing reports detailing exactly how much safer it was to ride Boston's trains now than it was a year ago, a month ago, last week. "It's safe to ride" was our campaign motto. We were pleasing the governor and, just as important, the public.

We were holding a press conference at the newly renovated Harvard MBTA station, detailing its new security system, alarms, cameras, and increased safety, when a reporter said, "Chief, Commissioner Joe Jordan has just been checked into a rehab facility in Rhode Island. What would you like to say about an alcoholic police commissioner?" There was a gasp. I ignored the question.

Joe Jordan retired, and the search for a new police commissioner commenced. I was one of those mentioned as a possible successor, along with my mentor, Mickey MacDonald, and several others. In the meantime, there was a mayoral election. Ray Flynn, a South Boston city councillor whom nobody gave a chance, pulled off the win, and now word was out that he had selected Mickey. Al Sweeney's and my happy response was, "Oh my God, it's Mickey MacDonald!" So we took him out to lunch. "Look," we told him, "we just got word from reliable sources that the mayor has selected you." Mickey looked at us and said, "You're out of your mind, I'm not going to be the police commissioner. The mayor told me straight out it is not going to happen."

"But we have heard clearly: It is Mickey!"

And it was. Mayor Flynn selected Acting Lieutenant Mickey Roache, my former sector-car partner and college classmate, the guy I'd encouraged to take the sergeant's test and had brought into headquarters, a very quiet, introverted, humble guy. He and Ray Flynn were South Boston boys, and there was an element of comfort between them that few could approach.

On the first Sunday of his being named commissioner, Mickey Roache quietly invited me and Al up to his office and asked for a perspective from the outside looking in. What does the Boston Police Department look like from two respected, former superior officers who are now chief and deputy chief of the MBTA Police?

I launched into the program that had worked consistently well for me.

"I think you need new equipment, new cruisers, I think you need to re-imagine the organization. I think you need to give the officers a good reason to go out and do their police work. They are demoralized under Joe Jordan. You've got to pick a new command staff to do all these things."

Mickey turned to Al, who took a different approach. "You can do all the cosmetics that you want to do," he said. "And they are necessary. But like *This Old House*, you can do all the vinyl siding you want, and you can put a new roof on, but if the structure and the foundation needs attention and is rotting, you need to fix that first. I think you need to deliver the services. You're getting hit with story after story of officers having really nasty, negative interactions with citizens; we need to get police officers back to being good police officers, and paying attention to that, and holding people accountable. All right? We have seen too much of the negative side." This was the difference between Al and me; I was transformational, Al was developmental. Strategy versus tactics. That's why we made a good team; between the two of us we were usually able to cover all the bases.

Who did Mickey Roache install to do the job? My team. Jack Gifford was named superintendent-in-chief, Al Sweeney became superintendent of internal affairs, Mickey MacDonald was appointed chief of the Bureau of Field Services. I had spent years envisioning my own administration, and they were all in it. But I was now on the outside looking in. Commissioner Roache had the right guys—but in the wrong positions. This lineup needed a shuffle.

Jack Gifford was tough and smart, but he was the most *disorganized* organized person I'd ever met. He'd have been perfect controlling patrol forces or internal affairs, but I didn't think he could keep all the necessary balls in the air. Sweeney could do that in his sleep; he'd have been my superintendent-in-chief. With my systems, Sweeney's organizational abilities, Gifford's control of the streets, and MacDonald's maturity, we could have made a real difference to the city.

I let it be known to Commissioner Roache that I would very willingly step down as chief of the MBTA to be a BPD superintendent in some capacity, but I wasn't invited in at all. My team was running the Boston Police Department—*without me!*

My good friend and classmate from the recruit class of 1970, Tom Maloney, replaced Sweeney at the MBTA Police, and we continued to grow the organization and decrease crime. It didn't take long for the job to demand little more than maintenance. Crime was down, accreditation and size and equipment were up; I had turned it around and was ready to move on.

The Metropolitan Police, the Mets, was a division of the Metropolitan District Commission not known for its rigor, and the third largest police department in Massachusetts, behind the BPD and the state police. The Mets were responsible for parks, beaches, playgrounds, and property throughout a wide swath of Massachusetts. Governor Dukakis wanted to change the image and the way they did business. When I got the call to be superintendent I jumped at the chance to lead this six-hundred-person agency.

The Mets were one of the worst police organizations in America. Badly organized, badly equipped, and unaccountable, they were lacking in procedures and discipline, with a growing high-level corruption scandal. One of its captains had broken into the Civil Service Commission offices and stolen the exams that determined promotion, then sold them for three thousand dollars a shot and, in a final gesture, downgraded the scores of people he didn't like and upped the ones of people who were paying him. He was also involved in a major bank break-in in Medford over the Memorial Day weekend. Plus, my predecessor as superintendent was doing four years in federal prison for perjury. If that was the top, you can imagine the extent of the corruption down the chain.

I brought in an array of policing talent. I appointed Kathy O'Toole, one of my protégées whose career at the Boston Police Department had stalled, deputy superintendent for administration. I promoted Metropolitan Captain Al Seghezzi, who had fallen out of favor in the previous administration, to chief of patrol; he became a second Mickey MacDonald to me and welcomed the opportunity to reclaim his career. As my second-in-command, I named Tom White, a career veteran of the department, who welcomed the chance to restore the Mets' integrity and capabilities. Recent Northeastern University graduate Peter LaPorte shaved off his beard to become my staff assistant.

When we extensively analyzed the department we found it was even worse than I'd thought. It had poor facilities, with leaking roofs and falling plaster, and a radio system that hadn't been updated in decades and left Met officers with worse communications than cab drivers. They were supposed to investigate traffic accidents, but they never really looked into their own; of the 113 marked cruisers, only 25 had no body damage. No one was held accountable, few officers were disciplined, most just didn't care.

The exam scandal left officers convinced their supervisors had bought their jobs and had not earned their respect. The rank and file knew they could get away with anything, and as a result, they did. The Mets were tremendously demoralized and ineffective at their mission.

I have great faith in cops, even dispirited ones. I arranged to be picked up at home and brought to work by a different officer every morning. On the drive I asked each for their sense of the place and their ideas for bringing the Mets into the modern world. In my experience, cops didn't lie down on the job; I needed to know what had gone wrong. We wanted our officers to have pride in the Mets and themselves.

I gathered their thoughts, identified the department's strengths and weaknesses, identified the modern-world changes, and along with my staff developed a forty-six-page plan of action. For a downtrodden group of people, what was needed was a central purpose. We came up with a written statement:

METROPOLITAN POLICE VALUES

- The Metropolitan Police Department exists to protect and serve the public.

- The Department and its members will maintain the highest ethical standards of conduct.

- We will treat all citizens with dignity, respect, and courtesy.

- We will safeguard each citizen's rights to free expression, movement, and constitutional liberty while within the Metropolitan District Commission jurisdiction.

- We will use only minimum necessary force when performing our lawful duties.

- In applying the law, we will exercise discretion with consistency and equitableness.

- We are committed to giving each employee the authority to make decisions and to hold them accountable for their actions.

- The Department is committed to creating an environment that is productive and satisfying and of which its members can be proud.

Change has to be more than words, however. Motivating police to improve also takes training, accountability, and equipment. For example, cops like cars. Whoever was designing the Mets vehicles could not possibly have actually met a cop. A few years earlier, their cars had been orange and blue; the cops looked like Howard Johnson's delivery boys! No wonder morale was in the toilet. Who wants to be a cop in a HoJo car?! After that, because they patrolled the parks, the cars were painted green and white. Still awful. Now, MDC commissioner Bill Geary, my boss and an incredibly talented and creative manager working to overhaul the commission, helped design the markings on the new police cars and gave the Mets the best-looking police cruisers in Massachusetts. When the cops finally liked what they were riding around in eight hours a day, the quality of their work increased in proportion to their satisfaction. We also received $800,000 in state funding for eighty-nine cruisers, eight Suburbans with push bar bumper plates to push disabled vehicles off the highways, five patrol wagons, and a dozen motorcycles. It took some convincing, but eventually the Commonwealth ponied up $2.5 million for a new state-of-the-art radio system, including computer-aided dispatching and data processing and a citizen emergency call-box network. We offered to share it with the state police, but the Staties said they didn't need it.

I got us uniforms the Mets could actually show off, and distributed them to all levels of the organization. Look good, feel good. Top to bottom. I made promotion ceremonies into celebrations instead of bore-a-thons.

I also established discipline to get the cops' attention. Oral reprimands would be read at roll call; if you screwed up, the squad would know about it. You didn't want to do that twice. I gave out more oral reprimands in a single year than had probably been given in the organization's one-hundred-year history. And what happened? The auto accident rate decreased big-time, and fewer officers got injured. I knew I was onto something when the jokes started to appear. The officers gave me a T-shirt that read: I SURVIVED THE REPRIMANDS OF 1987.

I was learning how to run an organization. The key elements were attainable goals, discipline, elimination of corruption, equipment upgrades, responsiveness to officer concerns, and the shared sense of satisfaction for a job well done. My turnaround strategy: Talk to the officers and find out what they want and need. Get the funding to put those ideas into play. Keep a sharp eye on every detail and have an answer for every conceivable question. Once you complete those tasks and check a number of items off the wish list, a good commander can then start asking his troops to perform, and they will respond. I was confident in my policing concepts and believed the best way to implement them was first to meet the needs of the officers, then get their buy-in on what had to be done. We developed our own training as well. Dedicated staff spent three years significantly improving the curriculum. We improved facilities and worked hard to make the Mets feel like they were real cops again. The Mets' good work was rewarded and their job got more enjoyable.

And crime went down.

The modernization, improvement, and growing reputation of the Metropolitan Police began to piss off the much larger Massachusetts State Police, to the point that the Staties decided to attempt a formal absorption and thus get rid of us. They were the old guard—larger, more traditional, with a highly politically connected union. We were the Cinderella department. I didn't think the Staties could run our shop nearly as well as we did, and I fought the merger for a solid year. The fight grew bitter, and I sensed we were losing. It also became clear that when the merger came through I would lose my command and wind up in at best a second- or third-level position in the command staff of the Massachusetts State Police. After the hands-on thrill of turning around the Mets, that was not a job that excited me.

And then, out of the blue, I received an opportunity courtesy of Robert Kiley. Bob had a résumé straight out of a novel: CIA, Police Foundation, deputy mayor of Boston, CEO of the MBTA. Now he was the new chairman and CEO of the New York City Metropolitan Transit Authority, the agency responsible for the New York Transit Authority, which ran the city's subways and buses; Metro-North, a commuter rail line serving Westchester and other counties north of the city; the Long Island Rail Road; and a number of the city's bridges and tunnels. The MTA is one of those unique Big Apple creations, along with the Port Authority and co-op apartments, that couldn't really happen anywhere else. The result of dozens of public and private companies competing and merging and devouring one another, the MTA is a public benefit company. And although the bulk of its operations are in New York City, ultimately it answers to the governor of New York.

Bob was trying to fix the New York subway system, which was a disaster. Between 1945 and 1975, it had received zero capital investment, and as any New Yorker could tell you, was filthy, crime ridden, actively decaying, and dangerous. Cars careened by with walls and windows covered in what some called urban artwork, but to most was plain-and-simple graffiti vandalism. By the time Kiley became chairman, there had been half a dozen attempts to get graffiti off the system—Mayor Ed Koch had tried all sorts of maneuvers, including painting the cars white—but nothing had worked. The thirty-year absence of capital investment had contributed to ridership falling basically in half, from two billion people a year in 1945 to about 1.1 billion in 1975. New York's shift economy had changed substantially in that time—the city had once been a 24/7 manufacturing and shipping center—and Robert Moses had built parkway after highway after expressway, but that said, the subway was falling apart.

In 1975, the *Daily News* famously ran the headline: FORD TO CITY: DROP DEAD. The decay had continued through the 1980s. Even as crime was rising and the tabloids trumpeted each felony, what was also exploding on the streets was disorder. Visible disorder. There were homeless encampments that approached the Hoovervilles of the Depression. A hundred people lived in what was basically a cardboard city in the park adjacent to the United Nations, men and women camped out on packing boxes, and parks throughout the city were overtaken. There were five thousand homeless men and women living in the subways; many stations had cardboard flophouses at one end, and riders steered clear as best they could. Confrontations could become ugly. A hard-core population of about three hundred significantly drug-addicted or mentally deranged people were living not on the platforms but in the tunnels with the trains. On average, 120 people died in the subway system each year: twenty to murder and a hundred run over by trains, frozen to death, or overdosed.

So the governor, Mario Cuomo, brought in Bob Kiley, and Kiley brought in David Gunn as president, and they went to work. Kiley contracted with Bob Wasserman and George Kelling to look into the advisability of the Transit Police merging with the NYPD. Their investigation in 1988–1989 produced the recommendation that the two forces not merge, and concluded that such an arrangement would lead to a decline in the number of officers, and that any advantage to the subway cops would be lost. Kelling and Wasserman, as social scientists, also gravitated toward the issue of homelessness. They had not been hired to do anything about it—in fact, the homeless had not been mentioned in their marching orders at all—but the issue was inescapable and their interest led them in that direction.

Having tried and failed to gain control, Kiley called in the heads of the three MTA police departments—Transit, Long Island Rail Road, and Metro-North—and said firmly, "Do something about the homeless." The chiefs all detailed their previous attempts, none of which had succeeded. *We tried all these things,* they told him, *and nothing worked.* Kiley blew up and slammed his fist on the table. "Goddammit, get them out of there!" And that was the end of the meeting.

Kiley's chief of staff, Trish Moore, called Kelling right after the gathering broke up. Kiley and Kelling knew each other personally as well as professionally, and as Moore described the scene, she said, "George, you've got to get here and talk to Bob." Kelling came down from Boston that afternoon and was ushered into Kiley's office.

"George, I didn't know you were in town," said the chairman.

"I wasn't," said Kelling. "I understand you had a meeting with the chiefs today."

"Yeah, they really irritated me. All they did was tell me what they couldn't do."

"I understand you told them, 'Get them out of there'?"

"Yeah."

"Bob, they are going to do that, and then what are you going to do?"

Kiley understood. This would be dirty work; perhaps he ought to rethink. He told Kelling, "They have a meeting planned for a few days from now. Why don't you crash it?"

Kelling arrived at the gathering to find a proposal on the table that the police get high-powered hoses and "clean" areas where the homeless were encamped. After the scourging waterworks, the police, in support of the cleaning crews, would eject the people living there. At the end of the meeting David Gunn asked Kelling what he thought.

"Well," said Kelling, "I really don't think much of it, but I'm certainly going to watch TV on the day that it gets done, because what you are going to have is little old ladies hitting police over the head with their umbrellas. You are going to have demonstrations. This is really going to be quite a show."

Gunn was silent for more time than Kelling expected.

"What do you think I should do?"

Kelling said he didn't have the slightest idea, but that maybe they had defined the problem wrong. Maybe the problem in the subway wasn't homelessness, but lawlessness. "We really ought to try and figure out what the problem is before we do something about it."

A task force was created but didn't get far. The Transit Police wanted to schedule a December crackdown to restore order. Kelling reminded them that, no matter what their intentions, *The New York Times* and others would not fail to mention that this large-scale dislocation of people, particularly those in genuine need, would be occurring during holiday season. They would literally be throwing people out into the cold. Merry Christmas, Scrooge McTransit. If they were going to start a program, Kelling advised, it had to be in October, well before the weather turned, with ample time to make provisions for people's safety and well-being. It became quite clear to Kelling, however, that the Transit Police leadership was not prepared to implement such a program effectively.

Sure enough, not long after its October inception, the plan was attacked by the New York Civil Liberties Union, which provoked confrontations by having representatives walk into the subway, lie down in front of the turnstiles, and tell the police to do something about it. Transit Police command staff would not come down, so there was a sergeant standing off against the NYCLU in front of the media, television cameras rolling, the MTA looking heartless and unprepared. Kelling and Wasserman went to Kiley and said, "We need new police leadership."

"How do I find someone?" he asked.

"We ought to be thinking about this guy from Boston, Bill Bratton," Wasserman said. Kelling seconded him.

Kiley had been a deputy mayor in Boston when I was just a beat cop, but he knew who I was. I had received the second annual prestigious Gary P. Hayes Award from the Police Executive Research Forum (PERF), for turning around two different police forces, and Kiley, Gary Hayes's mentor, had been among the presenters. He said, "Do you think he would be willing to do it?"

They said they would ask.

Kelling and Wasserman invited me to breakfast at the Bostonian Hotel and said, "Would you be willing to go to New York as the chief of the Transit Police?" I almost fell off my chair. The Transit Police, with four thousand officers, was twice the size of the Boston Police. And I wasn't afraid of a mess. I immediately said of course. I was thrilled.

David Gunn invited me to visit the city before taking the job, and when I arrived we went straight into the subway in midtown. He wanted to show me what I was facing.

The line to buy tokens seemed endless, and when I finally tried to put the coin into the turnstile I found the mechanism had been purposely jammed. The slam gate beside it, the automatically locking emergency door that could be opened only from inside the station, was held open by a seedy-looking guy with his hand out; having disabled the turnstiles he was now turning that misdemeanor into cash. At the same time, one of his cohorts had his mouth on a coin slot, sucking out the jammed coins. The next person who put a token in there was going to get a handful of slobber. People who hadn't paid streamed through the open door, either giving over their token or ducking their head and stealing the service. Others were vaulting or going under, or had learned the little urban dance by which you pulled the stile back halfway and shimmied through without paying. The MTA was losing $65.5 million a year on this free ridership. Nobody seemed pleased to be there. And that was before they even got inside.

On the platform, people were sprawled on the benches, either waiting for the train or just having taken up residence. Once inside the car and heading downtown I took in all the men spread-eagled on the seats, asleep. One sleeper who smelled like he hadn't bathed in weeks could clear out half a car by himself. In a subway system that shuttled more than three million people a day, no one made eye contact. A stream of beggars stumbled from one end of the car to the other, some with stories to tell, others just holding out their hands as if everyone he was panhandling had heard their tales before. The entire ride was unsettling and I was happy to get back into the street. Gunn had made his point; all the cleaned-up cars and power-washed stations would make no difference if there weren't a transformation of the system itself.

I surely wanted the job. New York was the world's biggest stage, and if I successfully turned Transit around—if I could make it there—there was every possibility I could place myself on the short list for New York City police commissioner, the highest-visibility police job in the country. By this time I knew enough not to say that out loud.

Before my hiring was finalized, Gunn was replaced as president by Alan Kiepper, who had been recruited from Houston, where Lee Brown had been the city's first African American police chief prior to taking his current position as NYPD commissioner. Kiepper wanted three problems addressed by the Transit Police: fare evasion, disorder, and crime. I waited six months to hear whether I got the job, and studied New York every day. What did Transit mean to the city? *The New York Times*, I found, influenced the agenda, and the *New York Post* was read by the cops. Where was the power? Which reporters were significant, which were there to cause trouble or promote the cause?

Between subways and buses, five million New Yorkers rode transit every day. From what I could tell, each of them had a personal stake in my job. Crime, disorder, and fear were skyrocketing. Whoever turned that around could be knighted. Let it be me.

In April 1990 I got the job.

CHAPTER 5

Transit

New York. Just like I pictured it!

A Boston boy out of Dorchester, I got a big kick out of being in New York. The hotel where I was staying for my first month was around the corner from Grand Central Terminal, and at about 5:30 on my first night in town as Transit chief I went out for a walk. A police officer was lounging against an aging office building across from the station. He looked miserable. Shaggy hair, five o'clock shadow . . . from two days ago, wrinkled shirt, scuffed gun belt with his hat hanging off the holster, clip-on tie askew. The patch on his shoulder said he was one of mine, and even the patch was beat up.

I like introducing myself to officers; I know how much it meant to me when someone high up in the force noticed me. I looked at the nameplate below his shield, stuck out my hand, and said, "Hi, Officer Smith. I'm Chief Bratton, how're you doing?"

He gathered himself a bit.

"What's your post?" I assumed he would give me a several-block radius.

"Right here, sir."

"Right here?" He was standing in front of an office building. "What are you doing here?"

"I'm guarding the token booth, sir. That's my responsibility."

We were standing on 42nd Street. "Where's the token booth?"

He pointed to an entrance forty feet down the block, left into a marble corridor, inside a building.

"What are you doing out here?"

"My radio doesn't work in there, sir."

Here was the Transit Police incarnate. Nonexistent morale, soul-killing assignment, disrespect for his organization and himself, shoddy equipment, sloppy uniforms. He put himself back together, saluted, and went back to his post. At the station house, if he told the story of meeting the chief on the street at all, he wouldn't offer it with any amount of pride.

The transit cops felt terrible because they were treated like crap by the NYPD. Every police recruit takes the same civil service test and goes to the same Police Academy. Two weeks before they graduate, the entire class is gathered to hear their assignments. In 1990, there were three separate police agencies in New York City: the Transit Police, under the control of the New York City Transit Authority; the Housing Police, under the New York City Housing Authority; and the NYPD, under the New York City police commissioner. An official company instructor addresses them and gives them the news: "You seven, go to the street. You two go to Transit, and you go to Housing. That's your career. Have a nice day."

The street, the NYPD, was the brass ring. Transit and Housing, which were separate departments for the subways and the public housing developments, were not. The men and women who got Transit were usually not happy about the assignment, where they might have to spend twenty years working in the subway system. And be treated like dirt. At that time, when a three-star Transit chief would call a sergeant in the NYPD Chief of Department's office—a three-star chief talking to a sergeant—he would hear, "What do you want, Transit?" Infinite, undeserved disrespect, and nothing they could do about it. That's just the way the city worked. Transit was treated like shit. Absolute shit.

Transit cops were known as the "Ohhhh" Police. They were not part of the NYPD, but a smaller agency with none of its prestige and glory. They were not thought of as New York's Finest. People would ask cops in social situations, "What do you do for a living?"

"I'm a police officer."

"Oh, where?"

"City of New York."

"No kidding! I've got a brother who's a cop. Where do you work?"

After a while they could hear it coming.

"Uh, I work in Manhattan."

"Oh, yeah. What precinct?"

"I'm with the Transit Police."

"Ohhhh."

The "Ohhhh" Police.

That was going to stop.

At my first meeting with my command staff I told them, "I didn't come down from Boston to lose. I intend to win. I believe in working hard, and I am expecting all of you to work hard with me. I also believe that we should have some fun. My intention is to succeed and to have fun succeeding. We should enjoy our time here.

"I know how you feel." (And I did. I hadn't liked getting kicked out of BPD headquarters one bit.) "You feel like you are third-class citizens. Well, I'll tell you—you are going to be the Marines of New York City policing. This is going to be the best police department, not the worst, not the disrespected, not treated like shit! You are going to be second to none!"

Kelling had missed the speech, but Bob Kiley reported back to him. "By the end," Kiley told him, "if Bratton had said, 'Now take City Hall,' they would have taken City Hall!"

In the months preceding my appointment, Kelling and Wasserman had given me a rundown of the department that included a list of several talented people in the organization. I will take all the information I can get. I have no problem making a decision; give me the information.

The Transit Police's general counsel, Dean Esserman, a civilian, had taken an unusual path into the police profession: New York City private schools, Dartmouth, PERF, NYU Law, Brooklyn assistant district attorney, and then general counsel to my predecessor, Transit Police Chief Vinny Del Castillo. Esserman was a straight-up progressive—smart, networked, and possessed of an encyclopedic knowledge of New York City police history.

Highly decorated Chief of Detectives Mike O'Connor (also known as "Iron Mike") quickly got on my good side by offering to go with me out into the system anytime day or night. Director of Media Services Al O'Leary gave me strong and accurate advice on how to deal with a vital element, the press: "Don't play games with them, tell it to them the way it is. Always tell them the truth." Director of Planning Phyllis McDonald had been hired a year earlier by Del Castillo at Wasserman's recommendation and wanted to move more quickly than the department had allowed her; I liked her drive. I brought computer whiz Athena Yerganian with me from the MDC as a consultant, and her ability to analyze the charts, diagrams, and data she produced was prodigious.

For months we struggled with the creation of a Transit Police Plan of Action. Some of the best writers I knew weren't delivering what I was looking for, including Wasserman and Kelling. Then I met a young writer, Bill Andrews. Bill brought intellect, extraordinary writing skills, and the ability to articulate complex ideas. He wrote the department's Plan of Action, and I have had the continuing good fortune to work with him for more than thirty years, in every department that I have led and many for which I have consulted.

We all met frequently in my hotel room during my first weeks on the job. Within two months the command staff had shaken out. I asked every commander above district level to tell me who they were and what they did. In an organization that felt unrecognized, I wanted all levels in the spotlight. I got a quick but thorough overview and drew upon the found talent.

With this new personnel insight I proposed a major organizational restructuring. I made Mike O'Connor chief of operations and gave him full authority to run the department day to day. We were in good hands, and I was freed to examine the big picture.

First, we were fighting fatalism. I admired and respected New York's governor, Mario Cuomo, particularly for his leadership. However, at a press conference in 1989 when he was thinking of running for president, Cuomo stated what almost everybody was thinking. As Fred Siegel writes in his book *The Future Once Happened Here*, when asked about the crime situation, Cuomo said words to the effect that "maybe this is as good as it gets." He didn't get a lot of disagreement, except from me.

Nineteen ninety was the worst year for violent crime in the history of New York City, and indeed one of the worst years for crime in the history of America. It was also one of the worst in the history of the subway system; in the 1980s going into the '90s, crime in the subways was awful. Not as awful as what was going on in the street, but the confined spaces of the subway system made it seem worse; once you went in, it was very difficult to get out. There were thousands of homeless people living on the platforms and trains and in the tunnels. Robberies of token booths were very frequent and fare evasion was epidemic: 250,000 documented incidents every day by the riding population of just over three million. Graffiti, vandalism—it was not a very inviting place. And on top of it all were the horrific physical conditions—breakdowns of trains, track fires caused by rubbish thrown on the tracks. Even coming from the turmoil of the streets above, it was like walking down into Dante's Inferno.

When Kiley had taken over in 1983 he had gone to Governor Cuomo and said, "I need a thousand managers outside of union protection to run this place." Of the fifty thousand Transit Authority employees, maybe a dozen weren't in the Transport Workers Union (TWU), which essentially meant there was no independence, because every member of the TWU of America, a branch of the AFL-CIO, would cover for the others. "So I need you to go to the legislature and get me those guys," he had said. "And if you don't do that, I'm leaving." Which was Kiley's way. He would say, "It's okay, I'll just leave." Cuomo got him the thousand independent managers.

To avoid corruption on construction projects—at the MTA, everything was about no corruption—the Transit Authority historically did not hire general contractors, who could often be mobbed up, preferring to handle jobs itself. The problem was, the TA wasn't any good at it. The people in charge could never get the plumbers to come in sequence with the electricians, for instance, so nothing would get done. Kiley and Gunn hired general contractors and held them accountable: "You better hit your dates or we are not paying you. In fact, you are going to pay us." And they did. They began to get the system moving.

John Linder was the head of marketing and corporate communications for the MTA when I got there. He was in his early forties, as was I, with curly, graying black hair and the look of a man who was constantly worried. Which he was. He seemed to be aware of every possible pitfall, smart enough to be both wary and prepared. Linder all but wrung his hands when he spoke. He took me out to dinner in Chelsea one night at a century-old restaurant with mahogany paneling and green velvet seats. He turned out to be my kind of guy.

Linder had convinced Bob Kiley of the need to advertise the improvements he was making, and was given a $10 million budget to change public perception of the subways. In 1989, the MTA wanted to provide President Gunn with a graffiti-free subway system for his birthday, so they eliminated graffiti from 6,200 cars and left 10 for comparison. Kind of the intentionally dropped stitch in the otherwise perfect tapestry. Linder fielded a survey to find the results of the cleanup.

Eighty-three percent of the people in New York, Linder discovered, said they were seeing graffiti on trains often or somewhat often or on occasion—when only 10 cars out of 6,200 in the system were actually still tagged. He also found that the public didn't notice the other improvements made to the system during Kiley's stewardship, as many of the much-needed infrastructure repairs were being made down in the tunnels at night. A deep cynicism had set in. In the public's mind, getting around New York on public transit was dangerous through and through. New Yorkers were using the transit system to go to and from work, but not for discretionary trips. Nobody rode during the day, nobody rode on the weekends, and they sure as hell didn't ride at night.

Women were terrified. Linder did focus groups and asked, "What percentage of the city's crime do you think happens on the subway?" Women said 40 percent. "What percentage of murders happen on the subway?" They said 50 percent. He said, "If I were to tell you the truth, which is that one percent of the city's murders and three percent of its crime happens on the subway, would that make you feel safer?" Not at all, they told him.

Linder had a system for uprooting deeply ingrained negative perceptions, based on social science research done in the 1970s and early '80s. The MTA had never spent millions of dollars on television advertising. Kiley told him, "You know if this doesn't work, this will never happen again and you will be out of a job."

Linder first went to one of New York's top ad agencies, but Kiley hated their mock-ups.

"Do you want me to fire them?" Linder asked.

"We'll show them the elevator shaft," said Kiley. CIA talk. They hired a different agency.

Part of Linder's unique talent was to find a buried value, underactivated in people's awareness, that once called to their attention would result in behavioral changes. He called it his cultural diagnostic. Presented with the fact that they had not been acting on an important value, people would respond with positive action. For example, studies had found that for four months after one airing of a specifically designed television program in eastern Washington State, people who watched were twice as likely to give money to the NAACP, the National Organization for Women, and the Sierra Club as people who hadn't, or who had gotten up and gone to the bathroom and missed it.

Linder searched his survey data for a buried value that could benefit the

TA. Three quarters of the New Yorkers surveyed didn't like the subway service, he found, and had rated it fair or poor. When household income hit forty thousand dollars, they said, "People like me are too rich to ride the subway, I have to ride around in cabs."

The buried value Linder unearthed in the research was that 70 percent of the people of New York agreed with the following statement: Riding the subway is part of being a New Yorker. From that nugget he extracted the message we would use in our advertising campaign: It used to be bad, it's getting better, it's not perfect. And if you don't like it, move to Des Moines. Because this is New York.

Using a hot young director who was doing cutting-edge handheld work for *Saturday Night Live* at the time, we spent $1 million shooting four commercials about the Transit Police on four different kinds of film stock and aired them where New Yorkers would see them.

During the recession under President George H. W. Bush, when New York City lost 150,000 jobs, subway ridership had decreased 6 percent. After we ran the ads, it started to go back up. Kiley, who spent every August at his house in Martha's Vineyard, came back after the summer and said, "My mail has totally changed. Television is the nuclear bomb of advertising!"

Always looking for a way to be noticed, Linder suggested radio spots featuring me and my Boston accent. I had one then, still have one now. I didn't think about it, I was busy going about my business, but I definitely didn't sound like a New Yorker. You think of the subway, you think of someone who's been on it forever. I'd just come to town and I sounded like a caricature. Linder was looking for something that would make people stop and think, *Come on, who is this Boston cop who's talking to me on the radio in the morning when I'm in the shower?!*

We recorded several spots and had the budget to make them inescapable. And it worked. Don Imus, the very popular radio commentator, even mimicked one of them. I was at the Lord & Taylor department store information desk not long after they went on the air, asking for directions, when the woman behind the counter said, "Excuse me?" I repeated my request and she squealed, "You're the voice! You're the voice!"

We also needed to motivate our officers, who on the odd times they saw themselves on television were portrayed badly. So we used exactly those people—good, hardworking cops with strong outer-borough accents, who sounded like they had grown up in the city—to serve and star in our Transit enterprise. If we could turn around crime and *fear of crime*, we could make a big difference in subway ridership.

In addition to the effort to reach the public, we also needed to reach the cops. So Linder, Bill Andrews, and a talented young producer, Tony Lopresti, worked with me to produce a weekly video with Sergeant Jimmy O'Neill—who ran the Transit Police video training unit and later became police commissioner—that was distributed to every Transit Police district, describing the changes we were making or were about to make. The cops loved them.

The ads opened people's eyes, and the videos helped boost morale. But most important of all, my team and I and the cops brought crime down. How did we do that? Broken Windows policing.

In response to the urban rioting the state had experienced in 1967, New Jersey established the Safe and Clean Neighborhoods Program. The "Safe" part was the expansion of foot patrols in twenty-eight cities around the state. Governor Brendan Byrne liked foot patrols; they were throwbacks to a time of amity and community that he longed to reestablish. The "Clean" portion was money to upgrade the many New Jersey neighborhoods that had fallen into decay, including getting rid of abandoned houses. Cities couldn't take the "Safe" money unless they did the "Clean." Having transitioned to the whiz-bang pace of life in cars, most police didn't want a foot patrol assignment, filled as it was with paperwork, bad weather, and fallen arches. The upside was more engagement with the community; the downside was the decreased possibility of making a great arrest, or what was known in the trade as a "good pinch." As a result, foot patrols were isolated sights in New Jersey police departments. George Kelling decided to do the Newark Foot Patrol Experiment.

He was struck by his findings. The 1972 Kansas City Preventive Patrol Experiment found that nothing the police did while riding around in cars seemed to make any difference in the rate at which crime was committed, but what struck the social scientists was the fact that fear of crime was substantially reduced in areas where a foot patrol was installed, and increased where it was withdrawn. The quality of a neighborhood's life improved with the increased presence of cops on foot. Same thing with appreciation for the officers. In Newark in 1978–79, the old riots were still fresh in the minds of the both the citizenry and the officers. As before, most of the cops were white, while Newark remained a primarily African American city. And yet where foot patrol was installed, again an appreciation for police increased. Where foot patrol was withdrawn, appreciation for police decreased. These were powerful findings. And again it didn't have any impact on crime, but Kelling was struggling with the question "Why did fear of crime drop?"

Kelling found that, at core, what the cops did in Newark was maintain order. There were certain rules of the street—you couldn't drink on the main streets, but if you went off on the side streets the police wouldn't bother you; you could sit on the stoop of a building, but you couldn't lie down; panhandlers could approach people who were moving, but they couldn't approach them in front of or waiting for buses. Cops enforced this social contract.

Ed Flynn, who ultimately became chief of the Milwaukee Police, was a beat cop in the same program in Jersey City that Kelling studied in Newark. A white cop in a Black neighborhood, he wanted in the worst way to get in a police car and chase 911 calls, but instead found himself walking around talking to people. *What a pain in the ass*, he thought. But he found that most people were very nice to him. Assigned to a high-crime area, he found community members were overwhelmingly glad to see him—until they turned about sixteen. They aged out of that antagonism at around age thirty-two. "That was the bump," he said, "when they weren't thrilled to see me going up and down the street and imposing my will. Older folks, kids, merchants, the regular users of the street would stop me five times a night and say how happy they were to see me there."

So Kelling did not find that foot patrols had any impact on the levels of street crime in a given area. What he did find was that people in those neighborhoods *felt* much safer than people elsewhere. That comfort affected their conduct and had a lot to do with neighborhood stability. Flynn enforced the informal street rules and was able to preside over order through the presence and potential for, but very infrequent use of, arrest. If you're going to drink on the street, it's got to be in a paper bag around the corner, hear me? If you're going to have a dice game, do it behind the bar, not in front. Got it? You cannot lie on a park bench, you can sit on it. And if somebody got obstreperous, the general community did not automatically back the guy getting ornery, they supported the cop; he was the ref, he called the foul. The community valued order as much as the cops did.

When Kelling published the findings of his Newark Foot Patrol Experiment, one of his readers was James Q. Wilson, a professor of government at Harvard who had made a close study of issues of crime and social order in America. Wilson read and enjoyed the work, especially the summary chapter, and thought it would make a good magazine piece. He contacted Kelling and suggested they collaborate. Wilson was more widely known and respected in the field than Kelling, who thought the invitation was extraordinarily generous. He said, "All you have to do is to cite me." Wilson told him, "No, no, let's do it together." Their collaboration, published in the *Atlantic*, was entitled "Broken Windows." It became arguably the most important policing theory of the past fifty years.

As synopsized by Kelling, its three major points were:

1. Neighborhood disorder—drunks, panhandling, youth gangs, prostitution, and other urban incivilities—creates citizen fear.

2. Just as unrepaired broken windows can signal to people that nobody cares about a building and lead to more serious vandalism,
   untended disorderly behavior can also signal that nobody cares
   about the community and lead to more serious disorder and crime.
   Such signals—including untended property, disorderly persons,
   drunks, obstreperous youth—both create fear in citizens and attract predators.

3. If police are to deal with disorder to reduce fear and crime, they
   must rely on citizens for legitimacy and assistance.

I didn't know it at the time, but Wilson and Kelling relied heavily on
Robert Peel's Nine Principles. In an American context, their focus on disorder as a concern equal to crime was revolutionary. Until that publication,
the American police establishment had essentially concerned itself with
crime alone. I believed strongly in the thrust of their ideas—it had all been
demonstrated in the Boston-Fenway Program, after all—and now that I
had the platform I moved to put them into practice.

"Broken Windows," in the popular lexicon, has now become an activist
shorthand for racist police behavior and zero-tolerance policing. It is neither. Somehow the cops' intention to make the streets more hospitable to
the people of the neighborhood has been turned into a willful intention to
mistreat people of color. And the idea of addressing lesser offenses ahead of
serious crime has been misinterpreted—and sometimes misapplied—as
enforcing against every lesser offense. These have never been the point of
Broken Windows, nor its result. Broken Windows is just plain logical; people think it isn't, but it is. Unaddressed disorder leads to petty crime, and
then more serious crime, and finally violence. Stopping small things before
they become big things is key, as is recognizing that many neighbors actually care more about the former than the latter. Why? Because even during
the city's period of highest crime, victims of major crime or violence were

a small fraction of the city's population—but everyone could see and sense the disorder.

The analogy centers on an abandoned building. It has no tenants, no street traffic; it is sitting there unattended, in the same condition it was the day the last tenant left. Intact and shut up tight. You've seen it. A factory, a warehouse, an apartment building awaiting demolition. Then someone puts a rock through a window. If that window remains shattered, a second will go in a heartbeat, then a third, and what was once a community fixture will quickly fall apart. From pristine neighborhood icon to flophouse hellhole in the blink of an eye. As Wilson and Kelling explained:

> Social psychologists and police officers tend to agree that if a window in a building is broken and is left unrepaired, all the rest of the windows will soon be broken. This is as true in nice neighborhoods as in rundown ones. Window-breaking does not necessarily occur on a large scale because some areas are inhabited by determined window-breakers whereas others are populated by window-lovers; rather, one unrepaired broken window is a signal that no one cares, and so breaking more windows costs nothing. (It has always been fun.) . . .
>
> Untended property becomes fair game for people out for fun or plunder and even for people who ordinarily would not dream of doing such things and who probably consider themselves law-abiding. . . . We suggest that 'untended' behavior also leads to the breakdown of community controls. A stable neighborhood of families who care for their homes, mind each other's children, and confidently frown on unwanted intruders can change, in a few years or even a few months, to an inhospitable and frightening jungle.

This is not pernicious racist demagogy, this is empirically demonstrable social science. I put it to work.

Linder said, "I've got this advertising that is about to launch in three weeks. It's kind of a problem. We are going to launch it in the summer, it is going to be hotter than hell on the platforms. Would you mind putting cops on fixed posts at the turnstiles, so that people can't jump the turnstiles and ridership will go up?" I told him, "No, I'm not going to do that." There had to be a good reason for all deployment. If I was going to station officers at every turnstile in the city, there had to be a better reason than hyping stats for an ad campaign.

And there was.

Fare evasion was the biggest broken window in the transit system. People were going over the turnstiles like it was some kind of urban Olympic event, making abiding by the law seem like a fool's game and costing the MTA tens of millions of dollars a year. Fix that window for good, demonstrate that the Transit Authority did care, and the system could be brought back to health, and maybe the city with it.

It was a huge pain in the ass for cops to arrest fare beaters. What were they stealing? A dollar twenty-five a ride. By the time an officer made the arrest, issued the summons or Desk Appearance Ticket (DATs, known to all as the "disappearance ticket" because so few arrestees ever showed up in court to answer them, after which a warrant would be issued but rarely pursued), did the paperwork, took the perpetrator downtown to Central Booking to be held for arraignment, sat at the courthouse until they were arraigned, then testified and watched the person they'd worked hard to collar either walk out the door or pay a miniscule fine—that cop was out of the system for sixteen hours. Two days' work. For what? As far as they were concerned, instead of doing all that, they could actually have been working!

How could we attack fare evasion, stem disorder, bring down crime, and improve morale?

The fare-evasion minisweep.

Some high-traffic subway stations were being treated like free-fare freeways. This had to stop. First, we warned riders that there would be a crackdown. We weren't looking to run people in; this was not calculated to be a high-arrest program. The essence of Broken Windows is the effort to maintain order and to stem disorder, and the goal of our program was not to put people in jail but to get them to stop ignoring the fare. So we spent a lot of time and effort to get people to desist.

I put a sergeant and sometimes as many as ten cops in uniform and plain clothes at these stations day and night, and they collared a couple of dozen people at a time as the scofflaws came vaulting over. They cuffed them, lined them up against the walls outside the turnstiles' line of sight, and waited for more. When their nets were full they marched the jumpers upstairs in a daisy chain and put them in wagons to be taken downtown for processing. All neighborhoods. Citywide. For the record—and in anticipation of knee-jerk accusations of racial animus—the only factor we used to determine which stations we chose was high rates of fare evasion. Interestingly, the Wall Street station was among those high-evasion locations.

Response was excellent all around. The cops loved being cops again, making arrests, getting noticed. Riders in every neighborhood, who had bridled when they followed the rules and others didn't, finally had a reason to cheer. Officers heard a lot of "Go get 'em!" "Great job!" "About time!" Transit cops had forgotten what that sounded like.

An epic enforcement effort is much more effective when everybody knows about it. As the Kansas City and Newark experiments showed, when community members felt there was someone present who was on their side, they felt better about the quality of their lives. Riders had become inured to the daily assault on their comfort, and when that assault was noticeably decreased . . . they noticed! We advertised our success, and as the word got out that the Transit Police were serious about fare evasion, the fear of being arrested increased and behavior began to change. Fare evasion began to decline dramatically.

We also found that many of the people we were arresting were the same people who were causing other problems once inside the subway system. When they stopped jumping the turnstiles and riding the trains, lawlessness decreased as well. It came to be understood that if you were going to avoid the fare, you stood a very good chance of being arrested. We changed behavior, and it stayed changed for thirty years. By focusing on disorder we were preventing crime. Kelling and Wilson were being proved correct every day.

Whenever police pull someone over we check identification and warrant status. That's standard operating procedure; we want to know who we're dealing with, and we want to know if they're wanted. By arresting fare beaters we were uncovering a significant number of wanted criminals with whom we would not otherwise have made contact. During the first weeks of minisweeps, when word to stay home had not yet filtered out, we were raking in offenders. One out of every seven had an outstanding warrant for a previous crime. One out of twenty-one was carrying some kind of weapon, from box cutter to knife to gun.

At first, cops had a field day. Where they had largely been disengaged from their jobs, now every Transit officer wanted to be the one who came up with the big find. They kept opening gift boxes. What will I get this time? Got a warrant? Got a knife? Got a gun? All kinds of good things could happen on a minisweep. We had no problem with officer buy-in and public support for the effort. After a while, the criminals wised up and either left their weapons home and paid the fare or didn't ride the trains at all. If cops were going to be out in force, why take the chance of getting caught? Either was fine with us; arrests weren't the point—the bottom line was fewer weapons, fewer crimes, fewer murders, fewer perpetrators, fewer victims. Less crime, less fear. We had created a safer, less-threatening public transit system. And all because we fixed a broken window. Success!

We had broken the code. Cops *could* do more than chase crime; we *could* prevent it! How? As Sir Robert Peel had written 160 years before, by recognizing the link between crime and disorder.

Why was disorder important? Because disorder was what people saw every day. Every twenty-four hours, sixty or seventy people were victims of a serious crime in the subway; but every day, more than three *million* people saw the rampant disorder that was not being addressed, and that made them fearful and it made them angry. That rage was poisoning the city as much as the river of crime.

I knew the issues of public order and crime were inseparable. My experiences as a young sergeant in Boston in the 1970s, running a Neighborhood Policing program and finding out at community meetings that despite my crime statistics, people wanted to talk about disorder, informed my decision making as Transit chief. The prostitutes, the gang on the corner, the graffiti, the abandoned cars that were never removed—this is what people cared about. And so what I brought to New York in 1990 was an appreciation that to deal with serious crime you are first going to have to deal with disorder. Transit had tried to do it the other way around for twenty years and had failed miserably.

The sweeps presented the unwelcome problem of what to do with the offenders once we cuffed them. The delay in the courts was awful. Each man or woman still had to go downtown for disposition, a proposition that continued to take sixteen hours out of an officer's workweek. We were losing vital manpower. Some cops liked it because for sixteen hours they sat on their ass out of the subway and made overtime. Others hated the idea of sitting on their ass for sixteen hours. That would have been me; I would have gone out of my mind.

Several staffers were brainstorming our options when the thought struck: *We're in transportation. Why don't we take the processing to them?*

And so we created the Bust Bus. We tore apart one of our own city buses and turned it into an arrest-processing center. Four cops, a lineup of telephones and fax machines (the cutting-edge technology of the day), fingerprinting and photographic facilities, a holding pen—a full-service mobile district station. We led our daisy chain of fare evaders up the stairs, past the civilians in the street, around the corner, and onto the Bust Bus. The men and women who had made the mistake of coming into the subway system armed or sporting outstanding warrants we deemed "keepers" and shipped downtown. If the others had proper identification, we gave them DATs and sent them packing. Instead of sixteen hours, a fare-evader arrestee could be in and out in an hour, still a major disruption for them but not for us. Our cops could go right back downstairs and restore order.

We were not unmindful of the impact an arrest would have on citizens trying to keep their jobs—arriving late, perhaps skipping a day of work altogether because of the time it took to get booked—but we had warned them. Every attempt was made not to arrest people; all they had to do was obey the law. The point was: Don't do this. Do not evade the fare. Obey New York's laws and customs, and save the taxpayers the tens of millions of dollars that fare evasion is costing.

One of my favorite Bust Bus memories is standing outside as a string of handcuffed arrestees kept winding forward. New Yorkers have a fascination with crime scenes; they expect to hear the cop mantra "Nothing to see here" but will always ask some uniformed officer, "What's up?" An old woman pushing a wire shopping cart read the sign on the side of the bus: ARREST PROCESSING CENTER.

"A jail on wheels!" she exclaimed. "Why don't you bring that on up to my neighborhood? You can lock 'em all up!"

Once I had a handle on the state of the department, I decentralized power and mandated each of our ten district commanders to come up with new ways to control fare evasion, disorder, and crime. I wanted them out in the system searching for ideas, then I visited their districts and encouraged presentations. When they began to compete for the best, I knew I had them.

Having been neglected for so long, Transit needed a full refurbishing. New uniforms, new squad cars, updated weaponry, cleaned-up police stations. I invited the city's movers and shakers—politicians, business executives, members of the media who regularly covered the transit system, police buffs—on a Disneyland tour of the subways and buffed them up real good. I showed them our desperately underequipped communications room with the dead spots in the middle of Harlem; I showed off our canine unit; I took them on a train and asked them to pick out our undercover officers. (They usually got about two out of eight.) Then we took them in the tunnels.

You really do not want to go into the New York City subway tunnels. They are dark as a coal mine, wildly hot in the summertime, icy cold in winter, and because you're standing at ground level, the trains roaring by are eight feet higher than they look from a platform in the station—and they're rocketing. A subway train, careening from side to side, leaving little room to press your back against a filthy wall, is a thundering and threatening vehicle. Our officers had to deal with them daily. Between the omnipresent rats, the filthy mattresses, crack vials, and discarded syringes, the stench of urine and feces in alcoves where some unsettled and not necessarily lucid characters had set up living spaces, this was a vision of Transit Police life that was news to all.

I was lobbying for funds and attention. When they got back to the surface I wanted the powerful representatives of the city's business, political, and media life to consider the burdens we were working under and to understand, when they were chatting at their dinner parties on the Upper East Side or out in the Hamptons, what it's like for a cop trying to make sure all New Yorkers get home safely.

I've got to say, even with all these challenges—or perhaps because of them—I was having the time of my life. I was exactly where I wanted to be, in a position to make a difference in millions of lives. What more did I need?

General Counsel Dean Esserman strongly suggested, "You want to meet the head of the robbery squad, Lieutenant Jack Maple." We met him for dinner at the famous River Café under the Brooklyn Bridge.

Maple was an outlier in Transit. Born and raised in Queens, he had signed on with the department before he could vote and became a detective at age twenty-seven. He had worked undercover in Times Square in the eighties, which all but qualified as combat duty. By the time we met he had made four hundred arrests and become something of a Transit legend when he and all his eccentricities had been profiled in *New York* magazine. Still in his thirties, he looked like nobody I'd ever known. He was the fat little cop, as he called himself, in the homburg hat, sharp suit, bow tie, and polished two-tone wing tips that made it look like he was wearing spats. Five foot eight, two hundred twenty pounds, he was squat, sturdy, tough as nails, and had been known to roll on the ground getting perpetrators under control. One Friday night in the tough East New York section of Brooklyn, waiting on a robbery suspect, Maple and Esserman were first through the bodega door, Maple knocking the guy down and Esserman piling on. Detectives ran in with guns drawn, it was a scene. Maple got the guy in a headlock, looked up at Esserman, and said, "It's better than sex, isn't it!"

He was quite a character. Quick with a phrase, a connoisseur practitioner of wiseacre banter, he was not particularly popular with superior officers because he had better ideas than they did and basically didn't give a damn what they thought of him. He respected the chain of command mostly because it could make his life difficult if he didn't. So he was walking a thin line because the Transit Police was pretty much his only life.

He was also a policing genius. Despite what was going on in most of the Transit Police at that time, Maple was having success. His decoy squad was producing numbers as he focused on those who were actually committing crime in the subway. He had a lot of creative ideas. He figured he'd see what I was made of.

Maple and his executive officer, Tommy Byrne, developed a ten-page document for reducing crime and improving the department. Among his concepts were targeting fare beating, warrants, wolfpack robberies, interrogation, interviewing, crime analysis, and coordinating deployment between detectives and plainclothes and uniformed officers. All on the money. I told him, "The reason they brought me here is to reduce crime." He said, "If we go by this plan it's going to happen."

He admitted our minisweeps were good for department morale, but he didn't think we were getting what we could be getting. It was Maple who suggested we check for outstanding warrants. "If you run a warrant check on everybody," he said, "there's a greater propensity that you're going to catch not only people with prior fare-beat warrants, but really bad people. It's going to knock crime down. And then you're going to create an environment in the subway where the criminal element is going to say, 'It's just not worth doing robberies there.'" Seemed obvious, except no one else had thought of it. All ideas are new if you haven't heard them before.

It pissed him off that we'd had felons in our grasp and let them disappear. If people had committed crime, he said, let's serve the back warrants and get them. Maple felt we were missing opportunities to increase pressure on the criminal element. Many criminals felt that once they'd been arrested and bailed out, we would never go after them. Transit crime was one big free ride.

Officers in Transit's warrant unit were assigned to the NYPD, and not only was the larger organization not producing, the city squad prioritized crimes and served warrants on the most significant cases, which were rarely, if ever, ours. Transit warrants were basically not being served. The NYPD wasn't doing a hell of a good job as it was; it could take four to six weeks to get a warrant into a warrant officer's hands. And warrants were only served Monday through Friday, 8:00 a.m. to 4:00 p.m.—basically when no one was home. I took my people back from the NYPD warrant unit and set up our own independent unit. NYPD First Deputy Commissioner Ray Kelly responded, "Take them away, but we're no longer going to have anything to do with your warrants." Fine with me; they weren't serving my warrants anyway.

We streamlined the process. Dean Esserman found that from the time a judge issued a warrant to the day it showed up at the NYPD as "new," thirty to forty-five days would elapse. Using his contacts to stay with the paper, Dean shortened that to forty-eight hours. We used a computer system, believed to be the first of its kind in the city, to change the warrant process from being paper driven to something approaching electronic. Now, when someone didn't show up, they no longer had a month's head start. We were right on their tail.

I gave those returning warrant cops to Maple. Having worked under the auspices of the NYPD, they weren't so happy to be back at Transit, but Maple transformed them. We went after criminals seven days a week, starting at 3:30 in the morning in Maple's office to go over the game plan. Description, crime, layout of where they were going. At 4:00, led by a sergeant, a half dozen or more detectives wearing Transit Police windbreakers started banging on doors. Loudly, so the neighbors could hear. This was no polite request; we wanted the community to know we were on the case. *Transit Police! Open up!* If it woke some people, they'd know we were working. And if we went back every morning, sooner or later someone in the neighborhood might shake loose some information and we could catch our criminal.

We made gains in multiples. We increased both our arrests and our presence. We partnered low-performing officers with high performers and improved the quality of the force. And by catching bad guys we closed the loophole through which people were disappearing from the justice system. Crime went down, morale went up. Transit came back.

Maple's creativity and understanding of the subway world was extensive. He believed not that there were a lot of criminals, but a lot of recidivists. It was his idea, as they were coming out of jail for having committed an offense in the transit system, to greet them with his robbery squad detectives and say, "Welcome back. We know you're back, and if you start up your old tricks again, we are going to be looking for you." There was a core group that committed a large percentage of crime, and he wanted to focus on them. These were the same lessons I had learned in Boston in the 1970s and '80s. At a time when almost everybody in New York City government and policing had given up on the idea that something dramatic could really be done about crime, Jack was a true believer that cops—and he in particular—could make a difference.

With Jack, I met a soul mate. Because of his look and his outrageous behavior, some of the smartest people in New York criminal justice had written him off. What the hell could that fat little lieutenant from the Ohhhh Police know about anything? Fortunately for me, I met Jack, and fortunately for Jack, he met me. And fortunately for the subway system, the City of New York, and eventually the country, that bond began to be built.

The country was undergoing a time of resignation, not unlike President Jimmy Carter's "malaise" in the period directly before Reagan. And wasn't that how Ronald Reagan ended up beating Carter for the presidency, with optimism? It was not that I discovered in Jack a miracle worker. What I discovered was a guy who basically thought like I thought. We were simpatico. He had maps on his wall; he put dots on the map (sound familiar?). He was the man who coined the phrase "cops on the dots"!

Policing crime in the subway system was different in some respects from policing crime in fixed geographic areas like housing developments or on the streets of a precinct. Crime in the transit system wasn't stationary, it moved up and down on the lines; there were four hundred-plus stations, but a lot occurred on the trains. Jack knew where every crime was. Each complaint report contained a pole number—in the subway system, each pole is numbered; we didn't have street addresses, we had pole numbers— stating exactly where on the platform the crime had been committed, down to what staircase had been used.

In 1990, there were sixty reported felonies a day in the subway system. Considering what was going on aboveground, the NYPD scoffed at the number, but sixty was a tremendous amount for Transit. The NYPD spoke with pride about the carnage that surrounded them, as if there were some sad badge of honor in saying that you worked in a command that faced a hundred murders every year. It was disgraceful.

Jack Maple believed he could do something about crime because he believed, as I did, that the cause of crime is not poverty or lack of opportunity, it is people. The root causes of crime are criminals—or people who, in a moment of emotional passion, commit a crime.

There are other elements. We do need to improve our education system; we do need to worry about fair or unfair access to jobs; we do need to worry about the health of entire demographic groups. We know, for example, that Blacks are far more likely to die early than whites, and far more susceptible to asthma, diabetes, heart disease, and now diseases like COVID-19.

But in the end, nobody is robbing someone because he's got diabetes, he is robbing somebody because he chooses to rob somebody. Police can prevent that robbery if we are not tasked with running to take a report about the last one, but instead are driving around—or even better, walking around—thinking about the conditions under which crime can happen, and being in the places where we know crime is likely to occur. It is my firm belief, borne out by a lifetime of experience, that people's behavior can be changed by good police work. Jack, like me, was not happy with just responding to crime, he wanted to stop it.

That's where Jack and I bonded; Jack focused on the criminals—not the large majority of people who were living within the law, but the smaller number, including recidivists, who were operating outside it. In New York's quaint terminology in the nineties, they were "mutts" or "skells." Jack's focus was on the bad guys. I got a big kick out of one of his favorite sayings: "It's not that we are so smart, it's that they are so dumb!" We are fortunate a lot of criminals are pretty dumb, because they leave traces behind for us to snatch them up.

And he was, undeniably, a character.

Maple had a tiny little boat that he docked in the East River. He liked being at the helm and taking folks out on the water. Jack, Al Sweeney, and I were zipping down the East River and around the tip of Manhattan in the mouth of New York Harbor. We passed the Statue of Liberty and then turned north up the Hudson. It's a beautiful sight from the water, one most people don't get the chance to see. The day was sunny; salty spray swept into our faces. Sweeney was a Boston guy, he didn't know the local geography. There was a huge city over his left shoulder. He knew it wasn't New York because lower Manhattan's entire impressive financial district was looming to our right. "Jack," he said, "Jack, what's over there?"

Jack said, "That's New Jersey."

"Yeah, what city is it?"

"It's New Jersey!"

"I know," said Al, "but what *city* is it in New Jersey?"

"How the fuck do I know?" said Jack. "What does it matter? It's fucking New Jersey!"

Brian Watkins was a twenty-two-year-old from Provo, Utah, in town with his family to see the United States Open tennis championships. At 10:20 Sunday night on Labor Day weekend in 1990 they were standing on the D train platform at Fifty-Third Street and Seventh Avenue when a wolfpack, as they were known at the time, of about eight kids robbed them at knifepoint. His mother was punched and kicked in the face, his father's wallet was slashed from a back pocket, his brother and sister were smacked around. Watkins was stabbed in the chest with a spring-handled butterfly knife and died trying to run up the stairs to get their attackers. The killer claimed, "He ran into my knife." The gang ran off with $203 and were found hours later dancing at the club Roseland. Good police work brought in arrests within two hours, but that wasn't going to heal the horror.

Two days later I got a call from Governor Cuomo's criminal justice coordinator, Richard Girgenti. The governor understood the implications for New York's safety and tourism. "Can you put together a proposal as to what you would do if we were to give you forty million dollars?" I was asked. "Believe me," I told them, "I can get that together for you very quickly."

The money arrived. The first ten million bought each cop in the department a new, more powerful and reliable walkie-talkie. Ten million went to desperately needed repair of dead spots in the radio system; no longer would my officers be out of touch. A couple of million bought the new vehicles we needed. Two million upgraded the Transit Police Academy. I put money away for new weaponry, because that was an issue on the horizon. And ten million went toward overtime pay, putting the hourly equivalent of two hundred extra officers in the system.

Within a few months, due to our increased manpower, new strategies, better communications, and improved equipment, the crime rate began to plummet.

New uniforms were already in the pipeline. I encouraged input from all officers, and their suggestions yielded a more practical coat with a distinctive look. For years transit cops had tried to hide, to seem like city cops. We also gave them commando sweaters with epaulets, very sharp. Our patch, which before had hidden the word *transit*, was redesigned to feature it. Our recruitment posters read "Second to None. Join the Force on the Move." The former tunnel rats liked that. The new highly equipped cars we bought for them were the envy of the other two police departments.

For their part, our Transit officers received better training, better equipment and uniforms, and looked and acted like professional police officers. They worked hard and were rewarded. The Transit Police, the conscripts of the New York law enforcement world, were becoming its Marine Corps.

We needed new weapons. The NYPD standard-issue .38 six-shot revolver was outdated, and New York City cops of all stripes felt they were overmatched and outgunned by the armaments routinely carried by the city's bad guys. More than half the U.S. police organizations, including thirty of the thirty-one largest, plus six major transit police departments, the FBI, and the Secret Service had made or were in the process of making the changeover to the semiautomatic. It was more accurate, had greater capacity, and was easier to load than the .38.

But when I requested an upgrade from the MTA board of directors I walked into a political buzz saw. Mayor Dinkins was adamantly opposed, as was NYPD commissioner Lee Brown. NYPD first deputy commissioner

Ray Kelly was concerned about the cost of retraining his entire department. The editorial page of *The New York Times* stood firmly against the change.

I was very careful in presenting our case, emphasizing both public and police safety. NYPD cops partnered up and traveled in twos, so there were always two guns on the scene. Transit cops primarily worked solo. All officers were permitted their regulation-issue weapon and a smaller second pistol, often in an ankle or waist holster but not visible; we couldn't have cops walking around with a holster on either side of their belt, looking like Dodge City's Marshal Matt Dillon at high noon. In effect we were permitting officers twelve rounds; I was asking for one weapon that carried seventeen.

We would integrate the semiautomatic into Transit in a carefully conceived and staged training program. In additional to physical training in the use of the firearm, we would reinforce and emphasize the department's deadly force policy principles. Our highest priority was the protection of human life; our firearm was a defensive weapon, not a tool of apprehension; and our officers would be instructed to use every other reasonable alternative before resorting to firearms.

We were asking for something the NYPD didn't have. This was a first for Transit. I think the NYPD command staff didn't trust their officers or their own ability to train their department; they just didn't seem to believe in the professional abilities of the cops they were leading. I trusted mine.

The vote came down to one man: Dan Scannell, eighty years old, vice chairman of the MTA, a former cop—who carried a 9-millimeter.

We won. I announced it over the radio in my car. "Chief Bratton here. I just want to notify members of the department that the board of the MTA voted to approve the issuance of nine-millimeter weapons to Transit Police officers."

Transit cops around the city went wild. I had taken on the mayor, the NYPD, and *The New York Times*, and we had won.

We outfitted the department with the Glock semiautomatic. I was in uniform with my adjutant, Sergeant Cal Mathis, on one of my ride-alongs one night, when a couple of teenagers checked us out on the platform. "Hey, man," one said as we passed, "you guys got Glocks!" These kids knew their firearms by sight. Word got out: "Hey, Transit's got nines!"

There are critics who simply do not trust law enforcement. To them, my main impulse for improving our weaponry was to bolster department morale. Or worse, to terrorize the populace. Well, yes, morale did skyrocket. Transit had things the NYPD could only dream of: better cars, commando sweaters, 9-mm pistols, and a chief who trusted them. But this was no Machiavellian plot. In fact, the new weapons served our needs, and the cops, the subway system, and all its riders were safer because we had them. Safety prevailed. And crime continued to fall.

And sometime after Ray Kelly was appointed police commissioner, the NYPD got their nines.

CHAPTER 6

NYPD 1994–1996: The Turnaround

When I arrived at Transit, subway crime had been rising steadily for years, with robbery increasing two and a half times faster than in the city as a whole. With Broken Windows policing and advances in theory, tactics, matériel, and morale, in two years we decreased felony crime in the subways by 22 percent, with robberies down 40 percent. Fare evasion was cut in half, and ridership and rider confidence had grown significantly.

In 1991, Bob Kiley resigned as chairman of the MTA and was replaced by Peter Stengel. Stengel was a railroad guy, and it appeared to me that he wanted to return to simpler days and just post cops at turnstiles. I felt my Transit journey pulling into the station.

Lee Brown wasn't going anywhere, so the NYPD commissioner position wasn't open. In Los Angeles, however, the Rodney King riots had put Chief Daryl Gates's job on the market, and that looked like exactly the type of extreme rebuild and turnaround that appealed to me. (Plus, frankly, at $175,000 it was the highest-paying police chief's salary in the nation.) I threw my hat in the ring.

I was on a list of eleven finalists when I took my hat back out. The legendary LAPD was being criticized, with some justification, for a pattern of deeply ingrained racism. It became clear to me that the people running the nomination process wanted Gates's successor to be African American, and that Philadelphia's Chief Willie Williams was going to be that man. Also, since during the course of selection the list of final candidates would be released, I was not willing to damage Transit morale unless I was fairly assured of getting the job. I would have taken the risk if I'd thought I had a direct bead on it, but there was no reason to upset my department needlessly.

Then Boston opened up. A *Boston Herald* front-page story said that the St. Clair Commission, established to investigate the Boston Police Department and headed by President Richard Nixon's former counsel, James St. Clair, was about to recommend that Mickey Roache be replaced as commissioner because of incompetent management. It was New Year's Day, and I knew where to find my old sector-car partner: at his desk.

"Mickey, how're you doing? Bill Bratton."

"Hey, Bill, how're you doing?"

"Well, I've been reading the paper, all the problems with the St. Clair report. I think I might have an option you might want to consider."

Mickey had been reading the same paper and knew more than I did. We talked for a couple of hours. "It strikes me," I said, "that I can do something for you and you can do something for me.

"I've got a pretty good reputation for turnarounds and management. I'd like to come back to Boston and help you put the department put in shape. Would you consider bringing me into the organization as the number two?"

Mickey was a smart guy. Several days later I met with him and Mayor Ray Flynn. They made me an offer. I would be superintendent-in-chief, the highest-ranking uniformed officer in the Boston Police. I accepted.

The Boston Police Patrolmen's Association immediately went to court to prevent me from returning. As the face of the Proposition 2½ layoffs, I was persona non grata. I was surprised; only the year before I had been named the New York City Transit Police Benevolent Association's Man of the Year for my work on its members' behalf, but they do know how to hold a grudge in Boston. They lost the suit, but our relationship did not begin auspiciously.

Once inside, I found the St. Clair Commission was on the money; the place was in true need of an overhaul. I had thought Mickey Roache could not survive, but my presence gave him the political cover to hold on to his job, and his boyhood friend Ray Flynn was generously loyal.

Mickey was not as supportive of my turnaround ideas as I'd been led to believe. For decades, an executive bathroom on the sixth floor of the historical headquarters building had been traditionally shared by the police commissioner and the superintendent-in-chief. Lockable from both ends, in it was a shower stall and a private commode so the top two people in the department would not have to use the public restroom. On the day I arrived, I called Al Sweeney. "Do you know what he's doing?"

"No," he said.

"He's walling up the door." Mickey Roache had sent the facilities people to eliminate my access.

"Wow," said Al. "His cooperative spirit ended already?"

"Well, it's going to be a little more challenging than I thought, isn't it?"

Nevertheless, I had to go through Mickey to get things moving. I imported John Linder, who had left the MTA and set up his own shop, and George Kelling, to help write a plan of action. I brought my old friend and trusted colleague Lieutenant Bob O'Toole as my adjutant. We instituted the neighborhood-policing program. and between 1992 and the following summer, using the same techniques that had worked in New York, began to bring the Boston Police back.

NYPD commissioner Lee Brown announced his resignation. Although he didn't reveal it at the time, his wife was seriously ill with cancer and they chose to return to their family home in Houston. Over the summer, I secretly interviewed with New York City mayor David Dinkins for the commissioner's post, but it went to Ray Kelly. The next spring, Ray Flynn resigned as mayor to accept his appointment as the U.S. ambassador to the

Vatican. Mickey Roache resigned almost immediately and announced he was running for mayor. (Police commissioners will do that; we all think we can run the show.) A few days later I got a call at seven in the morning. Could I be in Mayor Flynn's office at eight?

The mayor was in shirtsleeves. He and his closest aid, Joe Fisher, spent fifteen minutes talking about what they had tried to do with the BPD. I couldn't tell if they were keeping me on or letting me go. After all this, was I getting the ax? Finally the mayor said, "Bill, I'm going to announce your appointment as police commissioner later this afternoon."

From a toddler directing Cambridge traffic on Mass Ave. to Boston Police commissioner: I could have jumped in the air for joy.

I finally had the opportunity to put my own team in place: Paul Evans as superintendent-in-chief, Jack Gifford at Operations, and Bob O'Toole, always at my side. James Claiborne became Boston's first Black superintendent as chief of the Bureau of Field Services. Significantly, I named Al Sweeney commanding officer of the Academy, knowing he would change the military culture of the department into the community policing culture we had developed and he had taught throughout the country. Al was the best person for that job and I was happy to be able to promote him, my good friend, after having had to lay him off during the budget cuts. I was letting it be known by word and deed that we would be running a new, more progressive BPD from the ground up, open to all races and mavericks. Along those lines I brought Jack Maple up from New York as my executive assistant, to begin the transformation of the detective bureau.

Boston's new interim mayor was City Council president Tommy Menino, as local a guy as you ever could imagine. His nickname was the "urban mechanic," and as far as he was concerned, the world ended at the Boston border—even the state of Massachusetts didn't exist; there was only the city. He was busy campaigning for a full term and did not make any attempt to politically influence the department, which was ideal for me. As a result, my staff and I dealt directly with the office of the new governor, William Weld. Through the good lobbying work of former George Kelling student Joan

Brody, who I had brought on board as a special assistant, I was also able to open lines of communication with Bill Clinton's White House. Among Clinton's top priorities was a national crime bill and the hiring of a hundred thousand more cops nationwide. Brody cold-called the White House to lobby for some of our efforts . . . and succeeded. In late 1993, I was honored to represent American police chiefs and stand with President Clinton in the Rose Garden when he initiated the crime bill legislation. In early 1994, as NYPD commissioner, I returned to the Rose Garden for the signing of the bill and was privileged to escort Hillary Clinton into the ceremony.

Tommy Menino and Rudolph Giuliani won election on the same night. I, along with all other Boston department heads, was asked to submit an undated letter of resignation to the new mayor. I was the only one not to hand one in. I am very much a team player and had every intention of working closely and well with Menino, whom I respected, but I had several years left on my five-year appointment and did not feel the need or desire to be under the gun. Mayor Menino and I were not off to a smooth start.

Giuliani asked to see me. He had campaigned on the issues of crime and quality of life, and since I had succeeded in New York already, his representatives told me I had visibility and stature. I had passed on the opportunity to interview for commissioner with him once, but when I was no longer applying but being recruited, bypassing the selection committee and going straight to the top, I drove down.

An observation is necessary here about Rudolph Giuliani. Who he is now—a pariah, a caricature—is a corruption of who he was then: personally flawed, divisive, and sometimes vicious, but an effective, rational actor. Back then Rudy could be charming when he wanted to be. He said he admired my work in Transit but wondered whether it would work in the streets. I told him the NYPD was ripe for exactly my kind of turnaround; cops had to be motivated, equipped, energized, and directed. But, I said, the city's issues of appearance, graffiti, aggressive panhandling, and street peddlers demanded parallel changes in the Parks, Transportation, and Consumer Affairs departments. With the expected increase in accountability, the district attorneys and Department of Corrections also had to be on board. Rudy didn't have to be convinced.

Giuliani said he wanted to put my name up for consideration and led me to believe I was his choice for the job. I agreed to appear before the selection committee. I told them, "We will win the war on crime. We will successfully move against street-level drug dealing within twelve months. We will reduce crime by forty percent within three years. We will reduce public fear measurably within four years and let people feel that they can walk the city's streets.

"We will win by transforming the systems and practices of all the departments. We will empower and make precinct commanders accountable for all police activity in their areas. We will reward success, not merely the absence of failure."

We would broaden the number of units empowered to make drug arrests, encouraging anticrime units and every uniformed officer to do so, and keep cops on the streets by reducing their time in court. We would treat guns like drugs by interrupting their flow at every point of supply, sale, and use. We would pursue everyone involved in the commission of a crime with a gun. We would identify the source of the weapons in the city and use stings to attack dealers.

We would fundamentally change the way the NYPD ran its investigations. We would look for connections between crimes and try to make three cases per perp rather than one. We would train all officers rapidly and systematically so they would be committed to the new strategies and new ways to do their jobs. But, I stressed, the changes must come from inside the department first. "The cops must know their mission," I said, "and have the skills to carry it out."

Word was out. When I was scheduled to fly from Boston to New York to meet with the committee, the press was at the gate in both cities. In a subsequent trip to Washington to meet with a group of mayors and police chiefs and the president about the crime bill, I was asked at a press conference, "Commissioner, what if you don't get the New York City job?"

I smiled. "Well, you know, Boston's a pretty good consolation prize."

What a foolish thing to say. Beyond foolish. Stupid. I was a hometown boy, I treasured the Boston commissioner's job; I had worked my entire professional life to earn it. It was in no way a consolation prize, it was my lifelong goal fulfilled. I was being glib, trying to make a joke. It was not the least bit funny, denigrating the position I had worked so hard to achieve.

The clip was all over the news, and with devout Boston loyalist Tommy Menino as mayor, it was a continuing disaster. Red Sox-Yankees, Patriots-Giants, Celtics-Knicks—the rivalry was serious. The mistake still haunts me.

Mayor Giuliani offered me the job and I accepted. I had won the big one: police commissioner of the City of New York, the most important police job in America.

My transition team, headed up by Bob Wasserman and including Jack Maple, Dean Esserman, John Linder, Al Sweeney, Bob Johnson, Joan Brody, Peter LaPorte, and Bob O'Toole, took a deep dive into personnel. Wasserman, in particular, put together a Who's Who of the NYPD. Aside from having a good working relationship with Lee Brown, as Transit chief I hadn't been particularly welcomed into the department's halls of power, but now Wasserman and Maple introduced me to the up-and-comers I was looking for. Maple, as an unregenerate Transit tunnel rat, was not saddled with the vested interests or organizational baggage of a lifetime NYPD cop. Besides, most conversations with Maple were interrogations, so he was in his element. He became Deputy Chief for Crime Control Strategies.

One-star deputy chief Mike Julian was not a knee-jerk cop defender. Articulate and argumentative, he had earned his law degree at night while a plainclothes cop in Crown Heights, Brooklyn. Smart, good-looking, remarkably funny, he had a talent for problem solving. As an attorney he had represented both police officers and the city, and had prosecuted cops for misconduct, which didn't win him any friends in the department. Not that he cared. Maple told me, "Julian is brilliant, you need him around. But the cops hate him. Why don't you make him chief of personnel? Nobody likes the chief of personnel." As I overhauled the department, training would be critical. We were confident we could lower the crime rate; the more difficult task would be to do it respectfully, without antagonizing the public—particularly minority communities—and Julian would be well placed to seed the department with people who could be taught the same vision. I promoted Mike to three-star chief of personnel, but he was essentially my Chief of Big Ideas.

I was supposed to like one-star deputy chief John Timoney. He was about my age, born in Dublin and never truly lost the brogue, which became even more pronounced when he got excited, which was often. A marathon runner, he looked great in his uniform and had the craggy face of a throwback cop who'd seen his share of brawls. Which made his intelligence all the more striking. He and Julian were unlikely good friends. "He looks and sounds like a tough Irish cop," was Maple's evaluation, "but his message and his programs are extremely progressive."

Timoney was chief of the Office of Management Analysis and Planning under Ray Kelly. OMAP was effectively the commissioner's personal think tank. He had been on the job more than twenty years, could be counted on to act in the department's best interest, and was respected as a leader throughout the department. He intended to be NYPD commissioner someday soon and had the self-confidence to believe he was better than any of his competitors. Timoney was on his way up. "If Bratton only bumps me from one-star to two-star," he told friends, "there's no way I'm staying. One-star to three-star, maybe . . . Unless there's some super-duper offer, I'm going into business with Kelly."

John Linder uses the motivational technique of "strategic intent," presenting seemingly unreachable goals and challenging job applicants to create means to attain them. He told all the chiefs being interviewed, "We want a dramatic decrease in crime. Ten percent the first year. Fifteen the next. Twenty-five percent in two years." We had run the numbers, and with our strategies we felt this was within striking distance.

"Can't be done." Several chiefs gave up the ghost right away. "You can have decreases. Crime goes down two to four percent, we can continue that trend. But ten percent? No chance." Ray Kelly told Linder, "You want to reduce crime? I can reduce crime. You give me fifty men and suspend the Constitution, I'll reduce crime." We would not be following that path.

The popular wisdom is that crime skyrocketed under Mayor Dinkins, but that's just not true. It had risen consistently under twelve years of Mayor Ed Koch, and continued while Dinkins was installing his new community policing initiatives. But crime had fallen 2 to 4 percent annually in the last three years of the Dinkins administration.

In fact, getting his Safe Streets, Safe City program through the legislature had won Dinkins funding for six thousand new cops. In a huge political miscalculation that probably cost him reelection, he had spent two years of that money on social-service initiatives instead of hiring cops right away. The public wanted to feel protected, they wanted to see more cops on the streets, and with Dinkins fighting the reputation for being "soft on crime"—race may have had something to do with that image—Giuliani successfully pilloried him. If, however, Dinkins had had photos and press stories of him at Madison Square Garden presiding over the swearing in of two thousand new officers and then fanned out the fresh recruits throughout the city in the final months of the campaign, it might have given him just the slight increase in votes he needed to win. Poor political planning. Giuliani was a more effective go-for-the-jugular politician. After he was elected, Rudy attended two police graduation ceremonies and was pleased to take credit for Dinkins's 4,200 additional police officers on his watch.

Only Julian and Timoney thought the decrease was possible.

"Yeah, it can be done," said Timoney, "but you're going to have to change everything about this place. If you really change the whole department, you can bring it down significantly."

Julian was even more succinct. He told Linder, "This car is operating on two of eight cylinders. If you get it on four cylinders, you can reduce crime twenty-five percent."

Maybe I'd been overhyped, but the first time I met Timoney I was not overwhelmed. He seemed very full of himself. On top of that, I had a hard time making out what he was saying. "The guy's from Ireland," I told Linder. "I can't understand a word he says." Apparently he wasn't so impressed with me either. He told Julian, "The guy's from Boston, he talks funny." At our next conversation, however, I was struck by his forthrightness and honesty. He wasn't afraid to contradict me in order to present his view of the facts, and he didn't let his friendships cloud his clear appraisals of fellow officers. I needed someone who knew the department and could run the day-to-day operations while I changed the organization as a whole. A chief operating officer to my CEO. When I told him he would be chief of department, a one-star-to-four-star jump, he seemed to expand in front of me.

At the announcement of my appointment as commissioner I had stood beside the mayor and told the press, "We will fight for every house in this city. We will fight for every street. We will fight for every borough. And we will win." Five weeks later, with my team in place, I had quoted Dr. Martin Luther King Jr. at my swearing in ceremony: "The ultimate measure of a man is not where he stands in moments of comfort and convenience but where he stands in times of challenge or controversy. That is how we should be measured." My first night on the job, I had walked in on the roll call of the multiethnic, multiracial 103rd Precinct in Jamaica, Queens—Governor Mario Cuomo's home precinct—and told them, "I want my cops to be cops. I want them to be assertive. I don't want them walking by or looking the other way when they see something. No matter what the old rules were, I expect you to see something and take proper police action." All lessons I had learned as a young officer in Boston.

"I expect you to be honest. I expect you to uphold your oath that you took on the first day. If you get into problems doing your job, and you're doing it right, I'll back you up. If you're wrong, I'll get you retrained and back to work. If you're dirty or brutal, I'll see to it that you're arrested, you're fined, and you're put in jail.

"I like cops," I told them. "I've been with cops most of my adult life. I want to bring three things to this department: Pride, commitment, and respect. I want you to be proud of your city, of your department, and of yourselves. Proud that you're cops in the greatest police department in the world. Commitment to do the job. It's not enough for you to uphold your oath. When that man or woman next to you is brutal or corrupt or stealing, it is part of your oath that you just can't stand by, that's not enough.

"We will be sailing into harm's way as we take back this city together. We're going to work very hard, but all our good work can be undone by one cop who treats a citizen disrespectfully. We have to keep the public's respect for us. If we do our job brutally, if we do it criminally, if we do it thoughtlessly, then we're going to lose the public's respect and all the good work you do will be overshadowed by the sense that we're a brutal, corrupt force. You can't break the law to enforce the law. Pride, commitment, respect."

We had a very good first week. I personally evicted some guy from the subway who was panhandling and frightening riders, I supervised a very tense confrontation at a mosque between police and followers of Black Muslim minister Louis Farrakhan, and began to broker an improved relationship with the Black community, and I began to create a good working relationship with the New York media.

In this effort I was assisted tremendously by the hiring of John Miller as my deputy commissioner of public information. Miller was Maple's recommendation. As a well-known television-news reporter for the local NBC affiliate, he had world-class reportorial skills, great contacts, and a lot of balls. He had made his bones by getting on Mafia don John Gotti's good side and getting him to talk. Miller dressed expensively, was a connoisseur of New York nightlife, and yet was happy to take a half-a-million-dollar pay cut to be my DCPI. The cops loved him, but for that alone they questioned his sanity.

Miller was a born storyteller with an impressive repertoire, and now he was in on the action. He helped me write an op-ed for the *Daily News* explaining department thinking on the mosque incident and outlining my thinking on race relations. He arranged for an interview by *Daily News* reporter Patrice O'Shaughnessy, at which I said, "My number-one priority is fear reduction," and on Sunday the headline to her profile read: TOP COP WILLIAM BRATTON: I'LL END THE FEAR. Giuliani had run on exactly that platform and I was putting his agenda forward.

I should have known. Maple, Miller, and I got called down to City Hall *that night* and were read the riot act by the mayor's right-hand man, Peter Powers. "We will control how these stories go out," he told us. "The mayor has an agenda, and it's very important that everyone stay on message and that the message comes from the mayor." In fact, the mayor and I had discussed his agenda fully before I was hired, and we were getting good press for advancing it. Clearly what Powers and his boss were objecting to was that the mayor wasn't in these stories. "I'm his best friend," Powers said, "and *I* couldn't get away with this stuff, he'd get rid of *me*."

Some bosses, some managers have the good sense and good grace to take pride in the accomplishments of individuals in their workforce. After all, the successes of valued staff members reflect extremely well on the person who has been smart enough to hire them. Think of it as the seeds of the candied apple. Rudy was apparently not that guy. What kind of person demands all the attention? And sends his best friend to do his dirty work! I pocketed my awareness of the man with so little character and tucked it away for another day.

I don't like being threatened, and I could have walked. But I had spent my professional life getting here, and I was finally well positioned to have a far-reaching impact on the policing profession in America. The greater good was served by staying. I had a big job to do.

Jack Maple was sitting at a table at Elaine's, the Upper East Side watering hole that seemed to function as a clubhouse for a rolling roster of intellectuals, celebrities, and the press, as well as civilians looking for a good meal and good conversation. He and John Miller introduced me to the place and I fell for it hard. I'm not a drinker, but several nights a week I sat with Maple and Miller and drank my Diet Cokes as they played hard after working hard. Maple was trying to figure out how to stop crime. He didn't seem to do much else. That night he was doodling on a napkin.

He had decided that fighting crime came down to four elements:

1. Where are the crimes happening? What days of the week? What times of day? Map it.

2. Once we know where crimes are, let's coordinate detectives and plainclothes, get there fast and catch the bad guys.

3. What do we do when we get there? Buy-and-bust? Warrant enforcement? What works best?

4. Is it actually working? It's the precinct commander's job to reduce crime in his or her area. Do they know their precincts? Are they getting it done? Is crime going down?

The napkin read like a tablet. On it Maple had written the commandments of policing. To control crime, we must at all times have:

Accurate and timely intelligence

Rapid deployment of personnel and resources

Effective tactics

Relentless follow-up and assessment

These are the key elements upon which New York City policing was turned around. They deserve attention.

Accurate and timely intelligence. If police know where crime is occurring, when it often takes place, and often who is committing it, we can deploy officers—put cops on the dots—and deter it. Crime can be prevented! As trends and patterns are identified, our likelihood of success increases exponentially. The involvement of the public is vital in this regard and must be encouraged. People in every community know their neighborhood intimately, and their assistance can be of critical importance. Knowledge of two or three incidents can mitigate against their becoming twenty or thirty and forestall the newspaper headline reading: CRIME RAMPANT IN BED-STUY.

Rapid deployment of personnel and resources. Once a crime pattern or trend has been identified, get cops on the dots fast. Because crime is rarely contained to a single person or area, coordination between patrol and support personnel and investigators can combine and maximize expertise in a hurry. Expedited preparedness will cut off crime's lifeblood.

Effective tactics. Find what works and do it. In order to bring about permanent change, these tactics must be comprehensible, flexible, and adaptable to the shifting crime trends we continue to identify and monitor.

Relentless follow-up and assessment. We can never rest. Success must be analyzed; so too with failure. We will incorporate the best, jettison the worst, and maintain forward movement. Like a doctor treating a cancer patient with chemotherapy, as the condition changes, the medication must be adapted.

Think of a serious illness. Cancer. You go to a doctor, she does an examination. She spots something. It might be a basal cell, it doesn't look right, and if she waits too long it might metastasize. *Accurate and timely intelligence.* So she immediately does a test. *Rapid response.* The test comes back, it is a basal cell. If it is not treated early, it is going to become a more serious cancer, just as an unattended broken window or quality-of-life issue can lead to a more serious crime. What does she do? *Effective tactics.* She has choices. Does she want to cut it out? Does she want to prescribe chemo? Similarly, in policing, we have a variety of solutions, different medicines to deal with the identified illness. And like a doctor, after she hopefully cures you of your cancer, every six months she wants you to come back and be examined, just to be sure the treatment has worked. *Relentless follow-up and assessment.* The same for policing; you want to be constantly scanning to see whether that first dot on the map, or the second, appears again. Or if a third dot shows up. And when you get your CT scan, if the doctor sees the dot has diminished, perhaps she decreases the chemo to account for the progress made, or if it's still a problem maybe she wants to go right back in and remove it for good. The professions are joined at the hip, both guided by an original principle: First, do no harm.

Jack had been relentless as a cop, and he continued to be relentless at headquarters. He understood that what policing had done for so many years was take the easy way out. It was accepted procedure that when you made an arrest, even if there were ten perpetrators, you could take the clearance with only one, and for all practical purposes the crime was considered solved. At Transit, with the wolfpack problems and gangs of ten to twenty kids running rampant in the subways and on the streets, Jack wasn't satisfied getting just the first kid. He developed systems to go after everybody. Relentless follow-up.

At Transit, Jack had known where all the crime was. When an officer filled out a complaint report it included a pole number; Jack knew the exact location on each subway platform of every crime that had been committed, down to which staircase had been nearest. He'd had stats and maps, and was on top of it all. Accurate and timely intelligence. We needed the same information and oversight at One Police Plaza. He asked OMAP for the official crime statistics and was told they would give him what they had, but that they were eight or nine months behind. Jack was incredulous. He said loudly, "It's Christmas. So you're telling me how the crime was last spring? How can I do anything with that?!"

Jack Maple did a lot of sub rosa interviews setting up my new NYPD team. He had heard good things about Lou Anemone, a one-star deputy chief who had done innovative work in creating new training protocols for disorder control after the Crown Heights riots.

Anemone reported to headquarters, sat in the anteroom, then came into my office and sat on the big leather couch. John Timoney, whom I had already selected as chief of department, sat in a chair to one side, I sat on the other. "So," I told him, "you are going to be chief of patrol."

"What? Excuse me? I thought this was the interview." No, he had the job. He was going from a one-star to a three-star chief. Double jump, king me.

I had a very simple agenda, I told him. "We're going to reduce crime."

"I can do that, Commissioner." An NYPD lifer with a trove of knowledge and an abrasive side, Anemone didn't know how long his shelf life would be in his new position and wanted to get right to work. "I've got a lot of good ideas."

"We're going to reduce the fear of crime," I continued.

"I'm not so sure about that," he said.

"And we're going to improve the quality of life."

"I know I can get that. I've been a precinct commander for years now, I know what the people are complaining about, I know what they want, I know what they need. I know what the issues are. But lessen the fear of crime?"

"We are going to build on our success," I told him. "We are going to get a lot of good press from our success. We are going to let everyone know the good that we are doing. And that alone is going to make people feel safer."

Like most cops, Anemone had never thought the department could either measure satisfaction with the police or do anything about it, but he took on the task gladly.

Anemone wasn't a headquarters guy, he was a street guy, a creature of the patrol side. Even when he was working disorder control for Commissioner Kelly, he had not worked at One Police Plaza but operated out of a precinct office in the Bronx. He had been in narcotics as a captain, but most of his time had been in uniform, on the streets.

Early on I told him, "Three rules: It has to be legal, it has to be effective, and it has to be moral."

Anemone could live with that. "I know what the Constitution says. I can police constitutionally. I can get our people to do it. And if it's not effective, we are not going to do it; we will switch, we will change, whatever has to be done."

Maple had never met Anemone before he walked into the chief of patrol's office in early 1994. Bow tie, two-tone shoes. He took off his homburg and introduced himself. Anemone had heard the stories. Maple had his own moral code and was an inspired judge of character. "I'm looking for a partner," Maple said. Someone with a department pedigree so he would be listened to. The NYPD, like most police organizations, is very tradition bound and respects its own history. Coming from Transit, from the Ohhhh Police, he had none of that. "I'm an outsider," he said.

Anemone told him, "That's not a problem."

"Louie," he said, "that *is* a problem. I am not a blue blood like you. But you and I maybe can become partners as we're moving forward."

"All right, what do you have in mind? How are you going to help me, Jack? I know what I have to do."

And then Maple dazzled him with tactics.

"Let's say, for example . . . Are you ready to give the seven-five precinct another two hundred and fifty cops?"

"What are you, crazy? Why would I do that?!" The 7-5, the Killing Fields, was in the poor, unnoticed, and underserved Brooklyn neighborhood of East New York.

Maple said, "What about if the seven-five precinct was situated on East Fifty-First Street, would you have any qualms then?" The Upper East Side is a well-heeled portion of Manhattan in a highly visible precinct that got a lot of attention.

"So what are you saying?" said Anemone.

"The seven-five has the *crime*! They need the *help*! The commissioner said *reduce crime!*"

He had Anemone there. "I'm going to do it."

"We can't just do this," said Maple. "We've got to do this systematically. Will you help me?"

Anemone signed right up.

Maple went straight at it. "Do you have some help? I don't have too many people in the office."

"Well, I have John Yohe and Bill Gorta. They're pretty sharp guys."

Jack and Anemone would close the office door and scheme. Anemone liked to get out of 1PP and visit cops; he wanted to be on the road. In order for him and Jack to run around and play cops and robbers, he needed an anchor in the office to do his paperwork and run the bureau. His guy was one-star chief Pat Kelleher. Kelleher was an effective manager; he had held many ranks in the building, spent several years at the Organized Crime Control Bureau, and knew both how to get around things and how to get things done.

Jack's obsession with timely and accurate statistics became Kelleher's problem. One day, the two were in one of the computer rooms with Sergeant John Yohe, a computer whiz who had studied in a seminary to be a friar, earned a master's degree in German studies, and had taken a liking to computers in the early nineties, when few others in the department knew about them. At that moment Yohe was writing a Community Police on Patrol (CPOP) program for the Community Policing Unit. Working with him was Lieutenant Billy Gorta, a borough administrator brought to headquarters by Kelleher. Looking over Gorta's shoulder, as much to get Jack off his back as anything else, Kelleher asked, "Is there any way we can get some sort of daily crime statistics monthly?"

"Yeah," said Gorta. He gave a technical explanation of what it would entail that went right over Jack and Kelleher's heads.

Jack almost fell over. Kelleher said, "Okay, well, if you're so smart, do it."

And Gorta did. Gorta and Yohe came up with a program. It was only the second week in January 1994; it wasn't that hard to go in the drawer and pull out the previous year's crime statistics and compare them to this year's count—it was only two weeks' worth of data.

Gorta, Yohe, and Lieutenant Gene Whyte built the program in a couple of weeks. They were working on the DOS file one night in February during a mounting snowstorm. You really don't want to get caught in a snowstorm leaving Manhattan late at night; traffic can be a nightmare. Gene Whyte, who was giving Gorta a lift home, kept saying, "Let's go. We gotta go."

The computer system was primitive. Officer John Blancotto, who was organizing the files, said, "I can't close this out until I have a file name. I have to put a file name."

Whyte chimed in, "Put 'Fuck you, it's snowing.'"

"No," Blancotto told him, "it's gotta be eight letters." Blancotto jotted down "compare statistics '93 vs '94" and named the file CompStat. And so CompStat was born. There are many origin stories out there, but this is the real one. It means "It's snowing, let's go home."

The results were highly secret. The NYPD had a history of being resolutely tight lipped and keeping its statistics to itself; God forbid they were bad and the department had to answer for them. Ten copies of the original CompStat book were made, the first printed on February 15, 1994.

There is an old expression in policing: Two things that cops hate are change and the status quo. There is comfort and safety in the status quo; there is risk and danger in change. Cops resist change for the most part. And often, accountability. And yet they're rarely satisfied because things could always be better.

One Police Plaza used to worry about what, inside the building, was called the Fatal Flaw theory: you hand something to a chief, he looks at it, finds one mistake, and says the whole thing is invalid, and now he doesn't have to abide by it. If the arrest numbers were incorrect, for example, then all CompStat information would be deemed a mistake and nothing had to change. The resistance to innovation I found in the department was, at first, very strong.

Yohe, Gorta, and Whyte were afraid people would photocopy and distribute the CompStat books before they were ready, in order to make the changes being suggested more difficult. To guard against this sabotage, they inserted secret codes on the original ten CompStat books so they would not be messed with: a star in the corner of a few pages that wouldn't be noticed in the jumble of numbers, for example, or an inverted symbol—a secret watermark to protect against their being photocopied and shown elsewhere. Gene Whyte would drop a book with a chief's secretary and pick it up at the end of the day. This was proprietary information, not for distribution.

Sometimes it was difficult to ascertain whether the information had been reviewed at all. The team took to gluing several pages together, and when the books came back intact there was no question. "I don't think some of these guys are reading them," Whyte told Maple. "I don't think everybody is taking our numbers seriously."

After the crime book came together, Maple and Anemone asked for the arrest numbers. That effort did not go well either. The data provided was inaccurate, to say the least. Apparently, at the time, no one in the NYPD cared to get the arrest numbers right.

This was not difficult information to cull; it was a draw from a computer, siloed information, it should have been easy to do. But Maple and Anemone were getting resistance from the agencies. "What are we going to do now that we know that there were three murders in the Thirty-Second precinct in October?" was the question. "What are we going to do about it?"

A commander was really only required to possess two pieces of vital information about crime in the precinct: the number of robberies (the academics had written that robbery was New York City's bellwether crime) and the number of red-light summonses. A red-light summons was given to a motorist who went through a red light. The figure played an outsize role in the mayor's management report, because the city gets a very large sum of money from the state based on that enforcement, which goes a long way to funding the mayor's budget. The question was phrased: "How are your red lights?" In cop lore, the push for summonses is always about money for the city. A forecast projection for red-light summonses is budgeted in the mayor's management report.

Each borough held a monthly crime meeting, and Anemone and Maple decided to go to one and talk directly to the officers about crime data. After months of scheduling difficulties, Anemone finally said, "You know what? We can never go out. Find out the next borough robbery meeting and tell them we'll have it here!"

We held the gathering in the press room, large enough to handle a crowd. Gene Whyte sent the message to all the precincts in Brooklyn North, at the time a high-crime area. His phone lit up immediately with commanders wanting to know why they were coming to headquarters. "I don't know," he told them. "They want to talk about the borough crime numbers, including robberies and red lights."

"Why do they need to know about the red lights? Our numbers are good." Meanwhile, Brooklyn North was leading the city in murders. But their red lights were good, so their asses were covered. They didn't care.

We were going to do something different. Pat Kelleher said, "We're going to invite the whole building to the crime briefing." They wanted the department to watch and learn. Notices were taped up all over the building, on the first floor, in the elevators. "Come to the crime meeting. Press room." It looked almost like flyers for a college concert. Reporters were also invited, but interestingly, none came.

There was a podium at one end of the room and two reserved seats, for Anemone and Maple, in front, near the door. The meeting was scheduled for 2:00 p.m., and everyone arrived at 1:30. The meeting began and the Brooklyn North borough commander stood waiting for his cue. "Okay," Anemone shouted from his chair, "take it away! Let's hear from our precincts. Tell us about your commands."

The borough commander began in first gear, describing his borough— its geographical size, the population, the number of officers assigned. Anemone stopped him immediately.

"This is not a community council meeting! Tell me about your GLAs!"

"GLAs?" The commander couldn't understand why the brass wanted to know about his grand larceny auto numbers.

Maple called sharply, "Where are they recovering them?"

"Recovering?" Nobody even thought about tracking them. A car gets stolen, maybe it's taken to a nest, a chop shop, and taken apart. The whole idea of getting it back was way over the line. "I don't know."

Two more questions were asked and not answered. Around the room you could smell the fear.

Anemone jumped up and started waving his arms. He'd had enough. "That's it! We are coming back. *You* are coming back! And you are going to talk about crime. *Everybody* is going to talk about crime!"

Kelleher set up a rotation. Every precinct in the city would cycle into this new meeting called CompStat, and they'd better be prepared.

Anemone had said it out loud: "We are going to talk about crime." *Crime?* thought the commanders. *We don't talk about crime, we talk about red lights.* Not anymore.

Everything old is new again. In Boston in 1975, with my maps and dots and Billy Boards and directed patrols, I had always been talking about crime. Now almost twenty years later I was running the NYPD—the iconic center of American policing!—and that idea was fully taking hold. It was not that I necessarily had brought this idea to Maple and Anemone; we had all come up with it independently. What I provided was an opportunity for them and others to put into practice the concepts they had been developing. With Maple at the Transit Police I had had the intimacy of tracking sixty crimes a day. At the NYPD the number was over a thousand, but the ideas were the same. We created an environment, a world of policing devoted to preventing crime and disorder. Much as Bob Wasserman fashioned an opportunity for me to be creative in the seventies, we unearthed the Anemones and Maples of the world and created an opportunity for them to thrive. We began the transition of the NYPD from an organization in which people were afraid to do anything original, to a community in which men and women with good ideas were encouraged to pursue them.

Maple and Anemone brought Brooklyn North back for another meeting. The room was set up in a U shape this time, inviting all present to see and be seen by the entire gathering. The press was again invited, and this time some showed up.

The first presentation was made by Deputy Inspector Joe Dunne of the 7-5 precinct, probably the city's busiest in terms of violence; it had the nickname the Killing Fields, and in one year recorded more than 150 homicides. With Brooklyn's other precinct commanders watching, Maple and Anemone started their interrogation.

"Tell me about your homicides."

Dunne answered everything.

"How about your shootings?"

He answered it all, rattling off his statistics. Dunne knew his crime.

There are some people of the opinion that Jack told him beforehand what they were going to ask. Maple and Anemone needed someone to demonstrate that success in this room was possible, someone to perform in the clutch, to set the standard. Experienced commanders all realize that in the police department, if you order someone to do something, they will do it but it will take some time. On the other hand, if you tell them a secret—*"They are going to ask for this, but you didn't hear it from me"*—they will do it immediately. Sometimes it's good to present the vision of an attainable goal.

The effect was like wildfire. Commanders sat there thinking, *This guy was good. I need to know crime.* Joe Dunne was the first presenter and he knocked the ball out of the park. He had not been given the answers; he had done his homework. He ultimately became first deputy police commissioner and did a tremendous job leading the department during the horrific days of 9/11.

The next guy up, however, was horrible. There was still plenty of work to be done.

I knew that whatever I said at my first CompStat would be on the grapevine immediately and would hit every station house by that afternoon. I informed the commanders, "I expect a five-percent drop in crime this year." They were ashen. "Buckle your seat belts," I told them, "it's going to be a bumpy ride." My favorite Bette Davis line. In fact I wanted 10 percent, but I gave them a number that would shock but not overwhelm them.

The department rose to the occasion. I asked for five; in my first year they delivered twelve. The following year we did fifteen; a 27 percent decrease in crime in two years. By the time I left, in April 1996, it was thirty-nine.

CompStat became a means of measuring the effectiveness of everything we were doing.

Jack's idea was to have Yohe and Gorta pin-map every crime in the 7-5 precinct—every day, starting the next morning, for a week—and clock how much time it took. Look at the crime stat, find it on the map, and physically put a dot on the map. The 7-5 was the busiest precinct in New York City, and they found this job took two guys a total of twenty minutes a day. Jack was preemptively decimating the precinct commanders' excuses. "Now," he told Lou, "when we ask them to bring their maps down here to headquarters, so that we can talk about crime?"

"Yeah?"

"We know they can't argue that they don't have enough people, that it takes too much time, because we know in the seven-five, it is only going to take twenty minutes. What's it going to take for them to do it in the seventeenth? Three minutes? Four?"

The commanders carried their easels with their maps and the overlays of the crimes. And sure enough, they tried to talk their way out of it.

CompStat started at 7:00 a.m., Wednesdays and Fridays. Don't be late. And after that first week, with Maple embarrassing them as they walked casually through the door several minutes after start time, nobody was.

Maple and Anemone, who were running the show, wouldn't tolerate lateness, discourtesy, or anything that sounded like a bullshit excuse. Lou was good at detecting it, Jack was world-class. When they heard something that wasn't right, they were bulldogs.

They brought down a different borough for each session. It took awhile for the precinct commanders to get the idea. Some figured, "There are ten precincts here today, it's only going to be a three-hour meeting. Maybe they won't call on me." And some did get by . . . for one month. Maybe they even got by the second month. But sooner or later they all got their chance.

Maple and Anemone had to be on guard because if anything wrong was left unchallenged, there were a hundred people in the room getting the wrong message. That couldn't stand. A commander might get up and say, "You know, Chief? You want us to conduct these canvasses at the scenes of these shootings?"

"Yes."

"Well we did, but you know how it is. This guy was a bad guy and he had a lot of enemies . . ."

Here was an inflection point for the men running the meeting. If they allowed this commander to proceed to the next question, everyone in the room would be thinking "public-service homicide"—a bad guy gets killed by another bad guy—and from that point on, no one would want to break a sweat on that kind of case. Corpses would pile up as word got out in the criminal world that the cops weren't working small-time homicides. Maple and Anemone could not let that become de facto department policy.

"Hey, wait a minute, Captain," said Anemone. "Every life is valuable in this city. Good guys, bad guys. Everything counts. So we want you and your guys to get off your asses and get out there in the street and solve this!"

Or a commander might say, "Commissioner, the guy that got shot and showed up at Coney Island Hospital at three o'clock in the morning on a Saturday? He was uncooperative."

If they let that go, because the commanders of that borough's precincts were all in the room listening, being "uncooperative" would become the excuse du jour—for everybody. They were watching their peer being grilled, but they were also watching the chief and the commissioner running the show, searching for clues.

"Well, what did you do? What makes this guy uncooperative? Does he have a criminal record? Is he on parole? Did you speak to his parole officer about his lack of cooperation?" And everyone in the room is thinking, *Okay, we're not getting away with that one.*

Maple and Anemone had to know that each precinct was doing the right thing. Most were on board, but personnel gets moved around all the time in the NYPD; people retire, new commanders come in, someone who understands the urgency of fighting crime our way might be replaced by a new person who doesn't. It took constant vigilance to see and learn: Are they good? Are they not so good? Is their heart in it? The evaluation process never ceased.

Anemone was not a patient man. If, after mandating a change, he didn't see improvement after two meetings he'd want to know why. In a room of a hundred people, sometimes the questions became pointed.

A cop from the Street Crime Unit, Officer Kevin Gillespie, had been murdered in the Bronx, around 9:30 at night, on the Grand Concourse, not far from Yankee Stadium. A transit cop was shot in the throat and survived. Two of the bad guys were caught, two others got away. Chief Anemone was out with the search all night, and as it continued he kept getting calls about the next morning's meeting. "Are we going to have CompStat?" Yeah, they were going to have CompStat.

Anemone slept an hour on his office couch and went downstairs to the meeting room. During a back-and-forth about a burglary, a deputy inspector who had recently been promoted from captain got testy. "You know how tough it is?" he told the chief. "You want us to do an extended canvass for that—" This burglary was not a big crime to him. "You know how hard that is? I've got to get people, I've got to get—"

"Stop right there!" Anemone wore distance glasses to see the maps, but if while someone was answering a question he took them off and pinched the bridge of his nose, regulars in the room knew the fireworks were about to start. That was his tell.

The glasses came off.

"You are telling me you got it hard? I just came from St. Barnabas Hospital, where Kevin Gillespie gave it all for this city, but you have it hard? How about the people living up in your neighborhood trying to raise their kids? Trying to get the kids to school, stepping over the junkies or dodging the bullets from the guys having the shootouts on the corner? You want to talk about hard? That is fucking hard, mister. Don't give me this bullshit about hard. You have got to get out there and do what you have to do!"

The right answer, and the one he then received, was, "Yes, sir. Yes, Chief."

From day one, Maple and Anemone created a sense of urgency in the organization. Every meeting, every time they saw people, command officers had to understand: We are on a mission. I felt we had a lot of good people just waiting for leadership.

CompStat could be a nightmare if a commander was unprepared, but it was an opportunity to be noticed positively for those who chose to take it. I had Anemone keep a scorecard of precinct commanders: Who moved up? Who moved down? Who moved laterally? It wasn't all negative. For example, Joe Dunne, who did so well as a commander in Brooklyn's 7-5 precinct when we came in, eventually retired as first deputy commissioner. Joe Esposito was another CompStat star. He became chief of department.

The NYPD had not previously operated in this manner. Anemone had only met the previous chief of department when summoned to headquarters to be berated. That was how a precinct commander would meet the top brass, when he was being called on the carpet. CompStat became an excellent personnel tool. It enabled Anemone not only to talk to and get to know every precinct captain inspector, but also lieutenants and sergeants, people in Patrol, Narcotics, and the Detective Bureau. This was valuable contact for the officers, and it gave the chief of patrol a feel for who in the department had good policing in their heart, who understood, who could explain their actions and reasoning, who had the drive to do this job. The NYPD had been an enormous organization with no communication. We opened it up.

Information had been held in silos—various segments of the department hoarded theirs out of distrust or fear or ego, and that is a continuing battle that has yet to be won—but the ability to pursue two-way conversations about subjects that were critical to the success and survival of the city with seventy-six precincts times two commanders, plus their sergeants and lieutenants and others from various units, made CompStat extremely valuable. Inclusiveness was a much better management principle than exclusiveness.

We drilled down to specific crimes and specific people on specific streets. "All right, talk to us about the robbery dots. What are you going to do about those robbery dots? How many of those are committed by the same guy? Are you looking for patterns?"

Early on we drilled into everyone in the room the fact that as few as *three* cases with similar features constitutes a pattern. Anemone and Maple developed pattern books, with each pattern given a number, and would ask commanders to discuss the growing patterns in their precincts and what they were doing about them.

In the old NYPD there were no patterns unless the newspapers pointed them out. There was reluctance within headquarters to indicate patterns. Why? Because there would then be pressure to solve them. How would officials go to lunch or dinner if the news media was calling, wanting daily updates? The brass did not like the pressure or the oversight, and were not looking for detectives to add to their burdens.

And yet front-page cases, the ones that led the 6 o'clock, 10 o'clock, 11 o'clock news—high visibility, sexy, likely to contribute to reputation and promotion—those were the ones most often solved. It was the ordinary cases, the ordinary patterns, that Maple insisted be handled with the same intensity. "There are people being victimized all over the city," he told Anemone. "In incredible numbers. Let's fix it."

CompStat was where community policing was tested. Everything is local. New York may seem from a distance like a huge monolith, but it is all alive at the local level. I let the precinct commander be the quarterback. At One Police Plaza, we had our complex relationships at the top with Rudy and City Hall and different city agency commissioners, but our individual precinct commanders were our best emissaries to the city, and it was important to support them in getting done what had to get done.

Say the issue was calls to 911. "What were your top ten calls last month, Commander?"

"Noise complaints, Chief."

"Where?"

He named ten at one location, eight at another.

Noise complaints might come from street sales of narcotics, or loitering inside city-owned or private buildings. We would find locations with ten, fifteen, thirty, a hundred calls a month, the same address. How long can you let that go?

"What are you doing about it? Why are they calling? What's going on over there? How are you handling it?"

Once a problem was resolved, the calls would cease. "Last month there were thirty calls about quality-of-life issues, now there are none." That was an indication that this commander was doing something right out there.

Anemone had a small team of people at headquarters who, if he hadn't been to a precinct in a while, would drive over and take photos that gave him a flavor of its quality of life. He knew the bad spots, he'd been around long enough to know them throughout the city.

"Go out to Nostrand and Flatbush, I want to see what it looks like at rush hour. Last time these guys were down here at CompStat they talked about a social club they were going to take care of. I want you out there at three o'clock Saturday morning, I want to know what's going on. Is there illegal parking at this club? Are they still working without a license? What are the cops doing?" The team would come back with photos, and word would spread—at the meeting and then throughout the city: *They're looking.*

"Graffiti. You told me you were going to handle that gang stuff. How come—put it up on the screen. This is fresh graffiti!" Gangs often marked their territory with graffiti. Analyzing the tags was an important intelligence-gathering tool, but once their import had been understood it was also important to the health and tranquility of the neighborhood to get rid of them.

"Sorry, I'll handle that, Chief. I'm going back now right after this meeting. We are going to get that done. Somebody told me it was already done."

"Okay, good. We will see you next month. That better not be there next time."

As good as they were, there wasn't a precinct commander who didn't at some point have a similar issue—and it was a testament to the intelligence and preparedness of Maple and Anemone that they knew about it. Sometimes the commanders fixed the problem, other times they tried to finesse it. That never went well.

"You know, Chief, how hard it is to convene at the community board to ask for the paint to get the kids from the Youth Corps to go out—"

"Yeah, I know it's hard," Anemone would tell them. "It's hard work. Try living there, try raising a family in city housing, see how hard that is."

Until then the accepted wisdom in American policing had been that cops could do nothing about crime except respond to it after the fact, so setting a numerical goal for crime reduction was historic. Even Giuliani was scared to death. He did not want me publicizing a numerical goal, because it had never been done and he didn't want to be the face of failure.

Anticrime activity in each command—the quality-of-life teams, the specialized units—is run by the Special Ops Lieutenants (SOLs). These guys were the real crime fighters in the command, the boots on the ground doing the bulk of the enforcements. Maple wanted to meet with every one of them throughout the city. If Manhattan South was coming in, all its SOLs would be summoned to headquarters the previous week. Many had never met a deputy commissioner; some had heard about this guy with the bow tie and spectator shoes. Jack would grill each of them. "What's going on in your command?" Because they knew their stuff, they knew what their problems were.

"I am not able to run warrants."

"How come you can't get this done?"

"I don't have a mobile digital terminal."

"Why?"

There were only two or three of these devices in each command. "They're not working. If I had that, I would be able to do more."

Maple would send Gene Whyte to the eighth floor to bring back the headquarters technician who handled that piece of equipment. "We will have a guy come over and fix your thing today, right now, at the end of the meeting," Jack told him. Soon the SOLs trusted Jack and would tell him when they had problems, so when their bosses came in the following week Jack could say, "How long has your mobile digital terminal been broken? You can't run warrants, can you?" And the commander would sit there stunned, thinking, I *don't know that, how did* he *know that?*

A month later, we had the executive officers make the presentation, not the precinct commanders. We wanted to see the next layer, the guy who was watching the command when the CO was sleeping. People got recognized.

CompStat has now grown into an internationally utilized policing accountability system, but one aspect that has gone largely unnoticed is its use as an effective personnel management tool that allowed me, as a leader in charge of a fifty-thousand-person organization, to get down into the weeds and find talent. Twice a week I would sit in the CompStat meeting room and watch the interaction. It quickly became apparent who knew what was going on in their precinct and who didn't, who had ideas and who didn't, who were the resisters and who was on board. It was the ultimate transparent system; convened in one room was everyone who had anything to do with our primary goal of fighting crime, from the cop all the way to the top.

One of the great powers of the NYPD commissioner is control of personnel promotions and assignments. In 1994, new to the department and determined to turn it around, I was faced with a large number of promotion decisions for captains and inspectors. There were about fifteen hundred in the department, and even though they had personnel packages on my desk, they were mostly just names to me. As I sat in CompStat, certain people would stand out, and when I saw the promotion list I would think, *I remember them.*

On side two of the CompStat precinct statistics page I had my staff develop a profile sheet that included pictures of the captain, the inspector, and eventually the sergeant in charge of burglary, the sergeant in charge of the drug unit, the sergeant in charge of the Robbery Intervention Program unit. Each was accompanied by career information: years on the job, previous assignments, statistics relating not only to crime but to time control, sick-time control, and other behavior of the officers under their command. CompStat ultimately became extremely useful not only for crime-fighting accountability but also for pinpointing how effectively these leaders were managing the resources in their precinct, their platoon, their squad.

As computers became more powerful, as algorithms were developed to improve the visualization of dots on a map and information was provided in a more user-friendly format than a stack of paper, the benefit to a police commissioner, a department, a borough chief, a precinct commander became substantial, and eventually transformative.

When the city wouldn't fund our search for expertise, Gorta, Yohe, and Whyte reached out to the deep resource of New York City's colleges and universities. This may have been outside the lines of standard department procedure, but all it actually required was Jack Maple's approval, which he did not withhold unreasonably. When we needed an upgrade in mapping technology to inform CompStat, for instance, Hunter College sent a professor of geography and several graduate students to help amass information. An NYU statistics professor informed CompStat that its charts were wrong, that it needed sixty-seven points of data, and that it was actually comparing last year's Saturday to this year's Sunday and had to redo the books. In return for their help, the educators were permitted to claim credit in their academic journals for having assisted the police department. It worked for all of us.

Nevertheless, there was resistance. One objection was, *You can't let them in the building, they are going to see our crime numbers!* Or, as they say in *Dr. Strangelove,* "They'll see the Big Board!!"

So what? A guy with a beard is coming to subvert the NYPD?

By the fall we had a good sense of the relative value of the NYPD personnel and made significant changes, putting people in charge of the precincts who had performed well at CompStat and knew our goals and how to achieve them. This was a major upheaval.

Crime maps, with their overlapping sheets of acetate, went up in all the precincts. The idea was to switch from reacting to crime and measuring success only by the number of arrests and the decrease in response time, to preventing crime from occurring in the first place. Instead of waiting until there were twenty or thirty dots to indicate where the problems were, cops in the station house could walk in, see two or three or four dots on the map, and say, "Hey, what's going on there?" and then go out and do their job.

In management, you give people clear-cut goals to strive for. CompStat was one of the systems to measure how we were doing. The basic mission for which police exist is to prevent crime and disorder. We weren't doing a very good job preventing crime, and we were doing nothing about disorder. It was the old policing adage again: You can expect what you inspect. It became clear—nobody was inspecting.

There were plenty of ways to do well at CompStat: know your precinct, decrease crime, avoid scandal and brutality, be held in high regard by the people you were supervising and those you were policing. But there were more than a few ways to screw up. Commanders would not necessarily be punished for crime rising on their watch, but if they didn't know that it was going up—if they were ignorant of what was happening in their precinct— that was a mortal sin. Jack Maple and Louie Anemone had the whole city to worry about; commanders had a three-square-mile precinct. If the commissioner and the chief knew about a pattern or trend in their precinct and the commander didn't, that was unforgivable and sometimes impossible to recover from. Some people are excellent crime fighters, some are better as administrators. The organization was big enough to accommodate both.

We distributed each precinct's crime stats to the entire department. We had a room full of competitive professionals; why not give everyone a peek at other precincts' numbers as well as the strategies that were being used to deal with those numbers? That woke the place up. The natural competition was strong, especially for younger officers or people looking to take on greater responsibility. It didn't matter how old you were, if you wanted to move up, you could seize the opportunity by working hard. Where else in the history of the department would you have the commissioner, the chief of the department, the super chiefs, borough chiefs, civilian deputy commissioners, down to sergeants and detectives all in one room talking and sharing ideas on what worked, what didn't work? You could be seen at CompStat. It would become apparent: This person is ready for command. Everybody knew who was going to become a star and who never would.

In 1994 and '95, between CompStat and the new crime-focus leadership of Timoney, Maple, Anemone, John Miller, and countless others, crime plunged. Our commitment to manage the prevention of crime, not just the response to it, was working. If we acted appropriately, with accurate and timely intelligence, rapid response, effective tactics, and relentless follow-up, we would find tools to prevent crime from growing and make sure it didn't come back. During the twenty-seven months of my commissionership, crime went down 39 percent. We reached the tipping point. In fact, the crime decline was so dramatic it became the inspiration for Malcolm Gladwell's book *The Tipping Point.*

I don't believe anyone involved in the birthing of CompStat had any understanding of how it would morph into the internal combustion engine of American policing. We were trying to solve a specific problem. It turned out that both the problem and the solution were universal. CompStat has now thrived in New York for more than twenty-five years, through a succession of seven police commissioners and four mayors. And while people have tinkered with it, they never shut it down. Why? Because it works. Any police commissioner or mayor who tried to get rid of CompStat today would get run out of town on a rail.

Intrigued by the widely reported declines in New York City's crime and disorder, it didn't take long before other police departments started coming to CompStat meetings and adapting the system to their own needs. I am pleased that our ideas have made a significant impact worldwide. No longer is the image of a police investigation the detective with notes in his pocket that he doesn't want to share. The beauty of the system is its adaptability to local conditions, which is why CompStat has many different variations throughout the world—some more successful than others. It has become institutionalized. It has changed the police profession.

In 1996, the John F. Kennedy School of Government honored our program with the Innovations in American Government Award for the most significant innovation in public policy in America. The award reflected not only CompStat's significance but the speed with which it was spreading through policing. Crime was decreasing around America, but it was falling most dramatically in New York City. New York being the news capital of the world, the rapid change was attracting widespread attention.

Even now the public may not fully grasp the importance of CompStat in their lives. Neighborhood crime information is put on the web by the NYPD on a daily basis so that members of the public, the press, academics, or those politicians with an interest can access fairly intimately what is going on in the department from day to day. The idea of instant retrieval of information is commonplace today, but when I arrived in the 1990s the department couldn't find that information even for internal use on a monthly basis, let alone daily or sometimes even hourly. It was unheard of to share that type of analysis with the rank-and-file cops, and now we are sharing with the wider public not only the crime stats, but the analysis of the stats.

We had a dream team of American policing. Jack Maple brought outrageousness, an important quality needed to take on a department that thought a lot of itself. He brought force of personality and he brought smarts. Jack was the smartest person I have ever met as it relates to crime; I would match Maple up against any criminologist or academic on his basic understanding of crime and what to do about it. He may not have been as smooth or as articulate, he may not have had their writing skills, but boy did he have the instincts.

Louie Anemone brought passion, knowledge, intensity, and credibility. He was so smart, and he understood the NYPD intimately. As chief of patrol he brought command presence and had the imprimatur to bring about change. Louie often seems to have operated in the shadow of Maple, but no, they were truly a team. Jack could not have been as successful without Louie as his partner. Louie eventually became my chief of department when John Timoney was promoted to first deputy commissioner.

I could not have been as successful as commissioner without Maple and Timoney and Anemone and Andrews and Miller and the whole cast of characters. There was no one single personality, but a combination of many very different personalities who combined to revolutionize the NYPD. Fortunately there is a big stage for this band, because a lot of people deserve credit. My contribution was to assemble that orchestra of previously overlooked virtuosos and make them all sound good together.

Over the course of two years we systematically implemented seven crime-control strategies, to include Guns, Drugs, Youth Violence, Domestic Violence, Quality of Life, Auto Crime, and Integrity (Anticorruption).

Written largely by John Linder and Bill Andrews, all were innovative improvements on anything the department had instituted in the past, and all were founded on our four basic principles of policing. And New York City turned around. A city that had been considered throughout the world to be an urban wasteland filled with murder and mayhem was transformed—in reality and in the public eye—into a thriving, safe haven: its mayors could brag that it was the safest large city in America. Companies that had only recently been threatening to leave and take their tax revenue with them were now competing for office space. Tourists who had been terrified even to consider coming to the city began to show up in droves, spending money, supporting jobs, and taking back to their home states and countries the message that New York, the Big Apple, was once again Fun City. None of that happens without bringing down the crime rate and restoring order, and allowing New Yorkers once again to feel safe and comfortable in their homes, at their jobs, and on their streets.

Echoing Jim Collins's popular management book, *Good to Great*, we had gotten the right people on the bus, the right people off the bus, and the right people in the right seats. It was going to be quite a ride.

But it didn't last long.

Jack Maple had a plan that would win the war on drugs. He canvassed chiefs across the city, asking, "If there were no drugs in New York City, how much do you think crime would go down?" The answers came back between 30 and 90 percent. He took the most conservative. Only fifteen hundred cops, 4 percent of the department, were assigned to Narcotics. "Why don't we just put ten thousand people in Narcotics," he said, "and blow the place up?"

Research found that it would take only five thousand to do the job. We had the staffing; we developed the plan.

Previously, the drug battle had seemed like guerrilla warfare; now we would level them. The NYPD wouldn't go after users, we would simultaneously and systematically attack the low-level street dealer, the midlevel operator, and the high-level kingpin. We would overwhelm them at all times on all fronts. We called it Operation Juggernaut. We were going to wage a comprehensive, aggressive campaign against all aspects of the illegal drug problem in New York, and actually win. What a thought.

We invited the mayor and his inner circle to the CompStat room for our presentation. We brought in maps and charts and revealed our attack plan for the entire city. We even produced a video to visualize how we would do it. We ran the numbers and told them the cost.

From the time I assumed command of the department, we had had weekly one-on-ones at City Hall. Maple, Timoney, John Miller, First Deputy Commissioner Dave Scott, and after he left, Lou Anemone and I would walk over. Giuliani wanted to know everything. "What about the crime?" "What about these demonstrations?" "What is coming up next week?" He or his staff would find a nugget, either as a result of a meeting with someone in the PD or from the newspaper clippings with which he was surrounded. The topic du jour would change but Giuliani always wanted to know "what's going on with the crime stats?" He had won his mayoralty on the issue of crime, and wanted to make sure he would not lose a second term because of it.

Giuliani was adamant that arrests were going to have to go up to keep crime going down. We tried to explain to him, "No, it is the opposite. As crime goes down there are fewer arrests—because there are fewer criminal events occurring, because we will have prevented them from happening." Giuliani had a hard time taking this in. He was of that mindset that more is better, when actually more was not better.

At one of these meetings directly after we rolled out the Operation Juggernaut battle plan, the mayor had said, "It's money well spent. Let's do it."

That Sunday, in bold print on the front page of the *Daily News*, "New York's Hometown Newspaper," the headline read: BRATTON'S JUGGERNAUT. A smaller headline said: COMMISH'S '94: YEAR OF SUCCESS & SYMBOLISM. My picture took up about a quarter of the page. Maple saw it and said, "I knew the world was over." He called Miller, who had arranged the coverage; he started laughing.

Two weeks earlier, under the headline RUDY PLANS WAR ON DRUGS, the operation had been laid out and we hadn't heard a word of complaint. Now the mayor pulled the plug.

"Well," Giuliani told Miller, "I'm not really sure about this."

"We can't have these leaks," he went on. "Where did they come from? This isn't the way we do policy. It's a leak, and I want the people responsible found, and I want them dealt with."

It was a given among my command staff that if the headline had read "Rudy's Juggernaut," the plan would have been put into action and the city would have seen historic crime decreases and remarkable increases in civic contentment.

From that time on, City Hall made a concerted attempt to break the police department and put it under Giuliani's thumb. When he failed to mention the mayor at his promotion ceremony, Timoney was called down to City Hall and upbraided. I know, because I accompanied him; I didn't want him getting fired without a witness. "I thanked him and shook his hand before the press conference," he told Giuliani's chief of staff Peter Powers. "I thanked him and shook his hand after the press conference."

"Yes," said the mayor's hatchet man. "But when the TV cameras were on, you didn't do it."

Timoney was incensed. "What are you, nuts?"

They cut staffing at Miller's press office by 50 percent, causing Miller to submit his resignation. "[City Hall] said," he told local news channel NY1, "because of what's been in the papers, that the people here couldn't be trusted and that therefore we shouldn't replace some of the cops but all of the cops. They were going to ask me to throw everybody out of here. Now, loyalty is important. Loyalty runs up. I'm loyal to the mayor, I'm loyal to the police commissioner . . . but there were loyal Nazis, too."

Crime was plummeting. Overall crime was down 12.3 percent. Shooting incidents fell by 16.4 percent. There were 18.8 percent fewer murders and 385 fewer murder victims. The city was significantly and measurably safer because of the changes and innovations my team and I had put in place. "I think that City Hall should understand that positive publicity for the police department reflects well on them," Miller said.

That point was apparently lost on Rudy. One local interviewer referred to the NYPD as my police department. "The fact is," Giuliani said with great conviction, "it isn't his police department, it's the mayor's police department. The mayor of the City of New York is in control of the police department, [and] I am fully capable of doing it."

Giuliani: Maple nailed him early on. "Rudy," he said, "is the kid who would go to school and the other guys would beat him up and take his lunch money every day. Now he finds himself in the mayor's office. The biggest city in the country. The largest police force in the country. And he is going to get back at everybody." He went out of his way to be disagreeable to people, to communities; he didn't make my job any easier. Following his belligerence, we were the bad guys, the cops who had to handle the blowback and continue to work amicably in the neighborhods.

CBS News vice president Jerry Nachman, a good friend of John Miller's, said, "It almost seems like this is some former East-bloc country that you're covering, in which the chairman's picture has to be in every story you do."

I lasted twenty-seven months as police commissioner. *Time* magazine put me on its cover, looking badass in a trench coat, collar up against the cold, standing under the Brooklyn Bridge at night. The headline: FINALLY, WE'RE WINNING THE WAR AGAINST CRIME. HERE'S WHY. Needless to say, that about tore it with the mayor.

City Hall began tearing at the independence of the commissioner's job—overseeing promotions and using them as bargaining chips in negotiations with the unions; inserting itself into the transfer process of midlevel personnel; micromanaging the budget. When they launched a campaign to embarrass me over finances and began impugning my ethics after I signed a book contract, I decided it was time to go. I recommended the mayor promote John Timoney to commissioner and Maple to first deputy. He did neither.

There was a terrible crime on 125th Street in Harlem. In December 1995, a Black Pentecostal Church, the United House of Prayer, which owned a retail property on 125th Street across the street from the Apollo Theater, asked Fred Harari, a Jewish tenant who operated Freddie's Fashion Mart, to evict his longtime subtenant, a Black-owned record store called the Record Shack. Al Sharpton led a protest against the planned eviction and told protesters, "We will not stand by and allow them to move this brother so that some white interloper can expand his business."

On December 8, one of the protesters entered Freddie's with a gun and flammable liquid, shouted, "It's on now!" shot several customers, and set the store on fire. Because he was firing bullets, the fire department couldn't get in. The NYPD had to stay outside because we didn't have hoses. The gunman fatally shot himself, and seven store employees died of smoke inhalation. It was a terrible scene, made worse by the fact that we could not do anything about it.

In the aftermath, among the steps we took in an attempt to prevent any similar occurrence, Chief Anemone procured a surplus Air Force fire truck. When the purchase was reported in the newspapers, a furious Howard Safir, the fire commissioner, apparently feeling his authority was being threatened, demanded a meeting in my conference room with me, Maple, and Anemone.

"Listen, Commissioner," Anemone told him, "we need it because we don't know if your people are going to be equipped to handle something like Freddie's. I don't want to ever be there standing helpless, not being able to put out a fire."

"Well, there were shots—"

"I understand. So we are going to take this fire truck, and we are going to use it. If we have, God forbid, a situation like that again, I have cops who are willing to get out and pull the hose and put the fire out."

Two months later, I had retired. Maple went up to Anemone and said,

"Good luck, Louie." Giuliani had hired Howard Safir to be the new police commissioner. In a show of support for me, Maple resigned not long thereafter—but his heart remained with the department and the city. Anemone would continue in his role running CompStat, and Jack suggested promoting Deputy Chief Ed Norris to step into his own role and copreside as Deputy Commissioner for Crime Control Strategies. "What do you think, Louie?" he asked. "Will you back it?"

"Sure, I'll back it. I like Eddie, he's good." Anemone stayed on the force and they both suggested the promotion to Safir. The response: "Well, I'm not sure that I'm going to continue with CompStat. I want to see it work."

For five weeks, CompStat was in mortal peril. Anemone had no help in administering it. No Jack, no Ed Norris, just him with Safir sitting beside him, watching. Safir, who was not a believer, was looking to pull the plug.

With Maple gone, there was only Anemone to ask the pointed questions. When he'd shared the role, while Maple was doing one interrogation, Anemone might read ahead and take a look at the next, but he couldn't do that at a live meeting. Anemone found it very difficult. It had been hard enough while working with Jack, but working alone was more than twice as tough; not only did he have to be on his own game, his was the only game in town. CompStat was hanging in the balance.

Was it any different for those five weeks? Did CompStat crackle with the same intensity?

Even more so, because now Anemone was cranky. He started the day cranky! No helper, no partner. Anemone was pissed.

But the NYPD continued to do great work. The men and women of the department responded to every challenge.

After five weeks, Norris was interviewed and got the promotion. "Okay," Safir told him, "you're going to do this, but remember, you are *my* guy. You are *my* guy down there, you are not *Anemone's* guy." CompStat was saved.

As essential as CompStat was and remains in controlling crime and disorder throughout the city, it was not without its critics. Many in the department thought it was too tough on personnel, too abusive and disrespectful, particularly as Anemone and Maple practiced it. Others felt the pressures that it placed on commanders, concerned that their careers could be negatively impacted by poor performance, resulted in a few playing games with the numbers.

CompStat also became a focal point of attack by civic groups when, many years later, Commissioner Kelly inserted stop, question, and frisk into the metrics to be measured, and pumped the numbers. They felt this addition incentivized precinct commanders to dramatically increase SQFs, leading to their significant growth. It has been linked in some quarters with the rise of mass incarceration, and in an unintended consequence, the creation of arrest records that would prevent some who were stopped from getting decent jobs and affordable housing and creating a viable economic future. People tend to forget, however, that in New York City in the 1990s, there were half a million serious crimes—rapes, robberies, murders—committed every year. To break the back of that crime problem, to reduce that terrible number, we had to find the people who were committing those crimes—and at that time there were a lot of them—and put them in jail. I could not effectively do that without arresting people. If you could find a better way of doing that, if you could find a vaccine, fine. We had arrests. The fact that people went to prison, that was what was supposed to happen.

At the same time, New York State was operating under the extremely harsh Rockefeller drug laws, which mandated sentences from a mandatory minimum of fifteen years to life to a maximum of twenty-five years to life for possession of minimal amounts, putting nonviolent drug offenses on a par with murder. These laws were a major piston in the New York State engine that helped to drive mass incarceration. CompStat was not intended to serve that function. Around the country, other states had adopted three-strikes-and-you're-out laws, reflective of the public, media, and political get-tough-on-crime attitude that was driving police to be much more proactive in trying to turn around the problem. Compounding this, at the federal level, the battle against drug use, sale, and distribution and the crime associated with it caused laws to become more punitive. We know conclusively that the unfair discrepancy in punishment for cocaine possession in its rock form as opposed to in its powdered form—the Anti-Drug Abuse Act of 1986, ill-advisedly supported at the time by Harlem's Congressman Charles Rangel in an effort to stem the drug epidemic plaguing his constituents—had an adverse impact on minority communities.

How much of an impact did our work have on crime? From 1990, the height of New York's violent crime, through 1996, after CompStat and Broken Windows made their first, dramatic impact, New York's overall crime fell 46 percent. Nationally over the same period, the drop was only 6.8 percent. Put another way, New York City's crime drop constituted 33.4 percent of the nation's crime decline. Over the following decade, from 1997 to 2006, as my methods were adopted by more and more police departments, the nation began to catch up, although even then, New York's decline was 42.25 percent for the period and America's was 13.2 percent. The idea that New York was part of some national trend was a fiction: New York *was* the trend.

I loved being NYPD commissioner. Felony crime was down throughout the city by 39 percent over my little more than two years on the job, murders were down by 50 percent, and with initiatives in place to broaden hiring practices and decrease drug trafficking, we weren't done yet. Sadly, though, I was.

There was talk of me running for mayor of New York, and I must say the prospect of running against Giuliani, bringing CompStat to all city agencies, and having the authority to move the city in a good direction was very enticing. But ultimately, fortunately, I didn't run. I'm a police officer, not a politician.

CHAPTER 7

LA Law: Getting to the Heart of the Black Community

F eeling my police career was over, I reluctantly stepped away from policing and went into the private sector. For six years my work focused on consulting for and advising police departments nationally and internationally. I was not satisfied, because I wanted to work in the public sector to accomplish things that impacted people's lives, and in the private sector I couldn't create a system; I could only advise. I found consulting very frustrating. I went in, I made recommendations, I left. The implementation was done by someone else. That was not enough.

I met and married a wonderful, smart, accomplished woman, Rikki Klieman. A noted attorney who earned great attention and acclaim as Court TV anchor for the O. J. Simpson trial, Rikki noticed me as she was leaving a breakfast meeting at New York's Regency Hotel. I kissed her on the cheek and said, "If you were single, I'd marry you." Soon she was and I did.

We were living in New York, and I was working with Kroll Associates, a risk solutions company, when the planes hit the Twin Towers on 9/11. Many of the companies we were advising were headquartered in the financial district, near those buildings. I felt completely powerless. I had no department, no function, no role. I was near the action but not part of it. "Who am I?" I asked my wife. "Who am I now? I knew who I was when I was police commissioner. I knew who I was when I turned around five police departments, but I don't know what my identity is anymore."

Cops have always been taught that we don't back down. We have an obligation to keep moving toward danger. In most states, civilians are required to exhaust all options prior to using force; private citizens must be backed into a corner before they are allowed to do so. A police officer, on the other hand, having been trained and authorized by the state, need not exhaust all other options. Cops are taught that ultimately, for the proper level of order to be established, their authority has to be maintained. Every cop-citizen encounter concerning an illegal act has a tacit dialogue:

"Stop doing that."

"What are you going to do about it?"

"Whatever I have to."

In LA, the cops were very assertive, very cold professional, very focused on officer safety and maintenance of control, which created many of the tensions with the Black community. That attitude for many years had been condoned and gone too far.

John "JT" Thomas grew up in South LA, the first generation of his family born outside the South. He remembers clearly riding in a car and hearing his grandparents say, when they saw Black officers in LAPD vehicles or on the street, "That's progress." He recalls being a little boy and thinking, *That is a good thing.* Much as I did in Dorchester, Thomas grew up to see policing as an admirable profession that he wanted to be part of.

He grew up in a poor family, on welfare, with a single mom, but blessed with brains. He went to Crenshaw High School, took the right classes, and had enough people investing in him so he could succeed. He was one of those kids, the pride of the community, doing everything any kid in the suburbs was supposed to do to get ahead. He was a young man who was going places.

When JT was fifteen years old his family lived around the corner from the Southwest Division police station. He and a friend were coming home from playing basketball at the elementary school a few blocks away when, out of nowhere, police black-and-whites descended on them, cut them off on the sidewalk. Cops jumped out and threw down on them, ordered them to put their hands up, then proned them out.

"Proned out"—stopped because they "fit the description of . . . ," and then forced to lie facedown in the dirt, publicly humiliated. Most often for no good reason. A too common occurrence in South LA in those years.

Being African American and growing up in South LA, no one he knew had great respect for the LAPD. They all knew what it felt like to be man-handled. Few young men in the Black or Latino community had not been worked over the same way, or worse.

This time it was directly in front of his grandmother's house.

The cops handcuffed JT and threw him in the back seat of one police vehicle, his friend Clarence in another. After a few minutes they brought over a middle-aged African American woman who had had her purse snatched. This was what's known in police parlance as a "field showup," a prelineup intended to identify possible suspects.

The woman looked in the car and said, "No, that is not the boy."

"Look closely," said the officer. "I'm pretty sure they were the guys, they fit the description."

"No," she said. "that is not them."

Thomas's grandmother saw what was happening out her front window. She rushed onto the porch and just lost it.

"That's my grandbaby, what did he do?"

She rushed toward the car. In a stern voice, the officer ordered, "Get on the porch!"

His grandmother was shrieking. There were boys in the neighborhood who had been taken away and not come back for years; she knew what was at stake.

"That is my grandbaby! Tell me what is going on!"

The officer snapped, "Bitch, get on the porch or you are going to be in the back seat with him!" Thomas was angry already. He knew he hadn't done anything, but to hear that hard malevolence toward his grandmother, who was only trying to find out what was happening . . .

This was life on the streets of South LA.

After a while they let him go. He knew enough not to challenge the cop, but it's now forty years later and he can relive the scene intimately.

Thomas finished high school and graduated from UCLA with a BA in political science, then completed graduate course work in criminal justice at the University of Virginia. He joined the LAPD, worked the Gang Enforcement Detail in South LA, worked undercover narcotics enforcement, and eventually was promoted to lieutenant and assigned as adjutant to Chief Bernard Parks. I had the good fortune, when I became to chief, to work with JT as my adjutant for two years. He retired at the rank of lieutenant after twenty-one years on the job to accept the position as Chief of the University of Southern California's Department of Public Safety. I hated to lose him. He was and is the best.

"When I think back," he says, "if that woman said, 'Yeah, that's the guy,' my life would have taken a whole different turn. I would have been arrested, and never having been in any trouble, probably taken a plea deal from a public attorney who would have told me, 'This is the best I can offer you: we'll plead this down and you will have to do thirty, sixty, ninety days.' From then on I'd have had a criminal record. No UCLA, no police department—all that would have gone away. That was the reality for so many of my friends. And I came that close.

"And no way I would have been telling this story to the chief of police."

Beginning in the 1950s, television shows like *Dragnet, Badge 714*, and later *Adam-12* had popularized the image of the no-nonsense, "Just the facts, ma'am" LA cop that had been religiously maintained for decades. But in 1991, the Christopher Commission—occasioned by the beating of Rodney King—exploded that myth. The Christopher Commission Report detailed Los Angeles Police Department abuses that were well-known and tolerated in the white community and by white politicians, and were no secret at all to its communities of color.

Mobile Digital Terminal transcripts of conversations between cops in sector cars and station houses revealed a horrific culture, unearthing crime-reporting acronyms like NVN—*nigger versus nigger*—and NHI—*no human involved*—and presenting an everyday stream of epithets, sexism, anti-Semitism, homophobia, and a rainbow coalition of racism that NAACP Legal Defense Fund attorney and noted legal activist Connie Rice calls "screaming neon outrageous." The language and attitudes were so repugnant that the commission, in presenting its report, proclaimed the worst of it would be stored beyond public access at the University of Southern California and not released for many years. The commission held, in essence, that the LAPD had to cease being an openly racist, gratuitously abusive force and move from warrior-gladiator policing to community policing. It recommended "the most fundamental change of values within the LAPD" and the establishment of community policing, which "treats service to the public and prevention of crime as the primary function of police in society." Instead of viewing "the community as enemy," community policing would emphasize "patrol officers interacting positively with the public." From as far back as the Boston-Fenway Program, I promoted and embraced this approach.

Not so much the beating of Rodney King—that, in and of itself, was sadly not at all unheard of—but the videotape of the beating of Rodney King, and then the acquittal of the police officers who had administered that beating, spelled the end for LAPD chief Daryl Gates. Los Angeles was enveloped in the riots, and at the moment when the streets and community needed the greatest protection, the LAPD chose to stand down.

Why? Two reasons: First, Chief Gates was so out of touch with the

Black community that he was unprepared with either manpower or strategic planning to predict or control the civic rage at the not-guilty verdict. Second, the LAPD was so reviled that a show of force in that situation would have been considered not protection but provocation. So Chief Gates and the LAPD were not around when Reginald Denny was pulled from his truck and almost beaten to death on the corner of Florence and Normandie in the Black neighborhood of South Central LA. They had been there but had pulled back in the face of the growing crowd and anger.

In New York, the police department can flood an area with cops in an instant. In LA, there just aren't enough of them; one or two officer cars might be patrolling twenty or thirty square miles. Because of its relatively small size, the LAPD had for many years adopted one of the most assertive postures in American policing, using excessive force and intimidation to police the city, particularly in communities of color. When, for the first time in their history, the police pulled away, a message reverberated throughout the community: "The cops are gone, we are in charge." It was the first time this had ever happened, and we saw the results. Watts started to burn.

The Christopher Commission's X-ray of LAPD culture ultimately revealed its rot and led to Chief Gates's resignation. Voted into law by a 2-to-1 margin, Charter Amendment F—the commission's reforms—placed selection of a new chief in the hands of the mayor, with the support of the newly empowered Los Angeles Police Commission and the City Council.

Because of the extreme racial difficulties between the department and the public, there was significant sentiment that the new chief should be African American. Such a selection—a Black chief heading an almost all-white organization—would send a message to the city that change had arrived. Willie Williams, who was at the time the first African American police commissioner of Philadelphia, became a leading candidate. The choice appeared to be between him and LAPD assistant chief Bernard Parks. Parks, also African American, had spent over thirty years on the force and carried himself as if he were smarter than everyone. He considered himself the heir apparent.

But Parks was imperious and didn't get along with the troops. People within the department thought of him as part of the old machine. They saw Bernard Parks as the Black Daryl Gates. Mayor Tom Bradley, who had no love for Gates, had no intention of offering him the job.

Williams was not a perfect candidate. He didn't have a high school education, only a GED, and no college training. While around the country the movement was toward a chief with a degree, that was not the requirement for this particular job in Los Angeles, allowing Williams to be eligible. It appeared that the fix was in.

But worse than his educational shortcomings was Williams's management background. He wasn't particularly good at what he was doing. He had started as a parks policeman in Philadelphia and come up through the ranks of the Philadelphia Police Department at that time, one of the most incompetent and inefficient and least sophisticated departments in America. During his tenure as chief, crime grew out of control. His time in Philadelphia in no way prepared him for the issues he would have to deal with in Los Angeles. LA was desperate to have Daryl Gates's successor be a Black police chief. And they got him.

From the start, Williams had problems. First, within the department there was anything but unanimity that Chief Gates had been bad for the force. Gates's fourteen-year administration had recruited the majority of its current officers. (Boston recruits its officers from the Boston area, and New York from the tristate area. In the 1950s, Chief William Parker created the LAPD prototype by recruiting heavily from Marine Corps bases in California and from the Midwest and the South, the vast majority of officers being white. The image of the tough, bigoted, brutal, white LAPD cop dovetailed with the Southern police stereotype, and Gates had refined that model.) Gates had his backers, and the department's routines and culture were deeply ingrained and highly resistant to change. Plus, while most officers believed fully in the sanctity of the chain of command, there was no great affinity or desire within the ranks for a chief of color.

The LAPD had been beyond the influence of the mayor's office for decades; it ran its own operation without fear of interference, an insular force with its own very specific set of rules, which had to be learned and lived by. It was exactly that insularity that had brought the department down, but the attitude remained. Willie Williams was an outsider. Worse, an East Coast outsider. Worse still, a Black East Coast outsider. An overweight Black East Coast outsider.

At three hundred pounds, Williams did not look like an LA cop. Heading a department that prided itself on its image and appearance, he didn't look good in the LAPD uniform. Chief Williams revised the uniform design to include a double-breasted blazer just so he could camouflage his girth. (The command staff hated that blazer so much that one of the first things they did when he finally left was get rid of it.) In a culture of powerful fitness, he didn't fit in. It was more than just a metaphor. Rabbi Gary Greenebaum said, "People would say to me, 'Oh, the department hates Willie Williams because he's Black.' And I would say, 'Well, they don't particularly like Willie Williams because he's Black. But the main reason they don't like him is because he's fat.'"

Williams wasn't one of them, and he made little attempt to identify or satisfy the cops' needs. It also did not go unnoticed by the people in the department when he refused to take the mandatory Academy tests necessary to authorize him to become a police officer. Minus that certification, Williams was not empowered to make felony arrests in California, which held him up to additional scorn from the rank and file.

Willie Williams was well intended. I knew him, I liked him, he was a good guy. A lot of the Black community liked him because he was trying to bring about his version of community policing, which was not focused on crime but on making life better for the people in the street. He was also popular with a large part of the white community. In his first two years he was able to create a community policing initiative, hire more officers, and reduce crime, to the satisfaction of the public and the media. But later in his term things began to unravel. He chose not to cut short a Las Vegas vacation to attend the funeral of a police officer who had died in the line of duty, a serious violation of protocol for any chief of police. It was also rumored that during an earthquake he wouldn't come out of his house to go to headquarters. He just didn't seem to know how to do the right thing.

And Chief Williams bumped heads immediately with Bernard Parks.

Assistant Chief Parks very much resented having been passed over; he felt deeply that he should have gotten the chief's job, not this guy from the outside. Parks had grown up in South LA, where he still had family. His dad was a cop in the port. He was a proud Black man, a representative of progress who had come up through the ranks of a racist organization and prevailed over generations of discrimination, helping other African Americans as he climbed. He was a known commodity. In fact, many white American police chiefs liked Parks more than other Black chiefs because they saw a Black guy who basically was more white than Black in their world. He was bluer than Black.

Parks understood how to intimidate—he knew how good he looked in uniform; he knew the power of the gun on his hip and how that frightened people. He was an intimidator and he set about orchestrating the ouster of Willie Williams. Familiar with the intricacies of LAPD culture, Parks held the levers of power and set up a shadow chief's operation in police headquarters at Parker Center. It was rumored that evenings after work, Parks held court with his immediate staff down in the basement and laughed at the new chief—at his physique, at the mistakes he had made that day, at everything. In his anger, Assistant Chief Parks acted as though he thought, *You got my job and you are not qualified.*

On a good day, Parks was like a coiled spring. Now he uncoiled. There were leaks to the media, bad-mouthing in the community.

There was also the matter of Daryl Gates, still alive and active at the time, still hovering, trying to extend his life in the public eye as a radio broadcaster. Much of the LAPD was still under Gates's influence. When he attended department events he was widely applauded. He and Parks were both very rigid in their defense of the organization to which they had devoted their lives; as far as they were concerned, the LAPD could do no wrong and they didn't want anyone from the outside telling the department anything. The cops loved them for it.

Yet Chief Williams also did a lot of good. He encouraged the idea of community policing, problem-solving policing. Although his reign is today considered a disaster, the LAPD's current core values originated under Williams. The present LAPD preamble and mission statement sprang largely from his determination that the department had to build trust and engagement with the community, and that crime prevention was more important than simple law enforcement. During his first two years, he was able to bring down the terribly high crime rates.

In many respects, Willie Williams was not allowed to be the chief of his department; Bernard Parks was de facto chief during the Williams years. In some respects, Parks functioned like Rudy Giuliani did vis-à-vis Trump's State Department. He was Daryl Gates with a bigger brain and a more menacing future.

A Los Angeles police chief's term runs five years, and 1992 through 1997 were ultimately a tough five years for the department. In '97, when the Los Angeles Police Commission decided not to renew Williams's contract, he accepted a severance package and stepped down seven weeks early. While Director of Operations Bayan Lewis served the interim term, the search for the next chief began. Bernard Parks finally ascended.

Parks did not become any less rigid during his years as chief. Things were his way or the highway. He brought to the LAPD an attempt to reinstill some tougher expectations of the rank and file, but he had his own challenges. Very soon after he was appointed, Parks went to address a roll call in one of the district stations. It was reported that one of the officers raised his hand and asked, "What are you going to do about morale?" Morale was miserable; everybody knew it.

"That's not my problem," he said, "that's your problem. My morale is fine."

From a morale standpoint, Parks was saying, "I control me, I don't control you." But that hard-ass imagery of self-reliance was a throwback to the old LAPD, and out of line in so many ways. Morale can be controlled, and the ability to affect it positively is one of the most important strengths a leader can bring to an organization. How does one provide support, assistance, and guidance without it? Word gets around quickly in a police organization, and Parks lost the force almost on the first day. Things got to the point where they were doing "drive-by policing," cops breezing by in their cars with no interest in getting their hands dirty, getting jammed up. The expression was "drive by and wave." The department that had been legendary for its assertiveness now became one of the country's least assertive. They had consciously disengaged, taking their time responding to calls instead of being proactively involved. Rising crime rates reflected that disengagement.

Parks cracked down on petty abuses among the rank and file while major crimes were being committed. He was so draconian, so out of touch, that the officers began to hate him, and worse, began to fall down on the job.

Chief Parks debated with several other African Americans in the department whether the LAPD actually engaged in racial profiling. "Profiling does occur," said JT Thomas as they were driving down the street. "You cannot say that it doesn't, because I have experienced it."

"JT," said the chief, "tell me what race those people are in that car in front of us." Thomas couldn't see and didn't know. "So racial profiling can't exist," the chief told him, "because the officer can't make that determination before pulling someone over."

"Good point, sir," said Sergeant Thomas. "But what would happen with me is they would drive past and see me, and then U-turn and get right back behind me." From JT's perspective, once they had confirmation, it was very clear the only reason he was targeted was that he was African American and driving in a location where, from the cops' perspective, he shouldn't have been.

And yet Parks's popularity within the Black community was extremely high. It was a source of great pride that a Black man had fought his way up in the notoriously racist LAPD and prevailed. Parks was a symbol of Black success and was brilliant at cultivating that image. The Black community loved him, loved the power of his position, the height to which he had risen—maybe even more so because of the failure of his predecessor, Willie Williams.

In 1998, an investigation of the department unearthed what became known as the Rampart scandal, in which a number of officers from and associated with the Community Resources Against Street Hoodlums (CRASH) antigang unit of the LAPD's Rampart division were found to have beaten up and shot civilians, extorted from drug dealers, stolen eight pounds of cocaine from the LAPD evidence room, robbed a bank, and committed perjury to cover the whole thing up. The trials of individual cops were just starting to come together. The investigation had originated with the Rodney King case, but the Rampart scandal added jet fuel to that fire.

After Rodney King, the United States Department of Justice had agreed to fund a $160,000 project under which the LAPD would develop an early-warning system to identify at-risk officers. A considerable fight ensued between the police department and the City Council over which vendor would be used to fulfill that contract, and ultimately, after much wrangling, the LAPD never spent the money. At some point, the head of civil rights for the Justice Department, Assistant Attorney General Bill Lann Lee, had come to Los Angeles and interviewed Bernard Parks and people from the mayor's office and the City Council. Gerald Chaleff—a progressive criminal defense attorney, former public defender, and American Civil Liberties Union board member who was surprised to have been named president of the Police Commission—had also been interviewed. Now he received a phone call saying, "Don't tell anybody, but the Department of Justice is sending us a letter and we are meeting on Monday in the city attorney's office." The city was heading for a consent decree.

A consent decree is an agreement between involved parties submitted in writing to a court. Once approved, it becomes legally binding. In this case, the consent decree involved oversight of the LAPD by a federal district court judge, who would appoint a monitor to coordinate the reporting of its compliance. The DOJ notified the City of Los Angeles that it was prepared to file a civil suit based on the pattern and practice of the LAPD's false arrests, unreasonable searches and seizures, and inappropriate use of force.

Police consent decrees were still a relatively new phenomenon at this time, and very contentious. A lot of the leadership didn't want it. The mayor didn't want it. Parks in particular was rabidly against because it implied that he had been doing a bad job with the department, which he had; crime was soaring, morale was miserable, the union was in revolt.

James Hahn had been elected Los Angeles city attorney, and in that role handled all civil litigation, running an office of approximately two hundred lawyers, about twenty of whom were assigned solely to defending police cases. Over the years, Hahn's office had defended a large number of civil rights lawsuits filed against the LAPD, many involving shootings and deaths. He had represented the officers and was very familiar with the department.

In the Rampart scandal, Officer Rafael Perez and other officers were not only found guilty, but as a result of their crimes the city was forced to litigate and ultimately pay out a significant amount of money in civil cases. Criminals convicted as a result of their testimony had to be set free. Chief Parks wanted to come down very hard on Perez and the officers involved; however, he got into an argument with District Attorney Joe Garcetti and threatened to refuse cooperation because he didn't think the cases were being handled correctly. Hahn found Parks a difficult man to deal with, very stubborn, with his own way of doing things. As his lawyer, Hahn told him, "Well, you kind of have to cooperate with the DA, that is kind of our job."

The Justice Department filed a lawsuit against the police department as they had done in other cities, New Orleans among them. Its basic premise was, "The LAPD has a systematic pattern and practice of depriving people of their civil rights." If the case went to trial and the city lost, the LAPD would be taken over and run by the U.S. Department of Justice, obviously not a desirable outcome. Hahn examined the law and quickly realized that the threshold required to demonstrate such a pattern and practice was very low: two incidents, a very low bar indeed. He told the mayor and City Council that they couldn't win and recommended entering into a consent decree that would put in writing what changes the LAPD would promise to deliver, while also establishing that if and when these changes were effected, the Department of Justice would withdraw its suit and the LAPD could continue to run its own shop. Hahn also felt that, rather than simply being an agreement between the city and the Justice Department, the consent decree would function as a tangible indication to the Black and Hispanic communities that the department was finally preparing to change. It would be a testament to the communities to get them to trust the LAPD. And the LAPD would have to earn that trust, because trust had been lost.

Chief Parks and Los Angeles mayor Richard Riordan fought hard against entering into a consent decree. They felt such a move would constitute an admission of guilt, which they were not prepared to make.

As a charter city, LA has a unique governmental structure. Under its charter, the City Council, not the mayor, holds the decision-making responsibility for litigation. So even though the mayor's and the chief's strongly held position was: *Do not settle. We can try this case and win. We are not racist, we are not violating people's civil rights, we are improving every day; we should not enter into a consent decree under any circumstances*, in September 2000 the City Council voted to accept the deal. As a condition of the settlement, a judge would appoint a federal monitor to compile information and report to the court on the LAPD's compliance with its obligations.

A consent decree is only as good as its monitor. I have mixed feelings about the practice because there is a group of so-called monitors who have made a profession of the job, in many instances getting into a police department and never wanting to let go. (Also, some are just not good at what they do. In my opinion the city of Oakland, in particular, has not been well served.) Gerry Chaleff felt the consent decree was needed "because we weren't going to get it done otherwise."

Presiding federal judge Gary Feess agreed. He was intimately informed, having been counsel to the Christopher Commission. He said words to the effect that "we have been trying to reform the LAPD for fifty years. You ignored the Christopher Commission report, but you are not getting out from under this decree until the Black community says things have changed." Judge Feess also had the wisdom to give the Police Commission oversight powers, and its vigilance effectively kept the department within the guardrails the consent decree established.

The Los Angeles monitorship contract would be the largest in the U.S. history, and highly skilled lawyers and former Manhattan assistant district attorneys Michael Cherkasky, Jeff Schlanger, and I went to California representing Kroll and presented as police subject-matter experts. We got the job.

Negotiations between the DOJ and the city over the terms of the monitorship started in May and ended in November 2000. Among the contentious provisions was financial disclosure. There had been very little vetting for officers' entrance into the CRASH antigang unit—where most of the illegal activity originated—other than a department search for complaints lodged against them. It was decided that because of the potential for dishonesty—the units were very freewheeling at the time, as the Rampart scandal revealed—officers would be required to fill out detailed financial background forms, which could be checked periodically when searching for the kind of net-worth increase that payoffs and drug transactions could produce. It was preventive anticorruption, so officers wouldn't be vulnerable—or weren't actually taking money to begin with. The department had similar requirements for people in vice and narcotics, but none for CRASH. The union objected—strenuously, going so far as to file suit to block the provision—but to no avail.

Another major issue was the physical safety of criminal suspects. A culture of casual brutality had been standard operating procedure for decades. Now an officer was obligated to bring suspects for booking in front of a supervisor to make certain they weren't injured coming in and there was a clear record of what they were being arrested for.

Ultimately the consent decree targeted nine substantive areas: Management and supervisory measures to promote civil rights integrity; Incidents, procedures, documentation, investigation, and review (including eight subcategories); management of gang units; confidential informants; mental illness; training; integrity audits; operations of the Police Commission and inspector general; community outreach and public information. Teams were set up within both the department and the monitorship to look at the relevant provisions and understand what was necessary for the city to deliver the appropriate data and documentation, and ultimately for us as monitors to come to a conclusion as to whether or not the department was in compliance with that reform.

We organized ourselves into teams to work with our LAPD counterparts, each with an individual leader. One dealt with use of force, a second with accountability, another with the early-warning system, another with pedestrian and vehicle stops as regards to racial profiling. Jeff Schlanger and I oversaw those units. We had protocols to measure the degree of compliance with each of the individual reform initiatives, and we would report quarterly on their progress.

With regard to pedestrian and vehicle stops, for example, officers were mandated to conduct themselves in a way free of racial profiling, otherwise defined as biased policing. Stops could not be based in any part on an individual's race or religion or sexual orientation, but rather had to be neutral in those categories, with the one exception of having specific suspect information; if a call went out for a crime in progress when the perpetrator was a Black man, police were permitted to focus on Black male suspected perpetrators. Otherwise not. The allegation was that Blacks were being stopped at a rate ten times that of whites, and as the process was to first get a handle on those statistics, the department was mandated to enter into a data-collection exercise, to be done electronically, which at that time was very novel. The data was then to be analyzed to determine whether the LAPD was engaging in biased policing and to support protocols that would provide training in how to do the work without engaging in bias.

One problem with consent decrees as a concept is that they become data-collection entities; their goals are statistical, not societal, and they are not set up to accurately measure the impact on the problem they are created to address. As a federal monitor, I found the Los Angeles decree measured success by the degree of compliance with the terms of the consent decree, not the impact on the issues that the decree was seeking to resolve. For instance, data was compiled to answer the question, Was use of force reduced? However, the more important question—Why was that reduction a goal?—was not asked. Clearly, since it had been held that a majority of the improper force was directed against minorities, the goal was to improve community and race relations. But were community or race relations measured? No. Did race relations improve? No one was asking that question.

In researching the assignment, we had spoken extensively with Jim McDonald and Sharon Papa, both of whom I had known previously and respected, Jim as a civilian clerk in Boston District 4, and Sharon as chief of the LA Transit Police when I had headed up Transit in New York. They were current members of the LAPD command structure but had come from police organizations outside the LA area, lending a perspective and recognition that LAPD lifers didn't necessarily possess. Jim and Sharon were candid about the department's problems and told us to expect resistance in the upper ranks. That was timely and accurate intelligence. The department didn't want us. The reception was as cold as a coronavirus vaccine freezer drawer.

Our team entered police headquarters at Parker Center (named after former LAPD Chief Bill Parker), received our IDs, and met with Acting Chief Martin Pomeroy, who had been appointed to serve out the remainder of Bernard Parks's term of office and made it quite clear that he was not happy about the LAPD being monitored by anyone. He was a gentleman, but he didn't make any bones about it. "This is something we don't think we need or deserve. And we really don't feel that we need advice from you on how to police the city." We had our work cut out for us.

It quickly became clear that the gap between where the department was and where it was supposed to be was significant. During our first month, for instance, we went on a ride-along to the Watts high-crime housing project, Nickerson Gardens. As one of the officers unfastened his seat belt to exit the sector car, he repositioned his weapon for ready access. It was not an idle gesture, and represented to us the officer's mindset. His answers in conversation bore that out; he approached his job as being part of an occupying force, not a representative of community policing.

James Hahn was elected mayor of Los Angeles in 2001. While the DOJ negotiations were proceeding, because of the findings by the Christopher Commission, the means of selecting a police chief were redesigned. Previously the chief's job had been a civil service post, with legal restrictions making unseating a chief virtually impossible. Under new regulations, it became an appointed position with a five-year term. The Police Commission would conduct a candidate search, after which three names would be submitted for consideration to the mayor and City Council. (A sitting chief would still be required to reapply for a second term.) The mayor would then make the selection.

Bernard Parks's term was to expire in 2002, and one of the major issues in the mayoral campaign had been whether Hahn would reappoint him. Chief Parks wanted and expected a second term. Mayor Hahn was not so sure. Parks had been quoted saying, "If we see four Black men in a car late at night and it doesn't seem like they should be there, we're going to pull them over and see what is going on." At a meeting in Hahn's office, the mayor told the chief, "That is racial profiling." Parks said, "Look, who commits most of the crimes in this city? You think it's a good police practice to make sure that people aren't carrying guns?" Hahn answered, "You know, if a white chief said that, people would be up in arms." Parks didn't seem to mind.

At that meeting, Hahn addressed another central issue. "The morale of the department is terrible right now," he said. "They don't like you, Chief Parks. They think you pick on them for small things and your discipline is unreasonable. They are very unhappy and are leaving faster than we can hire them."

"Well," Chief Parks told him, "the morale of the troops is not my problem."

"If General Patton had said that in World War Two," said Hahn, "people would have said he was crazy. Of course the morale of your troops is important!" Parks thought cops got paid well, that they should be happy to have a job—end of story.

Parks was adamantly opposed to the community policing model Willie Williams had installed. He wanted to do away with the Senior Lead Officer program—volunteer problem-solving officers who effectively don't answer calls but work the neighborhoods, developing relationships. They walk community beats working on quality-of-life issues as well as serious crime. Hahn wanted to keep the program. "Those guys sit in the trailer and drink coffee," Parks said. "We need people out on the street." This attempt by Parks to do away with the program did not sit well with a large portion of the Los Angeles population. After much deliberation, Hahn realized he could not work with Parks and would not reappoint him at the end of his term.

His staff told him, "Are you crazy? You've got eighty percent of the Black vote; no white politician ever gets that. If you don't reappoint Parks, you will lose the support of the Black community, you'll never get re-elected." Hahn said, "I can't let this situation continue. The department is shrinking, crime is going up; that is not a trend I can tolerate. And it is clear to me that Bernard Parks is not going to follow my lead on the things I think would work to turn that around."

"Okay," they told him. "It's your funeral."

Hahn agonized over his decision. He liked his job and loved the city, and wanted to make it safer and cared about its people, who were being victimized by crime. In life, he felt, you have to play the hand you're dealt, and sometimes it's a crummy hand. Maybe letting Parks go was not a winning proposition politically, but, he figured, sometimes a man has to be able to look at himself in the morning.

Hahn had a bloodline in public service. His father, Ken Hahn, who served the city in many elected capacities, had been the only Los Angeles public official to greet Dr. Martin Luther King Jr. after King had faced down water hoses in Birmingham, Alabama. Jim Hahn had been a Los Angeles elected official since 1985 and was realistic enough to realize that this decision might cost him not only his job but his legacy.

The Police Protective League, the police union, had backed Hahn over his opponent, Antonio Villaraigosa, with the hope that, if elected, Hahn would fire Parks; they felt he was destroying the department. Parks had over a third of the department under internal affairs investigation. He was firing people who should have been fired—the corrupt and brutal cops from the force's previous generations—but he also turned a vindictive eye on people who wouldn't kiss his ring.

Police Protective League president Ted Hunt called Connie Rice, a Harvard-educated litigator and legal activist par excellence. The journal *California LawBusiness* had named her one of California's top ten most influential lawyers. Over the course of nine years at the NAACP Legal

Defense and Educational Fund, she and her teams of lawyers filed class-action civil rights cases against the LAPD that changed the department's policies regarding police abuse of force, and in race and sex discrimination wins forced LAPD to diversify and eventually become a majority minority department. In between her legal assaults on LAPD, she led a team that won $2 billion in bus improvements on behalf of the Bus Riders Union, which California state librarian Kevin Starr noted was the largest civil rights settlement in the history of American civil rights. And later, she and her law partners at English, Munger & Rice won $750 million for new school construction in Los Angeles—money previously ticketed for less crowded, more affluent suburban school districts. In toto, her leadership of multiracial coalitions of lawyers and clients resulted in more than $4 billion in injunctive relief and damages. She was very good at what she did.

The union was so desperate they called to have Rice help push back on Parks's own internal Rampart scandal analysis. She knew it was bad when the head of the union was calling "all these liberal-ass civil rights litigators who sued the department for forty years." As Rice recalls it, Hunt said, "You have no reason to take my call. I have treated you like dirt for ten years, but we need your help." An unlikely alliance of liberal panel and conservative police union was formed. Rice's organization, the Advancement Project, issued a report stating in essence, "Parks is blaming the rank and file. We are pointing our finger at the brass and the culture and the mindset that is passed on. You are blaming the lower-level officers, you are not giving them due process, you are sweeping everybody up in a vacuum."

Hahn called Parks into his office and defined his new administration's agenda. "Bernie, we have known each other for a long time. I am the mayor and I want community policing to move forward."

Parks refused to sit down. He said, "You are not the law when it comes to LAPD. I am the law and I'm going to decide what is happening—and none of that is happening." Parks was harkening back to an era when the chief was effectively appointed for life, but that time had passed. Also in the room, Hahn's adviser, attorney Bill Wardlaw, stood up and said, "You don't speak to my client that way. You can leave your badge and your gun, because you are gone."

However, to fire Parks, Hahn felt he needed racial cover. The Black community loved Parks because he was Black; it had no idea of the reactionary, racially retrograde dynamic he wielded inside the department. For example, once he became chief he refused to exempt African American officers with razor bumps medical disorder from having to shave, even though knowing they could be subject to facial scarring and life-threatening infections. Even the U.S. Marine Corps exempted its Black officers from that requirement. In a deposition for a lawsuit on behalf of Lieutenant Kevin Williams, an effective crime fighter, Parks testified, "I don't care if he gets an infection, let him take antibiotics." He simply refused to back down at any level.

As a representative and defender of the Black community, Connie Rice had faced off against Hahn multiple times when he'd been city attorney. He told her, "You have sued and beaten me often enough. You and I both understand that this city will never be right until this department gets reorganized. Parks isn't going to do it. I am firing him."

She said, "You know you're going to be a one-term mayor."

Hahn recognized the stakes and accepted them. "If that is the price that I have to pay. This is our one chance."

During her many years of activism, Rice had earned extensive access to the press. If she, as a leading, iconic Black civil rights lawyer would assure Los Angeles's wealthy liberal west side that firing this charismatic central-casting-looking Black police chief was the right thing to do, then Hahn could overcome the Black community's fury and real change could begin. "But if you don't get out there," he said, "we're not getting it done." She accepted the challenge. "I didn't have that many clients," she says. "I had no money, no congregation. All I had was a big mouth and determination."

"Connie," Hahn told her, "you are going to pay a higher price than I am."

She asked what he meant.

"You're going to be excommunicated from the Black community."

"I have already been excommunicated from the Black community," she told him. "I am not losing anything. I am asocial—I hope I don't get invited to the Christmas party! There are many Black communities here and I have never really been a part of them. I am not anything, I'm just a social gadfly on the edge. They understand my power in terms of civil rights law but . . . Jim, no, you are paying the higher price."

"And I had the media wired," she says now. "I played the racial shield."

Against everyone's advice, Hahn made his position clear: he would not reappoint Bernard Parks. He thought there was an outside chance he might win respect and reap some benefit for taking this stand. It was a noble viewpoint. People often say, "Politicians always do what's in their own interest, they never do what's right. I would support somebody who does what's right and consequences be damned." But they didn't. And it did indeed cost him.

Some Black community leaders had approached Hahn while he was preparing to make the decision and said, "You have to get Parks out of there. He is terrible. He won't listen to us; he supports his cops over our community. He was a protégé of Daryl Gates, and we need change at the top." Yet after Hahn made the decision, some of these same leaders blasted him as being a racist. This was Los Angeles politics.

Hahn's mistake was that he couldn't take off his lawyer hat. As mayor he had the right not to reappoint Parks; he didn't need a reason. The desire to install a chief more aligned with his policies would have been an understandable rationale if widely presented. Yet when Parks went to the media and the churches, attacking the mayor and promoting himself, Hahn kept quiet. He didn't find it necessary or proper to go out of his way to criticize Parks; he didn't see any point in trying to tear the man down. He was probably also concerned about publicly attacking a Black public servant and the criticism that might bring.

Hahn told the chief that if he would simply retire he would praise him to the skies, tell the press that Parks had been the best police chief in Los Angeles history, and offer as a reason for not proffering a second term the civic platitude about needing to go in a different direction. Hahn offered Parks the carrot—"I'm sure you will do very well consulting in the private sector. And if you retire I will say nothing but good things about you." But he refrained from threatening the stick. He didn't say, "And I will tear you to pieces if you don't."

Parks waged war. He was well connected, and his one-sided battle with Hahn began to take on a life of its own. "My mistake," Hahn says now, "was not realizing I was in a political fight. I just said, 'I made my decision and want to go on.' If I had it to do over again I should have gone to war against him."

Beginning when he was a little boy with his father, Hahn had spent Sundays visiting churches in the Black community, stopping by and talking with people, being a responsive presence. Now Hahn received letters signed by many of the ministers whose churches he had visited his entire life, saying, "You are not welcome, Mayor Hahn, to come to our church anymore." John Mack, head of the Urban League and for thirty years the most outspoken critic of the police department, sent a letter saying, "You are not welcome to attend our Urban League dinner." Hahn found this deeply hurtful.

Jim Hahn was right to let Parks go. With department morale at a monumental low, with crime on the rise and community relations going from bad to worse, the chief had worn out his welcome. His own union spent a million dollars—billboards, radio advertisements—trying to get rid of him! As Gerry Chaleff put it, on the day that Parks wasn't reappointed, for the department it was like the sun came out.

W ho would be the new chief?

As the federal monitor, I was in and out of the mayor's office delivering reports, discussing results and perspectives. Mayor Hahn was facing the first momentous decision of his administration. I told him, "I know who you should hire as chief."

"Oh, really?"

"Yeah," I said, "but you would never hire me." He had no idea I was interested in the job.

Hahn wanted to change the culture of LAPD. He wanted a department that was respected by the communities in which it worked, and was interested in solving crime problems and making communities safer. He was looking for a change agent. I felt I had more to contribute, that I could go into that job as the only person in America who would turn the department around, the only one who knew what to do. I could change people's lives, save hundreds of lives, make the city safer and make LAPD's officers proud again. The community deserved and needed them at their best. I wanted to forge a partnership based on trust. I could prove in LA that cops can reduce crime and improve race relations. As corny as that sounds, that's what I wanted to do. It was what I did best, and I missed it. I felt Mayor Hahn and I were a good fit.

The mayor was adamant about involving the City Council in the decision-making process. The Police Commission, headed by businessman-entrepreneur Rick Caruso, examined the city's crime statistics. When Caruso placed the city crime map side by side with the county crime map, he found the city's crime rate to be twice as high—in areas across the street from each other. He also found a serious management problem, starting with Parks himself. The commission interviewed widely and narrowed the field to three nominees—two whites and a Latino, all men, one of them me. There was considerable public discussion, particularly in communities of color and among City Council members, about whether the list showed sufficient diversity. Mayor Hahn's highest demand, however, was that he be presented with the best possible people for the job.

Hahn met the finalists individually at the mayor's mansion. He didn't live there, but the office was an impressive place to conduct an interview. Each candidate brought his ideas for making the city safe. When I detailed mine I told him, "I'll bring crime down by twenty-five percent or I'll quit." He said, "Nobody makes predictions like that." I was very confident, having gained a deep understanding of the department's strengths and challenges as its monitor, that I could produce that turnaround. "If you are going to be bold and brash enough to say something like that," the mayor told me, "how can I lose?"

The betting was that Hahn wouldn't pick me for fear of being overshadowed. Almost all politicians have big egos, some bigger than others, and he was certainly aware of my history with Rudy Giuliani. Hahn had more self-confidence than that notoriously thin-skinned mayor. And yet, his parting words to me when I left the mansion that day were, "I'm not going to read about this in a book someday, am I?"

I was very pleased to get the job. Rick Caruso was solidly in my corner and highly instrumental in my selection. Rick became a strong partner in our time working together and remains a close friend. As chief of the Los Angeles Police Department I would have tremendous responsibility and, as opposed to working in the private sector, the opportunity to have a positive effect on a wide portion of society.

60 Minutes interviewed Hahn not long after the hiring, with the idea that they would come back every six months to see how it was going. They never came back. Correspondent Ed Bradley asked if the mayor had a problem with my history of getting and enjoying attention. Hahn answered, "It's fine with me that Bill likes the spotlight, because anybody who likes the spotlight is going to be on the spot. They're going to have to deliver."

In one long weekend less than a month after I went on the job, LA saw fifteen homicides. It was an extraordinarily tough three days—in addition to the murders, several other young men died in confrontations with the police—and it really knocked me back on my heels. The spate of violence caused me to think, *What the hell have I gotten myself into?* What also surprised me was how indifferent the city had become to this level of violence. This wasn't in Afghanistan. This wasn't in Lebanon. This was on the streets of the second-largest city in this country. And yet the carnage was going largely unreported by the media, as if it were to be expected. This had to stop.

As the new chief I had three priorities: reduce crime, prevent terrorism in the aftermath of 9/11, and comply with the consent decree so we could earn the government's stamp of approval. I wanted to come back into policing, particularly in a large city, to show that cops do count and police matter. In New York, we'd showed that with the right amount of police, and policing in an appropriate fashion, we could drive down crime dramatically. I also believed we could not only reduce crime, but at the same time improve relations with the minority community—that we could have both at the same time. I desperately wanted to prove that concept, and thought of New York as a missed opportunity. We were moving forward when I had left; all I'd needed was more time. The police had been the flash point for most of the racial violence in the past century; wouldn't it be wonderful, I felt, if we were the catalyst for the healing? I looked forward to the day the Justice Department would stand next to me and declare: "The LAPD isn't a racist, violent, dishonest police department anymore."

One of the first statements I made to LA's officers when I went on the job was, "The citizens of this city need you back in those streets. They don't need you smiling and waving, they need you out of those cars, taking back those streets that unfortunately—so many—have been lost." I wanted only officers who were willing to work toward my goals. The three causes for dismissal from the department, I said, would be corruption, racism, and brutality. "You cannot break the law to enforce the law," I told them. "Under any circumstances. If you're in this organization, getting money from the taxpayers, you're going to work for it. So all this bullshit is going to stop right here and now. Get with the program. If you don't want to work in this department, get the hell out, because there are a lot of people in here that want to do the work."

I installed CompStat so everyone would be accountable. I brought in my team, and as I had done in both Transit and the NYPD, used Bob Wasserman's assessment process, ordering all officers at the rank of captain and above to submit documents stating what they did and why they were necessary. I made it very clear that everybody had a clean slate; if you were producing, if you were moving in the direction I was taking the department, there were opportunities to be had. I wanted the LAPD to build relationships and work with communities in ways to which it may have given lip service but never really acted on. I said the word *partnership* so often that some on the staff started mocking—with affection, I'm told—my Boston accent. *Pahtnuhship. Pahtnuhship.*

This deep dive into the department had the intended effect of unearthing its best people and allowing me to put them in positions where they could do the most good. I cleared out some deadwood and promoted three of the contenders for the chief's job—Jim McDonald, Sharon Papa, and George Gascon—to the rank of assistant chief, the second-highest position in the LAPD. How many chiefs would put their competitors into the highest ranks of their department? I did, because I wanted people of that caliber.

I recruited John Miller from his TV anchor role with Barbara Walters on *20/20* as my deputy chief of counterterrorism. (Several years earlier, Miller had interviewed Osama bin Laden in the mountains of Afghanistan, earning great cred.) I also recruited Mike Berkow, chief of the Irvine Police Department and a friend of twenty years, to head up my internal affairs department. Once again I was getting the right people in the right seats on the bus.

One of the people who could not be on that bus was the amazing Jack Maple. Jack had died of cancer in August 2001. The world lost an inimitable character and one of its greatest crime fighters and policing strategists.

I put into practice all the programs I knew would work. I made a concerted effort to fix things immediately. The LAPD had an iconic history, and as a result often stood on tradition and followed precedent almost blindly. That needed to change.

Mayor Hahn wanted to be informed about promotions and transfers, but he never involved himself in the process. Even in high-profile discipline cases, he felt it was the chief's responsibility, not his, and stayed out of them. I appreciated both his way of doing business and the confidence he showed in me and the department.

My predecessor had gotten rid of the entire level of assistant chiefs and effectively attempted to run the department by himself. I found, when I arrived, a decision-making system that was barely functional. When a request or report was made by a captain at the division level, it would be sent up the line for approval. If, as often happened, the commander above him made a change or some minor error was found, it would be kicked back to the captain, retyped, and sent back up. With each alteration the document went up and down, up and down, sometimes taking months before finally getting to the decision maker, who was always Parks himself.

In the days before the consent decree, if a division commander wanted to run an undercover operation, he had to run the request all the way up to the chief of police for authorization. While Hahn was city attorney, a string of commercial burglaries were committed on York Boulevard in the Northeast Division. The division commander wanted to put some officers in plain clothes to stake out the businesses at night and catch the thieves. By the time that request made its way through the chain of command and finally received Parks's approval, it seemed as if every small business on York Boulevard had been burglarized.

Parks's organization chart was in the shape of a hexagon, with the chief's office in the middle. It was literally a stop sign. He had decided that, in order to ensure quality control, he needed to micromanage everything. It wasn't an effective way of running the department; the lack of trust undermined staff initiative, leading to command atrophy and an institutional distrust of one's own abilities.

I believe in delegation: find good people, hold them responsible, and let them run. I go to great lengths to find people best suited to the jobs they are assigned, and then I encourage them to work to their fullest. Their results are monitored. I have rarely been disappointed in the outcome. Parks,

I understand, used to go home with two legal briefcases of paperwork every night. I can honestly say that, in both the NYPD and the LAPD, I never took a piece of paper home with me.

Mayor Hahn was very impressed by CompStat when he accepted my invitation to attend. In an organization that had all but eliminated individual accountability, the fact that division commanders would be called upon to defend their actions was an eye-opener. No one ever combined police work and theater like Jack Maple, but Assistant Chief Jim McDonald ran the early meetings with a firm hand. He had control of the facts and went around the room, grilling every commanding officer.

"So it looks like commercial burglaries are going up in your area, what's that about?"

"Well, we think we have identified the suspects."

"Are they in custody?"

"No."

"Why not?"

We held our people accountable. That's how CompStat ran. "If you can't get it done, I'm going to get somebody else to do it." This was a big change. Hahn didn't think they had ever been talked to that way. *Oh, you mean I don't have a pass here, my job is now on the line every time I go to a CompStat meeting?* In the LAPD, this was a new way of doing things.

I made it clear to the department that we were going to do more than abide by the consent decree, we were going to comply fully and be so vigilantly adherent that we would make it go away. To that end, I brought in Gerry Chaleff, made him a two-star civilian Deputy Chief of the Consent Decree Bureau, and installed him on the sixth floor, alongside all the other chiefs, in an office right outside mine. A sixth-floor office was a big deal in the LAPD; it denoted power. I made him a direct report, responsible only to me.

Gerry was in the lion's den, much to the chagrin of some people there with him. As a criminal defense attorney, he had spent a professional lifetime on the other side of the table. He had defended the Hillside Strangler and the Alphabet Bomber, and served on the board of directors of the ACLU. He was a smart, aggressive advocate who had given the department a hard time. Just the man I wanted on the inside.

Soon Gerry began promoting people out of my units, demonstrating that the path to the top passed through the progressive wing. The message I was sending was that we weren't giving lip service to reform; we were serious.

I also brought in Connie Rice. After years of both suing and representing police, she concluded that society gets what she calls the "containment-suppression" policing it has asked for ever since the beginning of slavery, and that the DNA of today's policing reinforces, aggravates, and amplifies the toxic racial dynamics that stem from slavery. From thirty thousand feet up, she's clear that "Southern policing is plantation policing. You keep the niggers in check. That is the purpose of American policing." But, per her usual complexity, I would learn this meta view had nothing to do with how she views the individual valor, courage, and decency she freely says she has found in the many cops she has represented and made into her partners for police reform.

People whose opinion I respected told me Connie and I should speak. She had recently written an op-ed in the *Los Angeles Times* saying, essentially, "It's not Broken Windows, it's broken families and communities." We met at a New Year's Eve party and I found her dynamic, highly intelligent, and very persuasive. Her opening gambit was, "Welcome to LA, Chief. Don't take it personally but I will be filing another lawsuit next week." As I did with the city itself, I found myself faced with the choice between hostile response and considered reaction. I chose to listen.

"You don't need to file another lawsuit," I said. "Why don't you come inside and help me?" She had exactly the voice and persona needed to inform the department.

She then had a similar choice: she could remain an outsider and continue to rail or she could move toward the center of power and try to have an effect. As she recalls it, "I had to really think hard, because I had to stop what I was doing; it wasn't just the police who had to change how they were behaving and what they were doing in the community; I had to change what I was doing and get in the boat and row."

That was an eventful New Year's. Connie was brimming with solutions. "I want you to think about talking to Gang Intervention," she said, referring to a department division. "I don't need to just talk to Gang Intervention," I told her, "I need to talk to actual gangsters."

Connie thinks of the big picture. She wanted to know what she might be getting into. "What is your vision?" she asked. Was I going to wage war on gangs and neighborhoods, continuing the LAPD's history of militarization and attack, or did I have something else in mind?

"My vision," I said, "is that by the time I leave here, the African American community will say they no longer hate us and they will trust us when we do our job." Judge Feess had said the consent decree would remain in effect until the Black community verified sufficient improvement to let it go. That was my goal.

"That's great," she told me, "but I don't want you to say that at the Urban League dinner, I need you to say that to the white police unions."

Connie chose to come on board.

I think of myself as a good police leader, but without the consent decree I don't think substantive changes could have been made in Los Angeles by me or any chief. It was the lever to tip the department. The necessary changes couldn't have been put in place without effectively being able to say, "We're going to do this because it is the right thing, but also because it's required and we really don't have a choice." I knew some elements were difficult, that's why I got the complaints all day long about what a pain in the ass they were. To which I'd say, "If you don't get it done, it's going to be worse." And, I thought, when the decree was ultimately lifted—as I was very confident would happen—it would be as if the department had been given a diploma, that we were now the best.

The consent decree drew a good map of where we were and where we needed to go. Embracing it also provided me with a great set of shields. When under siege, the ancient Roman legions would interlock their shields to create an impenetrable wall—the testudo, or tortoise formation, they called it—so no attack from any position could harm them. I felt similarly protected. Gerry Chaleff was a shield, an activist with a fine legal mind, whose liberal bona fides were unassailable. Connie Rice saw Los Angeles and the world in ways that, having grown up as a white male, I didn't and couldn't. She had spent much of her professional life attacking the LAPD and was now working with us. She was a very effective shield. As was John Mack, head of the Urban League and a righteous critic of the department, who was named president of the Police Commission, effectively my boss. I had as advocates the leading criminal attorney, civil rights attorney, and civil rights leader. Their presence and stature, and the goodwill we all shared, helped blunt criticism and gave me room to maneuver behind the scenes. I hoped Los Angeles's communities of color would think I must be okay if I had earned their trust, and hold off putting us under siege until we could prove our worth.

Plus, Judge Feess's consent decree mandated specific actions, which I could use for cover if necessary, so I had the leverage and authority of a judge to obtain funding for programs that were necessary but might not have been immediately popular. The expanded budget was not a pay increase for the officers, but a large stash to be used for improvements in department conditions and matériel. Personal money is important, but most people come to work to do a good job; they want to succeed and they want their organization to succeed. When police officers—when any workers—are presented with elements that enhance their ability to get results, it produces very positive results. I was fortunate, when I came through the door, to have inherited a $1.5 billion construction budget, which we used to buy new sector cars and build twenty-one new facilities, which pleased the cops to no end.

A police chief must have the respect and goodwill of the department in order to succeed. It's a paradox; cops are devoted followers of the chain of command, and at the same time freethinkers. Given the nature of the LAPD, I was both owed respect and challenged to earn it.

Many cops were apprehensive about me. They wanted a chief who had their back, and I was an outsider; they didn't know who they were getting. Willie Williams hadn't worked out, and after the Parks years they wanted someone who had their best interests at heart. I was a double-department easterner, New York and Boston. Could be trouble. And I talked funny.

Periodically I would stop and speak with P2s, officers just out of training, within two or three years of first joining the force, to see what they were thinking. I thought it was a good way to get a ground-up perspective. Apparently this was unusual; my predecessors had engaged in very little of that kind of conversation unless it was at a roll call.

I asked JT Thomas, the cop who as a boy had been proned out in front of his grandmother's house, to be my adjutant. He told me, "I'll give it some thought."

Thomas had been an aide to my predecessor, but had little intention of sticking around. I was from New York, and the LAPD thought New York cops were corrupt—in their mind the total opposite of an LAPD officer. Word was, "They brought an outsider in before, and that didn't work out so good, so let's see what happens with this guy." Actually, there was very little doubt. "We know how this is going to turn out." And yet JT stayed.

As we got to know each other, JT and I would have good and serious conversations, and periodically still do. One night we drove to the scene of a crime at which someone had been killed. When we arrived I asked JT, "Why are we the only high-ranking people here?"

"Captains," he said, "they don't respond to homicides."

"You're kidding me. Someone can get killed in their division and they are at home asleep and hear about it the next day?"

I was appalled. This businesslike attitude signified that nobody cared about the lives that were lost, often Black and brown lives. The community was being denigrated. But when someone gets shot in the middle of the night and the captain jumps out of bed to get there, the troops hear it loud and clear: "This matters. This life matters. These people who are being killed matter." The level of accountability rises, and officers are made to understand that there are expectations, not simply, "Yeah, somebody got shot in South LA. Just another dead body." It reverberates through the organization.

Leadership is defined not only by words but by action. Now all of a sudden you have officers thinking, *This should have been fixed a long time ago. We've got to be here in the middle of the night, dammit, the captain should be here, too. Why do I have to brief the captain tomorrow when he or she should have been here?* The point I was trying to drive home was that we are all in this together.

Visiting roll calls and speaking through the media, I made it very clear to my cops that the old ways of treating people were no longer acceptable, that as of that moment there were new standards to which the department would be held. The community was not our enemy, I said; we would treat the people of all communities in Los Angeles with equal respect. And if anyone didn't, there would be hell to pay. I know for certain that most of my predecessors had told them nothing like this.

But cops have seen people say a lot of stuff. As far as they were concerned, my speechifying was only for the media; none of it meant much. "Is this guy for real? Let's see what happens when he catches some people doing some shit." That would be the test: what kind of discipline would I mete out?

When a commander did not perform up to expectations I let them know about it. I believe in accountability, and when someone has not done their job I will tell them. I wasn't brutal, but I was direct. One of my favorite phrases was "You guys in California are soft!"

For instance, at a staff meeting the day after someone had leaked department information to the papers, I showed what—behind my back—they called my "Chucky look." I was furious. This was a betrayal of the department and the people; if we couldn't develop our plans in private, we couldn't keep the criminals from getting one step ahead. I scanned the room, shaking my finger. "Okay, somebody went to the *Times* and they leaked this—and it's somebody in this room!" Nobody moved. "I'll tell you what. When I find out who did it, you better hit the hill!"

Despite JT's being a lieutenant and not normally privy to these scenes, I had no problem dressing down higher-ranking officers in front of him when necessary. If he was going to be my adjutant he needed to be well informed; I wasn't going to throw him out of the room every time I handed out a reprimand. JT heard me demand forthrightness many times, and at some point he felt sufficiently comfortable to tell me things he thought I needed to hear. Having witnessed my temper, he gave me an important piece of information and taught me something about LAPD culture.

"You're scaring these guys," he said.

I must have looked confused.

"When you yell at them," he told me. "They're not used to that."

"Get outta here."

"No, seriously. When you yell at them . . . they are not used to that." I gave him a look. These tough LA cops, these intimidators, were scared of a few harsh words? Having been raised under Boston and New York commands, I didn't think I was a pussycat, but I'd heard a lot worse. Apparently in the LAPD if you got mad at somebody, you held on to it for two or three years at least. You're probably still pissed off. If you pissed off some of the brass they would be angry at you forever but they would not raise their voice! Me, I'm not a grudge holder but I will say what I have to say with some force. Putting your discontent on simmer and keeping all mistakes current is a good way to stifle initiative and kill an organization. I would say my piece and let it go.

Community policing in Los Angeles began with Chief Ed Davis. Controversial and outspoken—his solution for hijackers: give them a trial and then "hang 'em at the airport"—"Crazy Ed" followed Bill Parker's militarization of the LAPD with a more community-oriented approach. Faced with a sprawling land mass, he divided the 480-square-mile City of Los Angeles into four police bureaus. Within each bureau he created four or five divisions, the equivalent of New York's precincts, and broke those divisions into sectors, which were called Basic Car areas. (As a Basic Car, think of TV's 1-Adam-12—one car assigned to a specific sector twenty-four hours a day.) There were 212 Basic Car areas. Staffing a Basic Car twenty-four hours a day, seven days a week required twelve officers, and the glue that held Davis' system together was the senior lead officer.

The role of the senior lead officer (SLO) was twofold. First, he (and at the time it was almost always a he; by the 2000s many of them were women) kept his officers abreast of what had been going on in their Basic Car area as they reported back to work after days off. Second—and this happened increasingly over time—he became a link to the community. The senior lead officer was not a walking officer per se, he had a vehicle; but he spent a lot of his time walking around the neighborhood, organizing and going to meetings, stopping at stores. He gave people his phone number, and later his email address, so they could reach him directly with their concerns about local crime and disorder. The SLO was thus able to keep the division commander aware of current issues. There were thirteen different ranks in the LAPD police officer structure, and the senior lead officer was the highest ranking police officer.

One of the issues that got Bernard Parks into great trouble was that, in his zeal to put more cops on patrol in the field, he proposed taking the 212 senior lead officers and putting them back into Basic Cars. This was just another reason why officers were leaving in droves—almost a thousand of them—and the department couldn't hire enough to replace them. The public, the media, and politicians all went wild on him. These officers had become so popular, so essential, that Parks's decision confirmed their view of his insensitivity and became another nail in his coffin.

When I came in, the Senior Lead Officer program resonated with me because it mirrored so closely what I had tried to do in the Boston-Fenway

Program in the 1970s. I reinforced the SLO program and sought to expand it by adding officers, because some of the Basic Car areas were so busy one person couldn't handle them.

I had made it a policy in the past to learn what my officers needed and wanted in order to do their jobs best, and then, if the request was reasonable, to get it for them. Uniforms, cars, and weapons had been consistent areas for improvement in my previous positions, and as I canvassed the force I found that assignments and scheduling were vital LAPD issues of the day. When I said the number *312* their entire demeanor changed.

"Three twelve" stood for a three-day workweek with twelve-hour workdays. A pilot program for this flexible schedule had been installed in several divisions around the city under Willie Williams and had gained wide support from officers, who liked the expanse of free time it gave them. The union was in favor and Mayor Hahn approved, but Chief Parks had pulled the plug on it. When the cops heard that I was fine with 312, they didn't care where I came from. From that time forward I had a relationship with the union that Parks never did. I even invited union representatives into some of our internal meetings.

Gerry Chaleff and John Miller and I were to gather for dinner one evening, but an officer-involved shooting occurred downtown, so they drove there first. (If you drive with John, you take your life in your hands, but Chaleff survived.) They spoke at the scene to Gary Brennan, the deputy chief in charge, and as they left, Gerry turned to John and said, "They're just waiting for us to leave, aren't they?" John said, "Yep." Just as the Boston cops had tried to wait out di Grazia, the LAPD was waiting me out. The men in the department had outlasted everyone in the past ten years who was different than they were—two chiefs of color and the accompanying command staff. They didn't figure we would last very long either.

ieutenant Fred Booker, an African American, was a smart man who had risen through the ranks to become the officer in charge of the Community Relations office, a position with the prime responsibility of creating a pathway between the department and LA's communities of color. By the time we met, Booker had had almost thirty years on the job. He had worked under Chiefs Gates, Williams, and Parks, and now here I was.

I knew I might have problems with the Black community. There were rumblings that after he had been denied a second term, out of pique Parks had marshaled all his contacts among the ministers and leadership to undermine me. He also advised the department's Black officers to quit.

I didn't know the half of it. Fred Booker did. According to word on the street, I was the white outsider, the stop-and-frisk commissioner, the abuser of the community, the racist; I was not to be trusted. Fred respected the post of chief, he was loyal to the department and loyal to his own code of ethics. He had been loyal to Chief Parks, and now he was loyal to me. He decided I had to know I was being set up.

But first he had to tell me who he was. He was waiting for me at my office at 6:00 a.m., having thought about it all night. I came in after my morning workout and he said, "Hey, Chief, I need to talk to you." It was important to him that I know he didn't just fall into his job, that he had earned the right to be there; that if he was working for me, he was fully committed. Booker was passionate and even somewhat emotional about his connection to the LAPD. He suspected, and he was right to suspect, that someone had been questioning his loyalty to me. He wanted me to know why I could trust his judgment.

Fred Booker grew up with no man in the house, just five women and his six brothers and a sister—thirteen people in one small house eight miles outside the town of Chester, South Carolina. He walked to his one-room schoolhouse carrying a yellow gallon bucket that held his lunch of buttermilk, cornbread, and fatback meat. The white kids drove by every day in school buses—the Black kids didn't have buses—screaming, "Nigger, nigger, nigger!" as they passed. Fred and his family were sharecroppers; they didn't stay long.

When Fred was nine they moved to a huge farm twelve miles outside Lowrys, South Carolina, population 300, belonging to a man named A. T. Morgan. A. T.'s brother Harvey Morgan was a high sheriff of that area. They had no electricity, no toilets, and no money. They were not paid for working the farm; as sharecroppers they lived on the land in exchange for a roof over their heads. Lamps were expensive, so they woke up each pitch-black morning and lit a dark bottle of kerosene with a rag in it. Now it's a Molotov cocktail, back then they called it a flambo—their morning and evening light. They milked the cows, put the milk cans in an old wagon, and took them to the road, where the milk truck would pick them up. Then they fed the animals, slopped the hogs, and picked cotton. There were crops of corn, watermelon, and peanuts. This was 1956. Fred had stopped going to school when they'd left Chester.

A. T. Morgan owned a huge new Cadillac. On occasion, if things were okay on the farm, he would hand Fred and his brother a nickel and drive them to the Lowrys general store. They couldn't ride with the family; Morgan put them in the trunk, which they held open to see out. He would let them out in town, where they could get some candy with that nickel, but they had to walk the twelve miles back by themselves.

Fred was the middle brother. The life was brutal, so when the two older boys turned eighteen they ran off the farm and went up north to places like New York and Washington, D.C., leaving the work to him and his older brother, Robert.

One Sunday morning Mr. Morgan came by in his pickup truck to check on his sows. When sows get pregnant and ready to deliver, they usually go off by themselves to have their piglets. The boys could not find that pig. Seven to eight piglets was money out of the man's pocket, and they couldn't find them. Cussing something fierce, Mr. Morgan reached into the back of his cab and pulled out a rifle. "Take those shoes off!" he shouted.

Fred and his brother were wearing Brogan shoes, the sturdy kind of footwear that slave owners used to issue to their slaves. The soles were run down. When a sole wore out, the boys would replace it with cardboard and use the rings put in a swine's nose to prevent the pig from rooting to secure it. The ground was covered with snow from a big storm the night before, but Mr. Morgan made the boys remove their shoes. Then he pointed his rifle at them. *"Get out there, go find the pig! Get out there!"* He started shooting over their head. Barefoot in snow, with a white man cursing and firing at him, Fred ran into the woods. He could hear the bullets ringing through the trees, and he got the hell out of there.

Mr. Morgan came back to the farm around four in the afternoon. The boys had found the pig and her litter. He gave each of them a small bag of candy.

Fred learned to read and write when he was thirteen years old and was the first in his family to graduate from high school.

He was my age now. We were both from working-class families. That was pretty much it for common experiences. About our only similarity was that each of us had joined the military. Me, the military police. He, the Marines.

In the early 1970s, as a twenty-five-year-old just out of the service, Booker visited Los Angeles and went looking for 77 Sunset Strip and Edd "Kookie" Byrnes, just like he'd seen on television. A friend convinced him to join the LAPD. Once inside, he found very few fellow officers who looked like him.

On his first night working East LA in the Hollenbeck Division, the watch commander in the briefing room called the roll to set up partners. He called everyone's name. Booker was seated in the front of the room. They called his name and no one said anything, nobody moved, everyone just laughed.

When it was time to roll, the Hollenbeck cops got up and left. Booker sat there, waiting for his new partner to identify himself. No one spoke to him, no one told him what was going on. He grabbed his gear and went to the gas pumps to find the Basic Car. He waited and waited. No one came by.

Suddenly a black-and-white cruiser screeched up. A cop got out.

"Get in."

"Okay."

"Put your stuff in the back and you sit here." His new partner pointed to the shotgun seat. Booker obliged.

"Let me tell you something," said the officer. "I will tell you right now, I do not like working with niggers. I want you to know that. So what I want you to do, I want you to sit here. Don't touch anything, don't say anything. Just sit here. You don't move until I tell you!"

Having grown up in small-town South Carolina, Booker had heard this talk before, but nevertheless he was surprised; he'd thought it would be more subtle on the job. "Okay," he said. "You are the boss." Booker told me this had happened twenty-eight years earlier, but he was telling me for a reason. I reached over and shook his hand and sealed the deal.

I needed to transform the image of the police in the Black community, and Fred was my conduit. He knew everybody, and over the course of my first few months, I got to know him. He's a smart, strong, honorable cop. There's not much better one can say about a man. He helped introduce me—and when Fred vouched for me, given his reputation, it went a long way.

"Chief," he told me, "the Valley and West LA are not going to hurt you. There are two places where you better spend a lot of time: South LA and East LA. Those are the places that are going to hurt you." Further, he said, "You need to go to not just the big events that you are expected to attend; they need to see you in the community at a level they are not accustomed to—at barbershops, churches."

Booker arranged a wide array of meetings with various citizen and church groups. Initially the reception was rough. Rather than take me at my word—and why would they? I was the chief of a police department that had proned out so many of the men and women sitting before me— the people who were interested enough to attend and meet me sat back and were not of a mind to believe me. Most supported Parks, and I had taken his place. But as I spoke to their issues and began to take action, they started to come around.

Booker took me to Lawrence Tolliver's barbershop. I was aware of the barbershop's place in Black society, and of Tolliver's in South Central LA. It advertised itself as "A Watering Hole of Truth and Knowledge. A Pulse of the Community." Tolliver's was where neighborhood people came for styles and opinions, where celebrities came to hang, where Black politicians came when they had something to say, and white ones when they needed to be noticed. The banter was nonstop. People were jovial in there, but they weren't fooling around.

Tolliver's had been open since the 1960s. In the '80s, when gang violence brought fear into the streets and a program called Safe Passages enrolled volunteers to walk kids to school, a sign was posted on the barbershop's door like a beacon, saying that if there was an incident they were running from they could "Come here and be safe." The people inside the day I arrived didn't expect much from the police chief; not a one had ever come through their doors—certainly not Bill Parker, who said, "We didn't ask these people to come here." Not Daryl Gates or either of the Black chiefs. So what was I doing there?

They didn't know whether I was a decent human being. They knew I was a white police chief who'd been a lot of places. They figured me for a racist showing up for a photo op.

It was not my way to storm the podium. At gatherings, I told Booker that I preferred not to speak first. I would watch the crowd, get a feel for peoples' needs and priorities, and then address them. I told meeting after meeting that I was there to reduce crime, to bring order back to their communities' streets. That I knew the history of the LAPD, that some of the people in the room had had a lifetime of bad experiences with cops who were now under my control, and that I took their experience seriously. "Look, people," I told them, "the future is not in handcuffs. That is not what we're about." (In truth, I borrowed that phrase from LAPD commander Bob Green. I think he was on the money; it completely encapsulates my feelings about policing.) I didn't get an overwhelmingly positive response, but I didn't get booed out of the room. They wanted to see if I meant what I said. Within a short time I had two opportunities.

A group of cops had chased down a Black car-theft suspect by the riverbank in the Southeast Division. The cops didn't realize it, but this being Los Angeles, where there were always news helicopters in the air, one caught them with a telephoto lens from something like a mile away, in the act of beating the daylights out of the man. Even on the grainy film you could see the cops working him over, the shiny shafts of their Maglites hitting *boom boom boom.*

The Maglite was a chrome-handled flashlight inside of which lay several large D batteries. The weight was all on its end, and using it as a weapon was like hitting someone with a ball peen hammer. Back in the day, the billy club was the police officer's nonlethal weapon of choice. New York had the long nightstick, then transitioned and trained on the PR-24 baton, which had a handle. But you couldn't hit people the same way with a PR-24—it wasn't balanced right—so in its place cops started carrying the Maglite. Anyone who had had a physical confrontation with a cop knew what a Maglite was.

As time passed, the Maglite began to grow in length until it capped out at around eighteen inches. No cop would get out of his car without his; before hitting the street they would grab that flashlight, whether it was day or night. Crack a couple of people over the head with that and it made an impression.

The flashlight beating was clearly over the line and unacceptable. The video played on TV constantly because it was so graphic and upsetting. It became a galvanizing news item, and for John Mack at the Police Commission, one of his first controversial cases.

My initial instinct is almost always to support my cops; I understand better than most the mindset of officers and the components of a police encounter. But this was unsupportable. TV news wanted my response to the incident and I said, "Look, there is no training in the Police Academy for use of the flashlight." I pulled the Maglite out of the department's work belt. In both image and fact, this was no longer something we should be wielding. As a result of the subsequent investigation I disciplined several of the officers and fired one.

Cops don't like having their tools taken from them. Young officers working the gangs at the time of the incident were using the flashlight as a secondary impact device, a last-chance implement with which to deliver a strike. They believed I had weakened their leverage and made them vulnerable. Maybe so, in which case they would have to find another, lawful way to get the job done. The Maglite had to be replaced.

Captain Terry Hara spent almost a year designing a rubberized device that is now known as the LAPD Flashlight and has become standard issue for many departments around the country. I expected blowback because the rubberized version was useless as an impact device, but I wound up convincing the officers that this smaller flashlight would be more illuminating and much brighter than the Maglite, and that every officer would get their own, plus a charger, that could be mounted in the sector car. Some of the new lockers in stations around the city were also equipped with chargers.

And here's a small glimpse into the often parochial world of modern policing. Because officers would be taking the new flashlights out of the station house, the union wanted the city to pay each cop for the electrical costs of charging them at home. They wanted the city to pay for electricity! When we gave officers their own personal walkie-talkies to improve safety and performance, the union demanded the same thing. The cops didn't have to take them home, they could be left at the station; but rather than acknowledge and be grateful for an extra safety feature, in both instances the union came after us, wanting extra compensation for a newly provided convenience. The change in matériel and concept played better with the community than it did with the cops. Go figure. You can't make this stuff up.

Not long after the flashlight incident, on Super Bowl Sunday 2005, a thirteen-year-old African American boy named Devon Brown stole a car, took it on a joyride, ran a red light, and jumped the curb. His passenger jumped out, he did not. When the car reversed and came in the direction of two officers, one fired his weapon and killed the boy. After two detailed and extensive investigations—criminal and administrative—it was decided that the officers had acted within department guidelines and would not be charged.

The African American community was understandably outraged—young man, joyride, police shooting, death—but I was very determined that the situation not boil over; nobody wins in that case. We made a good-faith effort to be transparent in all aspects. Brown's family was bereft, as one would expect. Ultimately, however, the facts determined that the officers would not be charged or reprimanded, which did not sit well with the community. For my part, I wanted to make certain this kind of situation would never happen again. I investigated LAPD procedures regarding shooting at a moving vehicle.

In *Tennessee v. Garner*, the Supreme Court ruled that officers who fear that their lives are in danger may be justified in using their firearm to take a life. Many police departments and cops have learned to rely on that justification. There are ample opportunities for bad faith to infect that defense, but that can be difficult to pin down. It was LAPD policy that if a vehicle was moving toward an officer and they felt it was going to be used as a weapon, that officer could lay down fire and shoot at the driver.

As a matter of strict department policy, no NYPD officer may shoot at a moving vehicle; that cop's job is to preserve safety. Plus, if a driver is coming at you and you shoot at the vehicle and take that driver out, you now have a three-ton piece of steel, with no one at the wheel, that can veer out of control and do wholesale damage. Why would you do that? Because the car is coming at you? Once the car has passed, then you can assess the situation more fully. Until then, get the hell out of the way! Aside from risking harm to the surrounding community, shooting is just not the right thing to do. We killed a thirteen-year-old. Why? I made a public statement to the entire force and introduced a new policy: we will no longer shoot at a moving vehicle; our job is to get out of the way.

Some officers were not pleased. "Get out of the way." What did that mean? They wanted to shoot, but we'd made them vulnerable again. "Hey, you're an outsider, you don't know us and now you are trying to make these changes to our LAPD. It's not yours!"

Unlike my predecessors, who did not explain their decisions happily, I sold the idea to the command staff, who then involved the patrol officers. Rather than simply issue a statement, I instituted physical training to introduce this new policy, and directed that it be explained—What did getting out of the way actually entail? What did it mean to return lethal force if necessary? What were the consequences?—every step of the way.

I brought in the union. I told the command staff, "Why do we need this? It is against organizational principles to fire at will. Do we want to go out there and shoot some crazy person in a car and have it run over some little old lady walking across the street? What would we look like? Who would we be?!"

(After a murderous incident on New York City's West Side Highway in which a terrorist intentionally ran down pedestrians, killing eight people and wounding eleven others, the NYPD did change its policy to say that if a vehicle was deliberately being used as a weapon against a crowd, shooting at the vehicle would be permissible.)

Not only did the officers get the message, the community began to understand as well. We were not intent on abusing or insulting or killing them;

we had their best interests at heart. I understood that this must have been hard to take from an organization with a history like ours—particularly in a community with a history such as theirs. I didn't expect to be welcomed quickly, I just kept trying to deliver the message. I figured I was making progress when I visited Lawrence Tolliver's barber shop and he told me, "I will work with anyone if you lower the crime rate. As a matter of fact, I will give you a kiss on the mouth in front of City Hall if you lower the crime rate." I said, "Just give me a handshake."

Gang crime in Los Angeles was rampant, and violence in the streets was causing terrible fear among all of the city's residents. The police were not responsible for the creation or explosion of Los Angeles's gangs, which were made up largely of young Black and Latino men. But we were responsible for dealing with the impact of their crime and violence and the fear they were creating. The LAPD throughout its history had been very aggressive in attempting to get them off the streets, and that history sometimes made it difficult to defend the proper and effective use of police force. I was at Parker Center on my way to a meeting at the mayor's office when there was an annual demonstration outside, protesting police brutality and aggression. My security detail wanted me to avoid the crowd by going out the back entrance. I said, "I'm not doing that. I'm walking out the front door!" I didn't feel the need to avoid the confrontation, and I certainly didn't want to appear afraid of or unwilling to respond to the public.

I walked through the crowd, and once they saw me they swarmed around and started yelling. The demonstration was filled with people shouting and holding signs, one of which said "Control your cops!" I said, "I'll control my cops if you control your kids!"

This served three purposes: First, it made a direct statement to the community that responsibility for order in the streets runs both ways. Accepting that history and society and economics and education make getting jobs and raising children more difficult in most minority neighborhoods than in white ones, there are still standards to be upheld, behavior to be encouraged, lives to be directed. Police can't be expected to raise children, only to prevent crime and disorder and try to point them in the right direction. Cops alone can't do a job that parents, teachers, ministers, and politicians have failed at; communities need to establish controls as well.

Second, it showed the cops that I supported them in the face of criticism, that if they acted in the ways they had been trained, I had their backs.

And third, the media ate it up. There were a couple of TV crews at the demonstration who caught this and presented my ideas widely to the public. That was a good day.

To make Los Angeles a safe city everywhere for everyone, to keep its children from being swept up into violence by gangs, would require everyone to share responsibility. Police can never do it alone. There's an old African saying, which I first heard from Hillary Clinton, that it takes a village to raise a child. This was as applicable in Los Angeles as anywhere.

I believe that one of the major challenges in American policing is to remove the Black face from the image of crime. I was living in Boston during the 1988 presidential election when Massachusetts governor Michael Dukakis's campaign got successfully derailed by the Willie Horton ad, in which an African American convict with natural hair and a big beard, serving a life sentence without the possibility of parole for murder, while out on a work-release furlough program approved by Dukakis's administration, stabbed a man, raped a woman, and was made to represent crime itself— the idea being that the Blacks were coming to get you so you needed George Bush to be president and protect white people. Cops are not immune to that image and that fear; in fact, it's as pervasive in police forces as it is in all other segments of society. Sadly, a majority of the major American race riots have begun with police actions, often a quality-of-life offense, a traffic offense, or breaking up a dice game.

If we could dramatically reduce crime, we could also dramatically reduce the number of young Black and brown lives that are being impacted by it. We were looking so closely at the crime numbers that we lost sight of the fact that, as an unintended consequence, many of the young men committing minor offenses were not going to jail or prison for long, but now had arrest records that would prevent them from getting decent jobs and affordable housing and creating a viable economic future.

We did have to fight for a number of years to put on a thousand new cops to give the city the coverage it deserved and needed. As we replenished the ranks of the thousand officers who had left during Parks's tenure, we were able to begin to influence change in the LAPD culture by significantly improving the training they were receiving at the Los Angeles Police Academy, as directed by the consent decree. We also had to fight for additional equipment, but fortunately Mayor Hahn and his successor, Antonio Villaraigosa, were willing benefactors. Some mayors see the police department as a potential liability, a bad headline waiting to happen. Both Hahn and Villaraigosa saw the successful reformation of the LAPD as essential to the success of their mayoralties, and thus supported the reengineering wholeheartedly. They were great collaborators.

Recognizing the need for more diversity among LAPD officers as well as the department's long history of racial controversy, I made a concerted attempt to promote those Black, Latino, and women cops who had been prevented from advancing, and to introduce more women and officers of color to the ranks. A member of my security detail, Officer Andre Clansy, who is Black, asked, "What exactly are your goals for African American officers on the job?" I told him I wanted to put African Americans in places they had never been. Our elite Robbery Homicide Division had never had a Black captain; I brought in Kyle Jackson as its commander. I promoted Earl Paysinger to three-star assistant chief in charge of operations. In both New York and Los Angeles, many minority officers felt their unions were not sufficiently aggressive in representing their particular interests as people of color and had formed fraternal organizations to help deal with their issues. I made it a point to work very actively with these organizations and try to address their concerns.

I didn't expect racial awareness from Daryl Gates, though in fact he did more to integrate the LAPD than he's been given credit for. Since Gates's departure the department had had back-to-back African American chiefs and yet had not been significantly successful in developing and promoting Black officers. When I found there was no feeder pool I strategically placed African Americans in positions for advancement for the chief who followed me, and those in future generations, to cultivate and grow. I spent similar time and attention on the issues of Latino and women officers. In a city that was increasingly Black and Latino, and a department that had been historically dominated by whites and had created tremendous friction with the African American and growing Latino populations, it was important to make significant efforts to increase the recruitment of minority officers and women into the department, and equally important to promote them to command positions. Throughout my time at the LAPD I continued to focus my energies and forcefully address those issues. As another part of that effort, I instituted training to put the first women on our SWAT team.

When talking about the gay community, Bill Parker's successor Chief Ed Davis had said, in essence, "As opposed to having some kind of relationship, they all need to go and see a psychiatrist." Though Chief Davis later had a change of heart, that still seemed to be the department's attitude of the day. I made a point of being open and accommodating to the LGBTQ community. My sister, Pat, is gay and I believed I had more insight into and empathy with that world than previous chiefs. I was very frank and up front, and we enjoyed talking with one another. As good as these relationships were, more important was how they changed LAPD treatment of the LGBTQ community, which paved the path to the department eventually even having a transgender advisor. The LGBTQ community had a lot of influence in Los Angeles, including money and voting power.

Chief Parks had fought with the media every day and given them nothing. That seemed self-defeating. Antagonizing the daily conduit to the people you're trying to influence just seemed like a bad idea. I made a point of developing a good working relationship with the media. To improve the badly damaged press relations with the *Los Angeles Times* and the city's other TV, radio, and print news outlets, including the very active minority media, I made it a point to respond to their invitations to meet with their editorial boards and reporters, and to make myself more available than my predecessors. I instituted a monthly open press briefing at police headquarters, where my command staff and I would respond to any questions the news media might have, and I was able to discuss my goals and contemporary news stories. We were attempting to be as transparent, responsive, and accessible to the press as possible. That kind of relationship made both their lives and mine easier, and we were likely to receive an improved hearing as a result. Relationships with the press improved significantly.

This was before the internet caught fire, but cops read the papers and watch the news, and making our case stood to improve both morale and the actual work. It helps to have the media on your side. I got on well with the publishers; my successor, Charlie Beck, continued that initiative and met with them regularly, to everyone's benefit.

I found there was a sizable portion of the Black community who believed the LAPD had been unleashed by the white power structure to make sure the undesirables of LA, with their violence and deprivation, stay where they are and don't come above Interstate 10 or west of La Cienega Boulevard. That the LAPD's mission was to suppress and contain, not to serve and protect; to keep those folks—and their gangs with them—where they are supposed to be. That this has been the political mission of the LAPD for over fifty years and was the principle reason for the tension between the police and LA's minority communities. As I saw it, having accepted the job, my mission was not only to reduce crime throughout the city but to elim-

My parents, Big Bill and June. I was always Little Billy. About a year after this photo was taken they found me directing traffic in the middle of Massachusetts Avenue.

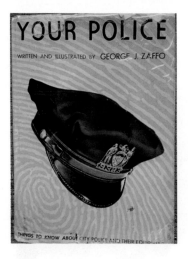

At eleven years old I read this book and fell in love with being a cop. Sometimes I didn't take it out of the library, just went there to visit it.

I was guarding the Long Binh ammunition dump in Vietnam on the first night of the Tet Offensive. I only spent two or three nights under fire, but that was plenty.

Swearing in for the first time, as a Boston Police officer by Commissioner Ed McNamara, 1970. A dream fulfilled.

My Boston Police recruit class of 1970. Very male, very white. Very soon the rules of the game changed dramatically.

Throughout BPD history, you had to wait almost twenty years to become a sergeant. In 1975, Jack Gifford, Al Sweeney, me, and Joe Saia were some of the first beneficiaries of Commissioner Bob di Grazia's progressive new rules.

As superintendent in chief under old-guard Commissioner Joe Jordan. The sign on my bookshelf said YOUTH AND SKILL WILL WIN OUT EVERY TIME OVER AGE AND TREACHERY. Boy was I wrong.

By the late 1980s subway crime and vandalism was out of control. Cars rolled by covered in in what some called urban artwork, but to most was plain and simple graffiti vandalism. After I got there in 1991 we decreased felony crimes by 22 percent and cracked down on Broken Windows quality of life offenses.

As Transit chief I was faced with homeless encampments in the subway system that approached the Hoovervilles of the Great Depression.

First-term NYPD transition brain trust: Bob O'Toole, Bob Johnson, Al Sweeney, Dean Esserman, Bob Wasserman.

What a great time! Times Square, New Year's Eve 1995, with the maestros of CompStat, Jack Maple and Lou Anemone.

JANUARY 15, 1996 $2.95

TIME

INSIDE THE
BUDGET TALKS

FINALLY, WE'RE
WINNING
THE WAR AGAINST
CRIME.
HERE'S WHY.

New York
Commissioner
William Bratton,
a leading
advocate of
community
policing

724404 1   0

No mention of Rudy. This *Time* cover is what destroyed my relationship with the notoriously thin-skinned Mayor Giuliani.

Having a great time knocking down crime. With key members of the NYPD command staff John Miller, John Timoney, and Lou Anemone.

Hollywood 2003 with George Kelling, City Council member Eric Garcetti, and Mayor Jim Hahn. I told Mayor Hahn we would reduce crime by 25 percent or I'd quit. I served two terms.

I promoted three of my contenders for the chief's job—Jim McDonald, Earl Paysinger, and Sharon Papa—to the rank of assistant chief, the second-highest position in the LAPD. How many chiefs would put their competitors into the highest ranks of their department? I wanted people of that caliber.

I was happy to share my LA swearing in with my son David and the love of my life, my wife Rikki Klieman.

Proud moment: My dad pinning on my LAPD shield at my second-term swearing-in ceremony, 2007, with Mayor Antonio Villaraigosa.

In 2009 I was extremely proud to receive the CBE, Commander of the Order of the British Empire—one step below knighthood—from the British ambassador at the embassy in Washington, DC.

Legal activist par excellence Connie Rice said, "Welcome to LA, Chief. Don't take it personally but I will be filing another lawsuit next week." Instead she became a valuable member of my team.

With President Clinton on his book tour. LAPD Lieutenant Fred Booker created a pathway between the department and LA's communities of color.

Lawrence Tolliver's barbershop in South Central LA, "A Watering Hole of Truth and Knowledge. A Pulse of the Community." People are jovial in there, but they aren't fooling around. I am honored to have my photo on his wall.

No white person can know intimately what it's like to be Black in this country. The highest praise I have ever received was from Watts community activist "Sweet Alice" Harris: "You really *see* us." Pictured here with co-author Peter Knobler.

Briefing Mayor Bill de Blasio with my executive staff in my executive conference room.

George Kelling, cocreator of Broken Windows policing. George was my theoretical rock. Activist shorthand for racist police behavior and zero-tolerance policing, Broken Windows is neither.

JT Thomas had been "proned out" as a teenager, a routine humiliation by that era's LAPD. He became my adjutant and retired at the rank of lieutenant after twenty-one years on the job.

The murder of Police Officers Rafael Ramos and Wenjian Liu, killed because they were wearing blue.

If we can learn to *see* each other, to see that our cops are people like Ramos and Liu, and that our communities are filled with people just like them too. If we can learn to *see* each other, then *when* we see each other, we'll heal. As a department. As a city. As a country.

The opening of the Jack Maple CompStat Center at NYPD head-quarters, 2015. Jack was a New York treasure, a connoisseur practitioner of wiseacre banter, and a legitimate policing genius.

With head of my security detail, NYPD Chief Tim Trainor and Deputy Commissioner John Miller. It is my firm belief, borne out by a lifetime of experience, that people's behavior can be changed by good police work.

Finishing up a gang takedown with Chief of Patrol Jimmy O'Neill, who succeeded me as commissioner.

Addressing roll call at Staten Island's 120th Precinct after the death of Eric Garner. The terrible death resulted in much-needed changes in NYPD training, equipment, and policy.

National Night Out promotes police–community partnerships and neighborhood camaraderie. Here with Deputy Commissioner Cathy Perez and a Brooklyn resident.

Ever since my Vietnam tour of duty with the Sentry Dog company I have loved law-enforcement dogs.

At each department I have led I upgraded the transportation. Cops work best when they're respected and well equipped.

The view from the new Freedom Tower. The country's daily safety is in the profession's hands, and although the country is now going through a social and racial upheaval, I am pleased to say I believe we are not far from achieving our goals.

At the NYPD we received
visitors great and small.
Saluting a future recruit.

What a way to go out! Kissing my wife on my last day at the NYPD.

inate the belief that we were there to harm them and replace it with a faith that we were actually present to protect and serve.

To that end, I began to bring community people into CompStat to show them what we were doing and how it would affect them for the better. We went so far as to run a CompStat at a large church hall next to Bishop Charles Blake's Church of God in Christ, with quite some success.

Effective policing depends on our developing relationships with community members in which they become comfortable enough to tell us what's going on. There are crimes we will never know about—and which we will be unable to prevent or solve—unless we are informed. We were reporting on a recent rape in the vicinity, and a woman who ran a local rape victim treatment center approached her friend Gerry Chaleff and said, "I think the same thing is going on in my neighborhood. Should I tell them?" Gerry encouraged her to participate, and using her knowledge—putting together disparate tracks from communities that might not have shared this information—we were able to solve a crime that would otherwise have eluded us. This was the essence of community policing.

So what did we do?

In 2003, as part of the consent decree in LA, we examined how the LAPD handled the emotionally ill. Often two cops would show up and either tase or beanbag or shoot them. The department had not thought beyond those responses. We put together what we called "smart cars": a single police officer alongside a clinically trained specialist professional, usually a registered nurse who dealt in psychological issues and could identify the person's condition—Is he schizophrenic? Is he bipolar? Is he off his meds? The clinical ride-along was not a cop and would be able to gain access to his medical records, which would normally be denied to the police for privacy reasons.

When I arrived at the LAPD and made a deep dive into personnel, as I did with all police organizations I led, Sean Malinowski was brought to my attention. A New Yorker with a degree in public affairs from Boston

University and a work background in advertising, he earned a master's degree in criminal justice and a PhD in public administration from the University of Illinois at Chicago, where his dissertation was on corruption in the Chicago Police Department in the 1990s. Malinowski became executive director of the Chicago Mayor's Commission on Police Integrity, then came on the job at the LAPD, where he was misplaced in internal affairs. He retooled the organizational behavior of my office, and for several years as a sergeant functioned as my aide as I set about changing LAPD culture.

I made a point of visiting the LAPD Command Development School when the up-and-coming lieutenants being trained to be captains were making their semester's-end presentations. Each team of five or six lieutenants was challenged to choose an element in the department and try to improve it. One chose streamlining the booking procedure, another took on recruitment, yet another examined how to introduce business intelligence into policing. That struck a particular chord.

Police have a motive to drive down crime just as business has a motive to drive up sales, yet we lagged behind in business intelligence. In policing there is very little thought of return on investment as regards technology. Using the best business intelligence tools, how could we improve our deployment and outcome? Coming from advertising, Malinowski was familiar with the concept, and in 2008 he and I collaborated on an article for the *Oxford Journal* concerning the idea. The phrase *predictive policing* came into being.

The LA cops were out working all day, every day, and there were always radio calls coming in, but when I arrived the department had no full-time command post overseeing the location and quantity of its resources. The department had a watch commander in each division, so it wasn't exactly asleep at the switch, but there was no vitally needed overwatch. We created the Real-Time Analysis and Critical Response Division (RACRD) as a communications link to the entire command staff. It kept them posted 24/7 and drove a sense of urgency I felt was lacking, and it also provided investigative services in the middle of the night plus previously unavailable data-mining capability.

But RACRD was really just a notification center. I wanted a real-time crime center and I sent Sean on a mission to work with academics and others to develop investigative, analytic technology to assist in determining our stats and how we could better deploy our personnel and resources. He had maintained his academic contacts and spent some of his free time with friends in the UCLA math and anthropology departments talking about their theses, so I sent him out there on city time to listen to professors talk about using mathematics to model natural phenomena, with the goal of testing interventions on the computer. He came back and told me, "You should see what they can do, Chief! They can model the migration of fish from the North Pole! They're trying to preserve the species, and they can model the effect of global warming on fish or of putting a power plant at a specific location. Before they ever do it in the real world, they can model it all on the computer and tell you the likely outcome!"

Sean came in excited about the migration of fish, and I pointed out, "That applies to us. We need to model what could happen with crime and then come up with interventions."

We brought in mathematicians who were in the midst of studying seismic behavior based on the prediction of earthquake aftershocks. Using what they called the self-exciting model, these academics took one event, and using research on human behavior in conjunction with routine activities theory, developed algorithms to predict what would happen next. They came up with a lot of Greek letters. The mathematicians strictly studied the fact patterns and found parallels between what they were seeing in the data and what was happening in crime, particularly when it came to repeat victimization. To translate that information into real-world action, I had Sean bring them together with the department's own subject-matter experts, burglary detectives. That must have been an interesting room.

Sean was neither a detective nor a mathematician, but he knew enough about each subject to function as an interpreter. Just enough to be dangerous.

Both sets of experts intimately knew their subject matter. Detectives could talk intensively about criminal behavior, and when the professors looked confused, think, *Who the hell doesn't know that?* The mathematicians were supremely smart about formulas, but didn't have a lot of social skills. This might have caused a problem, but cops are so used to dealing with a range of people with unusual personalities that it was easier than one would think. The hardest part was getting them to connect on what was needed.

The question was posed: What makes a house vulnerable to burglary? Burglary detectives had an accumulation of anecdotal data derived from talking to people who worked the streets. Researchers also talked to burglary suspects, and both came back with highly provable data that showed a direct correlation between home burglary and repeat victimization: If your house is burglarized, the likelihood that you will be burglarized again during the next two weeks skyrockets and then trails off. Cops will also tell you that the four houses immediately around your home are vulnerable to being burglarized within two weeks as well. The mathematicians said, "We will look for repeat victimization in the data." When they found it, they got very excited.

At the next meeting, the professors came in with theories about causality but wanted to talk to the cops and gather more information. Why did the original house get hit?

"Oh." The answer was obvious to the detectives, but they began to recognize that they had a perspective not held by the academics. Years of experience had taught them that, as a rule, the burglar knows he got in and out without getting caught, so he's confident, and maybe he didn't get everything, maybe there are still belongings inside that he wants. "And by the way, the house is very similar to the neighbor's house, and now that he kind of knows his way around one, it is very easy for him to get in and out of the other."

The results of that theory and practice and data analysis were incorporated into an algorithm that drove the department's ability to predict criminal behavior and then position police resources in a way to disrupt and prevent it from happening. Discussions with detectives from other divisions revealed that the same system of data collection and analysis could be used when pursuing all other major crimes. We called the program Predictive Policing, and it has been extremely successful. Within the first two weeks of the field test of Predictive Policing in the San Fernando Valley in 2011–2012, the LAPD saw a 25 percent decrease in burglary activity. At the end of the six-month trial, under controlled conditions, burglary and car theft combined were reduced by approximately 10 percent. Smart policing and predictive algorithms contributed greatly to crime reduction in Los Angeles between 2011 and 2014; burglaries declined by 2,167, while motor vehicle theft dropped by 500.

The LAPD did double-blind randomized control testing and found the algorithm yielded results consistently twice as accurate as those generated by human analysts, either in Hot Spot policing or intelligence-led policing best practices. When a department can isolate the areas in which crime is likely to occur down to a 500' x 500' box, put ten of those boxes out on the landscape, and police those boxes, communities become safer.

May Day is a big deal in Los Angeles. In Mexico, they celebrate International Labor Day, four days before Cinco de Mayo. In LA, there's a parade and partying and Mexican flags everywhere. It's a loud, vibrant, festive occasion.

MacArthur Park, near the city's downtown district, had fallen into disrepair in the 1990s, but through a police-public-private coalition had been brought back to life. Where not long before it had been trouble—drug dealing, gangs, homeless encampments, muggings—it had been rehabilitated as a Hispanic community resource. Through a collaborative effort involving political, business, and community leaders working to support an LAPD initiative led by Ramparts Division Commanding Officer Charlie Beck, the bandstand had been refurbished and remained unvandalized, a community watching out for itself. A summer concert series attracted a thousand people a night, and the soccer field with new artificial turf was getting enthusiastic use.

Los Angeles has for decades attracted a large influx not only of Mexicans but Central Americans, and in 2007 immigrant rights were high on the list of things to march for. A rally in support of immigrant rights, with permits from the city, was scheduled for May Day. In the late afternoon, about six thousand people arrived from a downtown parade that had attracted hundreds of thousands in a peaceful march. Four platoons from the LAPD's Metropolitan Division had been assigned to the event, but three had been released when it became clear they would not be not needed.

The park was buzzing. Spanish-language television was broadcasting, mariachi dancers were in full swing, families and singles and the full range of celebrants and demonstrators were on hand to revel. Some marchers left the parade line and gathered on Wilshire Boulevard, for which they had no permit. A small group of about twenty agitators started throwing things and yelling at the cops, making trouble. Officers directed them and the rest of the returning crowd off the streets. When efforts to move the large crowd failed, commanders declared the entire gathering an unlawful assembly. As the mass of people headed east into the park, someone in command decided, "Okay, we're clearing the park." By law, a dispersal notice must be given. The order was issued in English from the police helicopters hovering over the event, creating a storm with their rotors. The crowd was quite certainly not in a position to hear or understand the command.

The Metropolitan Division—Metro—is the most vaunted unit in the LAPD, the elite crime unit of which SWAT and the mounted patrol are a part. The Palace Guard. You tell Metro to clear the park, they are going to clear the park.

In riot gear, armed with batons and less-than-lethal weapons—2.5"-wide rubber bullets that pack a wallop—they started at the southeast corner and drove everybody with unrelenting force. They drove across the soccer field; they went right through the Telemundo TV tent, knocking down Pedro Sevcec, the Walter Cronkite of Spanish television, who was broadcasting live. Mothers were out there with their kids; it didn't matter, they were shoved around. Metro officers knocked down and kicked people in their path, including cameramen and reporters, and created a frenzy. Out of control, the Metro officers fired hundreds of rubber bullet rounds directly into the crowd, contrary to LAPD policy. Between getting hit by projectiles, beaten with batons, and trampled by the mass of fleeing people, 246 protesters and journalists as well as 18 officers were injured. Police struck civilians with their batons more than 100 times. At least 250 legal claims were filed against the city.

I was in a car with my detail, on my way to the airport, about to embark on a business trip to El Salvador with Mayor Antonio Villaraigosa, who was already in that country watching the event unfold on live TV, when my radio lit up. I immediately turned around. When I got to MacArthur Park I found the ground littered with rubber rounds. My first impulse is always to understand and defend my cops, but this looked unsupportable.

I called in internal affairs, the inspector general, and the federal monitor to begin an immediate investigation. I notified the mayor that he needed to return to LA at once. I met with the leaders of the event and promised them a full and transparent investigation. I then did the first of what would be many press conferences to calm the public and the Latino media, which felt correctly that they had been the subject of an unprovoked attack.

At an 11:00 meeting that night at Parker Center I convened about twenty commanders and Deputy Chief Lee Carter, who had been in charge. I met with captains, Metro, the media, all LAPD executives and officers, except for the inspector general. I quickly got the details and it became clear that what had happened was not acceptable conduct. I was in the middle of remaking the image of and building trust in the police force, and this outrageous treatment of the public threatened to destroy all the gains we had made. Ironically, my appointment to a second five-year term had been approved only the night before by the Police Commission.

I said to Gerry Chaleff, "Write a report with Hillmann." Chief Mike Hillmann, former head of Metro, had during the previous year conducted several days of intensive crowd and demonstration control training for the entire department. He was incensed at the behavior of his department and its officers.

"Okay," he told me, "but you know what you're going to get."

"That's what I want. I want a complete and transparent report that tells the truth about what happened." I also asked the FBI to investigate for civil rights violations. We would be held accountable.

The next morning I watched the accumulated video footage and was incensed. The policing of a peaceful demonstration had been fundamentally and violently mishandled. This could not stand, particularly from the unit that was supposed to be LAPD's best.

My security detail, all Metro officers led by Sergeant Tim Swift, reviewed the tapes. You can't be on the chief's detail unless you're in Metro, and they were disturbed by what Metro had done. As Officer Bob Donaldson of my detail was fond of saying, "I may not know if it's unlawful, but I certainly know when it's unethical." The city deserved better and would clearly and legitimately be demanding definitive action. I had a lot of fences to mend.

Transparency in these times is vital. I met with the immigrant community, I met with representatives of numerous communities around the city. I met with the news media, including flying to Sacramento to meet with a national organization of Latino media. I met with the police union, the ACLU, the rank and file, and the city's political leadership. There is a long and unfortunate tradition of leaders, chief executives, and people in high places finding finely worded ways of avoiding responsibility for their organization's actions. There are a million ways to place the blame elsewhere—each of them wrong. In times of crisis I find it is best to be completely transparent. You lose your credibility at the first inkling of making excuses. Take it, be prepared to be savaged, and have a plan for moving forward. There was no excuse; it was hard to defend a department that had used such wildly excessive force and arrested nobody.

I apologized to the public and the press. "A lot went wrong," I said. "I'm embarrassed for this department. I feel comfortable apologizing. Things were done that should not have been done. . . . I'm not seeking to excuse it. . . . As one human being to another, there were things that shouldn't have been done." Then I set about fixing the department. It is a great department in so many ways, but this was certainly not the LAPD's finest hour. Yet it had to be mine.

Every crisis is an opportunity. I redefined an ugly encounter as a chance to change the culture of the LAPD. Metro was the last bastion of the old department; under Gates and Parks they could do no wrong. Now I took them on. Less than a week after the May Day debacle I demoted Deputy Chief Carter, who had been in charge that day, to commander and assigned him to home duty. He resigned ten days later. I reassigned his deputy, Louis Gray, to operations and promoted Commander Sergio Diaz to deputy chief to replace Carter. I was not unaware that Chief Diaz was Hispanic.

I stood Metro down for a month and retrained them all. Metro needed to learn how things were done in the LAPD these days. This was unheard of. The rank and file thought, *Boy, if he got rid of the chief, what's he going to do with us?* They had never seen a chief get the ax before; usually it was the person lowest on the totem pole who took the fall. Getting rid of Carter was a bold move that resonated.

When the Chaleff-Hillmann investigation I had promised in the face of great distrust was released that fall, it criticized the department deeply and provided a series of recommendations complete with time limits. It received positive response from our critics and the department alike. I accepted the report as the death knell of the old ways.

And then there was "Sweet Alice" Harris.

Alice Harris was born in Gadsden, Alabama. Her mother had been mentally ill all her life, but Alice just thought she was mean. "Bad and mean," she says. "We didn't like her." Her father made the kids behave. There were eleven children in the house; her father had five when he married Alice's mother, who already had two. His children were being taken care of by his mother, a schoolteacher who lived in a nice neighborhood, but when he married she sent them to live with him in a poorer part of town. Alice's mother came home from work one day and found his five children sitting on her porch. Within two weeks the oldest boy had gotten hold of some matches and set the house on fire. Together they had four more kids, Alice among them.

Her mother told all her daughters that if they got pregnant, they would have to leave. By the time she was eight years old Alice was praying, "Lord, let me come up with a baby so that I can leave here." She was thirteen when she had her first child. A few years later she had her second. By that time her father had died, and her mother put her out of the house. Her father's car sat unattended in the front yard, so she slept there.

They called her "Nothin'." "Here come 'Nothin'," "There go 'Nothin'." At that time if a girl got pregnant and had a baby, she wasn't allowed to play with kids from the school she was attending, so Alice had to stay with the old folk.

A woman named Annabelle lived across the street and worked as a domestic for a wealthy white couple, Marvin and Ann Cohen. Annabelle got sick one night and had to be taken to the hospital. The next day, Mr. Cohen came around and honked his car horn in the street. "My wife is having a bridge party," he said. "Where is Annabelle?"

"She went to the hospital," Alice told him.

"Can you come up here and watch the kids for the day?"

"Yes sir, yes sir!" Alice left her children with her mother and jumped in the car.

She had never seen such a place as the gated community where the Cohens lived. Mr. Cohen told his wife about Annabelle and said, "I brought the girl across the street."

"You didn't bring the bad girl, did you?" So Miss Annabelle had been talking.

"You want me to take her back?"

"You can't take her back. People are coming in."

"Well, have the maid watch her." The Cohens had a maid, a cook, a gardener, a chauffeur. One of them would keep an eye on Alice. She didn't mind; she went and played with the kids. Long story short, the children took to Alice immediately, and she became their nanny.

After Alice had been working six months, Mrs. Cohen said, "My children won't need you all their life, but I want to help you." This was the 1950s; it was most unusual for a white employer in Alabama to think about her domestic's future. Mrs. Cohen knew from conversation that Alice had an interest in cutting hair. "You want to be a beautician?" Mrs. Cohen arranged for a tutor and twice a week had her chauffeur drive Alice to the beauty shop for instruction. In a year, she passed the state exam and got her cosmetology license.

Mr. Cohen was in the army, and when he was shipped out to South Carolina, Alice traveled with the family to help with their relocation. She found the children a nurse and remained until she was satisfied the new employee was satisfactory. When it came time for her to return to Alabama, she asked whether there was anything she could do for the family, whom she felt had been so good to her. Mrs. Cohen said, "I'm glad you asked me, because I was ashamed to ask you. But, yes, there is something that you can do for me."

"Tell me," said Alice. "I'll do it."

"This is what I want you to do," Mrs. Cohen told her. "When you find somebody wearing the same shoes that you were wearing when we met you, do for them what we have done for you."

Alice promised she would.

She arrived in Los Angeles with her children in 1959 at the age of twenty-five. A family friend worked at the Jordan Downs housing project and said she could find Alice an apartment so she wouldn't have to stay with her mother, who had moved there as well. Alice had never seen a housing project before. Once there, where other people saw dangerous conditions, she saw business clientele. Many Black women who needed their hair done. "Me making money."

Her mother told her, "You can't go there, you're going to get killed." So first she moved one bed, then had her brother bring her belongings, and finally her children. Once she was fully moved in, her mother refused to visit.

She began to fix the hair of the women in the project. She learned very quickly that she was tending to the mothers of the gang boys who were running in the streets, and all of them were complaining about their kids—they couldn't keep them out of trouble, they were ditching school. Mothers like any others who worried about their children. Then she started cutting hair for the community—women and girls, men and boys.

Alice began hosting "hot dog parties." She said she was doing it for the mothers, but she found a way to talk to their kids. Mindful of her promise to Mrs. Cohen, and in touch with her own sense of purpose, at these parties or in the barber's chair she would talk to the young men and women when they were calm. She would tell them, "You've got to go to school. You're not going to have nothing if you don't go to school. And if you go to school," she said, "I'm going to get you a pair of pants. And I'm going to get you a shirt." She was making decent money, she could buy them a little something. Alice is tremendously likable, and the young men who were causing so much trouble in the street began, very slowly, to move in the direction she was pointing toward. And somewhere along the line, probably because of her combination of demeanor and outlook and the wonderful way in which she carried herself, she gained the nickname Sweet Alice. Now everybody, even strangers, greets her with that lovely title.

Word started to get out and the police began coming by, wanting to know, "Who is this lady they're listening to while they're not listening to us?"

Sweet Alice started to organize meetings in the community. She tried to help people not to be afraid, not to run away. "You don't have to move," she told them. "You've got to improve!"

The 1965 riots tore Watts apart. They were physically and culturally devastating, a violent release of anger and frustration; another in a long line of explosions brought on by overaggressive policing. Sweet Alice saw an army truck roar down the block with guns protruding from canvas peep-holes like in World War II movies. At first the residents sat on their porches, but soon they ran indoors and stayed away from the windows. That was Saturday night. People were getting shot, and Sunday morning when they walked outside they saw blood in the streets running down the drains like water.

In the aftermath of the riots, real estate prices in Watts fell so low that Sweet Alice was able to buy a house for seven thousand dollars.

California governor Pat Brown created the McCone Commission to investigate the riots' causes and propose solutions. Ken Hahn, James Hahn's father and a another white member of the County Board of Supervisors, whose Watts district was largely Black and Hispanic, called to ask whether Sweet Alice would guide them around the neighborhood and participate in the process of making recommendations. By this time she had become a presence in the community and her reputation preceded her.

Among the highest community priorities were the creation of conveniently located medical facilities. At the time, if a child got sick, her parents had to catch two buses to get to a downtown hospital, and take two more to get home. If the child needed to be seen again the next day, that was another four-bus round trip. Ambulances were consistently late, if they showed up at all. If someone got hit by a car, chances were they would be dead before one got there. This was local knowledge in the Black and Latino communities.

Sweet Alice and others impressed upon Supervisor Hahn that medical facilities were necessary, and several months later he returned with a mandate to create some. "How are you going to do it?" she asked.

"You're going to help me."

Southern LA County is now home to Martin Luther King Jr. Community Hospital, thanks in no small part to Sweet Alice.

When Sweet Alice first moved to Watts, rival Black and Hispanic gangs would fight one another to the death for no good reason. "You couldn't have your children outdoors at two o'clock in the day," she recalls, "because if a Black or brown gang came past each other they were going to fight until you killed them in the street. And we couldn't have that." In an effort to ease the frictions and help change the lives of the community's disadvantaged young people, Sweet Alice and a Hispanic activist formed the Black and Brown Committee. Their credo was "Whatever we do for the Black we will do for the brown, and brown is going to do for the Black." At first they could not even understand each other's language, but they recognized the need to communicate and ultimately found a way.

The Black and Brown Committee evolved into an organization called Parents of Watts. They ran potluck suppers at which people who would not otherwise have anything to do with one another could meet, find common ground, share their different foods, and talk about how to do better for their neighbors. This was the essence of grassroots community organizing. Sweet Alice learned that to get anything done, they had to do it together— and that to understand someone else's needs you had to truly feel them, you had to see them.

Sweet Alice went to City Hall to ask Mayor Tom Bradley for help. If the city could provide jobs for these kids they would be less likely to be out in the street fighting. She was told to go to the third floor, where a uniformed officer stood guard. "Where is the mayor's office?" she asked the person at the desk.

"You're looking at it."

"No, that's the police." Her life had taught her not to be comfortable with the police.

"No, that is the guard. The mayor has a guard but he won't bother you."

She spoke in a pleasant voice to the officer—"How are you doing?"—as she walked passed him toward the office door.

"Come back, where are you going?"

"I'm going to see the mayor."

"You got an appointment? You have to have an appointment."

Sweet Alice had limited experience with government bureaucracy. All her planning and intention was going to go for nothing. She was representing a lot of people; her disappointment was overwhelming. *"Ahhh!"* She slumped to the floor.

Sweet Alice remembers the scene clearly. "A little white lady was passing by and she thought the officer had hit me! Finally I heard a voice say, 'Did you hit the lady?' And I looked up and here was a big old, tall good-looking man. He said, 'What are you doing out here sitting on the floor? Did the officer hit you?'"

"No, sir."

"Did you fall?"

"Yes, sir."

He told the officer, "Get the lady up and bring her into the office."

Sweet Alice announced her intentions. She didn't want to go into just any office. "I want to see the mayor," she told him.

He said, "You're talking to the mayor."

In his office, Mayor Bradley listened as she explained why she had come. She was working as a teacher's aide at a local high school but would have to quit her job in order to stay with and protect her children, who couldn't play outdoors for fear of being shot. She wasn't the only one, she explained. "I just need you to help me to keep the young people from killing and fighting with one another and let our children be able to play in their own yards. They can't do that anymore."

"Tell me just how you see it," said the mayor. And as she presented her ideas, he responded. "I'll tell you what," he said. "You say you work at Jordan High School?"

"Yes, sir. I am a teacher's aide."

He said, "I'm going to let you keep that job and let you work in your community. And I'm going to give you thirty jobs for young people. You know how to place them." It was springtime, but summer was coming and a large number of families would spend all day picking fruit in California's fields, leaving their children with time on their hands and nothing productive to do—a breeding ground for trouble.

The jobs Mayor Bradley offered involved physical labor—cleaning alleys in the neighborhood, which served the dual purpose of providing work and pay to people while at the same time improving the community's environment and quality of life. It was a start.

Sweet Alice turned her house into an office and started training the neighborhood's young people. "We were going to train them how to love each other," she says. "How to get along. They didn't have to be in the alley."

In order to qualify for one of the thirty jobs that Mayor Bradley had provided, kids had to agree to take academic classes in summer school. Her organization, Parents of Watts, brought in the principal of the Maxine Waters Preparatory Skills Center, and math and English teachers from Jordan High School. A high school Spanish teacher taught Black kids how to communicate with their Hispanic counterparts.

They started with tenth graders. Even the seating was inspired. In class, every kid was seated next to someone from the other culture—Black, brown, Black, brown. The Parents of Watts were trying to leave the fear and suspicion outside. They learned about one another. And they were fed lunch.

At the end of the summer, Sweet Alice went back to the mayor. He was ready for her with a new package of jobs, increased from thirty to thirty-five. They expanded to include eleventh graders. After a while these kids started going to college.

By the time I got there, Parents of Watts was a thriving community organization and Sweet Alice was a known presence. Because of her goodness of spirit, her work had become recognized in the media, which opened up fundraising opportunities, which in turn expanded the benefits she could provide. The year I arrived she was giving out forty turkeys to in-need neighborhood families for Thanksgiving and about twenty-five bicycles to kids for Christmas. When I asked to meet important people in the community, Sweet Alice was one of the first people Fred Booker introduced me to. When I rolled up, she gave me a big smile, hugged me, and proclaimed, "God done sent him to me! I asked for him and God sent him!"

I don't know that I was a godsend, but I wanted to know how she came to do such good work. She said, "I was told so often, 'You're going to get killed down there,' and I'm saying to myself, 'You don't know God like I know God.' God put me here. I wore the same shoes these people are wearing and I promised the one that God gave me—who helped me get my license to fix hair—I promised I would do for them what they done for me. And I'm still doing that."

Sweet Alice wanted to talk about how to help the kids stay in school and go to college. How to get them jobs. How to help their parents get out of jail, how to get the kids out of juvenile detention. She said, "We are out here working with the ones who don't have nothing to give us. And we don't have anything to give them. So we have to work on the love. And when we call people and tell them that we need help, the one who gives us that love back is the one who God always blesses us to stay with." I felt an instantaneous connection with this wonderful woman and did everything I could to help her. She might well be the most good-hearted woman I have ever met.

In later years she told me, "I stayed with you because whenever I would ask you for something, or needed to do anything, you had my back. You would believe me when I would tell you what I needed and that I am working for the community." To be believed was very important to Sweet Alice. She had faced a lifetime of distrust and dismissal, and was aware and appreciative when someone treated her with respect. The fact that I was a police chief was even more unusual. "I would tell you how a boy has changed and ask what must I do to get him a job, and you would be there. I could always get what I needed for the community."

My wife, Rikki, and I were both happy to become involved. We would drop in on Sweet Alice occasionally, and every year we participated in the holiday gift giving. Rikki and some of her friends would help Santa Claus distribute toys and clothing. She brought the wife of the British consul general to Watts. She introduced Sweet Alice to a wealthy LA woman who donated dozens of bikes and in turn brought celebrities like Kevin Hart and Ariana Grande, all of whom came down because of Sweet Alice. We made a point of spreading the word.

Rikki and I still remember a very distressed little eight- or nine-year-old girl—you could tell by the holes in her clothing that her circumstances at home were more than challenging—and how Sweet Alice took particular care to outfit that girl nicely with the clothes she was distributing, and made sure she received one of the bicycles. A pink one, I think. With tassels. The look on that girl's face was unforgettable.

Rikki and Sweet Alice developed a friendship that continues to this day, with Rikki telling people about the wonderful lady who was helping so many kids, and how they could become involved as well. The circle expanded. By winter 2019, the Parents of Watts were giving away five hundred turkeys and four hundred bicycles. Sweet Alice's power for good is very strong.

It feels good to be trusted. I was speaking to a community gathering at the 77th Street Division police station and in my remarks said something about "tribes." In the audience, Black Muslim minister Tony Muhammad from the Nation of Islam took offense at my use of that word. He rose to speak and tried to inflame the crowd by portraying me as insulting Black people—tribes, Africa, the bush, all the long-standing racist stereotypes.

But that was not at all what I'd had in mind. I'm Irish, and we Irish often refer to ourselves as coming from different tribes. I suspect Minister

Muhammad didn't know that this was my cultural reference—a commonality, not a denigration. He was trying to pick a fight and make me out to be a bigot.

Bless her, Sweet Alice was having none of it. She pushed back and refused to be intimidated. "Oh no, Chief, you're not doing that," she said to the assembled. "I know what you're talking about. I got your back." That shut the minister down. He and his following packed up their stuff and left.

In 2009, when I decided to retire as chief, I visited Sweet Alice to say goodbye. She hugged me and said in her delightful southern accent, "Chief Bratton, do you know why we like you and Rikki so much?"

I was pleased to hear that our affection was reciprocated. I would miss seeing her.

"Why is that, Sweet Alice?"

"Because you see us," she said. "You really see us."

I wouldn't dream of speaking with any authority about the Black experience in America. No white person can know intimately what it's like to be Black in this country. But what I think she was saying was that Black people feel that the people in charge, the holders of power, look at them without being truly aware of their individuality. That we look right through them and talk beyond them, not directly to them. That in some way we deny the power and legitimacy of their presence, as if their lives don't matter. And so her words have always stayed with me.

In some respects, isn't that the intent and demand of the Black Lives Matter movement: simply to be seen, respected, and responded to, not only by the police but by everyone?

I used the idea and importance of learning to "see each other" in my eulogy for Rafael Ramos. And Sweet Alice's compliment—"You see us"— was the highest praise I have ever received.

CHAPTER 8

NYPD II

For more than a decade, academics had been struggling to attribute America's dramatic crime decline to anything but our policing strategies. They proposed a host of alternate reasons: the economy had improved, so people had jobs and there was less incentive for crime; alcohol use decreased, so fewer crimes were being committed by drunks; mass incarceration had taken more criminals off the streets, leaving fewer to fuel the fire (although the academics held that mass incarceration had become a problem of its own); exposure to lead causes aggressive behavior, and since the Clean Air Act of 1970 had phased out lead from gasoline and paint, peoples' minds were clearer.

We had proved the academics wrong. I had gone to Los Angeles and said, "Okay, tell you what. Let's have a contest. You give me half the population of New York City and only a quarter of the cops. Throw in fifty thousand sworn gang members who want to kill each other every day, and I will show you again how it's done. It's not economics, it's not alcohol, it's not jailing half the population, it's not unleaded gas. It's us." Policing produced an overall 40 percent decline in violent crime, and a 70 percent decline in gang violence, trends that continued after I left, as my successors continued to refine and advance our systems and policies.

I retired from the LAPD in 2009, and Rikki and I returned to New York, where I accepted a position offered to me by Mike Cherkasky at a company called Altegrity. While there, I had the pleasure of working with George Kelling, Bob Wasserman, Pat Harnett, Joan Brody, Bill Andrews, and others, consulting with troubled police departments throughout the country, including Oakland, Baltimore, and Detroit. I was also consulting in Caracas, Venezuela, with George Kelling until President Hugo Chavez declared us counter-revolutionaries. Needless to say, that ended our consultancy. Rikki and I had a nice lifestyle. We were renting a new apartment in Manhattan and had bought a weekend place in the Hamptons. We had good friends, and if work wasn't life altering, it was satisfying. I had a national platform as a commentator on MSNBC and was doing some public speaking, so my expertise was being put to use and I was earning enough in terms of money and attention to please me. There was a brief moment in 2011 when my name was brought up in pundit circles in conjunction with an opportunity to lead London's Metropolitan Police. What an opportunity that would have been! Unfortunately for me, then–Home Secretary Theresa May said the post required a citizen of the United Kingdom. But if I didn't have a command, at least I had a voice, and in 2012 I cowrote a book about management practices, *Collaborate or Perish*, with my former colleague Zachary Tumin.

And then in 2013, New York City mayoral candidates started coming around. Michael Bloomberg was term limited, and after twelve years in office could not run for a fourth term. He had no natural successor. The Republican nominee was Joe Lhota, a former deputy mayor under Giuliani, so clearly he was not going to offer me the job of commissioner. The Democratic field included City Council speaker Christine Quinn, Comptroller John Liu, former congressman Anthony Weiner, former comptroller Bill Thompson, City Council member Scott Stringer, and Public Advocate Bill de Blasio. After several had reached out to me to discuss crime issues, I let it be known that my door was open to any candidate who wanted to discuss policing, and I had several conversations that led me to believe I could get a second bite of the Big Apple. The prospect was exciting. I felt my business at the NYPD had been left unfinished. Moreover, I was confident I could once again do what I had done in New York in the nineties and LA in the aughts: right the ship of a great department, sail it fast into harm's way, and make a city safer in the process.

Christine Quinn was closely aligned with Bloomberg and Ray Kelly, so there was no taste of an opportunity with her. Anthony Weiner, briefly the front-runner, self-destructed with his second sexting scandal. Bill de Blasio I knew only by reputation, and that reputation suggested he was far to my left on all political matters, so I'd be a long shot there. My bookmaking had Bill Thompson, who was well-known, experienced, and Black, as the winner. He was the preferred candidate of the business community and was doing well in the polls, and to my mind the tenor of our conversations suggested I had a good chance to be named his police commissioner.

In the first week of August 2013, however, the race turned. A lot of it had to do with a unique and incredibly effective ad featuring candidate de Blasio's teenage son, Dante. It spoke to people, promising a new start for New York, and hitting on stagnant wages, rising housing costs—and, as it was referred to at the time, stop-and-frisk.

From 2010 to 2013 as public advocate, an elected, citywide office, de Blasio had worked with communities throughout the city on what he thought of as the "stop-and-frisk crisis." He felt his constituency consisted largely of the city's underserved communities of color, and over the past several years he had been hearing from various groups that stop-and-frisk was a growing problem. When a minister from Queens approached him in 2011, de Blasio said, "Explain it to me why you know that."

The minister, an African American man in his fifties, said, "I will give you an example. A member of my church was going to a community meeting about this issue *and got stopped and frisked on the way!*" The more he talked to people, the more upset de Blasio became over Bloomberg's policies.

For most of Mayor Giuliani's two terms, Rudy had been a very divisive leader with aggressively racial overtones. In his response to 9/11, he had redefined himself as "America's Mayor." But the racial wounds persisted. Mike Bloomberg had to heal that. A technocrat faced with regaining economic stability after the worst terror attacks in history, he turned to business methods and data-driven solutions. But in the first years of his mayoralty, he went out of his way to change the atmosphere in New York City and overcome the many challenges around the issue of race created and deepened by his predecessor. He reappointed Ray Kelly, who had served under Mayor David Dinkins, as his police commissioner, and under their leadership crime continued to decline. Nevertheless, there were growing concerns in the minority community around the issue of stop-and-frisk. By 2011, many in the city felt Bloomberg was going in the wrong direction, particularly as regards policing.

Bloomberg allowed Commissioner Kelly a lot of autonomy to make law enforcement decisions. There's good reason for this: operational choices and even strategic plans are better when they're based on objective conditions and free of politics. Furthermore, in many ways, Kelly's twelve years at the head of the NYPD were remarkably successful, and he earned that autonomy: he created a world-class, first-of-its-kind counterterror capacity; he achieved continued if somewhat flattened crime declines; he introduced new technology like the Real Time Crime Center. He also accomplished all this even as he was required to allow his head count to plummet through attrition.

With regard to stops, however, there seemed to me to be an unwillingness to acknowledge that their diminishing returns insofar as crime control were not worth the damage they were doing to community trust. The situation was becoming increasingly dire, as people who had previously hoped they could at last forge a good relationship with the police were feeling that they were being set at odds on a regular basis. As it often is, the issue of trust was paramount. Rather than being recognized, many people felt what was often described as "the boot on the neck." The increase of stop-and-frisk made a bad situation worse.

As I'd grown to understand deeply in Los Angeles, parents and elders in communities of color work hard to bring up their children and teach them the right way to live in a challenging society. In LA, our gang units had used stops with great frequency, but they had focused them on specific actors, and the parents and elders saw that. During my tenure, stops never occasioned the kind of public outcry they did in New York, where too many young men being stopped were uninvolved in gangs and crime; to see their children and grandchildren treated like criminals even when they hadn't done anything wrong roiled the community's parents and elders. "It was endless stories," de Blasio remembers. "The kid going to school, the kid going to work; the kid could be a straight-A student, but it was just endless. Well before the actual fall 2013 mayoral campaign, I felt that something had gone very much awry. The overuse of stop-and-frisk . . . it was going to take a very big turnaround to restore the relationship between police and community. And the more that I understood that, the more that I understood that Ray Kelly had to go." De Blasio had come to understand that the election would largely be determined by that issue.

The conventional wisdom at the time, peddled by the tabloids and held by many in the city—including its mayor and police commissioner—was that in the absence of an aggressive use of stop-and-frisk, crime would inevitably skyrocket and there would be a return to the "bad old days." De Blasio did not believe that. From what he understood of the communities most affected, it just did not stand to reason. He did not find them fundamentally lawless. De Blasio and I did not know each other in any meaningful way, but he decided to consult me to contribute to his thinking. He knew that as the most progressive candidate, he would be cast as the idealistic "squishy liberal" and needed a bulletproof action plan to dispel that notion. He recognized that no one was going to accuse me of being soft on crime, and that my presence could go far in inoculating him against those accusations.

We met at my office on Third Avenue in Manhattan. I was pleased to find that the few preconceived notions de Blasio held about me were flattering ones. He told me he believed no one knew more about policing New York than I did, that I was the number-one reason that the city had become

safer, that I had been done dirty by Giuliani. Having worked on David
Dinkins's two mayoral campaigns, as well as being campaign manager of
Hillary Clinton's 2000 senatorial run against Rudy ("I don't believe he left
for health reasons," he said. "We ran him off."), de Blasio described himself
as "the all-time leader in campaigns against Giuliani. It is a very honorable
title." He had no illusions about why I had lost my job. "I thought it was as
simple as Bill Bratton got on a national magazine cover," he said, "and
Rudy Giuliani and his ego couldn't handle it." In fact, he gave me credit for
being fired. "That is my kind of guy," he said. "I think Rudy is an American tragedy."

He had checked my references in Los Angeles. Plus, because de Blasio
had grown up in Massachusetts, he didn't need a translator; he'd thought
I sounded normal from the first time he heard me.

For my part, I told him I was meeting with several mayoral candidates,
but that his questions had been particularly insightful. He was behind in
the polls at the time and I said, "When you're a candidate, you're looking
for any small glimmer of truth or hope." I thought we had found some
unexpected common ground. I saw a pathway to a safer city that other
people were not acknowledging. He found that compelling. It wasn't as if
we told each other, "Oh my God, my new best buddy," but it was very clear
that we could communicate.

I used a medical analogy to explain what I thought had gone wrong in
New York and how it could be fixed. I told de Blasio, "Police chiefs are like
doctors; you have good ones and you have bad ones. Cities are like patients,
no two are alike. The skill of a successful police leader is the ability to look
at his or her patient and develop the appropriate prescriptions and procedures to make that patient well." The difference between the treatment Kelly
believed was appropriate and the one I would put in place was dramatic.

To extend the analogy, when faced with our patient's symptoms—the
social cancers of crime and disorder—we both understood that radical care
management was sometimes necessary. Crime levels in the 1990s required
dynamic enforcement, equivalent to surgery or chemotherapy. But the city

of 2013 was not the city of 1993, or even 2003. Since returning to New York, I had watched as a private citizen and felt Kelly had been misdiagnosing the five boroughs. The twenty-first-century city was a far healthier patient. It needed less medicine. Instead, Kelly increased the dosage. The NYPD stepped up stop-and-frisk; it stepped up low-level marijuana enforcement; it stepped up other low-level arrests like criminal trespass. It created a plan, Operation Impact, that threw the newest, least-experienced cops at the toughest corners and neighborhoods. As I explained to candidate de Blasio, I think I had a more holistic view of the available remedies and a willingness to listen to the patient, who was clearly saying, "I don't feel so sick anymore, the streets are safer, and maybe there are medicines that keep crime down that don't have all these side effects." By 2013, stop-and-frisk seemed to have a lot of side effects.

What is stop-and-frisk? In fact, it's "stop, *question*, and frisk." I discussed it a bit, in reference to *Floyd v. City of New York*, Judge Scheindlin, and the PBA's anger at Mayor de Blasio. Reasonable-suspicion stops—stop, question, and frisk—are a cornerstone of excellent police work. We call them reasonable-suspicion stops because that's what they're predicated on: reasonable suspicion, a legal standard that falls between a hunch ("I think that guy may be up to something") and probable cause ("you're under arrest"). Reasonable suspicion means a reasonable, articulable, and specific suspicion that the suspect has committed, is committing, or is about to commit a crime. We also call them "Terry Stops," because, as I've explained, in *Terry v. Ohio*, the U.S. Supreme Court case ruled that they are constitutionally permissible and lawful. Stops are an essential part of being able to live up to Robert Peel's assertion that "The basic mission for which the police exist is to prevent crime and disorder." If officers had to wait for probable cause, they'd have to wait for crimes to happen.

The purpose behind reasonable-suspicion stops is to empower cops to deter crime. Police officers are trained to acquire—and ultimately obtain via professional experience—the ability to recognize scenes that look suspicious but have not yet risen to the point of criminality. Professional experience hones this ability. Imagine an officer sees a man on a street where neighbors have complained about automobile break-ins. Maybe it's dark, maybe it's broad daylight, but this person is proceeding down the sidewalk, peering into each car window. The cop is watching from a vantage point from which she can't be seen.

Here are the considerations: Is the officer observing random, innocuous activity? Who knows, maybe the guy is an automobile aficionado who just loves the burled walnut of the Jaguar dashboard or the tidy design of the new Chevrolet. Could be. On the other hand, according to statistics gathered and disseminated by the local precinct, in the past week this block has seen cars of all types broken into at an alarming rate. What do you do?

Our officer has two choices: one, she can wait for the person checking out the driver's-side windows to break in and rob the car. At that point she has a verifiable crime and an observed perpetrator; she can make an arrest. However, now there are shards of glass in the street, and a large amount of damage done to the vehicle, and that's not what the person who owns that car wants to have happen. Choice two: she can approach the person preemptively. The calculations she then has to make are constant and there are delicate rules that guide the appropriate level of interrogation. In addition to *Terry v. Ohio*, cops in New York State are accountable to a state case called *People v. DeBour* (1976), which outlines four levels of approach. It starts with the ability of an officer to approach and ask nonincriminatory questions: "Having a nice day?" It's followed by the "common-law right of inquiry"—i.e., more pointed questions, but not a detention. That happens at the third level, reasonable suspicion, which is required to stop and detain a person for a not-unreasonable length of time in order to ask inculpatory questions and potentially get enough information to move to the fourth level, probable cause, at which point an arrest can be made.

To justify a reasonable-suspicion stop, she'll need those "specific and articulable facts" the Supreme Court mentioned in *Terry v. Ohio*. She can cite the history of neighborhood break-ins. Maybe she can bolster that further by saying she thought the person she stopped fit the description of someone who had committed these crimes previously (if she has that information, that is, though car break-ins generally don't have descriptions because people don't break into cars when others can see them). "Fit the description" has also been overused at times, sometimes as a variation on Casablanca's "round up the usual suspects," and it's been characterized by some as a racial catchall, but in most cases police are guided by details coming from local citizens who call the precinct with eyewitness reports and alert us to characters who are causing trouble. Every valid, truthful, articulable reason for a stop clarifies that the officer acted lawfully.

And then there's the idea of furtive movement. Advocates despise the term, but it covers gestures and ideas that don't otherwise get considered. If the person moving from car to car is looking from side to side as if trying to see if he's being noticed, and that movement can be combined with the act of casing the cars and the history of criminal activity—that's grounds for a stop. In fact, if the cop doesn't make the stop, if she waits for the commission of a crime, on some level she would be remiss. She would have an easier case to make, but somebody will have had their property damaged and will have paid in time, aggravation, and money for the officer to gain that extra layer of certainty.

So the officer makes the stop. "Excuse me, my name's Officer Jones. Let's talk a sec."

She's not arresting him, but if she has articulable reasonable suspicion, he's not free to leave. She'll try to be calm and cool, to make him feel like he's sticking around voluntarily while they chat, but if he asks, "Am I free to go?" she can legally reply, "No." If she has to detain him physically, though, things get riskier for both of them. Since Officer Jones is smart, she keeps it low-key. For the time being, she has no valid reason to initiate a frisk; the person has done nothing to indicate he might be carrying a weapon, and breaking into cars isn't a violent crime.

Contrary to public belief, reasonable-suspicion stops were never about automatically frisking. About half never involved a frisk—a pat-down over the clothes, distinct from a search that goes into pockets. The operative concept, as I've said, was supposed to be stop, *question*, and frisk—and when you have reasonable suspicion but not probable cause, the question part is what's most likely to get you there. Maybe Officer Jones asks the right questions and the suspect ends up implicating himself in those car break-ins. Reasonable suspicion turned into an arrest. Maybe she just talks to him and he realizes he's being watched and leaves. Reasonable suspicion didn't get an arrest, but the cars on the block are safe for the time being. Maybe our suspect really was just a car aficionado. Now what's important is how Officer Jones treated him. If she was accusatory and brusque, he leaves feeling violated. If she was casual and informal, he may not even realize he was, technically, detained. They both smile and wave and the day goes on.

What if, however, Officer Jones notices that the large front pocket on the suspect's cargo pants is bulging? Based on the shape and weight, and the totality of the circumstances she observed, she has a reasonable suspicion that the pocket contains a weapon. She's not permitted to put her hands in the pocket; that degree of physical invasion is not yet warranted. But Officer Jones has a question: "What's that?" And she's within her rights to pat the pocket from the outside.

If the object feels harmless, the cop should not go further. Maybe it feels like a beanbag, the sort people use to keep their fingers strong because they just had hand surgery. The frisk ends. Maybe its size and shape clearly mark it as the one thing that so many in America now keep in their pocket: a cell phone. The frisk ends. But if Officer Jones isn't certain what it is, we get into more complicated territory.

Let's say the man gives an evasive answer. "Oh, it's nothing." And let's say the object feels heavy and hard and from the cop's experience is likely to factor into the suspected crime, and if the officer can articulate that she was fearful that the object might harm her, the cop can take it out. If it turns out to be a screwdriver, a judge might ask whether the man works with his hands and whether this is a tool of his trade. Depending on the judge, the suspect's record, and the cop's professional history, that ruling could go either way. If it's a car safety hammer, the kind that shatters windows, Officer Jones is going to call that a burglar's tool, possession of which is a misdemeanor. Here go the handcuffs, *click-click*, and the guy is under arrest. The man may or may not stay in jail longer than overnight for that possession, but that is one night he is not breaking into cars. Officer Jones did her job.

That's an example of a great use of a reasonable-suspicion stop. By 2011, however, the NYPD was doing nearly seven hundred thousand such stops a year, and the results were nowhere near what Officer Jones saw. Only about 12 percent of those stops resulted in a summons or arrest.

What about frisking for contraband rather than weapons? The law says you can't. When I came to New York as commissioner in 1994, in the midst of the crack epidemic, cops performing a frisk routinely found dealers' pockets full to overflowing with glass vials. (People don't carry crack in vials anymore. Now they sell cocaine in little ziplock baggies and heroin in folded glassine envelopes—a single-dose packet or envelope is a "deck," ten decks are a "bundle," and five bundles are a "brick.") Despite knowing full well that there were significant quantities of illegal narcotics lying beneath the fabric of the man's pants, officers were legally unable to examine the contents. According to the law, they were not supposed to do anything; the man goes on his way with his big baggie of crack vials. Nevertheless, in those days there probably wasn't a cop on the force who wouldn't have taken the drugs out of his pocket and placed him under arrest for possession.

From the perspective of a cop in the nineties, the law didn't know what it wanted in that situation. Should you play dumb—as if you didn't know what it was when you put your hand on it, so you had to go into the pocket on the grounds it might have been something that could hurt you—and take it out? Should you simply lie about how you found it? That's perjury, and the law knows damn well it doesn't want that, and so should you. So should you just let it walk?

Commissioner Kelly, in his efforts to keep crime declining, may have encouraged too many stops that unfortunately may not have been legitimate under certain constitutionally defined circumstances. A police department can't have a policy of demanding stops, because it can't predict where and when those circumstances will arise. It then becomes entirely reliant on the judgment of the officer as to whether reasonable suspicion of a crime has been established. Officers pressured to make stops are more likely to make bad judgments.

Much depends on how the officer has been trained. Old-school Police Academy training would prefer to avoid these kinds of nuances because they are complicated and will bog a class down. Instructors are charged with getting a classroom of thirty recruits through a lesson plan. Recruits will ask, "What if I think he's carrying contraband?" The instructor will say, "Stop it with the hypotheticals. You can't go into the pocket unless you have reason to believe it's an item that can hurt you. That's it."

"But what about . . . ?"

"But you also can't let contraband walk away. All right, next topic . . ."

So the rookie doesn't get it. The officer on the street, if he understands the distinction, would rather not talk about it because there is no right answer. The cop says, "What's that?" The kid says, "Nothing." So maybe the cop convinces himself that it could be a bag of acid, it could hurt me, and takes it out himself. Or maybe he just says, "Okay, take it out"—even though by doing so he proves he didn't think the item was dangerous. Would you have a perp draw and present the 9mm in his waistband? Still, the cop says, "Take it out." The guy obeys, and out comes a bag of marijuana.

If the nuances of stops could be confusing, the law was equally bewildering around marijuana—or "marihuana" as the New York Penal Law inimitably says. Marijuana enforcement was another example of the NYPD overtreating the problem. In 1977, the state decriminalized it, but left a number of caveats around weight and public use (burning in public) or public view. A dime bag in your pocket—if it somehow legally comes to light that you have it in your pocket; for example, if you're searched after you're arrested for some other offense—is a ticket, also called a summons; a dime bag in your hand is a misdemeanor, just like smoking a joint out in public. So a cop who said "Take it out" was essentially inducing a suspect to move from a summonsable offense to an arrestable offense. That tactic got so prevalent that Commissioner Kelly sent out an operations order in 2011 noting that "the public display of marihuana must be an activity undertaken of the subject's own volition." Even so, the NYPD made more than fifty thousand low-level marijuana arrests that year, to go with its nearly seven hundred thousand stops.

(During my years as commissioner, those arrests fell from about twenty-six thousand to about seventeen thousand; and in 2018 the NYPD and the city's prosecutors transitioned to summonses rather than arrests for all minor marijuana offenses. This was the result of better training and a recognition on the NYPD's part that a low-level marijuana arrest wasn't cost effective—an officer making one would be off the streets for hours with paperwork, and a member of the community might get a desk appearance ticket [DAT] or spend the night in Central Booking, and for what? The crime-control return on investment wasn't there, and neither was the public connectivity. But let's be clear that decreasing enforcement was only the objective when it came to minor marijuana offenses. The fact is that marijuana trafficking still has a lot of crime and violence around it, just as there's violence around any unregulated and unlawful but lucrative trade. And marijuana trafficking is a legitimate target for focused crime-and-disorder enforcement.)

Too many reasonable-suspicion stops and low-level marijuana arrests were two examples of overmedication. A third was criminal trespass arrests, particularly in buildings owned by the New York City Housing Authority, or NYCHA—i.e., the projects. These were a frequent outcome of "vertical patrols," officers patrolling privately or publicly owned high-rise buildings.

They were also the source of a lawsuit, similar to the *Floyd v. City of New York* suit around stops, called *Davis v. City of New York*. The *Davis* suit was overseen by the same Judge Shira Scheindlin who would ultimately be removed from *Floyd v. City of New York* for her appearance of partiality in favor of the plaintiffs. Like *Floyd*, *Davis* was looming over the department as Bill de Blasio and I discussed where policing might be going.

For a city that reaches to the sky like New York, a vertical patrol is the equivalent of a beat in a neighborhood. In Los Angeles, a cop in a sector car may be responsible for covering twenty square miles. If you are a New York City housing cop, your beat is defined by flights of stairs; your street runs from the first floor to the top. An entire community is contained in a half dozen eight-, ten-, and sometimes twenty-story buildings.

In a privately owned building, cops can only do verticals with permission. Under the Trespass Affidavit Program, building owners can register their property and basically give the police the run of the place. But in a NYCHA building, cops have not only the lawful powers of police officers, but also those of an agent of the Housing Authority, which are in some ways greater. Back before I took over the Transit Police, they'd been seen as an afterthought to the NYPD. The Housing Police were similarly situated: they too were "Ohhhh" Police. Even after I merged Transit and Housing into the NYPD in April and May 1995, some people still saw them as AAA ball instead of the majors. Not so! Housing, in particular, could be dangerous—the projects were populated by a great number of wonderful people trying to make their way in a tough city, and a small number of very bad actors, ruining it for everyone else.

To start a vertical, you enter the lobby, check for loiterers, and then take the elevator to the highest floor. Go to the stairwell, climb that last flight of stairs, push open the fire door, step out onto the roof, look around. In Housing they call the roof Pebble Beach because it's a flat tar paper surface covered in gravel, with waist-high walls low enough that anyone could get pushed over. It's not safe.

There's not supposed to be anybody out there, period. Presence on a roof is a criminal trespass; if you catch somebody, they are under arrest. Any individual on the roof can be locked up. But like the Drifters sang, when this old world starts getting you down, and people are just too much for you to face, you climb way up to the top of the stairs . . .

People go up on the roof for many reasons. They go up there to make out; they go up there to be away from mom, because mom is bugging them; or away from their spouse, because their spouse is just too much today. They go up there to sunbathe, to see the skyline; the city can be beautiful from a rooftop.

But other, less savory behavior takes place on the roofs as well. People will throw objects onto pedestrians below—Housing cops call it airmail. (Throw a lead pipe off a twenty-story, two-hundred-foot building and it hits the ground at seventy-seven miles per hour, enough force to kill.) People often go on the roof to shoot up or use narcotics. Rapes, shootings, up on the roof. Sometimes people throw people off, too.

One terrible story from the 1980s that has entered New York City law enforcement culture and gets in cops' heads is that of Officer Tony Dwyer, who fell in the very narrow airshaft between two buildings after fighting with a robbery suspect on a roof. Badly injured, he was wedged with his hip activating his radio. His agony was broadcast nonstop across the entire division's communications, and they had to divert everyone to an alternate channel in order to alert emergency response. By the time they got to him, he couldn't be saved. He died on the air. It happens.

These are the elements cops think about every time. They are not in the forefront of one's mind, because cops have tens of thousands of encounters, do thousands of verticals, make hundreds of arrests, and for most officers, none end up in tragedy, thank goodness. But the possibility is there. It's part of the training, part of the received knowledge cops get from other cops.

Let's say an officer and his partner get a foot post in the Castle Hill development in the Soundview section of the Bronx. There are fourteen buildings and they can pick any one. They ride the elevator to the top and exit into the stairwell.

On the landing of the top floor of every Housing fire stairs, there is a white stain on the concrete beneath the highest newel post. Because most heroin is cut with laxatives, when junkies shoot up they are plagued with horrible diarrhea. Where do they go to relieve themselves? To the roof, on the top landing of the stairwell. In their stupor, they wipe themselves on the corner. Cops know this; it is another part of the police life.

The moment when the officers open the door and enter the roof can be dangerous. They don't know what they are going to see; it could be dogs, guys shooting up, people arguing. No one out there is going to be glad to see them.

After surveying the roof, partners start moving down the stairs. Technically they are supposed to do this together, but depending on the layout of the building, there may be two stairwells, in which case they split up and pop their heads out every floor to make sure the other is proceeding safely.

Every now and then, they're not.

Officers don't get a full-body rush at this point, just a heightened state of alertness. They go to their partner's stairwell to investigate. Maybe she has found two guys sitting on the stairs. While not legally rising to the level of reasonable suspicion, such a seemingly innocent scene can raise doubt; every beat cop has had enough experience to know the location can often translate into trouble. So they ask the question, "How's it going?" Two women sitting having a talk, are you going to stop-and-frisk them? No, you're not. Is this evidence of police sexism, giving women the benefit of the doubt? Shouldn't the 51–49 percent female-to-male population divide translate into a parallel crime commission statistic? Police and those who critique the police don't even think about the idea of fairness along gender lines. Advocates want policing to be racially equitable, but they never ask that stops or any other kind of enforcement become gender equitable, because it is utterly intuitive that it is not. There are discrepancies in the rate of commission of crime, and those discrepancies are not concocted by the officers or the reporting system. Not in the real world. A preponderance of crime—street crime, white collar, domestic, armed, unarmed—is committed by men.

So two women sitting on the stairs will probably not be asked anything more probing than "How are you today?" A guy and his girlfriend clearly having an argument or an emotional moment—*I don't want to be with you anymore*—won't be questioned either, though if they are getting heated, an officer might step in and say, "Hey, is everything okay?" But two guys rolling a fatty are going to get stopped and told "Okay, you're getting one. Show me some ID!"

Often, officers react to reaction. If people see them and bolt, or immediately act suspiciously, dropping something with one hand while trying to act cool, or start kicking down the stairs something that had been lying on the step beside them—*Oh no, I'm not doing anything*—that will drive an inquiry. Being found in a Housing Authority stairwell does not meet the legal definition of reasonable suspicion, but experience teaches officers to be reasonably suspicious in all areas where crime is often committed.

So an officer pops his head out on the nineteenth floor and his partner doesn't pop hers out. He walks to her stairwell wondering whether something is up, and finds she's got two guys stopped. She sees him and tugs almost imperceptibly on the collar of her uniform, meaning she's got an arrest, a collar. Okay, one or both of these guys doesn't know it yet, but they're going to be wearing bracelets.

Her partner doesn't want to give away too much; maybe she doesn't want the men to be aware that she saw the knife in the man's pocket and knows, one, that she has a weapons arrest, and two, that one of these guys is carrying a blade that can potentially be used against them. He thinks, *I'm not going to make my partner articulate her reasonable suspicion, I'm not going to make her state her probable cause to me; I'm going to put the man under arrest the second she moves to do so.*

Partners trust and depend heavily on each other. You don't argue in front of the perpetrator or ask to make sure an arrest is legitimate; that's a sergeant's job after the fact, to ascertain and then deal with the outcome. If the sarge says, "Really? You had no right to run this guy in. I'm going to void the arrest, release him right here, and let's hope he doesn't decide to sue you," that's a worst-case scenario for later. In the moment, you have to trust your partner.

Verticals also yield a lot of trespass arrests. The value of them is this: a lot of people who don't live there go in and out of high-crime locations, particularly NYCHA buildings. Do random people wander the hallways, elevators, and stairwells of 820 Fifth Avenue, or the Dakota, or any other tony address in Manhattan? They do not. Are folks in NYCHA entitled to any less, asks the Housing cop? But an officer does not have the lawful right to ask just anyone if they reside in a given location, whether it's a single-family brownstone, stand-alone home, middle-class apartment building, or city housing complex. Cops should really not be asking that question; people in all American communities have the right to peacefully enter and exit their places of residence. However, if there is known criminal activity taking place at the location, the community not only has the right to know about it, they are well within their rights to expect that criminal behavior to be investigated and stopped. This is the police's job. So a cop keeps an eye out for when a person "knowingly enters or remains unlawfully in or upon a premises," as the penal law says.

There could be a perfectly legitimate reason for someone to wait outside the door of a development. He's a young man; there are two keys to the apartment, mom has one and dad's got the other, so Junior has to wait for the door to open because it's municipal housing, the intercom and buzzer never work, and he can't get buzzed in.

But there is a long list of illegitimate reasons as well. The cop knows there have been knifepoint robberies in the stairwells, and there's a drug apartment on the second floor. Narcotics is supposedly trying to build a case, but in the meantime, there's a lot of in-and-out traffic and most of it isn't legit. So when that person who has been waiting for someone else to open the door slides in, the calculus has changed and the cop now has a right to ask, "Excuse me, sir, I see you didn't use a key. Do you live here?"

The guy says, "I'm visiting my friend on five."

"What's your friend's name?"

Sometimes the guy says "I don't know." Because he's not going to five, he's going to the place on two that deals drugs, and he's not going to send the cops there because if he sends the cops to knock on a drug spot's door, he's never getting served there again. But sometimes he has a name ready to go. "Joe."

"Okay. My name's Officer Smith, by the way. What's yours?"

"John."

"All right, John. Five what?"

"Five A."

This goes one of two ways. Either the cop's partner waits downstairs with John while Officer Smith goes to 5A to verify that they're expecting company, or if the cop feels she wants to be fair, she says, "Come up and point it out to me." In that case the three of them, cop, partner, and John, go to the fifth floor. The partner hangs back with John near the stairs or the elevator while Officer Smith knocks on the door.

You never know who's going to open a door. You just don't know. Almost always it's uneventful, but it is within every cop's experience that sometimes it's not. So there is that moment after the knock.

Sometimes it's answered by someone who has no idea why the cops are there, who isn't Joe and who has no idea who John is. Now there's a moment of tension: John knows the gig is up. Is he going to fight? Sometimes it's answered by Joe. And Joe and John both look at the cop with eyes that curdle milk. Why wouldn't they? There have been more instances than not when John had indeed "entered and remained unlawfully." Officer Smith made an honest error, based on professional experience and an abundance of caution. But when everyone in the neighborhood has been or knows someone who has been a victim of that honest error, it will fundamentally alter that community's opinion of cops. *Davis v. City of New York* was the result of that alteration.

Stop, question, and frisk, low-level marijuana arrests, criminal trespass arrests—it was becoming clear to me that they were all driven by a belief that numbers mattered more than what the numbers represented. Comp-Stat used numbers, yes, but they were a means to an end, and the end was reduced crime and disorder. If officers could correct conditions without enforcement, well, Kelling and Wilson had lauded that very idea in *The Atlantic* and so had Jack Maple and Louis Anemone in the early days of CompStat. But officer discretion to make those nonenforcement crime-control decisions seemed to have been foreclosed by bosses who wanted more, more, more. The prime example of that was Operation Impact.

When I introduced Broken Windows policing to the five boroughs in 1994, New York City was still in the midst of a continuing crime crisis. While overall crime had begun to decline slightly, in small numbers, the public was not feeling the change. The patient looked and felt miserable and wanted nothing more than to be made well. Our statistical diagnosis had found what was causing New York's pain, and our strategies prescribed the dosage to bring the city back to health. Using an expansion of man-power that Mayor Dinkins had provided, we applied a heavy dose of police activity. With Broken Windows policing we were able to address quality of life for the first time in twenty-five years, and using CompStat we were effectively addressing the city's most serious crime problems. And we suc-ceeded. The patient, New York City, recovered and thrived.

De Blasio understood the need to focus more precisely on crime, while still keeping a focus on quality-of-life disorder. Other candidates who might have been expected to be forceful on police reform hedged on the issue. De Blasio didn't have a police vote to lose—the law enforcement community demonstrated very little interest in supporting his candidacy—so he felt no compunction about advocating a change in course. He felt it was necessary. I was not certain that he would choose me to do the job, but if he did I was ready.

De Blasio's progressive civic vision centered on New York's social fabric. He had seen the city divided during Mayor Ed Koch's three terms and had been in City Hall for four years as the Dinkins administration found difficulty healing the breach. He felt eight years of Giuliani had exacerbated the fundamental problems in that area and Bloomberg's countenancing the explosion of stop-and-frisk had made it worse, and that if the relationship between police and community was further undermined it would inhibit the path toward greater safety. He was committed to changing the workings of the police department in such a way that crime would not go up. (He was less certain he could make crime go down.) Between what he was hearing from the people he felt were his largest constituency and what he was seeing on the ground, he chose to make those changes the centerpiece of his campaign.

De Blasio understood the importance of combining quality-of-life policing with CompStat's attention to accountability and serious crime. I told him that by controlling behavior we could change behavior, which would in turn reduce enforcement by reducing the necessity for it. The challenge would be to control that behavior in such a way that we would not alienate the city's minority communities, as stop, question, and frisk had. We were going to have to police constitutionally, consistently, and compassionately.

Candidate de Blasio came away from our meeting seeing we had more in common than he might have thought.

He ran on a platform of police reform, and when he got elected he named me commissioner before he came in the door. When I heard the news I called Rikki and said, "We did it!" I was back on top of the world! I was now going to have the opportunity to finish the unfinished business of my first term and make my reform-minded progressive vision of policing a reality.

I n 2014, when I returned, I found a far healthier city than the one I'd left twenty years earlier. Starting in 1994, as a result of my tenure, and CompStat and the use of the policing theories and methods my team and I put in place, crime decline in New York City had accelerated every year for a decade by the time Bloomberg placed Kelly in charge. Having been away from the department for eight years, Kelly reentered in 2002, when the NYPD force was shrinking, while at the same time the pressures on the commissioner to keep the crime rate down, the city safe from terrorism, and the homeless population under control were increasing.

The idea of homelessness bears some discussion. The "homeless population" of New York consists of a number of distinct groups. The largest is homeless families, numbering in the tens of thousands, who through no fault of their own—eviction, lack of affordable housing—are without a roof over their heads. The second group are those suffering from alcoholism, drug addiction, and emotional and psychiatric conditions. The third consists of several thousand men and women who refuse city and private agencies' efforts to provide them shelter and choose to be on the street; they just will not accept services. A fourth group is made up largely of minority men, unemployed, many with prison records.

The problem began in the 1970s with the shuttering of mental institutions, which put thousands of people who needed treatment into the streets, where law enforcement was mandated to handle them. Now when their behavior crossed the line between acceptable and criminal, they were being incarcerated in prisons and jails, because there were no longer mental institutions in which to treat them. At the same time, veterans in large numbers were coming back from the Vietnam War with post-traumatic stress disorders and narcotics problems, and they became part of the homeless street population as well. That population was increasingly emotionally disturbed, and whether the city's social-service shelter system was adequate or lacking, they just wouldn't go in. George Kelling described them as "service resistant."

When I was Transit Police chief in 1990, we had been able to remove the vast majority of homeless and service-resistant people from the subways because I had the legal tools to eject them and a place for them to go. We created the NYPD Homeless Outreach Unit, a fifty-person team of officers specifically trained to deal with the hard-core resistant problem. As a result, the subways were very much safer and less threatening, and the people who had sought refuge there were provided more appropriate alternatives.

Kelly and Bloomberg faced significant challenges. The city was still dealing with the impact of 9/11 and the fiscal crisis of 2008 that decimated the tax base. They had done a phenomenal job of reorganizing the NYPD to deal with the terror threat, but the best-kept secret in New York City was that, in response to the budget crisis, Bloomberg was cutting the size of the police force to levels not seen since the 1990s. In the years after 9/11, the NYPD shrank by seven thousand cops, even as it was being asked to set up a one-of-a-kind, resource-intensive counterterror capacity. Kelly, being a good Marine, did not complain publicly; he tried to find ways to make up for the loss of manpower.

Over time, Kelly lost an average of fifty to seventy-five cops per precinct, and, still under pressure to keep crime going down, looked to solve these problems by using the successful medicine of the nineties, which had resulted in the abating of crime and disorder and the decline in quality-of-life offenses like public urination, graffiti, and prostitution. And what was one of the central elements for dealing with the continuing crime and disorder with fewer resources? Operation Impact.

Twice each year the Police Academy graduated twelve hundred to seventeen hundred cops. Under normal circumstances, these fresh recruits would be assigned to precincts throughout the five boroughs and teamed with experienced officers to continue the process of learning how to be cops. High-quality Academy instruction combined with good personnel already on the job would provide an ever-improving police force. This is how you build a positive and productive police culture.

De Blasio believed that in the world of Ray Kelly nothing could be debated. When he was New York City Public Advocate, de Blasio met with then-Commissioner Kelly to push him on Civilian Complaint Review Board reform. Kelly told de Blasio he understood the need for changes, but that they were highly unlikely because the department was very set in its ways. He said, "You know, Bill, this place is a lot like the Vatican." De Blasio thought, *What does that make you, Ray?*

Operation Impact poured each graduating class of rookie cops straight out of the Academy and into the city's twenty-eight precincts with the highest levels of crime and disorder, effectively flooding the zone, putting his cops on the dots. The idea was that they would focus completely on the needs of the community, which was laudable. Before General Petraeus ever thought of the surge in Iraq, Kelly was creating his own in New York.

Supervision of these recently graduated officers with no street experience, in the city's highest crime precincts, proved to be insufficient. There were too many officers with too few supervisors, who could not adequately oversee their activities. For the precinct commanders' part, while it looked on paper like each precinct was being beefed up, their frustration was the fact that they had no real control over their new officers; headquarters dictated where each Impact cop would be assigned, and they were not generally available for other assignments in the precinct. The idea was that they would be highly visible on an assigned post and not to be used for other purposes and taken away from that assignment. They were effectively in the precinct but not of the precinct. And what did headquarters empower and encourage them to do? Stop, question, and frisk. Compounding this problem, SQF activity was introduced into CompStat to document it. Precinct commanders clearly understood that they would be evaluated on the number of SQFs occurring in their commands, so obviously they encouraged its use. You can expect what you inspect.

But these kids were wet behind the ears and didn't have even a basic hold on how to comport themselves in the street, let alone in these hot zones that presented difficulty for even experienced officers. Left to their own devices, poorly supervised, many thought, *Well, Sarge wants "police presence"—I need something to show that. I can't stack up radio runs. So I need arrests, I need summonses, I need stops.*

Experienced cops, well-selected field training officers, can impart that humanity to rookies. We have cops on this job who are incredibly sophisticated about how to interact with and stop people; they could have been valuable resources to these recruits, but they were not deployed. So the green Impact cops were assigned to patrol tough-crime neighborhoods without meaningful mentoring or assistance. They walked down the street and everybody stared at them, and they were nervous so they walked in pairs, staring straight ahead or talking to each other. As George Kelling described it: "They had no idea what it is to have a felt presence."

One of the great deficiencies in American policing has been our inattention, and indeed inability, to fully train officers how to interact with the public in a positive manner. That training is vital, and it comes through good field training, with carefully selected field training officers and robust evaluation processes. Operation Impact was not a field training program.

When a cop walks down the street, he or she wants to touch everybody they pass. A nod. A smile. A quick, "How are you?" The entire realm of personal interaction that most cops take the job to experience. Impact rookies never learned how to do that. Instead, they locked their focus on suspects. If they saw a kid who might have a bulge in his pocket, they would stop him and be quite authoritarian. Sometimes, if they didn't find anything incriminating on the outside, they might say, "Empty your pockets." The kid would empty his pockets, the marijuana would be in plain view, and they'd arrest him. Combined with the ever-climbing number of stops, stories like that tipped the balance on stop-and-frisk and found the attention of the courts.

Cops often didn't truly understand the psychological impact of the stop, question, and frisk campaign. In some sense they felt, "I'm not really making your life harder; I'm not costing you money, like a summons. I'm not bringing you to jail, like an arrest. It's just a 250." (The UF-250 is the internal form on which officers record each reasonable-suspicion stop.) "I'm making your neighborhood safer." A significant majority of the stops resulted in no frisk at all, and there were times when they more than likely weren't truly stops. It was quantity over quality.

So generally, slowly, that's all those cops learned to do. For the first two years of their policing experience—six months in the Academy followed by eighteen months in Impact—they stopped people in the neighborhood, sometimes questioned, and occasionally frisked them in response to the department's priorities to get guns off the street and reduce crime. Every now and then they got a weapon or some other arrest out of it. But they didn't learn to deal with people as people; they didn't go to difficulty-breathing jobs and see panic in asthma victims' eyes or hold their hand while waiting for an ambulance. They routinely didn't go to a store to take a report about the burglary the shopkeeper had experienced, or the shoplifter who had victimized her. They didn't do domestic incident reports and come face-to-face with the realities of domestic violence. They just walked their beats, waiting for somebody to act like a knucklehead and make a problem of themselves so they could deal with that problem and generate their numbers.

One of the great frustrations throughout my career, with the single exception of my last three years as NYPD commissioner, has been the lack of time and/or money to adequately train our officers on the broad range of responsibilities we expect them to fulfill while keeping them contemporary with the changing needs of their job. One of the ironies of the "Defund the Police" movement is that among the first cuts made will be money for training. This seems entirely and obviously self-defeating. The second will be funding for Police Academy classes, negatively impacting the efforts to increase the number of minority and female officers.

As an example of training inefficiency, take a traffic stop. Until very recently, all over the country cops were taught that the first order of business is to be all business. Walk up to the car, and when the person puts the window down, say, "License and registration, please." Very likely the driver will ask, "Why are you stopping me?" The officer will then say one of two things: "Why do you think I'm stopping you?"—which is offensive—or just repeat, no nonsense, the approach we have seen so often on television and the movies, "License and registration, please."

Why? Because cops have been taught not to say anything until they have the license and registration, in case the driver runs off. They've been taught to take command, rather than to connect. It keeps them safe if, when, bad things go down. Even the way academies train people to stand—the "interview stance," feet shoulder-width apart, hands above waist and ready to move, gun-hip bladed slightly away from the other person to protect the holster—is a safety measure that serves to put physical, psychological, and social distance between the cop and the community member.

A major change in recent years is the prohibition, by most police departments, of officers wearing mirrored sunglasses. The public found looking at themselves when looking a cop in the eye to be particularly offensive. The image, the swagger—it was a brazen way to hide identity and reveal intimidation.

That thinking is fearful and assumes the worst of every encounter with a citizen. In fact, what works far more effectively is for the officer to walk up and say, "Hi, I'm Officer Carlyle. I pulled you over because you went through the red light back there. May I please see your license and registration." The whole dynamic may change. The hostility, both from and to the officer, is lowered. Belligerence and surliness are kept to a minimum and are less likely to lead to verbal or physical confrontation. The interaction becomes human. And very often we don't teach it.

A sizable portion of New York's pundit and business class believed that under de Blasio, crime was going to skyrocket. He was a liberal; he declared that the police department would not contest a consent decree but would accept it and go forward; he believed in affordable housing, he believed in taking care of the homeless, he believed in a range of ideas and policies outside the accepted thinking of the upper class. According to their precepts this was a crime wave in the making. The Upper East Side of Manhattan absolutely hated de Blasio; they saw him as Not Their Kind of Person. But he confused them by hiring me, because I was seen as a cop's cop, sensitive to their issues.

New York City has its own continuum. It goes through good stretches and bad, but it is always at heart a city on the cutting edge. One might expect, my having been away from the NYPD for eighteen years, for it to reveal itself differently than when I left. What had not changed, fortunately, was that the crime rate continued to decline. What had were the issues.

In 1996, the major issues confronting the city and the department had been crime and disorder. When I returned in 2014 the major concerns were terrorism; the threat of ISIS as it replaced Al Qaeda; social media as a phenomenal influence both on recruitment for terrorist organizations and the availability of information and opinion to the general public; and race as an increasingly volatile and dividing factor for New Yorkers, despite the fact that a mayor in an interracial marriage had just been elected. The department had successfully kept crime down over many years, and due in large part to the efforts of Bloomberg and Kelly had kept the city safe from terrorism. But because of its stop, question, and frisk practices and policies, they had alienated all levels of the minority community. De Blasio understood that; Bloomberg and Kelly apparently had not.

In 1994, we had been faced with a crisis of crime: Could the department do anything about crime and disorder? And we delivered for the next twenty-five years. Now we were facing a crisis of trust: Could the city be kept safe from terrorism, and could a community that felt it had been abused by its police force for the past twelve years be brought to believe in the good intentions of the men and women who were protecting them? The results were in no way a given.

As I had done in 1994, I quickly began to reorganize the department. I had a reengineering plan. I had John Linder working with me on a cultural diagnostic. I had Bob Wasserman working on the NYPD's training needs. I found the best and brightest in the department. Among them was Cathy

Perez, who had formerly worked on my staff as a sergeant in 1994. We reconnected in 2013 as I was putting together my transition team, which she headed up. Cathy, who had retired, had kept in close touch with the department and many of its members. She had her finger on the pulse of the organization and proved invaluable to me as I reentered—so much so that I appointed her Deputy Commissioner of Administration. Effectively, she was my morale officer, tending to the needs of the unions, the civilians, and all the department personnel.

We were significantly focused on continuing the crime decline and improvement of quality of life, while at the same time developing initiatives with the minority community. As I've always done, I also focused heavily on department morale, which at this time was very bad.

We set about changing how our officers were being trained. A generation of cops had grown up in a culture of enforcement, not one of relationship building. When I arrived, cops were still graduating from the Academy and going straight into Impact zones. With a new recruiting class about to hit the streets, Wasserman said, "Let's recruit a group of community partners, members of the community in every Impact zone, orient them, and have them introduce the recruits to the neighborhood." Excellent idea. Rather than entering as suspect strangers, the recruits would already know people in the community as they started to do their patrol.

Because of timing—summer was coming and we had to get these cops out there—we weren't immediately able to design a fully functional field training program similar to the one I had had in Los Angeles. Though it was under way, we could not put it in place for the first class, though we did clean out a lot of the old-line officers. To mitigate this in the short term, we ran special courses on how to patrol in these neighborhoods, and gave the recruits partner officers, who were more sophisticated, and community partners, who would walk with them and introduce them to people. By the second class, the field training program was operational. The idea worked so well we now have community partners in all seventy-seven precincts, and all recruits are paired up with field training officers.

When Wasserman introduced this training in Boston years earlier he had found that many recruits were coming on the job with no experience in inner-city neighborhoods and were learning about policing these communities without any real-world exposure to what they were about. We used that information in New York. Formerly, we had run a twenty-six-week training program, but we tweaked it so after the thirteenth week, recruits were sent for three weeks to the commands they would work when they graduated to meet the community partners, learn about the community, take classes, see how the station house ran, ride in the back of a police car, and observe its policing. They rotated through all three tours and saw the precinct from a twenty-four-hour perspective.

Recalling my own experience as a rookie in Boston, I was initially concerned about sending young officers out into the field after only thirteen weeks, but Wasserman persuaded me to give it a try and I was soon convinced by the results. The experience changed their world! They came back asking much better questions in class and saying, "Everything I'm learning, I see how it fits in." The reviews were fantastic both from the precincts, because they loved the new recruits' energy, and from the recruits themselves. The success was so substantial that we began to invite our community partners to attend graduations, and I made a point of acknowledging our community partners in my remarks and our videos.

I believe that as a profession we have never truly learned how to engage with the community in a way that gets them to share responsibility for what we are doing. We are much better at it than we were, but we still have a long way to go. At scheduled community meetings, for example, the commanding officer stands up and says, "Thank you all for coming. Let me go through the crime stats, all of the things that we are doing." We might include presentations by deputy commissioners on a variety of topics, like technology or collaborative policing, specific to the individual neighborhood on technology or collaborative policing. Presentation completed, the CO would then say, "Does anybody have any questions?"

That's not engagement. Engagement—and this is where the new policing model is hopefully going to take hold—involves sitting down with
representatives in the neighborhood and asking, "What are the key issues
that concern you the most? How do we jointly address those issues?" Done
properly, because the community has been involved in deciding what those
priorities are, this approach will start a sharing of responsibility for what we
in the police department are doing. That's a big step. It's the essence of
community policing: partnership, problem solving, prevention. Shared
responsibility.

This does run up against a prevailing police mentality that says, "I want
to take charge and do my job." Police have learned over generations that
you don't back down. Often, because of political invective, they have been
made to feel unwanted, unappreciated, as if they are the oppressor rather
than the guardians they want and feel themselves to be. But when officers
are presented with the opportunity to interact in a healthy manner with a
community with which they have not had a lot of experience, I have found
repeatedly in my fifty years of policing that they respond to it quite well.
They find that, far from wanting no police, the community wants the
safety and security that policing provides—they just want police who
know them and who treat them with respect.

All communities are scared of crime. All want to feel safe. Working-class
communities of color, often plagued by low incomes and high rates of criminal activity being perpetrated against them, as well as many other societal
injustices—bad housing, bad schools, bad health care, high unemployment—
are correct in demanding police who are responsive to their needs, who
treat them in a manner that creates the belief that we are going to do something about the neighborhood problems that really scare them. So much of
the despair in the community is visited upon the cops. The politicians, the
real estate agents, the people who won't hire Blacks, who won't fund the
hospitals—they aren't there in the community day after day, night after
night. We are. Police get the blame—and often the invective—because

we're there. We the police cannot solve many of the problems that plague the minority community, but we need to understand those problems so we can better serve it. We have to see each other.

The cops need to hear this as well. Periodically I would drop by a precinct station house, and when I spoke with the cops about their responsibility for the people they serve, their reaction was usually very positive. They got it.

Another negative result of the Impact program was that while the assignment was intended to last eighteen months, some cops stayed in it for two, three, five years and never had the opportunity to progress into other assignments. Some enjoyed the work, because there were elements that were engaging and interesting—they didn't have to do much paperwork or pursue multiple radio runs that often ended in dead ends; and they believed they were focused on trying to stop the bad guys!

But their understanding of who the bad guys were was tremendously diminished. If a young officer had a good sergeant—or was under the wing of the local crime or conditions teams, which consist generally of older, more elite, more experienced cops—then fine, they learned all aspects of the job. But otherwise they just stood there mistaking the idea that a weed smoker—or even worse, a kid with a dime bag in his pocket—constituted a criminal keeping a neighborhood from being safe and stable.

Kelly's increased emphasis on stop, question, and frisk had been a mistake. It didn't produce results worth the negative impact on the community. Crime kept going down, but he kept increasing the pressure. A doctor starts you off with a fistful of pills, and as they take hold you begin to feel better. But rather than examining the patient, finding him cured, and easing off the medication, Kelly kept increasing the dosage.

"Doctor, I don't think I need more pills."

"Keep taking them."

There's a similarity between the growth of stop, question, and frisk and the development of the opioid crisis. In one, doctors prescribed increasing numbers of painkillers in higher dosages, worsening their patients' conditions. In the other, the NYPD imposed stop, question, and frisk in increasingly higher dosages, worsening the conditions of New York City residents.

Disproportionate medicine brought about disproportionate enforcement. Stop, question, and frisk got way out of proportion to the issue they were trying to address. Kelly and Bloomberg were very slow to recognize its adverse effects. They were stubborn, in some ways almost a precursor to the attitude of President Trump, who never admitted a mistake. And what resulted? Widespread Black anger at the police in a city that throughout its history had already seen extraordinary racial tensions.

It would be naive to think there are no cops who abused their authority, and it was and is the department's job to eliminate those people from the force. But there is a knee-jerk reaction among some dedicated groups that don't believe in the basic goodwill of the NYPD or any other police organization. I've had a newly elected member of the state legislature tell me that the police saw its role in American society as protecting wealth, the working class be damned. I find that uninformed and unfounded and downright wrong.

At the same time, while some of the growing distrust of police was stoked by a sensationalizing media, it was in large part an honest representation of an honest community reaction. Overuse of stop, question, and frisk to satisfy a demand for numbers and the belief that it was truly necessary to decrease gun violence in the Bloomberg administration under Kelly had resulted in our stopping good kids, and the parents were sick of it; cops were stopping good working people, and they were sick of it. It must be said that crime did continue to decline, because the NYPD also spent its time wisely, using reasonable suspicion to stop characters who needed stopping, who people in the neighborhood said, "Yeah, you should stop that guy!" Still, the crime rate did not decrease in anywhere near the proportion that the stops increased.

But let's be clear: Stops were not made for biased racial reasons. That's not what we did and that's not what we do.

Now, it's hard to disprove a negative. Crime and violence continued to decrease throughout the 2000s. Did hot spot policing and Operation Impact have something to do with that? Perhaps. It certainly helped police keep on top of their responsibilities, even as Mayor Bloomberg cut the department head count by seven thousand. Was there a better way to do it? I certainly believe so.

Operation Impact used data analysis—Where was the crime occurring? When was it taking place?—and put cops on the dots. All well and good, but the cops they put on those dots in the twenty-eight toughest precincts had the least experience and were poorly supervised, with one sergeant per roughly a dozen fresh recruits. If these rookies made a mistake during the course of the day, as rookies can be expected to do, often no one was on hand to correct it. The first time they made a stop without reasonable suspicion, nobody corrected them. Seeing this behavior accepted, they did it a second time, and a third, and very soon, for some, stopping a citizen without having reasonable cause became routine practice.

Kelly believed that in order to continue reducing crime, and to bring down gun violence in particular, the NYPD had to keep increasing the number of stops; that if a hundred stops produced ten gun arrests, then a thousand would produce ten times as many. He made the same mistake under Bloomberg that Howard Safir had made under Giuliani when he came in behind me in 1996. Our Street Crime Unit had a hundred cops and was getting tremendous numbers of guns off the street. Safir increased the unit to four hundred cops, the quality of whose training declined, and whose numbers were not commensurate with the results. What happened next was the killing of Amadou Diallo: forty-one shots. Four poorly trained officers assigned to a car that night who had never worked together.

As the 2000s approached 2010, public and media unease about stop, question, and frisk had begun to boil over. In response, the NYPD began to step back from aggressively pushing SQF. By 2013, the numbers had declined from a peak of 694,482 to 194,142. Within the department, Sergeant Jon Murad observed that, as executives and supervisors foresaw the outcome of *Floyd*, they eased their performance pressures and many ceased seeking stops at all. Accordingly, the cops drastically curtailed the practice.

At the same time, Kelly–initiated Operation Crew Cut, a targeted enforcement effort begun in 2012, made significant dents in the violent crews that were disproportionately responsible for shootings and homicides. That effort evolved into an initiative we eventually called Precision Policing, focusing on the few who were committing the majority of violent crimes, rather than the tens of thousands who weren't. Those categories of violent crime fell significantly. The NYPD had found that you could diminish indiscriminate enforcement—a notion that was anathema to the prevailing wisdom and Commissioner Kelly's defense of stop, question, and frisk—and simultaneously, with precision, target impact players and significantly reduce violence. It was an important lesson for anyone who would listen.

For reasons I still do not understand, the department never really acknowledged a conscious effort to reduce the practice of stop, question, and frisk. They might have acknowledged to themselves that it had gone too far, but, as is so often the case, even if you're in a defensive posture for fear of the response of genuinely offensive people who are looking to demonize you whatever you do, if you don't admit mistakes, you ultimately lose the support of the reasonable people whose opinions you should and must take seriously. I have found throughout my career that it's always better to admit your mistake, apologize, correct it, and move on.

I am fervently tough on crime while always focusing on reducing disorder. To be effective in reducing the extraordinarily high rate of crime and disorder in the nineties meant more arrests, more warrant enforcement, and in a city that for twenty-five years had not restrained its population, the shock of being controlled. *You have to pay your fare. You can't urinate in public. You can't be a prostitute on the corner. You can't be a squeegee pest at every entrance to the island of Manhattan.* We were upsetting long-standing societal mores, and it was a shock to the city's system. Our prescription had been extremely effective, and for twenty years, starting in 1994, the city had gone into remission. Unfortunately, many symptoms had returned. That was the city and the NYPD I found when I returned in 2014.

When it comes to the mission of the police, again, I hold with Sir Robert Peel, whose first principle of policing states that "the basic mission for which the police exist is to prevent crime and disorder." For a police leader, there are three components to accomplishing that basic mission: paying deep attention to crime (and, in the modern era, to terrorism), to the community, and to the cops.

In 1994, amid rampant crime and disorder, New York City wrote a new chapter in American policing with the advent of the accountability system CompStat. In 2002, under the broadest federal consent decree to that point, Los Angeles changed its police culture, controlled its crime, and improved the relationships between its minority communities and its police. And now, in 2014, in the wake of the overuse of stop, question, and frisk, we combined the experiences of 1994 and 2002 with lessons from other eras and other departments to create a public-safety strategy designed to propel New York City to new standards of crime control and police legitimacy. We called it Precision Policing.

Precision policing was not a specific system, like CompStat, nor a criminological theory, like Broken Windows. It was neither a technological tool, like predictive policing, nor an operationalized community-policing model, like neighborhood policing. It was a combination of these things and more, in a new context.

Precision policing was an organizing principle for the complexities of structuring, managing, motivating, and leading a modern police agency. It was founded on the recognition that: a) the violent criminals who damage communities are a small percentage of the population; and b) working with the far larger percentage of the population who strengthen communities reinforces the fact that public safety is a shared responsibility. Precision policing depended on active collaboration between police, political leaders, and the public. Because it incorporated best practices from around the country and because it understood that local conditions have local solutions, it could be applied, with appropriate modifications, in any police department. We believed it could improve relations between law enforcement and the population, and make any city, town, or neighborhood a safer, fairer place.

Precision policing had a very large family tree. The term itself was coined by consultant Richard Aborn, head of the Citizens Crime Commission and one of a cadre of criminal justice experts with whom we coordinated, which included police leaders and community members, as well as stakeholders from government, nonprofits, and the private sector. We borrowed from police departments in Los Angeles and Boston, among others. We combined these with community input, political approval, and private-sector assistance. We incorporated lessons learned from three distinct eras in the police profession, stretching back nearly half a century, which we saw as a progression from CompStat's prevention to the LAPD's predictive policing to the NYPD's new emphasis on precision. In addition to the connection to predictive policing, its linkage to policing's history was fundamental to its efficacy. Its connection to New York was self-evident, because the core elements of CompStat and quality-of-life policing reached back to 1994, and even earlier, to my time with Jack Maple at Transit in 1990. The new command staff began quickly realigning the system and the philosophy with their original goals. Precision policing was applicable in any municipality in ways that shaped it to that city's conditions and needs.

Between 2013 and 2018, New York City's major crime—that is, the seven felony categories tracked by the FBI's Unified Crime Reporting— murder, rape, robbery, aggravated assault, burglary, grand larceny, and grand larceny auto—plummeted. This in a period in which America's overall crime decline had flattened. The year 2017 saw modern lows, with totals not seen since the 1950s in some categories. Robberies, shootings, and murders saw particularly steep drops, as did burglary. Comparing the five-year average from 2013 to 2017 to the previous five-year average, from

2008 to 2012, robberies were down 18 percent, shootings were down 29 percent, and murders were down 33 percent. In contrast, if we compare the 2003 to 2007 averages with the averages from 2008 to 2012, we see smaller drops of 16 percent, 4 percent, and 12 percent, respectively. In New York, "American carnage" had become an absurd myth.

At the same time, myriad initiatives unlocked new levels of officer engagement and public trust. Most of these initiatives stemmed from a comprehensive reengineering effort that we conducted at the NYPD in 2014. Reengineering functioned as a CAT scan of the NYPD, assessing what worked and what didn't. It involved a consortium of NYPD civilian employees and sworn officers of all ranks, along with a wealth of experts from around the country. The reengineering initiatives—including new technologies, new training, new recruitment efforts, a renewed emphasis on targeted enforcement, and most important, a new patrol paradigm called neighborhood policing—were components of the precision policing strategy.

One of the things we know about cops is that they don't like to volunteer. We knew we had a successful initiative when we saw the high numbers of senior officers volunteering to be Neighborhood Coordination Officers (NCOs), understanding that the job's responsibilities meant significantly increased levels of accountability to and expectation from the neighborhoods, and that success would depend on their engaging in partnerships with those community members to identify their priorities and problems and their recommendations on how to solve them,

Mayor de Blasio helped significantly by being generous in his funding. We put on the equivalent of 2,100 new cops through 1,300 new hires and 800 civilianizations (the placement of civilians into police positions), as well as receiving budgeting for training and overtime. Precision policing worked because it focused on the details, particularly those at the neighborhood level. The NYPD accomplished this focus through two parallel, overlapping efforts: targeted crime-and-disorder enforcement and neighborhood policing.

Targeted crime-and-disorder enforcement hinged on a revitalized version of CompStat. Twenty years after its initial inception, we brought CompStat back to its roots as a vigorous crime suppression accountability process that applied intensive analysis to individual cases and crime patterns alike, with the overarching goal of preventing violence and disorder. We focused not on the number of interactions with the public, but on the decrease in the amount of crime and disorder and the increase in public safety.

Neighborhood policing was an innovative operationalization of community policing. It borrowed aspects from the 1970s Boston-Fenway neighborhood policing initiative and the Senior Lead Officer program we had used in Los Angeles.

Two main aspects differentiated the NYPD's program from the LAPD's. First was the role of the NCO. Neighborhood policing worked in ways that community policing never did because it did not forget that police exist to prevent crime and disorder. Rather than making community relations the primary goal, it worked to achieve good relations as an outgrowth of making people safe. It sought common ground on local ground, by anchoring the same police officers to the same sectors within precincts, and making officers responsible for those sectors day in, day out, becoming intimately involved with their people, problems, and potential. (This had the ancillary benefit of providing new career paths for officers, ones that came with a host of training and eventual opportunities for promotion.)

Second was the comprehensiveness of the program. It was far more than just a new precinct-based position. Instead, the program restructured its precincts' geographical sectors, their organizational charts, and the very nature of how they worked with the community they served. Together with targeted crime-and-disorder enforcement, neighborhood policing was a way of preventing crime and disorder while also addressing the cops and the community.

For a cop, it's hard to help people when you are charged with responding to an endless barrage of radio calls. You are helping people to a degree—

THE PROFESSION

you are going to see the woman who got beat up and telling her how to get an order of protection; you are going to the person whose car was stolen and telling them how to file the proper paperwork—but there is no sense of completion. In community policing, cops were termed "problem solvers." Neighborhood policing gave cops the opportunity to feel like cops. They weren't going to crack the crime of the century, but they could earn the satisfaction of mounting small-scale investigations where they saw an incident through from beginning to end.

For example: A deli got robbed at gunpoint on two neighborhood policing cops' day off. Of course they knew the deli owner; he was a fixture on their beat, and when they came in the next day they saw that the whole thing was not getting much traction. The sense of urgency about this particular low-visibility robbery was not great; the precinct's detectives didn't have time to pursue the case actively and it just didn't gel. The officers looked again at the video and saw that the man with the gun had a shaved head and a goatee and was wearing red-and-black Air Force One sneakers. They started a systematic search of their area and within a couple of hours found the guy. Still wearing the sneakers.

They got out of their car.

"Can we talk to you?"

The man started to pull a gun out of his waistband, then ran. One of the cops caught up to him, knocked him down, and the pair took him into custody.

This was a simple little thing, yet it was a real investigation in its own way. The uniformed neighborhood policing cops performed a task that detectives, who are busy all day every day, rarely had time to do; they went out and walked the streets looking for a suspect. This is what neighborhood policing affords the community. One of the officers told Deputy Commissioner Bill Andrews, "Time is the greatest opportunity that we have. We know we can do this." It is part of the incentive to be a neighborhood policing officer.

A car-theft case fell low on the detectives' priority sheet so the neighborhood policing officers searched video from local street cameras. When they couldn't find anything, they used license plate readers (scanners placed by the City of New York at various locations around the five boroughs) to trace the car's route. They tracked the vehicle, went looking in pretty much the same area from which it had been taken, and found the guy who stole the car sitting in it. They arrested him and returned the car to its grateful owner.

The scanning system was a bonanza. A terrorist shot up a couple of people in New Jersey and drove into the city over the George Washington Bridge. His license plate had been fed into the scanner system and was in the process of being tracked when two Bronx cops pulled the car over because it seemed hinky. As they were running the plates, the information uploaded and they found they had stopped a terrorist. It had to have been the easiest terror arrest on record.

A woman walking in the street had her cell phone snatched by a man riding past on a bicycle. She called the cops. Prior to the advent of neighborhood policing, the responding officer would have told her, "I'm going to take the report. I'm going to give it to the detectives. But I'm going to be frank with you—we are probably never going to get your phone back." Detectives rarely had time for that low-level sort of assignment. But now— one of the benefits of giving every officer in the NYPD their own personal smartphone—he turned on the Find My Phone app. He and his partner traveled to the next precinct and arrested the bicyclist having breakfast, talking on the victim's cell phone. One of the cops told Andrews, "This was the greatest, man. Thirty minutes later we are back giving the woman her phone, telling her that the guy has been locked up!" Talk about satisfying!

A couple of technologically advanced cops programmed their smartphones to alert them instantly whenever a bank alarm came in. One afternoon, even as the alarm was being routed, before it was dispatched, they knew a robbery was in progress, and before the 911 alarm went out they were at the bank making the arrest.

It's simple: when police officers interact on a daily basis with the people and businesses in a neighborhood, both sides reveal their shared humanity and interest in each other. But cops who came up during Operation Impact were never truly trained to work with the community. I was familiar with that distancing. Some of the rules and regulations found in the Boston Police Department's Blue Book when I was on the beat told me that cops were supposed to be an objective presence in the streets; an officer wasn't supposed to engage unnecessarily with anyone while he was walking his post, I assume because headquarters didn't want their men getting corrupted. We had proven that idea dead wrong, but apparently the lesson needed to be relearned. Under neighborhood policing, we harkened back to the Peelian concept of the Constable on Patrol—the cop—who was a presence in the same neighborhood all the time. Everything old is new again—this was the idea we pioneered in the Boston-Fenway Program in the 1970s. We changed from objective policing to subjective policing.

An independent Harvard Kennedy School assessment, "Policing Los Angeles Under a Consent Decree: The Dynamics of Change at the LAPD," remarked, "Removed from the obligations to respond to routine calls-for-service, these officers become specialists in their neighborhoods, not only attending the usual panoply of community events, but building strategic relationships with community leaders, activists, and respected neighborhood residents." The same applied to our work in New York.

Community policing had been instituted with varying degrees of success around the country. The concept was sound—put cops in direct touch with the people they are serving and give them the opportunity to make a difference—but often a department would wind up with an isolated group of officers taking on all the community responsibilities in a given precinct. This presented two problems. First, there were never enough of them, so the community policing program was actually staffed only eight hours a day instead of twenty-four. Second, they had no effect on the culture of the rest of the police department. Ten people in the precinct were doing community policing work. Great—there were 180 others who weren't, and those officers were still behaving in the same ways they always had, still chasing calls and still feeling isolated, alienated, and to some degree resentful of the community. Community policing was not a philosophy, it was merely a program. Under those circumstances, it was going nowhere.

I had sent Jimmy O'Neill to see how the LAPD functioned. He was so impressed with the Senior Lead Officer program, in which they assigned sector cops to answer the 911 calls—all of them—that when he returned he used it as a template. O'Neill, his Chief of Patrol Terry Monahan, and their talented staff, including Rodney Harrison and Ray Spinella, designed the NYPD version of neighborhood policing. They addressed all these problems head-on. They considered and discussed how to retool in a way that was not simply a community policing program but a thorough, departmentwide solution and philosophy. They created manageable sectors, four or five per precinct, and assigned the same sector cops on the same tour, morning, evening, night. Four other cops, a second team, were delegated to back them up. Now there were two teams in each sector, ten total per precinct. Always on the same ground, always dealing with the same people. And because they were aware of their parallel assignments, the groups worked as a team.

One of the police world's big problems is how it thinks about time. Individually, shift after shift, cops may think, *I am here for eight hours, that is my job. I am here for eight hours, that is my job. I am here for eight hours, that is my job.* The work can be deadening, a steady stream of this little thing and that little thing, racing from call to call—some people are beating each other up and others are drunk and falling down. And every little problem ends the same way: Here's a report and off I go to the next problem. There are no solutions. This scattershot approach breeds a sense of otherness between cops and the community because they rarely see the end of the story. It can be difficult to develop a Big Picture. For almost fifty years, since the advent of 911 in the 1970s we had been doing it that way. It was time for a change.

Under neighborhood policing, connections between officers and shifts became better facilitated. In earlier days, if a cop ran into something in the afternoon and wanted to alert the midnights, she thought, *Who am I calling? Am I calling some sergeant?* Under the new program, she could call a cop who had her exact same job and would thank her for doing so. We also gave them off-radio time in which they could work on problems, get to know people, lay the groundwork for future crime solving.

Overlaid on this new range of sector responsibilities were Neighborhood Coordinator Officers, assigned two to each of these four or five sectors, working hours they set themselves. These were classic community policing officers in many respects, but with a large emphasis on crime fighting. As described by the department itself, the NCOs "serve as liaisons between the police and the community, but also as key crime-fighters and problem-solvers in the sector. They familiarize themselves with residents and their problems by attending community meetings with neighborhood leaders and clergy, visiting schools, following up on previous incidents, and using creative techniques and adaptive skills. NCOs function as adjuncts to the local detective squads, responding swiftly to breaking incidents and developing leads and evidence that might have been missed under the old patrol model. Most importantly, they feel a sense of belonging and responsibility that fosters a willingness to do whatever it takes to keep the neighborhood safe and secure."

The question, is how did we make that happen in the Big Apple? That is the whole trick. Otherwise we are fooling ourselves.

It began with Mayor de Blasio's head count increases, which were absolutely integral. Without an increase in manpower we would not have been mathematically able to put enough cops in the precincts to remove a certain number of NCOs from the radio. Sector officers were also given specific amounts of time away.

The NCO program had two ancillary benefits. First, in the same way that precinct commanders had been able to come together at CompStat and become aware of what was happening in the rest of the city in a way that they had not previously, now all NCOs received unified training and got a centralized awareness of the scope of the department and their shared part in it. One of the bellwethers was their being given the Criminal Investigations Course, one of the NYPD's crown jewels, effectively the department's tutorial on how to investigate crime.

CIC is the basic investigator course given to detectives. Three weeks off the street, they go to the Academy and put in eight-hour days of half-hour or hour-long blocks, with people coming in from other agencies, teaching police work to which they have never been exposed. CIC is the first instruction detectives receive after earning their shield and moving up to a squad. It's a huge deal. Previously, it had been given only to detectives upon promotion, a professional milestone. Giving it to all NCOs was a significant incentive.

Second, the Deputy Commissioner of Strategic Communications Bill Andrews maximized the utilization of social media. Bill's unit took the evolution and revolution of social media into the department, using smartphone capabilities as a conduit to get all types of information out to the cops. All cops now had smartphones and NYPD email addresses, they could communicate with one another via email and FaceTime, and we could reach them instantly with information and initiatives. NCOs became not only conduits for that information, they now had a mechanism to hear stories of what other NCOs were doing so they could remind themselves that *I am not just an arrest machine, and there are stories to be told about cops doing good work.*

None of this is to say there were still not malcontents, cops unhappy about pay or assignments or working conditions or any number of things that are just not right in the police world. No officer has ever sat in an RMP (Radio Motor Patrol, a squad car) and not had an eight-and-a-half-hour tapestry of complaint woven about them by their riding partner. Complaining is second nature to every cop.

Where in the past, community policing officers would concentrate on social and quality-of-life issues, now both sector cops and NCOs were doing preliminary investigations and sometimes solving crimes through to arrests. Rather than hand an investigation off to detectives, they might review video crime footage or check license plate numbers, follow a lead and catch the perpetrator. Previously, this had been rare because of the constant demands of the radio and the continuing need to address calls for service. Now smartphones provided access to unlimited streams of information. O'Neill's plan mitigated the issue of time spent on problem solving with the creation of response cars, precinctwide vehicles that picked up the slack for sector cops who were otherwise engaged.

The traditional means of answering calls would be to pull sector cars from all nearby sectors within the precinct. There would be no effort to maintain sector integrity, and no way to do so, because if there was a high demand there was no one else to send. As a result, before the evening was over, cars would be going all over the precinct. The creation of response cars enabled dispatchers to keep sector cars within their assigned neighborhoods (similar to the London Panda car concept I had brought to the Boston-Fenway Program). The returns from both the community and the cops were very positive; people in the neighborhoods appreciated the continuity and the cops loved the increased autonomy and discretion.

After I retired, precision policing continued to evolve and improve under my successor, Jimmy O'Neill. As a chief participating in the reengineering process, O'Neill was a primary architect of the NYPD neighborhood policing program, and, along with Mayor de Blasio, remained its most effective and passionate advocate. The efforts were also nurtured and enhanced by a core command staff spanning both administrations who shared my vision. This core included, among others, Chief of Detectives Robert Boyce and Chief of Crime Control Strategies Dermot Shea, who were arguably most responsible for the NYPD's targeted crime-and-disorder enforcement, and Chief of Department Terrence Monahan, the NYPD's highest-ranked uniformed officer. It also included First Deputy Commissioner Ben Tucker, the NYPD's second-in-command; Deputy

Commissioner of Administration Cathy Perez; Deputy Commissioner for Intelligence and Counterterrorism John Miller; and Deputy Commissioner for Collaborative Policing Susan Herman; as well as a large executive staff, of which Assistant Commissioner Jon Murad was a member.

When I returned to the NYPD in 2014, I immediately felt an expanding sense in New York's communities of color and across the country that the police were entirely indifferent to Black lives. That Black lives didn't matter to them. We called this the Great Divide. This alienation was reinforced by the way people of color were often treated on the street during routine encounters. In fact, the emotional discontent stemmed as much if not more from what was experienced as routine disrespect as it was from the actual killing of people in police actions. Neighborhood policing became vital to our response; when we initiated a communitywide conversation to discuss the implications of curt and rude and discourteous behavior, which was often believed to be discriminatory, this divide was an issue that had to be addressed.

Police have been called agents of oppression, a characterization with which they take great umbrage. I think the proper characterization of the relationship between the police and the community at the time was alienation. The cops didn't feel connected with the community, and the community didn't feel connected with the cops. Most of the problems grew out of this gulf.

Officer morale was not commensurate with the agency's operational successes: reduced crime, effective antiterrorism measures. Many cops felt unsupported by the brass because of overly punitive discipline, unstinting performance pressures, and the widely disliked Operation Impact. They also felt unsupported by the community and the city's political leadership because of a series of legislative actions and court cases directed at them, most significantly *Floyd v. City of New York*, which held that police stops were in part racially motivated. The fact that the cops felt that these cases impacted the officer on the street rather than the leadership in headquarters further undercut morale.

One of the major ironies in the clash between the rank and file and Mayor de Blasio was that many of the ideas the mayor ended up advocating—including the abating of stop, question, and frisk—were steps the police unions had been demanding of Commissioner Kelly for years. The unions themselves wanted wider latitude when considering whether to issue a summons or make an arrest. They felt they were being driven by numbers, not as a matter of civic necessity, but as a productivity measure. They were being told, "If you have a guy on a stoop drinking a beer and that is summonsable, *I want that summons!*" Why? Because their boss could take it to the captain, and the captain could show it at CompStat.

This was irrefutably true. As I've said, under Kelly, numbers had become too much the driver. Many commanders who ought to have been evaluated based on their efforts, leadership, and management felt they were being judged only on their numbers. Quality was trumped by quantity. They were not asked, "How'd you get there?" They were compelled to answer the question, "What've you got?" The NYPD pushed harder on the CompStat system and essentially pared it down to a single, implicit maxim: "More is better." This meant more of the enforcement inputs that the system measured: more arrests, more summonses, and, unfortunately, more stops. The numbers ceased to be a means to an end and became an end in and of themselves. Arrests and summonses are predicated on probable cause, but stops are predicated on reasonable suspicion. Like probable cause, reasonable suspicion is a constitutional standard but a more subjective one. Overemphasizing reasonable-suspicion stops through CompStat was a significant mistake.

The cop didn't necessarily want to stop members of the community, especially if it was a working guy on his own stoop. A common question among the rank and file was, "Why am I going to do this?" They wanted discretion returned to police officers.

I'm out there doing things. Whether it is the cop telling his sergeant, or the sergeant telling his platoon commander—*My guys are out there doing things*—or the captain telling his chief at the borough level—*We are out there doing things*—or the chief and the captain telling the super chiefs during CompStat at One Police Plaza, this was their credo. *We are out there doing things.* Now, if we did stop everybody, sooner or later every criminal would have been detained and the department would have put a dent in crime. However, we discovered through the experience of hundreds of thousands of stops annually that this exercise was wildly counterproductive, soured the police-community relationship, and ultimately was determined to have not been worth the effort. Facts demonstrated that police get better benefits by being focused and precise than by being indiscriminate.

The pushback from the cops who wanted stop, question, and frisk to be diminished was that this was make-work and they did not need to be compelled to do their job. The cops' issue was discretion. And the lack of it. "I am a grown adult," they figured. "I have an understanding of my own community; I know whether or not this guy deserves to be pulled over. I know the difference between suspicious behavior that needs to be controlled by a summons and behavior that deserves only a warning or admonishment. I know the difference out here on the street, Sarge, *and you don't, and neither does the captain!*"

The command default was, "You are going to issue that summons!" There was no explicit quota, and there was certainly no instance in which they were told, "Give this guy a summons for something he didn't do." But the individual police officer's discretion in choosing the level of enforcement had been severely diminished in the previous administration, and the union hated that; they talked about it all the time.

They had a hard time admitting this, but the unions' objections were not to de Blasio's policies, they were to his tone, to where he was coming from, to his politics. They had felt deeply insulted by the accusations of the mayoral race, in their minds a blanket statement that the reasonable-suspicion stops had not been legitimate in the first place and had been racially biased. With regard to community relations, the 2013 mayoral campaign had come to focus an outsize part of its rhetoric on the NYPD and its activities. Along with the August ruling in *Floyd*, the mayoral campaign drew attention to—and, in the minds of the cops, exacerbated—a drastic erosion of community trust.

When public opinion began to turn against the volume of stops, the NYPD defended their value. The department argued that UF-250s had contributed to important arrests and even helped exonerate suspects—for example, by showing that someone was stopped in the Bronx when he was alleged to have been committing a crime in Brooklyn. The department argued that nearly seven hundred thousand stops did not mean nearly seven hundred thousand people, because many suspicious people—pattern-robbery recidivists stalking victims, petty thieves casing parked cars, drug dealers peddling on the corner—were stopped repeatedly. The department argued that with more than fifteen thousand officers in enforcement positions, nearly seven hundred thousand stops meant fewer than one stop a week per cop—and if a police officer going about his or her regular duties doesn't see a single thing that is reasonably suspicious in the course of five work shifts, he or she might not be doing the job very well.

Moreover, the NYPD argued that nearly seven hundred thousand stops weren't really nearly seven hundred thousand stops—because some cops used UF-250s to document witness interviews, warnings, or even simple interactions such as, "Hi, how are you, can I get your name?" The department argued that only half the stop-and-questions included the more invasive frisk; it argued that the plaintiffs in *Floyd*—with years to find an army of complainants with glaring instances of abused authority or clearly unconstitutional acts—had instead found only a small number of complicated encounters whose subtleties were discernible in a judge's chambers in ways they were not on the street.

None of these arguments was successful. The NYPD's case for its reasonable-suspicion stops failed to win over critics. For neighborhoods that felt encumbered by experiences that didn't happen elsewhere, for individuals who felt humiliated by the stops, and for observers tallying the data, numerical context did not matter. Deep dives into the statistics did not matter. What mattered was that, in the communities that needed the NYPD the most, the fact of nearly seven hundred thousand stops with a 12 percent summons or arrest rate was unacceptable. It mattered, too, that the racial disparities in stop, question, and frisk were stark. The fact that Blacks and Hispanics are the victims as well as the perpetrators of violent crime at rates that far exceed their representation in the city's population—rates even greater than that at which Blacks and Hispanics were stopped—was obscured by the massive tide of stops and a profound sense that they were not applied equally.

By the time unease about stop, question, and frisk came to a head in 2013, with the mayoral election and a ruling against the NYPD in *Floyd*, the department had already begun to address the issue. As executives and supervisors foresaw the outcome of the federal trial, they eased their performance pressures. New review policies held that each UF-250 had to be examined and countersigned by a supervisor. Many supervisors ceased asking their subordinates for reasonable-suspicion stops. When sergeants ask their squads how many radio runs, complaint reports, summonses, and arrests they have for a quarterly evaluation period, but they leave out stops altogether, cops get the message. Accordingly, cops drastically curtailed the practice. From their high of 694,482 in 2011, stops fell to 540,453 in 2012, and to 194,142 by the end of 2013, when Commissioner Kelly's term ended.

In 2014, when I became commissioner for the second time, the NYPD began actively cooperating with the monitor appointed by the federal court to oversee the NYPD's internal policy around reasonable-suspicion stops. That scrutiny, as well as the more elaborate UF-250 that was developed with the plaintiffs, pushed stops lower still, to 22,939 by the end of my first year. By 2017, the NYPD had recorded 12,004 reasonable-suspicion stops, a 98.27 percent drop from 2011. Crime still fell.

From the moment he was elected, Mayor de Blasio was comfortable with the level of access he had to the leadership of the department. He never stuck his finger in the pie about decisions on which I would brief him, for instance regarding crime strategies or personnel. He never balked or sought to influence my authority. After my experience with Giuliani, I found that refreshing. He said he never had a problem with the NYPD. "I never say 'department,'" he told me. "I always say 'union,' because I think there is a difference."

De Blasio had a passion for certain issues and a willingness, not often found in chief executives, to explain his thinking. However, in his first year in office a series of events and decisions alienated the mayor from the rank and file and continues to this day to be the bane of his relationship with the department.

De Blasio's running on a police reform platform and criticizing stop, question, and frisk put the unions on guard right from the get-go. Stop, question, and frisk was viewed by some significant percentage of New Yorkers as racist—and cops therefore as racists—but the men and women walking their beats knew that, left to their own devices, they would not have been as aggressive as they had become, that it was Kelly's policies that had pushed them there, and they didn't appreciate being made the fall guys.

But, as I've mentioned, it was a decision early in his mayoralty that truly poisoned the well. In her *Floyd* ruling, Judge Shira Scheindlin found the NYPD's stop, question, and frisk practices violated New Yorkers' Fourth Amendment rights to be free from unreasonable searches and seizures and were racially discriminatory in violation of the Equal Protection Clause of the Fourteenth Amendment. I had much less problem with the first part of her ruling than with the second; the policy may have been ill managed but it was not founded on racism. This isn't to say that if a practice has a disproportionate impact on one community, especially a historically disenfranchised and brutalized one like the Black community, that impact shouldn't be taken into consideration. Of course it should. I was vocal about the fact that the policy had gotten way out of hand. But for a mayor himself to suggest that he thinks his police force is consciously racist—well, it's hard to come back from that. As I've noted, when de Blasio decided to drop Bloomberg's appeal and settle, as far as the unions were concerned, he was agreeing with the judge's assertion that NYPD cops were bigots. That tore it.

Community members, particularly in high-crime, low-income, majority-minority neighborhoods, felt simultaneously overpoliced and underprotected. That is a terrible place to be. It was also a paradox, in that every objective measure showed that even the city's toughest neighborhoods were safer than they had ever been, but it was a fact on the ground.

CompStat's crime-prevention outcome—its ends—was being confused with the enforcement inputs—its means. As designed, those inputs had been arrests and summonses, both predicated on probable cause. But they came to include stops as well, which are predicated on the lower, more subjective standard of reasonable suspicion. Used properly, reasonable-suspicion stops are integral to lawful, effective policing. Police need and must have the ability to "check out" people whose objective behaviors leads the officer to reasonably suspect they have committed or are about to commit penal law misdemeanors or felonies. Including them in CompStat, however, and the eventual overemphasis on them that led to nearly seven hundred thousand, was a significant mistake.

As I have explained, there was a significant overuse of the practice which tore at and humiliated majority-of-color neighborhoods, but it is naive to think everyone who was stopped was an innocent. Jon Murad was a precinct sergeant at the time and recalls, "There were guys I would do a 250 on almost every time I saw them, because they were dealers who hung out on the corner and I had a reasonable suspicion that they were committing a penal-law misdemeanor of loitering for the purposes of using or selling narcotics. No frisk, I wouldn't even touch them. I would just take out the form, 'What's your name again?' It was deterrence, prevention. Anything to make them close shop for the day, because any neighborhood resident watching from a window as a cop walks by a drug spot, who sees that cop not doing anything, will say, 'Why is that cop not doing anything?' They know who the dealers are. The neighborhood was watching us."

"And it wasn't innocent kids. This was a drug crew. We ended up taking them down in a multiyear wiretapping investigation that ended with an indictment of one hundred and ten counts and twenty-three arrests. The 250s helped document who was who on the corner. I had no doubt in my mind that these gentlemen were doing what they were doing; neither did the neighborhood. But again, these arguments are irrelevant, because citywide, the number of stops—and the racial disparity—was untenable."

When I returned as commissioner, the NYPD was a contradiction: a successful but rigid agency with well-deserved pride but low morale. As I have noted, cops were plagued by a sense that their efforts were unappreciated and even actively rejected. Tackling organizational dysfunction and compromised morale would require silo-busting, information sharing, and collaboration. It would require finding, recognizing, and empowering talent. And it would require deploying technological accelerators, accentuating training, and procuring new equipment.

Outside the department, contradiction reigned as well. Many in the city feared that crime control would falter if the NYPD eased off the enforcement throttle. Conversely, some observers were explicitly willing (for others) to suffer crime increases in the name of eased enforcement. "Let me put that more bluntly," wrote *Daily News* opinion writer Harry Siegel. "We should have a bit less policing, and a fair standard citywide for what's a crime—even if that means the numbers tick up." I never believed that was acceptable—nor did I accept the proposition. For me, safe and fair were compatible and had to be achieved in tandem. Safe and fair everywhere for everyone. But we knew there was a pronounced community dissatisfaction. Tackling police-community relations would require collaboration. It would require a renewed emphasis on seeing, listening to, and working with the neighborhoods where police were most necessary and where their presence was most fraught. And it would require projecting a strong optimism for what everyone could accomplish together.

I leveraged contacts within the NYPD and in New York's criminal justice spheres to solidify my understanding of the police department's status quo. I was aided significantly by a white paper entitled "The State of the NYPD and Proposals for Change," by Kevin Ward, then the chief in command of Patrol Borough Queens South, and Lieutenant Ronald Wilhelmy. (Ward became my chief of staff, while Wilhelmy was promoted to assistant commissioner.) As a sergeant, Jon Murad contributed to the white paper as well.

The white paper offered five prescriptions "to reinvent the department and possibly change policing across the country":

First, the department had to abandon the "zero-tolerance" misinterpretation of the Broken Windows philosophy that had taken root in the past decade. It had to also reject the belief that, with regard to enforcement activity, "more is better." New metrics facilitated this objective. While Jack Maple had said that "what gets measured gets done," the question of how we measure was just as important. When we measured only numbers, we got only numbers. We knew we had to move away from quantity and orient ourselves again on quality.

Simultaneously, I recommended an emphasis on offender-focused enforcement that hinged on deep data mining and efficient resource deployments. Unlike stop, question, and frisk, enforcement would focus on known offenders—who they were, what they were wanted for, and where they were located. This was the beginning of precision policing, the increased focus of attention on those who are committing the crime. Rather than stopping a hundred innocent Black men, we would focus on one guilty one.

Second, I proposed creating a decentralized management structure that truly permitted collaborative operations and investigations within the NYPD's complex bureaucracy.

Third, CompStat had to be reengaged using new metrics of accountability—quality of arrests, summonses, and investigations; citizen satisfaction; community stability; and the overall impact of crime. These new metrics would improve public safety in New York City, and ultimately served as a model for police organizations throughout the country.

I believed that new metrics would also help address officer morale, the fourth challenge facing the department. Officers wanted to make the neighborhoods in which they worked safer, improve community relations and residents' quality of life, effect meaningful arrests, and be evaluated on the quality of their work rather than the quantity. Morale would be further improved by creating a clear, unambiguous, and fair career path. Well-defined career paths would help to engender a culture of continuous improvement and innovation within the department in these four areas. If we succeeded, the fifth issue, the crisis of police legitimacy, would largely take care of itself.

Ward and Wilhelmy spelled out the challenge and the opportunity that lay before the NYPD. There was a chance to create cultural change, and to prove that doing right by the cops and doing right by the community could be the same thing.

Among my earliest decisions was to eliminate Operation Impact. We would give rookies the proper training to make them functional parts of a precinct through true neighborhood policing. We focused on trying to eliminate indiscriminate enforcement, in which cops made stops as if every citizen was a problem and every infraction deserved a single draconian response. Instead, through observation, intelligence, and casework, we would pick and choose and identify the bad guys, and focus on those people for hard-core enforcement. In handling less urgent disorder, we knew that trained cops have the ability to make proper enforcement decisions, and encouraged them to use their training and do their jobs.

The reality is that there is a great divide between the police and some people in communities that need us most. It was vital for the department to bridge that divide and advance the concept that the people and the police can be partners. To that end, we went about creating the Office of Collaborative Policing, which would work closely with the Office of Crime Control Strategies.

Dermot Shea grew up in Queens and took the subway every day to Xavier High School on Sixteenth Street in Manhattan. It was the 1980s—he developed street smarts and knew the city for what it was—pretty raw. He graduated from SUNY Oneonta with a business degree, and two days later was working a 32BJ Service Employees International Union job. He had no family policing background, but he didn't see himself sitting behind a desk for twenty or thirty years, and in his mind policing was a perfect fit. Shea took the New York State Police and NYPD exams and joined the department in 1991. As chance would have it, he and his brother came on the job at the same time.

Shea started out at the 46th Precinct in the Bronx, an area dotted with burned-out buildings. That was the New York he knew in those days. He was never much of a student, but he studied a lot harder for the NYPD promotion tests than he ever did in school. It was easy to get motivated when there was a pay raise attached. It took him only three years to be promoted to sergeant.

Shea rose through the ranks, earning several commands in the Bronx. As a lieutenant he served in the 24th Precinct, as well as the Manhattan South and Bronx Narcotics Divisions. Promoted to captain, he served in Patrol Borough Bronx and the Bronx and Queens Narcotics Divisions. He served as executive officer of the 47th Precinct, and then was designated as commanding officer of the 50th Precinct in Riverdale, a beautiful neighborhood, and the 44th in the Bronx, the Yankee Stadium precinct, one of the two or three busiest in the city. He was on the street for twenty years.

In the precinct, command is concerned with managing resources to handle the crisis of the day. "I was on the hamster wheel of arrest, arrest, arrest," he says. "Making many, many arrests and seeing everything that was wrong with the criminal justice system."

Promoted to inspector, he landed in police headquarters at One Police Plaza as commanding officer of Crime Control Strategies. The general mindset of police who are not in 1PP is to put out fires; it is the rare person who has a larger overview. Shea made the best of his opportunity. He felt he had developed a good base of information at the NYPD, but he made an effort to step back from the daily fight in order to see the bigger picture of the city and the department.

Much as Jack Maple's had before him, Shea's name came up during our search for quality personnel in the department. By chance I stuck my head in the door of a room in which he was being interviewed and he said, "I know you. You promoted me to sergeant about twenty years ago!" He was subsequently promoted to Deputy Commissioner for Crime Control Strategies, Jack Maple's last position.

Susan Herman graduated with a degree in political science from Bryn Mawr College and got her law degree from Antioch. She came on the job in the mideighties, and from 1985 to 1990 served as first assistant and then special counsel to three consecutive police commissioners: Ben Ward, Richard Condon, and Lee Brown. She loved her time in the department and probably left sooner than she was ready. She became an associate professor in the Department of Criminal Justice at Pace University and also served as the executive director of the National Center for Victims of Crime, Director of Community Services at the Enterprise Foundation, director of the Domestic Violence Division at Victim Services (now Safe Horizon), Director of Mediation Services at the Institute for Mediation and Conflict Resolution, and instructor at NYU School of Law and NYU's Wagner School of Public Service. She was a recipient of the United States Attorney General's National Crime Victims' Service Award. She had a great lefty résumé. Her husband, Jeremy, had been my deputy commissioner for legal matters during my first tenure as commissioner.

As a national spokesperson and advocate on behalf of, first, rape victims, and then domestic violence, child abuse, and homicide victims, Herman began thinking about what all victims had in common. She began to consider a global question: What do all crime victims need?

While at NYU, Herman returned her attention to the NYPD. When it appeared I might return as commissioner, she and I talked about what she might do in the department. She sent me a copy of a book she had written about victims, and I responded to her strongly held belief that part of justice is not only holding criminals accountable but also helping victims rebuild their lives. She believes this is an integral part of justice that we should all be providing to victims, and wanted to dig deep into how we could enhance the department's response to victims of crime. We needed critical crisis-intervention training.

This is not normally under police purview, but it made a lot of sense. Police had increasingly been seen as not only not on the community's side, but opposed to it. That had to change.

In the years since I had left, I felt the department had become disturbingly closed and insular. What had distinguished the NYPD was its can-do attitude that we could tackle any problem. But in the time I was gone the department had begun to exhibit the flip side of that confidence, the belief that we didn't need anyone's help and couldn't learn from anyone else's experience. This was not the department I wanted to run. I told her, "I want to air this place out, open the windows and doors, bring other perspectives into the NYPD, and put our agenda onto other people's radar." I wanted to strike a balance between empathy and enforcement. The question was, Where was that balance?

Herman had a background in mediation and conflict resolution. With

Zachary Tumin I had written a book called *Collaborate or Perish*, which taught how to reach across boundaries to share information and get results. (I appointed Tumin Deputy Commissioner of Strategic Initiatives.) Susan and I started talking about a concept we came to call collaborative policing. Her role would be to look at any problem or issue within the department and ask, "Would this problem benefit from the perspective of an outsider? Another city, state, or federal agency? A nonprofit? An academic institution? Community activists? Would our solution be better if we talked to other people?" I appointed her to the newly created position of Deputy Commissioner, Collaborative Policing.

As the concept developed between us and we discussed which outside voices she might bring in, she told me, "I have three buckets: contacting government agencies, speaking with nonprofits, and enhancing our response to victims of crime."

"Susan," I said, "you have four buckets. Your fourth bucket is enhancing collaboration within the department."

"I'm never talking about that," she said. "That's my stealth bucket."

Shea and Herman would seem to be oil and water, old-school police work and New Age idea gathering. A law enforcement Odd Couple. Susan's concentration was on dealing with the larger population in a better way; Dermot's focus was dealing with the worst part of that population in a better way. Yet when I put them together they formed the tip of the spear in puncturing organizational solitude and fostering an era in which the NYPD welcomed ideas from a broader circle. They tried to change the department's culture and mindset to nurture and grow the concept that nothing is simply what's in front of us; everyone in the organization has to look further down the road and think on a wider scale than their individual precinct. Everything is related. When Shea took over control of Comp-Stat he furthered that effort.

Most police departments employ at most a couple of domestic violence victim advocates. We contracted with the organization Safe Horizon to place two victim advocates—one for domestic violence and another for every other kind of crime—in every precinct and Housing police service area in the city. Where other administrations might have attempted to create this system from the ground up, our thinking was, *They know how to do this better than we do, let them do it.* Their numbers and wide range of expertise made our program even more powerful. The NYPD now presides over the second-largest victim service agency in the country.

And why is that important? Because our advocates not only help develop safety plans, mitigate trauma, and keep people informed, on a basic level they build trust in the NYPD as a whole. People being served, respected, and treated well by the police are so much more likely to work with us in other times of crisis. Beyond just being told, "Give us the information and we will see if we can solve the crime," they're hearing, "What do you need? Let us help you fill out that form for compensation. Let us help you get a ride to court. Let us help you retrieve some of your lost wages because you had medical expenses."

Programs to benefit victims, we found, were actually programs to help the public at large. We also needed to present ourselves as a caring organization—which, considering public sentiment, would take some doing.

We developed nonenforcement options for police officers, giving them more tools in their toolbox, and joined that with the precision policing movement to think about more creative uses of enforcement. While they agreed on goals, Herman and Shea often disagreed on the best way to handle criminal suspects—jail or some other remedy? As Shea jokingly put it, "I want to keep them in, she wants to keep them out." I thought that was a healthy tension.

We went about maximizing department resources. Much of Herman's time was devoted to getting other agencies to take on work that had fallen almost by default to the police. She negotiated with the Sheriff's Office to serve the thousands upon thousands of Family Court orders of protection we were handling annually. You don't need a cop to do that, and the sheriff saw it as squarely in his mission. Ironically, this was an early version of what some advocates for the Defund the Police movement are looking for. The buzzword of 2020, reimagining the police, is what we were doing in 2015. The responsibility for service of these orders had been dumped on the police years ago and could be handled by another agency that was better able and actually wanted to do it. We were happy to see it go.

Herman and Shea worked together on a project to have inmates' outstanding warrants checked at Rikers Island jail before they were to be released. It seemed simple, but this had never been done. When prisoners made bail at any time, day or night, it was common practice simply to release them out the door and onto the streets. Often they were suspects in other crimes and the courts had issued warrants on them, necessitating our searching for a person who moments earlier had been in custody. They didn't need a head start. Instead of hearing of their release after the fact, we created a checklist protocol for people at the Department of Corrections. *Call us before they step out so we don't have to go to the time and expense of chasing them around New York City.* The program protected the community from having a parade of criminal suspects in its midst, and it saved the city from looking incompetent at preserving safety and order.

Between them, Shea and Herman helped the department build stronger cases. Groping and sexual assault in the subways, for example, were a continuing problem; but because the victims were often tourists or people who for a variety of reasons chose not to press charges, arrests were not always made. But we were interested in pursuing them—these are exactly the crimes that unnerve and disturb a community and often go unreported. With the growing societal sensitivity and awareness about the prevalence of sexual misconduct and how few instances of sexual violence are reported, it became increasingly clear to the department that we needed to be more assertive and creative in our policing. In conjunction with the district attorney's office, Shea and Herman developed a victim impact statement to streamline the process of complaint. We would receive a statement right there in the subway, which often converted an assault into a criminal case rather than just a statistic. We requisitioned computer tablets to increase our capabilities.

Language access was made a priority. We created a Language Line, staffed it with officers whom we trained and certified, and stressed that the cops call it when encountering people whose fluency was not in English. To that end we brought Berlitz language trainers to the Police Academy for the first time—and out into the boroughs, rather than having officers travel to them—and added the incentive of career points for those who passed certification. In the past few years, we have doubled the number of officers certified as proficient in other languages. Because New Yorkers now know they have able translation officers, the program is good for police-community relations. Even more importantly, it helps build cases, making officers' testimony stronger when they are on the stand. Officers in recent years have also been assisted by smartphones with built-in language capabilities.

How do you reach people who are deaf or hard of hearing? We added sign language training, and we paid the license fees for certified ASL Language Line translators to be available on officers' tablets in their cars. The program started in the three precincts with the largest populations of deaf and hard of hearing people. It eventually expanded citywide. This is not only good public relations, this is crime fighting.

We developed a new relationship with Access-A-Ride, a service that transports people with disabilities. When Herman arrived, the general complaint was that Access-A-Ride was useless—individuals had to be preregistered to be on their list, the service took twenty-four to forty-eight hours before it would pick people up, and it required their being called in advance. When we wanted someone to come down to identify a suspect in a lineup, or if we needed to get someone to court, if they weren't preregistered, they would not get there—and we couldn't afford to wait. Through negotiation, the requirement for preregistration was eliminated and Access-A-Ride will come within two hours.

The NYPD worked with the Departments of Health, Probation, and others to develop these collaborative policing partnerships in support of public safety. When I got there, the criminal justice system interagency complaints were endless; the cops complained about the DAs, the DAs complained about the judges, the judges about the attorney general. The constant was that everybody complained up. There was a general sense that there was no point to working with Probation, they were good for nothing; there was no point in working with Parole. Gradually Herman brokered a cease-fire, bringing agencies in and having people see that they could work together, even be partners. Her best days would be when colleagues, either peers at the executive team or a precinct commanding officer or a borough commander or a neighborhood coordination officer—anyone at any level—called and said, "We have tried X, Y, and Z, and we don't know where to go with this. I can't get Parks on the phone, I can't get the Health Department. Are they the right agency?" And with help—direct or through another resource—they got the job done.

Under Shea, Crime Control Strategies used data to drive the agency and earn better results through efficiency. We were going to keep crime down by making fewer arrests but better ones. How?

Crime Control Strategies had lists of lists: Who had multiple gun arrests? Who shot the most? Who was arrested for shootings? Who kept getting arrested and having their prosecutions fall apart, which led to other discussions: "An arrest in that case is meaningless. Raise the bar, we need convictions." That ruffled feathers. "What do you mean, I failed?" "Well you had an arrest, but it accomplished nothing. That is not a success."

Over the course of time, Crime Control Strategies kept drilling down in an effort to find the roots of crime in each community. The same names appeared on arrest sheets over and over. Each morning, Shea would review the crime reports. As I monitored the course of crime and disorder in the city, anytime I saw something particularly troubling I would call or email him: "What's going on?"

"Here's what's going on. Eight shootings in the last four hours in a twenty-block area. Among the eight shooters, they have a combined hundred and fifty arrests and twenty prior gun arrests." We saw very easily what we were up against: Shea's "hamster wheel of arrests," consistent criminals going in, getting out, and shooting and getting shot again.

Amid the violence, Susan Herman and the victims' advocates were trying to find a way to handle homelessness, mental health issues, and mass incarceration. If, as was her mandate, we were intending to offer alternatives to incarceration for other than hard-core criminals, what were they and where would we put the people who would otherwise have gone to jail? She and Shea had many discussions about these alternatives. If they didn't actually fight, they engaged in intense searches for new paths. I felt something new needed to be done, otherwise crime would careen along with no end in sight. I told them, "Just get it done."

"I want you to promise," Herman told the agencies she was brokering, "that what you do with this small group of people who are involved in groups and gangs and crews will be something other than what you do ordinarily. Let's start with that, let's raise the bar." Shea was unconvinced. He wanted convictions. They found a middle ground.

New York City Ceasefire was a group-violence intervention program based on the work of criminologist David Kennedy in Boston. It involved pinpointing and talking directly to the small number of people in gangs and crews who were responsible for most of the city's shootings and homicides. These discussions took place with the actual groups causing significant problems in a particular area. The department knew who they were; it was our job to know.

Meetings were convened in local venues such as high schools and Masonic Temples. Herman represented the police department; the borough commander spoke; someone from the DA's office addressed the group, as did a representative from the U.S. Attorney's Office. All gave the message: *The violence has to stop.* They said it in a variety of different ways: *No more shooting, no more homicides. If you and your group continue to engage in these crimes—particularly the next homicide—or if you become a violent group, there will be consequences. And not for just one person; your whole group will feel it.* "We don't want to arrest you. We don't want to put you in prison. But if you continue going like you're going, you are going to get a lot of special attention from us, and it's going to be more than you're used to."

These were not idle threats. Where once a suspect was in our sights we had traditionally relied on our own resources—"If he spits on the sidewalk, instead of ignoring it, give him a summons. If he is jaywalking, instead of the summons, arrest him"—now we would be using more agencies to touch people. We could tighten their stipulations: If they were on probation or parole, we could make their curfew run from midnight to 7:00 a.m.; we could prevent them from leaving their home at all on weekends; we could put specific precincts where they had friends or contacts off-limits. If they were in the prison, we could listen in on their phone calls, move their cells, make sure they knew that we knew what they were doing. If they owed child support, get the sheriff to collect the liens. Make everybody feel some consequences. Impact their behavior. That was the enforcement message.

At the same meeting, we would bring in other agencies to offer help to anyone who asked for it. We had community members speak. We had a voice of redemption, usually a minister; a voice of aspiration, a voice of pain, for instance a parent who had lost a child to gang violence. We brought in a social-service provider to say, "There really isn't anything you could ask for that I won't try my hardest to get you. Try me."

Why was that important? Because our advocates were building trust with the people who were creating so much of the crime and disorder. They had never been listened to; now someone was helping with their problems. "What do you need? Let me help you get a ride to court." We were working toward change, redefining the cops and the city as potential allies. We weren't just there for the victims, we could be there for them, too. This alone could shake someone's world.

Offering the stick and the carrot, we presented the option of social services while at the same time investigating the actions of everyone brought into the room, so if they didn't accept, we had a leg up on following through with our promised consequences.

On the intragovernmental level, for half a decade the federal High Intensity Drug Trafficking Areas (HIDTA) had convened a monthly meeting of the NYPD Office of Management Analysis and Planning, NYC Department of Health and Mental Hygiene, and other city and state agencies—approximately seventy-five people—to share data about regional substance abuse problems, so everyone involved in the issue possessed the same information. In 2014, we began sending more parts of the department to these meetings, including Crime Control Strategies and Collaborative Policing. We listened for about a year and, as the opioid epidemic grew increasingly dire, finally said, "This is nice, to exchange data, but we have a crisis. What is everyone here actually doing? What are the plans? How is this changing behavior? Are our agencies sharing the data they should be sharing? Are our protocols what they should be? What are we doing?" We were greatly aided in this initiative by the head of HIDTA, Chauncey Parker.

The Department of Health and Mental Hygiene convened a new meeting, held in police headquarters' Jack Maple Room, the CompStat room, with hundreds of people from dozens of agencies around the table—Homeless Services, EMS, Fire, the prosecutors, representatives from the ambulances, from the hospitals. Dermot Shea's Crime Control Strategies shop shone a light on the big picture. It was a daunting task, the complicated nature of which made crime compilation pale in comparison, but they put together case studies of every fatal overdose and asked each agency, "What was your role in this case?"

For instance, one person who was staying at a city shelter OD'd. They got sent to the hospital. Maybe they lived, maybe they passed away. Twenty minutes later, someone staying at the same shelter died, not at the facility but around the corner, in the street. Off campus, if you will. Did the shelter know about the second death?

No.

We arrested a drug addict, but because they had a habit we gave them the option of nonincarceration and placed them in treatment. Three days later that person overdosed and died. Did anyone tell the treatment center? The answer to all of these questions basically was no; as a general rule, no one told anyone.

These meetings continue to today as RxStat, and can be very uncomfortable for the nonpolice people. We are looking at a PowerPoint presentation that describes real cases, and they are being grilled and often coming up empty. We have to break through the attitude of "Why are you asking me? I don't work for you. This isn't even a police problem, why is the Department of Homeless Services coming over to Collaborative Policing to talk about how much naloxone we give out in shelters? What's it to you?"

Our response: "That's fair, you don't work for us—but we are in this initiative together. We are all coming together voluntarily. Our mutual goal is to save lives. That's it—that's our goal. We are asking these questions because we think we can either identify gaps in resources and/or services or a pinpoint a problem. So I am just checking. Last month you said you were going to increase the amount of naloxone. Where are we with that, and what are we doing?" Essentially we were trying to find common ground for all to stand on.

Crime Control Strategies and Collaborative Policing brought problems to light at these meetings, then divvied up the issues and followed up with the relevant agencies.

The program started to work, but its success was difficult to gauge. When we made a successful criminal case, the violence stopped immediately; take twenty felons and put them in prison, they are not going to commit crime anymore. When they were still out on the street, was a crime drop attributable to their taking advantage of the new conditions or was there some other reason that wasn't obvious? One of several reasons why the impact was hard to quantify was that, as the department became aware of their potential, Ceasefire strategies began bleeding into non-Ceasefire initiatives. We took this as a positive development. A good idea, collaborative policing, was spreading.

Susan Herman left the department in 2019 to become senior adviser to Mayor de Blasio and director of ThriveNYC, a mental health initiative run by Chirlane McCray.

Dermot Shea was extremely good at his job. He was particularly adept at presiding over CompStat, and in 2018 was named chief of detectives. In December 2019 he became the forty-fourth police commissioner of the City of New York.

In 2014, my first year back as commissioner, with the success of community policing and the 98.27 percent decrease in stop, question, and frisk, I declared a "peace dividend." We made a concerted effort to have our officers act appropriately when dealing with what they understood was a crime being committed, or one that had been committed, so they were not needlessly getting engaged in negative interactions with the public. The public, of course, was being spared the inconvenience and indignity of the multitude of stops, and resources that previously had been spent in that regard could now be used in service of more meaningful programs.

We were dealing with three generations of New Yorkers: those under twenty-five years old, who had never known New York City as anything other than safe; those from twenty-five to fifty, who had experienced the difficult 1970s and '80s while growing up; and those over fifty who remembered the bad old days. Casual outside observers might have viewed my change in tactics as disingenuous. *Wait a second, isn't this the guy who was locking everybody up in 1994? Who had zero tolerance? Now he wants everybody to get a slap on the wrist and an admonition? What's up with that?* Well, you don't send the Red Cross onto the battlefield while the bullets are still flying, only after you have taken and secured the ground. Community policing, we came to understand, had been akin to sending the Red Cross onto the battlefield ahead of the infantry. You can't apply community policing to people who are afraid to be a community. You can't tell them *We want you to fix the crime. We want you to be the front line out there on the stoops, to gather and pass us information, to be engaged with your cops. We will solve problems together and the crime will go away.* When I arrived in 1994 people were too scared to come out onto those stoops and streets, they weren't engaging, and asking them to do that was not only unreasonable, but malfeasance. Put bluntly, there is a murder rate above which community policing becomes increasingly problematic.

That's what's going on in the country right now; people are afraid to work with the police, to be out on the streets, to be seen interacting with the police. How can you expect people to take back the streets when there are 2,245 murders, 7,000 people shot, a lot of them as a result of drug deals. They and their community group are going to go down and tell the drug dealers to get off the corner? They're going to get shot!

Community policing works best when an area has been made safe, when people can get out and enjoy the streets and engage with the police. Effectively, what Commissioner Brown had been attempting to do with his community policing initiative and what Kelly had been doing with Impact was asking the community to take back the streets before they had been made safe. That didn't work. Only after we exhibited the ability to focus precisely on those in the neighborhoods who were doing the most harm could we ask the community they were terrorizing to help us.

Once we used precision policing to successfully pinpoint the actual bad guys, we became aware of a new increase in community pressure for them to go straight. I don't think there's any denying that by making the community safer we make communities stronger, and that strength allows the community itself to have influence on its own world.

Consider a functioning neighborhood, regardless of economic status, where Mrs. Jones is not intimidated by little Tommy on the stoop and can tell him and his friends to knock it off when they start to get out of hand— and because of that neighborhood's prevailing culture, little Tommy and friends do what Mrs. Jones says. That is a strong neighborhood.

Time passes, however, and now Tommy and his friends have grown so strong and frightening that Mrs. Jones can't influence them. Unable to control her neighborhood, Mrs. Jones retreats inside and anonymously calls the police. Officers who are known to the community arrive and, whether by positive verbal influence or police action, reestablish the street's equilibrium. Depending on the depth of the problem this may take time, but the officers remain in contact with Mrs. Jones and others in the neighborhood who have expressed interest. Ultimately, they succeed. First they do the work for her, then they do it with her, and finally she is able to do it herself again, with the support of the police when needed.

There may be some truth to the idea that some neighborhoods can talk their disrupters out of violence, but that holds only if other systems in the community have been strengthened to the point where everybody is trying to support one another. In practice, community policing was often separated from crime fighting. You don't push the shared responsibility of public safety onto Mrs. Jones when Tommy has an Uzi and a murder occurs in the city every four hours. D-Day comes before the Marshall Plan. Neighborhoods had to be made secure before cops could ask people to come out and work with them. When I arrived in New York City in 1994 and began utilizing community policing, the police were doing it for Mrs. Jones. The key to precision policing in 2014 was learning to have the police at first act for Mrs. Jones and then have Mrs. Jones begin to develop the confidence that she can finally do that on her own and we will be there if she needs us.

The peace dividend paid off. In 2016, we had the lowest index crime total since the Giants left for San Francisco; one of the three lowest murder totals (with 2013 and 2014) since 1951; and up to that point the fewest shootings since 1993 (a drop of 110), the fewest burglaries and auto thefts since 1951, and the fewest robberies since 1965. Not only were we very much on the right track to bridge the gap between the public and the police—particularly that portion of the public that felt the police had not been responsive to their concerns—we had the real ability not only to bridge that gap, but to close it. Through observation and intelligence and casework we could pick and choose bad guys, focus on them for hard-core enforcement, and delegate to the cops, particularly our NCOs, the ability to make decisions about who should and who shouldn't get enforcement.

Precision policing is moving into the field of intelligence. As officers are given more leeway in whether an individual warrants a warning, an admonishment, a summons, or an arrest, they can be afforded increased access to that person's law enforcement history. The opportunity exists through the development of an electronic database.

I recognize this is controversial territory. As a society, our buying habits are continually monitored and monetized by private corporations. We see it every day when advertisements for products we may have browsed or purchased show up uninvited on our smartphones. *Isn't that something, the last thing I searched for on Amazon is popping up on my Facebook feed.* Millions of dollars are spent analyzing our behavior patterns in service of economic advantage. These are generally viewed as, at worst, a nuisance. When cops or the government perform the same analysis, however, people have visions of Big Brother disrupting their lives and freak out.

Unfortunately, in the twenty years I had spent away from the NYPD commissioner's office, the policing concepts of Broken Windows, stop, question, and frisk, and "zero tolerance" had merged in the public's mind. They are entirely different concepts. Broken Windows involves minute attention to detail at all levels and in all areas; valid reasonable-suspicion stops are responses to potential misdeeds; and "zero tolerance," an absolutist misrepresentation of the fundamentals of Broken Windows, was not about partnership and priority setting with the community, it was about the police alone deciding what should be enforced and how to enforce it.

In the 1990s we needed to surge arrests and focus on quality-of-life enforcement to take back the streets. Did we medicate for too long? Did we, in certain neighborhoods, medicate too heavily? Those questions were being asked and answered as we decreased the number of stops made and summonses issued. We performed a new diagnostic, analyzed the results, reassessed the prescription, and set about correcting the dosage. The heavy dose of police chemo, so necessary in 1994, was no longer needed. The patient had gotten much better.

We were accused of targeting minorities, specifically instructing the NYPD to go after Black and brown people. That's nonsense. We targeted criminals.

Nevertheless, some of the claims made by the Black Lives Matter movement about abuses by police have both historic and current validity. Slavery is America's original sin, and for hundreds of years of American history the police, among others, were called upon to enforce slavery laws, track down runaway slaves, and later enforce Jim Crow laws. You didn't see a lot of cops investigating lynchings, let alone stopping them. Cops have clearly been on the wrong side of history for a long time as it relates to racial justice. In every law enforcement category, Black people were at the short end of the stick. There are long, complicated, and sensitive arguments about how much of that was bias and how much was cause related, but it doesn't matter. If you are Black, you see this through the prism of oppression. "Why am I always the repressed one? Why do the cops stop me on the street but they don't stop the white guy who just walked by? Why do so many Black professionals have horror stories about being stopped by the police when few white professionals have had similar experiences?" When you then see cops "militarized," or you see police aggressively confronting Black protesters in ways they don't whites, that gives further life to the notion that the cops repress Black people.

Cops in many ways are the principal manifestation of government in America. The average citizen has more contact with police officers than any other representative of government. As a result, the way cops conduct themselves goes a long way toward forming the public's perception of government itself. If you agree with the idea that the cops are here to oppress you, you're more likely to have a negative perception of government as a whole. Thanks to these high stakes, this, to me, is the single biggest challenge in policing. What changes do we make to achieve a great goal of policing, to establish a healthy relationship between cops and communities of color, to make communities safe and fair everywhere for everyone?

Unfortunately in America, there are still places where policing has not progressed as far as I would like. We are the most visible arm of government, and sometimes because of our own horrendous behavior we create our own problems. Taken as a whole, however, progressive police leadership generally recognizes the historic injustices. The people who represent the Black Lives Matter movement on television and in the media will tell you that the communities of color disagree with that assessment, that we do not comprehend or consider those injustices. However, if we went into the Black communities of New York City or Chicago this afternoon and sat down and talked about their specific problems, while police misconduct would be discussed, problems of disorder and lack of safety would be paramount. And it would be demanded, quite correctly, that police do something about them.

I believe the vast majority of Black citizens have two problems with the police: one is abuse and two is underservicing. It has been law enforcement's experience that communities of color around America are as indignant about the underservicing as they are about the abuse. Unfortunately, when this issue is raised with the Black Lives Matter movement, they won't go there with you.

My concern has been for victims of crime and disorder. The first Peelian principle. Who are the disproportionate victims? African Americans. And who are the disproportionate perpetrators of crime and disorder against African Americans? African Americans. African Americans are more heavily victimized than any other portion of society, and they are victimized in large part by African Americans. (Most perpetrators of crime and disorder against white people are white people.) In order to protect African Americans, you're going to arrest more African Americans. It doesn't matter how you plan. If you police hot spots, if you put cops on the dots, if you perform predictive policing, what do you discover? You wind up in an African American community, concentrating on African American perpetrators.

At the same time, while there is no denying that African Americans commit the vast majority of crimes against African Americans, one can also look to the role of systemic bias in government that is inflicted on Blacks—whether in education, jobs, housing—and that factors into these actions. *The New York Times* even reported that in the average inner-city neighborhood, the temperature is as much as 10 degrees hotter than in other parts of town because there are no trees and public spaces have been paved over. Systemic bias, in this case the unwillingness and failure to put resources into poor Black neighborhoods, has created conditions more conducive to crime.

A s a precinct commander, if you don't address quality-of-life issues, you are dead. Dead. Not just within the NYPD, where high rates of crime under your command will get you chastised at CompStat and stymied in your career. You are dead in the communities, who will demand better. As a precinct sergeant, when Jon Murad attended community meetings in the 34th Precinct, those concerned attendees didn't complain in great degrees about homicides or shootings or robberies; they talked about the unacceptable number of people in the street smoking weed, about dogs defecating on the sidewalk. As with the citizens of Boston when I worked there in the 1970s and in New York in the early '90s, what was important to them were the daily disruptions affecting everyday life. That's what they looked to us to control, that's what members of every community look to the police to control. And as we were coming back month after month, we had better show some improvement or we'd get called out, and rightfully so. Classic Broken Windows! In the 4-4, with a population of 150,000 documented people within 1.9 square miles, on top of which you could probably add another 20,000 who had no papers, that's what the majority of community members were concerned about.

When people say we should abandon Broken Windows, as far as I'm concerned they are talking about abandoning the overreach of Broken Windows, and I agree. Zero tolerance, for instance, was never what Kelling and Wilson had in mind. Arrests were to be a last resort. "Broken Windows was never intended to be a high-arrest program," Kelling said. It was designed to use the threat of discipline as a means to influence behavior. A central tenet of Broken Windows is that fear and disorder matter. One of Kelling's most deeply held convictions, as it is mine, was that the role of police should be negotiated between the communities and the police. Zero tolerance is a toxic idea, and it did tremendous damage.

Kelling and Wilson were keenly aware of the potential difficulties. "We might agree that certain behavior makes one person more undesirable than another but how do we ensure that age or skin color or national origin or harmless mannerisms will not also become the basis for distinguishing the undesirable from the desirable?" they wrote in their original 1982 *Atlantic* article. "How do we ensure, in short, that the police do not become the agents of neighborhood bigotry?" They concluded: "We can offer no wholly satisfactory answer to this important question." You are still going to have some bad cops do bad things. It is our responsibility to send a very strong message, both internally and externally, that when we discover these cops we will do all we can to get rid of them. The fact is, however, that protections have been put in place by police unions, civil service, and even police commissions that makes eradicating some bad cops from the police force extremely difficult. The key to the creation and maintenance of a good department, Wilson and Kelling wrote, is in the "selection, training, and supervision" of the police. Most police chiefs will tell you that one of their greatest frustrations is the inability to get rid of bad cops.

But to suggest that we should stop doing order maintenance is just wrong. Order maintenance is an ancient function of police. We will continue to do it, and the demands that we do it will remain high. When you've got somebody pissing on your doorstep every morning, it doesn't matter whether you are white or Black or Hispanic or Asian or whatever, you are going to demand that something be done about it. You are going to demand that order be restored. This doesn't mean that police will arrest everyone who has to pee in public—there are guidelines that specify under which circumstances to give an admonishment or citation—but nonetheless, the demand for order remains high. The offense must not be ignored.

I wholeheartedly acknowledge and agree that some of the Black Lives Matter movement's concerns have a legitimate basis. But when members go to extremes and define the entire American culture and American policing as racist and hopeless and in need of overthrow, and advocate violence, at that point I believe they are making the same mistake that was made by radicals during the 1960s, when they took a sharp left turn and lost their credibility and constituency.

Do Black lives matter? I've seen the dance some people do when asked that question. They won't answer. They say "All lives matter." That is a meaningless evasion. Do Black lives matter? It's a yes or no question. Only a bigot would refuse to answer in the affirmative.

CHAPTER 9

The Ecosystem of Eric Garner

here was a human ecosystem in Tompkinsville Park. Named for Daniel Tompkins, nineteenth-century governor of New York and vice president under James Monroe, who settled that part of Staten Island and died of alcoholism, the park was a small triangular patch of grass and benches that sat, in 2014, at the juncture of Victory Boulevard and Bay Street. Women with strollers would bring their children to play and enjoy a slice of the New York City outdoors. On the streets abutting the park were a convenience store, a bodega, a pharmacy, a beauty supply store. And because it was one of New York's little oases where you could sit for hours and do whatever occurred to you, it also attracted a rougher crowd. The borderline homeless, junkies, and other people with time on their hands congregated as well. A twenty-two-year-old alleged drug dealer, Ramsey Orta, routinely made a living serving that portion of the park's society. There developed a pattern for the day: while the parents and caretakers were tending to the children, the more unsettled in the neighborhood would go to the liquor store and buy something on the order of a Colt 45, purchase a spliff in the park, and spend the day standing around arguing, nodding, or conversing in groups or by themselves. Between their booze and drugs, they wanted a smoke.

How much was a pack of cigarettes? There was the five or six dollars that the pack cost, plus the $5.85 cigarette tax that Mayor Michael Bloomberg had imposed in an effort to reduce a public-health hazard and raise needed funds for New York City. Eleven bucks was far outside the budget of the men and women frequenting Tompkinsville Park and trying to get wasted, so capitalism took over, and Eric Garner found a strong market on the block for the untaxed cigarettes he brought in from Virginia. Garner was part of a network that would pay people a premium to drive down south and buy cartons or cases, then drive them back up. He would sell these untaxed cigarettes individually—loose—at an even higher premium, though no-where near as high as the store owners, who had to charge city tax. He was making a living selling what were known on the street as loosies.

Complaints came into the 120th Precinct from both the parents in the park and the merchants surrounding it. "These guys are smoking weed, they're getting drunk, and because they're drinking their Colt 45s, they are pissing in the park. *We have people smoking marijuana and urinating, and nobody's doing anything!*"

Every precinct had a Conditions team. It was their job to deal with quality-of-life conditions in their location, and each day their supervisor gave them a menu of tasks to fulfill. The officers would target individuals and issue summonses, and when those summonses were ignored, as they were routinely, maybe a warrant would drop and if someone was caught with small amounts of narcotics they would make an arrest.

So what did they find each day at Tompkinsville Park?

You had Ramsey Orta, you had the liquor stores for the liquor, and you had the guy for the loosies. Orta was low-hanging fruit. The liquor store owner was an interesting figure; he had a liquor license, he was paying his taxes, he had an investment in the community, yet he was supplying the alcohol that was serving to disrupt that same community's calm. (This case was not unique to Staten Island; New York is home to many centers of disruption.) Usually the complainants are the store owners, who say, "I'm paying taxes and selling cigarettes at the tax rate and this guy is out here, not paying any rent, and he's underselling me!" In this part of Staten Island, it was the people who wanted to use the park who comprised the majority of the complainants.

Eric Garner's cigarettes were indispensable, and he became an important part of this ecosystem. In response, the precinct officers would summons and sometimes arrest him, depending on how much weight in terms of cigarettes he possessed. The local precinct cops knew Garner; he had been arrested more than thirty times on charges ranging from assault and resisting arrest to grand larceny.

On July 17, 2014, there was a fight between two people in the park, and it got called in. The Conditions team fielded the complaint. Lieutenant Christopher Bannon, on the desk, gave it to Sergeant Dhanan Saminath of Anti-Crime, a plainclothes unit that targeted violent crime, who walked back to the trailer behind the precinct where Anti-Crime and the precinct Conditions team shared space. Police Officer Justin Damico was on the Conditions team, but his regular partner was tied up with an arrest, so he was paired up with an Anti-Crime cop, Daniel Pantaleo. Pantaleo was not his regular partner. Lieutenant Bannon told Damico to "go do surveillance of the area."

As Pantaleo drove by the park, Damico eyed the scene. There was Garner. Damico looked at him. Garner did not make eye contact; it's not clear whether he "made" the unmarked car or not. In any event, Pantaleo and Damico set up on the right side of St. Marks Place and Victory Boulevard and began their "surveillance," as directed.

Damico knew Eric Garner. He had stopped him by the park a couple of weeks earlier when he was working Conditions. Garner had started flailing his arms and yelling at Damico that he wasn't doing anything, and that he was not going to be arrested, and that he was tired of being harassed. The tirade went on for about ten minutes. Damico told Garner he wasn't going to arrest him this time, and gave him a warning. "I was new to the area and

I knew I was going to be taking, you know, control over the quality of life in the park," Damico recalls, "and I felt that it was, you know, necessary and the right thing to do, is issue him a warning, let him know that I will be around the area and to do it someplace else."

Justin Damico never mentioned the prior encounter to Officer Pantaleo. It may have been because Damico didn't want Pantaleo to infer that Garner had backed him down, or it may have been simply that, at around 3:15 p.m. on July 17, Damico was focused on what he was seeing—Eric Garner selling loose cigarettes to two men on the street, who handed him money and then walked away.

Had Pantaleo known those facts, would he have approached the scene differently? Would he and Damico have skipped the rerun of the ten minutes of yelling and flailing and the crowd that gathered behind it all, by simply taking Garner into custody right away? And if so, would Garner have put up the struggle or simply figured out the cops meant business this time? We can never know. What we do know is Garner went into his now-practiced speech about harassment and his declaration that he was not going to be arrested. Even if Garner were "arrested," he was only going to be handcuffed, driven down to the 120th Precinct, and given a Desk Appearance Ticket (as I've noted, referred to by cops as a "disappearance ticket"). The whole process would have taken him off the street for three or four hours. Eric Garner would have been home for dinner by eight. If he kept his court appearance and paid a fine, it would be one more in a series of such arrests Garner had endured as part of the price of being in the untaxed cigarette business.

But that is not what happened. The events that followed would end Eric Garner's life and alter the lives of all those involved and many, many more.

Having witnessed the transaction, Pantaleo and Damico rolled up and told Garner, "You know the drill. You're going in."

Selling cigarettes is not the worst crime in the history of the world, to say the least, but they were confronted with a policing problem: Garner was a recidivist who ignored all lesser penalties. They couldn't give him a ticket because he'd ignore it. He didn't go to his court appearances; as a matter of practice he didn't show up. So what do you do with a guy like this? And now he was back doing it again. He was shouting at them, "You're harassing me!"

I'm not harassing you, you're breaking the law, and you've been breaking the law here on this corner for the last ten years, and you gotta stop! That's the friction between the two.

Then Garner resisted arrest, which doesn't look like much except he was twice the size of both Pantaleo and Damico.

What the cops didn't know was that Garner was the man who had broken up the fight that got them called in. He was excited and out of breath and sweating. Orta used the camera on his phone to record the encounter. Garner told them, "Get away [garbled] for what? Every time you see me, you want to mess with me. I'm tired of it. It stops today. Why would you . . . ? Everyone standing here will tell you I didn't do nothing. I did not sell nothing. Because every time you see me, you want to harass me. You want to stop me [garbled] selling cigarettes. I'm minding my business, officer, I'm minding my business. Please just leave me alone. I told you the last time, please just leave me alone. Please, please don't touch me. Do not touch me."

Eric Garner was six foot three, three hundred fifty pounds. Daniel Pantaleo is not a large man. Having watched Orta's video of the encounter, here is my impression of what happened:

Pantaleo thinks, *I've got to take this guy by surprise, I've got to take this guy down, I've got to get him off balance, because if he starts to fight with us, we are going to lose.* He and Damico talk to Garner for a fairly significant amount of time without taking action.

There may have been other calculations. If Pantaleo and his partner were yelled at by Eric Garner and then turned around and said, "All right, we'll you give a break this time" and walked away, Ramsey Orta and all the local miscreants would know, "These guys aren't the real police. All you got to do is yell at them loud and they will back down." This is not acceptable to any police official, certainly not the cop on the beat.

Pantaleo got on the radio and said something like, "We're going to need a little assistance here." One or two units were dispatched, not the whole world, but additional units were on their way. Watch the video carefully, you can almost see that he is aware they will be arriving but are not yet present.

Waiting for the backup units, Pantaleo and his partner were attempting a form of de-escalation in that, rather than rush him immediately, they were telling Garner, "You're going to have to come in." Garner protested, but ultimately they said, "No, you are under arrest." Garner's hands were up, indicating "I'm not going." Pantaleo waited until he felt the backup units were almost on site and then initiated the takedown.

One tactical error was clear from the beginning: they decided to take him out against a plate-glass window. This is an issue we always worry about; there are so many ways for that to go wrong, from cuts to decapitation. Unless there is no other alternative, it is always advisable for an arresting officer to try to move the action to a safer location.

Another may have been timing. Pantaleo and Damico appeared to know the backup was there, which may have freed them to move preemptively. Why did they not wait?

They made their move. In the struggle that ensued, police procedure would have Pantaleo attempting to apply what is called the seat-belt hold, taught to all cadets in the Police Academy, in which one arm is placed beneath the detainee's underarm and the other over his shoulder, to bring him under control. Garner was a large man, and Pantaleo seems to have had difficulty maintaining the hold, his arm moving from under the arm to around Garner's neck. Did it evolve into an arm bar? A chokehold? The NYPD patrol guide—the rules that NYPD officers must follow in carrying out their official duties—states, "A chokehold shall include, but is not limited to, any pressure to the throat or windpipe, which may prevent or hinder breathing or reduce intake of air." It is specifically forbidden and absolutely banned. Procedure would have taught Pantaleo to let go when he had his man under control or when resistance had ceased. Garner resisted. It took four cops to wrestle him to the ground. They struggled with him. He thrashed and said, "I can't breathe!" He said it eleven times. The cops kept trying to subdue him. Shortly thereafter, Eric Garner died.

D eputy Commissioner for Intelligence and Counterterrorism John Miller stopped at a light, looked at his NYPD-issue BlackBerry, and saw a note from Dom Williams, chief of staff to First Deputy Mayor Tony Shorris. In it was a link to an article on the *Daily News*'s website with the headline: THEY KILLED HIM. Ramsey Orta's video had been uploaded onto it. Williams was asking, "Do we know anything about this?" By the next morning, the encounter and death had become front-burner news.

I canceled the day's schedule and called several key people—Deputy Commissioner for Legal Matters Larry Byrne, Deputy Commissioner for Public Information Steve Davis, First Deputy Commissioner Ben Tucker— to meet in the executive conference room at One Police Plaza and review the facts of the case as we had them, most of which came from Chief of Patrol Jimmy O'Neill and Steve Davis, because press inquiries had begun to explode. I had questions that needed to be answered.

We went to City Hall because Mayor de Blasio was concerned that Staten Island could heat up quickly. It was summertime, and we had the death of an African American man in custody. Staten Island can be very brittle, depending on which neighborhood is affected, and the mayor was deeply aware that this situation could evolve into a crisis. We went over the essential facts and responded to the mayor's many questions. One of his aides, Emma Wolf, and several community representatives were in attendance and it was decided to make contact, on behalf of the mayor's office, with key religious and neighborhood leaders and push resources out into Staten Island. The mayor's wife, Chirlane McCray, and Chief of Department Phil Banks participated.

Immediately after the meeting I told Miller, "I want to go to the scene." You never really understand it unless you go there. I chose not to use the NYPD Police Commissioner Car One, driven by my security detail, and instead rode with Miller and Davis, with Sergeant Andy McGinnis at the wheel. I thought, *How is this going to play out? What do we need to do? How do we get ahead and not fall behind the curve?* All the way to Staten Island we once again went over the facts as we knew them and discussed the necessary outreach.

The NYPD Staten Island borough commander was Ed Delatorre. I knew Chief Delatorre from the first time I had been commissioner, when, as precinct commander in the Bronx, he had handled a challenging crime adeptly. A young girl on her way home from school had been killed in a crossfire shooting between two rival gangs. This wasn't a crime that would cause a riot, it was a moment in which people needed care as much as policing, and because of his devotion to the job and to that community, Chief Delatorre had developed a real connection to the neighborhood and made one with the girl's family. I had been impressed.

The conversation in the car centered on whether this was going to be called a chokehold death. It would not be the first time the NYPD had dealt with this issue in Staten Island. In April 1994, during my first tenure as commissioner, we had had an incident in the Park Hill houses, which was a center of crime, drug dealing, and violence. Remarkably similar scenario. A Street Narcotics Unit had been staked out, looking for a man with a warrant. When they spotted a suspect, the cops moved on him. A crowd formed around them and a large boom went off, might have been a firecracker or a gunshot. Officer Donald Brown moved toward the noise, which is what cops do. Brown was not some stranger who didn't understand the community; he had grown up in the Park Hill houses. Gun drawn, he saw two men and said, "Halt!" One of them was Ernest Sayon, a small-time drug dealer out on bail from an earlier shooting. Sayon started to run. Brown pursued him, tackled him to the ground, other officers piled on, handcuffed him, and got him out of there quickly before the crowd could mobilize. Sayon was taken to the hospital, where he died.

Initially the cause of death was thought to be a head injury, caused when he was tackled, but ultimately the medical examiner found that Sayon had suffocated while the officers were subduing him. Ultimately, Officer Brown and the other arresting officers testified before a grand jury and were not charged. *The New York Times* wrote, "The decision—one that reflects the frequent reluctance of grand juries to indict police officers for using force against suspects—had pitted a family and a neighborhood who regarded Mr. Sayon as a martyr, against police officers and their supporters who portrayed him as a dangerous if petty criminal."

"The confrontation with Ernest Sayon involved police officers who knew him in the community very well as a dangerous man in a dangerous situation," the prosecutor said. He noted, *The Times* wrote, that officers had wide latitude to use force in such a situation.

Those were the days of shots being fired at the police, cars set ablaze, bricks and bottles thrown. The demonstrations went on for a week. We were trying to prevent a recurrence.

In another incident around the same time as Sayon, in the Bronx, Officer Francis Livoti had killed an innocent young man named Anthony Baez using a chokehold. Livoti was acquitted of criminally negligent homicide but convicted of violating Mr. Baez's civil rights and sentenced to seven and a half years in prison. In response, the city medical examiner, Dr. Seymour Hirsch, began to increase the department's awareness of an issue of which we had no previous knowledge: positional asphyxia.

Positional asphyxia can occur when a person is fighting with the cops, and in an effort to subdue, officers pile on top while he is resisting being handcuffed. Police training instructs the placement of a knee in the back and the forcible restraining of the arms—one officer has a knee in his back, another has his arms, someone else is standing on his leg. But, particularly with the obese or people with breathing issues, officers are now compressing the suspect's lungs. So the suspect starts to yell, "I can't breathe, I can't breathe!" In the midst of this struggle the cops are thinking, *Well of course you can breathe. You're talking. If you can talk, you can breathe!* And as they compress the lungs, and what air the restrainee is using to say "I can't breathe" is leaving, they think, *Lots of people say that, he's just trying to get away, he is still resisting like crazy, he could get up and be right back in the fight.* What we learned from Dr. Hirsch is that the struggle starts as resistance to arrest but soon increases to "Get off me!" because of the utter panic felt when one can't get air. Unfortunately, in the moment, there is no way to differentiate between the two.

In response, after the Park Hill and Lavoti incidents, Dr. Hirsch worked with our training division and jointly put together a video detailing the perils of positional asphyxia and instructing our officers on how to arrest people who are resisting without blocking their airways.

My former first deputy commissioner, John Timoney, famously boiled it down to "Keep your arms away from the neck." But as we began the training on how to avoid the chokehold, Chief of Personnel—or as I liked to call him, Chief of Big Ideas—Mike Julian did an informal survey and asked, "Hey, after they eliminated the chokehold and somebody is resisting and you are losing that fight, where do you go to?" Cops said, "We go to the chokehold, because it works." When I moved on and other commissioners took over the post, the issue and training languished; little time was devoted to the cops' question, "Now that we know we're not allowed to use the chokehold, what are we supposed to do? What is the alternative for getting somebody who is resisting arrest under control?"

The idea that this had started in an African American neighborhood of Staten Island with a death in custody back in 1994 and you could flash forward twenty years and see it unfolding in an extraordinarily similar manner—also on Staten Island, also involving plainclothes cops, also involving an African American male—disturbed me greatly. In the car I tried to familiarize myself with the evolution of that training. I had been away for two decades and needed to get up to speed quickly. What were the current rules and why had the training we had put in place not been prioritized?

On the way to Staten Island I said, "When I get back, I want to see that training video." By the time we returned, the Training division had dug out the tape and run it down to headquarters. When we popped it in the tape machine later that afternoon, there was the very clinical, white-coat-wearing medical examiner with charts and graphs and demonstrations about compression of the neck. And there was Mike Julian, looking like John Travolta in *Saturday Night Fever*. It featured officers doing demonstrations of takedowns and the ME describing the phenomenon of positional asphyxia.

It was good as far as it went, but years had passed and times had changed. "We need to have this updated, with many more tactics," I said. "We need to develop this training, we've got to make sure that this training gets out to everybody. The plainclothes teams, do they not get in-service training? Doesn't every cop get in-service training?"

In-service training used to be about tactics. "You are in plain clothes, people may not know you are a cop, this is how to do a car stop. This is how to spot a gun." This was taught, but for several years before my return, under my predecessor, Ray Kelly, most of that instruction had been pushed aside to make room for training on how to stop-and-frisk. I believe this occurred because, after the controversy concerning the overuse of that tactic had reared its head, Kelly and his administration wanted to be able to avoid criticism and say, "We've trained everybody in the right way to do this." This single focus was drilled down even to the plainclothes people, who were getting shortchanged on other training as a result.

We would change that. We made some quick financial calculations, and by the next day's meeting with the mayor we were able to give him a timetable and the number of million dollars it would take to do this training.

My mind was going in three different directions: investigation, community outreach, and accountability. *What specific steps should we take involving this investigation?* Which was critical, because we were going to be under a public microscope and had to get it right. *What are we going to do in Staten Island to engage and make sure that we are not indifferent and that we don't lose the community?* And, *What are we doing to our cops when we say, "You can't use the chokehold"?*

When I reached the scene I told Sergeant McGinnis, "Slow down, let me take a look." There was the park, there were the stores, that's where it happened. Okay. I did not leave the car and inject myself into the scene, I did not usurp the authority of the men and women in charge; I got what I came for, a physical sense of the event's immediacy, which I could use when analyzing the actions that took place. At the 1-2-0 we met Chief Delatorre and the precinct commanding officer Joseph Veneziano, who brought me up to speed. They brought in the local councilwoman and assistant borough president for a wider discussion about a rally we had heard was being organized and a vigil to be held there. We spent a lot of time discussing potential community reactions and how best to deal with them.

The event had already begun to set off protests, but Chief Delatorre had such deep contacts in Staten Island that Eric Garner's grandparents became extraordinarily helpful. When outside groups from other boroughs showed up—there were demonstrations every day in Staten Island, large and small, and then some in Manhattan from antipolice groups—when things showed signs of careening out of control, they got on the bullhorn or the microphone, or took the podium and said, "You need to keep this simple." They became a giant help, for which we were extremely grateful.

I visited the office of Staten Island District Attorney Dan Donovan. It was important, to avoid accusations of a cover-up that often attach themselves when police actions are called into question, that the DA take the lead in the investigation. The district attorney's office had a panoramic view of the Staten Island Ferry Terminal and across New York Harbor to the skyline of Manhattan on this bright blue day. It was a multimillion-dollar view. Eric Garner died in police custody in Staten Island. Chief Delatorre and Captain Veneziano, the City Council member and the borough president and the community leaders would figure out the Staten Island part of it; the DA would be the face and voice and guiding leader of the investigation as it made its way through the criminal justice system.

But looking toward Manhattan, with its media and history and deserved reputation for driving things over the edge, it was clear to me that the story was going to be written there.

I said, "You have all the resources of the NYPD at your disposal, but you have to call the shots and be the public face, because whatever we do will be questioned. So use your DA's investigators"—who are not in the police department, although many were former NYPD—"and you have full access to my internal affairs, if you want officers brought in. You want witnesses found, you want anything, they are all yours."

The mayor called a press conference at City Hall, in which I participated. Fortunately, Staten Island held. Unlike after Park Hill, there were no police cars set on fire, no rocks, no bottles, no upheaval. Why? In 1994, Mayor Rudy Giuliani said, basically, "We are looking into the situation. We don't have all the information. Sometimes, at the beginning, events appear to have gone one way, and then a little later you find out they went another. So I would hate for anybody to jump to conclusions now." You could have changed the name on the quote to Bill de Blasio. And yet there was violence. The difference was that Rudy, because of his basic isolationism, didn't have Mayor de Blasio's community operation, didn't push his people into the streets to influence and assuage their known contacts— because they didn't have any. De Blasio and his staff were working Staten Island immediately. It was more than just words from the pulpit, there were real people making true contact. They were different mayors, clearly—one who had relationships with the Black community versus one who had just defeated the first Black mayor and shown a cold heart doing it.

I, as police commissioner, reviewed all Civilian Complaint Review Board cases regarding the conduct of NYPD officers. When I saw the video for the first time I said, "It appears to be a chokehold." Officer Pantaleo's arm did slip around Eric Garner's neck rather than under his armpit.

But as I considered the case I had to consider intentionality. Pantaleo may have used a chokehold under the broad definition, but was it intentional? If he hadn't intended to choke Garner, that became a factor. The death was ruled a homicide by the chief medical examiner. That ruling is technical. It is different than murder, which is intentional. It simply means that the medical examiner determined the death was caused by the actions of another person. Whether those actions were legal would be a matter for prosecutors and courts. Whether it was proper under NYPD's rules and procedures is something that the police commissioner would be the ultimate arbiter of.

The death was terrible. A man died needlessly, his family lost a loved one, for which the department will be eternally regretful. But this was not, as it would come to be claimed in the world of racial politics, a willful killing of a Black man for selling loosies. Eric Garner was not killed intentionally.

The confrontation's aftermath was not handled well. It was awful. Had the videotape revealed someone kneeling beside Eric Garner and showing empathy, the tape would have gone nowhere. If one cop—not simply Pantaleo, although he would have been best—if one cop had sat next to him and said, "Hey guy, hey guy, breathe, there's an ambulance coming, you're going to be okay. You're going to be okay. Just breathe," followed up with, *"Just check that bus, would you check that bus!"* and continued to show concern for the man on the ground—"You're going to be okay, okay?"—Eric Garner may still have died, and that is terrible and cannot be negated, and his death would have occasioned an investigation; but the city might not have erupted in the way it did.

But it did.

I never made a final decision on Pantaleo because, as I've said, according to NYPD custom and protocol, administrative processes involving officers are postponed until the criminal component has been adjudicated. From the outside this would seem unjustifiable—you have a cop whose performance demands evaluation; why is the department dragging its heels investigating him?

It's not as simple as it seems.

The administrative process and use of officers' compelled testimony from that process in subsequent court proceedings is complicated and critical to understand. In the NYPD internal administrative process, which starts with an Internal Affairs Bureau investigation, the officers must give statements, internally called GO-15s. The officers have no Fifth Amendment right not to answer in the GO-15s, because while these statements can be used in our internal administrative department trials, they cannot be used in criminal investigations, prosecutions, or trials. If the officers refuse to answer, they are fired.

We conducted the IAB investigation, and GO-15s were taken from Pantaleo and other officers.

At the request of the Staten Island district attorney's office and of first the U.S. Attorney's Office in Brooklyn and subsequently the U.S. Department of Justice's Civil Rights Division in Washington, D.C., we did not proceed with department administrative proceedings or trial. Deputy Commissioner for Legal Matters Larry Byrne and I together spoke directly with Loretta Lynch, first when she was United States attorney, and again after she became attorney general, and in both calls she confirmed that she did not want us to proceed until the federal criminal investigations were completed.

The main reason prosecutors ask us to hold off on starting administrative disciplinary proceedings until after criminal trials is that department trials themselves are open to the public and the media. The public revelation of GO-15s—through media coverage or leaks from defense attorneys—creates an insurmountable issue for prosecutors to show that their criminal investigation, criminal charges, grand jury process, and criminal trials have not been tainted by direct or indirect exposure to the statements of anyone involved (including witnesses). The same issue holds with the jury seated for the criminal trial and the grand jury members who return an indictment. Had we ignored the local and federal prosecutors' requests not to proceed and gone ahead with a department trial, we would have been accused of preventing a criminal prosecution from taking place. Others would have said that we deliberately obstructed the criminal investigations to protect Pantaleo. (This issue, known as a Kastigar issue and Kastigar burden for prosecutors—based on the U.S. Supreme Court's *Kastigar v. United States* decision—is not simply a theoretical problem, but a very real one. It was the reason Oliver North's criminal conviction on obstruction of a congressional investigation and destruction of documents charges was reversed on appeal.) This is why, as a general matter for many years, and in the Garner matter in particular, we did not proceed with the department administrative trial until much later.

On the evening after the Staten Island district attorney's office announced it would not prosecute because the grand jury had voted not to indict Pantaleo, then–United States Attorney General Eric Holder went on national television to announce an immediate federal criminal civil rights investigation. The decision not to prosecute in the Garner case took place shortly after it was announced that there would be no criminal charges filed in the Ferguson matter. After a five-year investigation the Department of Justice chose not to prosecute Pantaleo for civil rights violations.

Pantaleo's administrative case took five years to conclude. In that time Jimmy O'Neill ascended from chief of patrol to chief of department to succeed me as commissioner. Ultimately agreeing with the findings of NYPD Deputy Commissioner of Trials Rosemarie Maldonado that Officer Pantaleo "consciously disregarded the substantial and unjustifiable risks of a maneuver explicitly prohibited by the department" and that the use of the chokehold was "reckless" and "a gross deviation from the standard of conduct" established for an NYPD officer, Commissioner O'Neill dismissed Pantaleo from the department.

Pantaleo sued in New York State Supreme Court to get his job back, and the case remains pending in the Appellate Division. Pantaleo was found guilty by the NYPD Deputy Commissioner of Trials of recklessly causing physical injury to Eric Garner and dismissed from the department by

Commissioner O'Neill. The issue on appeal is whether there is a "rational basis" for the decision, which is a deferential standard favoring the department. In other words, it is unlikely that Pantaleo will get his job back.

Predictably, the PBA and rank and file were incensed by the decision. PBA president Pat Lynch conducted an emotional press conference blasting it.

Jimmy O'Neill said, "From the start of this process, I was determined to carry out my responsibility as police commissioner unaffected by public opinions demanding one outcome over another. I examined the totality of the circumstances and relied on the facts. And I stand before you today confident that I have reached the correct decision.

"But that has certainly not made it an easy decision.

"I served for nearly thirty-four years as a uniformed New York City cop before becoming police commissioner. I can tell you that had I been in Officer Pantaleo's situation, I may have made similar mistakes. And had I made those mistakes, I would have wished I had used the arrival of back-up officers to give the situation more time to make the arrest. And I would have wished that I had released my grip before it became a chokehold.

"Every time I watched the video, I said to myself, dozens of times: 'Don't do it. Don't do it.' I said that about the decisions made by both Officer Pantaleo and Mr. Garner.

"But none of us can take back our decisions, most especially when they lead to the death of another human being."

Over the course of years I overruled several Civilian Complaint Review Board chokehold findings, largely around the idea of intent. Was the officer attempting to apply pressure that would restrict the air, or in the course of a fight, when anything goes until you get control—and once you get control, you let up—was he trying his best to subdue a suspect in a lawful manner? This was the question I was continually asking.

We did change the training and the patrol guide, however. We chose not to alter the definition of a chokehold, but we established a three-day program to retrain the entire department in de-escalation techniques. Included was a full day devoted to rules and techniques for the physical takedown of suspects, emphasizing that at all times we try to avoid grabbing around the neck, but understanding that if you are in a life-and-death struggle, you are going to do whatever it takes to gain control. Central to this understanding was that, as a police commissioner or as a CCRB investigator, one must take into account the specific circumstances at the moment a hold is applied. We instituted a four-day training session for dealing with the mentally ill and people under the influence of narcotics, many of whom ended up being people of color. It was quite apparent that the department needed to do a much better job in dealing with the mentally ill so we didn't harm them or worse while we were supposed to be addressing their issues.

We also created a strong new emphasis on conflict de-escalation, one of the long-standing gains from the terrible death of Eric Garner. Not solace for his family, but a significant step forward for the people of New York.

We thought we had come a long, long way.

And then there was Ferguson.

CHAPTER 10

Race: Policing and America's Original Sin

T he police are not merely a 'spark' factor. To some [African Americans], police have come to symbolize white power, white racism, and white repression. . . . The atmosphere of hostility and cynicism is reinforced by a widespread belief in the existence of police brutality and a 'double standard' of justice and protection. . . . The abrasive relationship between the police and minority communities has been a major—and explosive— source of grievance, tension, and disorder. The blame must be shared by the total society. The police are faced with demands for increased protection and service [in minority neighborhoods]. Yet the aggressive patrol practices thought necessary to meet these demands themselves create tension and hostility."

That statement sounds like it could have been written yesterday. In fact it was included in the Report of the National Advisory Commission on Civil Disorders—the Kerner Report—published in March 1968 after a long, hot summer in which first Newark and then Detroit went up in flames and "brought racial disorders to American cities, and with them shock, fear and bewilderment to the Nation." These issues are still with us and it may seem, in times when America's problems appear intractable, that they will remain with us forever.

On August 9, 2014, a young African American man, Michael Brown, was killed in Ferguson, Missouri, by a white police officer, Darren Wilson—and all hell broke loose.

My reaction to stories of the day is tempered by the years I have spent leading police organizations as chief, superintendent, commissioner. As I've said, as bad as the images in a first story look, that's never going to be the last story. In every investigation I always seek to find the truth, and I've found from hard experience that it's going to take a while to get where the truth will take us. When I was a young cop, the received wisdom was that you had to protect the department's image at all costs. But while some in policing had a history of condoning all types of abhorrent behavior in that effort, that was not me. Each department's image is what it is: good, bad, or indifferent. And if there was, at some point in policing history, the opportunity to sweep things under the rug, that day is now thankfully long gone in most departments.

We thought we might handle the Garner difficulties, but Ferguson drove us over the cliff. There was so much animosity.

Slavery is America's original sin, with the arrival of the first slave on our shores in 1619, and the country is still atoning for it. In the United States, though I believe in the essential goodness of most citizens, there are bigots in low places and high office. There was in 2014, and there continues to be, a portion of the population that believes police departments across the country are largely comprised of racists who do not believe that Black lives matter. Technological advances—cell phone cameras, the internet, social media—have captured genuinely depraved behavior committed by police officers. They also have sometimes made terrible mistakes by officers appear to be intentional acts of violence, and because of the ease of their dissemination, made infrequent spasms of malevolence seem to be widespread evidence of institutional bigotry. In the face of overwhelming evidence to the contrary, there persists the image of the cop as a racist brute.

Early reports out of Ferguson seemed to confirm worst fears. Eyewitness reports indicated that Michael Brown had been walking away from Officer Wilson and been shot—at a distance, in the back, with his hands up in surrender—in an apparent racially motivated homicide. Could not have been worse. Paired with videos of other racial incidents around the country, what took hold was a popular image of cops indiscriminately shooting unarmed Black men. The rallying cry in subsequent demonstrations became "Hands up, don't shoot!"

The Ferguson Police Department did a lot of things wrong. They didn't know how to deal with a police-involved homicide. They left Michael Brown's body out in the street, covered only by a sheet, for far too long. The department had clearly had been doing other things wrong as well, including making revenue on the backs of the city's poorest citizens through summonses, warrant money, fines, and fees.

However, it seemed to me very unlikely that a police officer would summarily execute a young Black man in broad daylight on a street completely populated by other African Americans. The eyewitness first said Brown was shot in the back; however, that was disproved by the fact that there were no injury wounds in Michael Brown's back. Ultimately, three separate investigations found that Michael Brown did not have his hands up and was not trying to surrender. These investigations established that Brown got into a physical confrontation with Officer Wilson, who was in his patrol car, during which Brown reached inside the car in an active attempt to take the officer's firearm. The gun discharged inside the car, the bullet perhaps striking Brown. Brown fled some distance from the cruiser, but then turned on the officer and came back at him. He did not have his hands up; that lie was perpetrated by Brown's accomplice in a store robbery they had just committed, and by several eyewitnesses who didn't actually see what happened. Their story was that Michael Brown had his hands in the air and told the officer, "I don't have a gun, stop shooting!" Didn't happen. Both eyewitness and forensic evidence overwhelmingly supported the officer's story. Didn't matter; the damage had already been done. The media went with "Hands up, don't shoot."

Whether Officer Wilson was racially biased, I don't know. Whether Officer Wilson spoke to Michael Brown in a way that was derogatory or mean or cruel, I don't know. Whether Wilson had knowledge of the robbery is unclear. But Michael Brown knew he had committed the robbery, so when Officer Wilson tried to stop him—when Brown knew he had just committed a felony and was now about to be questioned by law enforcement—he decided to fight. Brown tried to take Wilson's gun, then walked away, turned back and came toward him. Fearing for his safety, Wilson shot Brown. Upon hearing that another Black man had been killed by police, the community erupted.

The Ferguson police chief, by all accounts, was a progressive, decent-hearted man who led a police department that had gotten entrenched in unfair policing both in terms of whom it was targeting and what it did to them. But he wasn't Bull Connor. And he had no knowledge of how to hold such a fraught crime scene. They should have never piecemealed out information; they should either have emphasized the robbery and their officer's safety concerns or countered the eyewitness statements with relevant facts of their own. One or the other. But they didn't know what they were doing, and small police departments often aren't accustomed to dealing with attention on that level. Instead, when protests took to the streets and the community began to be torched, the Ferguson PD and other surrounding police agencies suited up in riot gear, broke out the military hardware, and made matters so much worse.

"Hands up, don't shoot!" became a national rallying cry, a widely recognized hashtag. It fit the moment. But it wasn't the truth. When the Department of Justice investigation found the claim that Brown had his hands in the air and was shot while retreating to be false, even the activists gave it up. Less knowledgeable activists still shout the phrase, but Cornell

West and Black Lives Matter's DeRay Mckesson aren't using it, although I think they both still believe in a world in which such a cold-blooded killing could have happened, and I understand that.

What has taken hold is the popular image of cops shooting unarmed Black men in large numbers. That is a demonstrable numerical falsehood. "An Empirical Analysis of Racial Differences in Police Use of Force," a study by Harvard economics professor and MacArthur "Genius" Fellow Roland Fryer, found that white officers were less likely to use deadly physical force against African American suspects than against whites, regardless of whether they were armed or not. His hypothesis is that white officers may be more cautious because they see the possibility not just of legal consequences, but of becoming a Darren Wilson.

Professor Fryer did, however, crucially find that white officers use nonlethal force against Black and Hispanic suspects far more often than against whites. The casual use of force—making someone sit on a curb while you go through their car, rather than allowing them to stand; putting someone up against a wall—and the more intrusive, more potentially harmful uses, like putting hands on or pushing somebody against a wall, happen far more often. The question is, Why? Is it bias? Is it resistance? Is it resistance perceived by the officer because of bias? Is it actual resistance, because after generations of abuse, minority suspects are sick and tired of having been thrown against the wall and are now standing up and increasingly resisting officers? Professor Fryer found a terrible feedback loop in which each side does exactly what the other expects it to.

During my years in public service I have spent a great deal of time reflecting on the role of police in keeping America safe. Every day we confront what most of our fellow citizens fortunately don't—people's anger and hatred and vitriol and violence. Most of all we confront fear. Our neighbors', our own. One way or another, fear is at the foundation of America's discord. Americans fear the loss of our jobs, the loss of our income, our homes, our standing in the community. Some of us live in precarious neighborhoods and regularly fear for our safety and the safety of our families. Some fear random acts of violence and crime. Some fear acts of terrorism. Fear overwhelms our reason, even when—perhaps especially when—it exists wholly out of proportion to the facts. Fear of immigrants, fear of other so-called outsiders, fear of false conspiracies and fake bogeymen. Fear of the police. Sometimes fear is justified, as I well know: to have a long career in this line of work is to see on many occasions the worst side of human behavior. There have been some very bad days. The problem is that it's human nature to focus on your own fear, as opposed to understanding someone else's.

And what is the policing solution?

One thing we know for certain is that we need change. Gandhi said, "If we could change ourselves, the tendencies in the world would also change. As a man changes his own nature, so does the attitude of the world change towards him . . . We need not wait to see what others do." We can only get so far telling the other guy that he has to change first. It's up to us to step forward. I know this: Cops are born leaders. So, isn't this a place we can lead?

That might be a tough sell to many cops. They might say, "How about a little more respect for police, who have a tough job?" "How about not ignoring the police when you're given a lawful order?" Or especially, "Don't fight us when you're being placed under arrest!" And they might be right.

I have also heard from citizens in three different cities where I have run police departments; they've told me about indignities they've suffered under the authority of cops who worked for me. There are parts of any argument where both sides can be right.

All that said, I've been around a long time and I've seen a lot of change in this business. And much of the best of it started when we, the police, decided to be the change. Let's start now.

It is incumbent upon the police to change the way we operate—and we are doing so. Departments around the country are working on de-escalation techniques, on being less hands-on. The NYPD has signed a contract for all members of the department to be trained on unintentional implicit bias. "You can see it on their faces," said one of the teachers, describing many sergeants as they entered her classroom for the first time and sat, arms crossed, stone-faced. "They are waiting for us to call them racists." That recedes, she said, when she tells them "that implicit bias is a human issue, not a law enforcement issue."

Among the most recent advances is the introduction of precision policing as an organizing principle for the complexities of structuring, managing, motivating, and leading a modern police agency. Its two most important components are focused crime-and-disorder enforcement and neighborhood policing. As I've explained, they recognize that: a) the violent criminals who damage communities are a small percentage of the population; and b) working with the far larger percentage of the population who strengthen communities reinforces the fact that public safety is a shared responsibility. Precision policing depends on active collaboration between police, political leaders, and the public.

While the advent of precision policing seeks to diminish the overall number of stops, summonses, and arrests, the number of warnings and admonitions has skyrocketed, replacing enforcement actions. The cutting edge of police theory is working not to increase tension but to eliminate it. The leading police thinkers are working to stem disorder before it leads to crime itself.

None of that was in place in 2014.

Garner and Ferguson became conjoined in New York street demonstrations. Garner died in July, Ferguson happened in August. Demonstrations around each were organized in New York, but for the most part we handled them successfully, allowing protesters to express their views without their engaging in significant displays of street violence. They did not metastasize. Then, in November and December, the grand jury decisions of "no true bill" to indict the officers in either Garner or Ferguson fell within days of each other. The Black Lives Matter movement had gained attention and stature, and this time, in addition to New York, a wave of protests broke out in San Francisco, Boston, Washington, D.C., Baltimore, Minneapolis, and Atlanta.

From a cop's perspective, the demonstrations became deeply poisonous.

These were not simply generic protests against racism in America; cops felt the street actions were highly organized attacks directed personally at the police officers themselves. Cops who had extensively and actively dealt with protesters had never, at least in the memory of any man or woman on the job, been the subject of those protests individually. They were used to manning barricades, but now they faced hate-filled people screaming in their faces. The target was not the Israeli consulate or the Republican National Convention at Madison Square Garden, at which the officers had tried to maintain order. No, this vitriol was directed at them personally. Whether the officer was white or Black or brown, it didn't matter. They were the targets of the hatred.

The large majority of people in those crowds were, as Mayor de Blasio accurately described them, peaceful protesters. They were engaged citizens who decided to mass in the streets and indicate by their presence their strongly held belief that justice had been denied, that injustice had ruled far too long, that it was time these facts were recognized and things be made right, and that if they marched in solidarity and gained attention for their cause, things might change. They had every right to protest.

That was the majority of the people in the street. Many were angry, many may have disliked cops and called them "pigs" and "fascists," but the majority were not the ones making trouble. Small groups of intense activists, some from Black Lives Matter, with institutional roots in the Occupy Wall Street movement, the "Battle in Seattle," and G8 Genoa summit disruptions, made it their business to torment the police. There were professional protesters, many not from New York City.

How did we know? From checking IDs while locking them up. We locked up eighteen hundred people, and nothing that we did was unprovoked. If a crowd was marching in the street, or if they were in a park, we didn't make the mistake of arresting everyone. They had the right to protest, but also the obligation to respect other people's rights. When they blocked vehicular or pedestrian traffic, when they prevented other New Yorkers from going where they needed to go, that's when we took action.

The activists' assumption seemed to be that all police, from brass to rank and file, were integral components of a racist power structure, and therefore fair game. I was monitoring activity in Times Square the night the grand jury decided not to indict Officer Wilson, when a professional agitator hit me and my security detail with a quantity of fake blood. The operative idea seemed to be that whatever we got, we deserved.

Cops see it very differently. Stop, question, and frisk actions, for instance, are mandated by commanding officers. Cops will fight to their dying day to say, "I recorded every stop because my boss made me, but I never stopped anybody for less than true reasonable suspicion. And I never did it because I was suspicious of him or her because they were Black or Hispanic and not white. The racial disparity that exists in all those stops was a function of where I am deployed, who commits a crime in the city, and the realities of the disparities in violence among New York's ethnic groups. Not because I, Officer Smith, am a bigot."

When an officer has a crowd of two thousand people screaming at her individually, and she doesn't know where the situation is heading, the scene can be difficult. When it gets personal, it ups the ante. No distinction appeared to be made by our accusers between the NYPD's record as a department with the lowest use of force of any in the U.S., and the entire rest of the country. Every viral video that came along added another thousand people to the next demonstration on the streets of Manhattan, and this became what the *New York Post* called a "War on Cops."

The provocation was visceral. Knowing that officers were constrained by law from initiating contact without direct physical cause, demonstrators would get right up in their faces and scream or blow shrieking whistles, hoping to goad cops into reacting with force and expanding the image of enforcement lawlessness, which would then be captured on video by other demonstrators positioned for exactly that purpose. Some provocateurs cold-cocked cops, punching them in the face and then running away.

The same dynamics happened across the country. There was plenty of vitriol and plenty of video showing officers trying, to the best of their ability, to remain stoic and impassive. Most often the situations were serious, but sometimes they were funny. One video showed a demonstrator blowing a whistle in a cop's face, just blowing as loud as he could. Finally the cop reached up, grabbed the chain hanging off the whistle, yanked it out of the guy's mouth, and tossed it into the scrum of cops behind the barricade. The guy looked at him and didn't know what to do, then he just started screaming. The cop gave a little smile. The things they think they're allowed to do to a cop! It's similar to people trying to get a rise out of the Queen's Guard outside Buckingham Palace, except fueled by hatred.

Hateful provocation is extremely hard to deal with. On a human level it can be painful to neither shout back nor speak reasonably. Nothing works. In a perfect world one individual might try to reason with another, but there is no reasoning in that environment. The adrenaline is up, as is the feeling that one is about to be beset. One tries to control the fear. There is the high-intensity human instinct of fight or flight, but a cop cannot fight back and cannot flee. It is incredibly stressful. No individual should be subjected to such sustained bombardment for an entire night. Commanders learned to rotate their officers off the front line every twenty minutes.

The possibility of violence is a constant. Once a crowd becomes physically unsettled it may not be controlled without violence, and yet violence is antithetical to good policing. Police violence is evidence of unpreparedness; in establishing control, one should have all possibilities thought through. Police riots like the ones at the Democratic National Convention in Chicago in 1968 or in New York's Tompkins Square Park in 1988 reveal shoddy command and can also cause counterescalation; the next thing you know you have burning cars and overturned vehicles.

One solution is to allow the crowds to move. With or without a permit. Cops will say, "What are you doing? Listen to them, they're standing here screaming at us like I'm a murderer. Screw this! Why are we letting these guys march?!" This was a delicate job, making certain we were giving protesters enough room while containing them, and simultaneously giving the cops enough room while containing them as well. We could have flamed out like Baltimore or Ferguson, but we didn't.

The police line may have a very difficult time accepting it when the brass hits the escape valve, something Mayor David Dinkins became synonymous with when he supposedly said, "Let them vent" and allowed Crown Heights to live under siege for three days. (This is apocrypha—Mayor Dinkins did not say that and didn't intend it—but many cops believe the story.) Crowd movement functions as a safety valve, dissipating energy and not allowing a riot to explode. In the days after Ferguson, crowds marched down the street screaming, *"What do we want? Dead cops! When do we want it? Now!"* That's not apocrypha, that's on videotape, and it is beyond the pale. You shouldn't do that in this society. That is hate speech, that is riot speech, and two weeks later Rafael Ramos and Wenjian Liu were dead in a squad car, murdered by a man from Maryland.

The Black Lives Matter movement is the postmillennial version of the civil rights movement, which, at its genesis in the 1960s, focused on enforcing constitutional rights—voting rights, economic rights, political rights, and social rights—that had long been denied to the Black community. Police at that time—most visibly in the South, but in the North as well—were identified as obstructions to change, and were often rightly vilified. It became a matter of faith among some that cops were inherently and institutionally brutal, and part of the civil rights movement's success was in identifying and curtailing the use of police as agents of what they considered a corrupt state. In some segments of the modern left wing and communities of color, that faith has endured. While the policing community has gone to great lengths to examine its role in society, and has undergone tremendous growth and change in the past fifty years, many activists have been slow to acknowledge our advances. They don't see us. They think they do, but they don't.

Unfortunately, despite the many advances we have made, all too frequently bad cops do terrible things that fuel the raging racial fires. Sometimes cops make mistakes, they do stupid things. That's not what I'm talking about here. As the killings of George Floyd and Breonna Taylor can attest, terrible incidences of inappropriate use of force by police still occur. There is no explaining them; they are indefensible. Unexplainable police brutality, indifference to life—the incidents are not widespread, nor are they in any way police policy, but when they happen, with social media as an accelerant go viral, they poison every good deed and intention of the entire policing profession. They make us all seem like killers, and they contribute to the fracturing of American society.

Throughout the country, we in policing take this seriously. We are clearly using less force than we did in previous years. Our use of gunfire, for example: in New York, a city with 35,000 cops, in 2019 there were 35 incidents; back in the 1970s there were more than 900 annually.

Sadly, there is an element in the radical community that seems to relish these dreadful episodes, as if each confirms their anarchic worldview. Others use police violence to condone the use of their own. This too is unacceptable.

When I came on the Boston Police force in 1970, street demonstrations were usually convened by established organizations with specific goals and accountable leaders. They massed their forces via telephone and printed flyer, and often applied to local municipalities for permits to gather. Once on the scene, they were led by people who had a general idea of where they were going, while we cops—trained to handle exactly such situations—literally manned the barricades. Documentation of these confrontations was done by the professional press, which was generally trusted to be relatively unbiased and accurate. For better or worse, all that has changed.

The advent of social media has allowed crowds to gather almost instantaneously, including in flash mobs, with no one specifically tasked with having a strategic or tactical overview. Texting has made organizers more anonymous, wildly more tactical, with impressive powers of mobility. In years past, a crowd would head steadily to its predetermined destination.

Now, with a single text, thousands of people can take an abrupt left, and we need to be nimble in response.

In performing crowd control, when twenty thousand demonstrators were blocking major vehicle arteries, we initially had the option of having cops either walk or run along the perimeter. We found our people would wear out trying to walk with these groups. In response to lessons learned from policing the moving demonstrations that became the norm following Garner, Ferguson, and the murder of our two officers, we created a Strategic Response Group (SRG) of six hundred officers who would be highly trained in crowd control techniques, and outfitted several hundred of them with bicycles to increase their mobility and functionality. In a crowd, when trying to steer people in the desired direction, a cop on a bike is the equivalent of three cops on foot, so bicycles became force multipliers. Not only did bikes give us increased speed and the ability to head off or outflank demonstrators, they could be linked to create barriers and deny access.

The ubiquity of the cell-phone camera and viral video has encouraged not only legitimate documentation of police and crowd behavior, but also provocation for political ends. Political polarization has done away with any generally accepted version of the facts. What has caused a schism between police and Black Lives Matter? Anger at the cops. "Putting wings on pigs" was a murderer's mantra. In 2014, I needed to understand BLM but found no one to represent it.

Black Lives Matter, as it was starting to be legitimized and institutionalized, celebrated its leaderlessness like its predecessor, Occupy Wall Street. Conceptually and purposely decentralized, it emphasized the importance of local organizing over national leadership. This made our lives difficult, as it is next to impossible to negotiate with an organization when no one is there to hold up its end of a bargain. You can't have a long-term movement without leaders; that's why Occupy Wall Street collapsed. As BLM has continued to evolve, recognized leadership has begun to appear and speak on behalf of the movement.

In the arc of history, 2014 saw a transformational change in the activist movement and at the same time a transformational change in policing. This was the most significant crisis of my career. I had almost fifty years of experience. I had a tremendous team of policing professionals to help strategize and implement our actions. I had experience with communities of color in several major American cities. Could I turn this around?

I was dealing with national movements, racial perspectives, local issues, union contracts, history. We had a country in turmoil: deaths of Blacks at the hands of police; police officers assassinated for who they were—police officers.

We had cops who were under siege, feeling personally assaulted and insulted, and a union trying to present its intransigence as emotional anger, when behind the scenes its issue was about one man winning reelection and pressuring the mayor for a better contract. We had the media basically trying to get hits and sell not only newspapers but their political goals, with Rupert Murdoch's conservative *New York Post* going directly after New York City's progressive Mayor de Blasio. We had the Black Lives Matter movement trying to save lives, change the political dynamic, and gain legitimacy. We had the NYPD trying to maintain order in the belief that we really could save our city.

Dr. Martin Luther King Jr. said, "The arc of the moral universe is long but it bends toward justice." President Obama said, "I believe that. But I also believe that the arc of our nation, the arc of the world does not bend toward justice, or freedom, or equality, or prosperity on its own. It depends on us, on the choices we make, particularly at certain inflection points in history." The arc of American policing runs from catching crooks to preventing crime. From chasing criminals to preventing disorder. From performing accounting to being accountable. This was the heart and soul of that arc, and the bending of it continues.

CHAPTER 11

Implicit Bias

There are two kinds of people: those with explicit bias and those whose biases are less obvious. We are human, we all bring our cultural background with us.

Explicitly biased racist individuals are fortunately not widespread in America. There are some people who do adopt biased behavior, philosophies, and principles. For example, white supremacists and members of the Ku Klux Klan. But it is fortunately generally unacceptable to do so.

However, no one among us is without bias.

Not that most people will admit to that.

Most modern human beings, if you accuse them of being a racist, will say, "No, I'm not. I'm not a racist. I am a good, well-intentioned human being." We have all heard this before: "I have friends of different races in different cities, I can't possibly be someone who makes judgments on people based on race." As human beings, none of us believes we have biases; we reject the concept that we hold animus, hostility, or hatred toward specific groups of individuals. Particularly cops, who have been accused of it often and increasingly.

There comes a moment at any given police department when it becomes clear that implicit bias training is necessary. It may come after a bad incident that occasions community outcry and the need for a police department to do something drastic. This is training under duress, and it is happening with increased regularity.

Or more preferably, it may come with the recognition by a department's command staff that change is necessary for the organization to move forward. At its inception, implicit bias training was most often decreed or mandated by the U.S. Department of Justice during the imposition of consent decrees. Departments had to be dragged to it. But over the years, as the results have been favorable and effective, the ratio has changed and now most training is proactively arranged by innovative police leaders who want to do something before it becomes a problem.

Because of the history of policing in America and the growing concentration on the fact that Black lives matter, in 2015 we in the NYPD decided to face the issue head-on and incorporated a program designed specifically to deal with implicit bias in our ranks.

Blacks comprise approximately 13 percent of the American populace. In New York City, the Black population is a little over 24 percent, but 85 to 90 percent of the people who shoot police are Black. So there are two kinds of bias. There is conscious, unregenerate racial bias. And there is implicit bias, which says, "I don't hate anybody, but when I see a Black person coming toward me, because I know there have been a lot of robberies in my neighborhood and they have all been by male Blacks, I might cross the street." Translate that to a cop who says, "A large majority of people like me—police officers—who get shot, or shot and killed, are shot by male Blacks." Factor that into what is going through their mind when they make a stop. They may think, *Why am I treating this guy different from a white guy? My hackles are a little more up because when I look at the white guy, he is soft, he doesn't fit any of the descriptions that came over the radio tonight; he is not the character or cliché of the man who shot the last fifteen cops in New York. I go on more crime calls where the guy is described as a male*

Black. I know that every time a cop is shot, there is an eighty-five percent chance, at least in New York City, that the perpetrator is a male Black.

The flip side of that is, say, a wealthy Black entrepreneur who might get pulled over while wearing casual clothes and driving a Mercedes. He may have a different experience from the police at that stop than, let us say, a white dentist driving the same car—even though he may have fifty times more money than the dentist. The cop is calculating, "I have got a casually dressed Black guy in a Mercedes. I know the percentage of male Blacks involved in crime. I am being more cautious because I know assaults against police are rising." Part of the policing dilemma is how to adjust and soften the effect of human nature on police officers when they must calibrate their own human experiences and feelings of threat. It is wildly complicated, involving calculations few other professionals in other businesses have to make.

If you approach a training curriculum with cops and tell them, "You are a racist pig, you are the embodiment of institutional racism in this country. It's all your fault!" what do you think they're going to do? They are going to block you out, and you will never be able to change their hearts and minds.

Think about the public health education around smoking cessation. To change smokers' and presmokers' attitudes and create the idea that change was possible, health officials and the U.S. government had to show that smoking will kill you—and then hope the new knowledge would lead the public to positive behavior. That's the theoretical framework.

The NYPD curriculum was developed by Anna Laszlo and Dr. Lorie Fridell for Fair & Impartial Policing LLC. I met Anna in Boston when I was a lieutenant in charge of the Community Disorders Unit and she was director of the prosecutor-based Victim Assistance program at the county prosecutor's office during the race riots over school busing. Her husband, Gil Kerlikowske, a highly respected retired police chief and federal law enforcement official, and I have been friends for over forty years. Anna became Fair & Impartial Policing LLC's national training director and managing partner. She and its CEO, Dr. Fridell, crafted an interactive curriculum that is now used by many police departments around the country.

Primary in any discussion of bias is the need to accept that it exists. In the NYPD's implicit bias training program, race doesn't get talked about until the afternoon of the first day.

It starts with a showing of a video of Susan Boyle on *Britain's Got Talent*, singing "I Dreamed a Dream." She's the matronly looking woman who walked onstage, sang a song, and overwhelmed expectations. Those five minutes demonstrate everything you need to know about implicit bias.

Look at the audience in that video, the officers are told. Those are good people, they are not bad people. They are you and me. But if you watch their reactions—they roll their eyes when they see her walk on stage. They smirk. They didn't consciously sit there and say, "I think I'm going to roll my eyes and smirk now." It just happened. They took one look at her and made an assumption: this woman is unintelligent, she is not talented, she is a slob, she can't sing.

But of course she could sing. She could sing extraordinarily well! And the moral of the story: We all have our implicit biases.

What does the Susan Boyle story tell us about our humanity? It tells us that bias is a normal human attribute—it can be unconscious or explicit—and our implicit biases can impact our perceptions of people and our behavior toward them. That is what the audience and the judges did; they made a judgment about her based on what? On her age, on her size, on how she looked. Which had nothing to do with her talent.

In thinking about my own implicit bias I'm reminded of my Boston State College art appreciation class, in which Dr. Arvinites taught me to look beyond my preconceived notions and initial impressions in order to truly see the art and its intentions.

The next step in the training, an examination of other situations in which human beings are stereotyped, uses interactive exercises. The cops are shown a quick batch of photos of people, and told, "Give us your quick response, your gut response to them." A photo of an elderly gentleman is flashed on the screen. "Okay, really quickly, what is your immediate take on this man?" Cops shout out, "He is weak!"

"He's frail!"

"He's senile!"

Next comes a series of pictures of two young African American males wearing shorts, T-shirts, baseball caps, hoodies. "Response?"

"They're basketball players."

"They're rap artists."

"They're gang bangers."

"They're drug dealers."

The trainer, Anna Laszlo, goes back to the beginning. "Okay now, let's remember what we talked about. This elderly gentlemen." It turns out the weak, frail, senile old man is 101 years old and holds the world's record as the fastest bicyclist in his age group. The officers are shown photos of him bicycling in the Grand Prix.

The young Black men who were assumed to be gang bangers and drug dealers are actually Juilliard-trained violinists and members of the group Black Violin, who perform Bach with rap. In fact, they recorded an album called *Stereotypes*. Proved wrong but not blamed for it, the cops laugh. It is indeed laughable how far off base their presumptions turned out to be. Laughing, the cops are now more at ease.

The discussion moves to stereotyping in their professional field. It's a fun exercise in which the trainers hand out index cards with occupations like defense counsel, prosecutor, state police, and FBI, and the cops identify the stereotypes they hold of those people. Defense counsel? *Sleazy*. Lawyer? *Can't trust*. FBI agent? *Arrogant*. Some are funny, some are true, some are funny *and* true. Anna Laszlo says, "The exercise serves to demonstrate the learning point that all of us in that training room are well-intentioned people; we see ourselves as nonprejudiced, but we do stereotype people. We have just been doing it for the last ten minutes, starting with Susan Boyle! We all have implicit biases that are affecting the way we see the world." That eases the path, so to speak.

Cops are notoriously skeptical. They deal all day long with people who swear up and down that they're innocent. Even if most people they meet in the course of a workweek are entirely guilt-free, the ones who aren't—the surprises, the disappointments, the bad guys—are the most memorable. It's just the way the job works. So they walk in suspicious, but once the trainers capture their attention and they start having a good time—once they are having some fun—they start thinking, *Maybe this won't be so bad. At least I will give these people a chance.*

The bulk of the department's training relates to the decades of social science research documenting the existence of implicit bias and how it is manifest in our culture. People of all races have implicit biases. Black people have implicit biases against Black people and white people, just like everybody else. There are implicit associations we all make based on age, gender, race, ethnicity, religious affiliation. We also know that implicit biases exist in all professions; volumes of literature look at doctors, real estate agents, lawyers, judges, probation officers, prosecutors, and law enforcement. Doll studies from the 1940s, replicated in 2012, have revealed that even young children have implicit biases.

A solid chunk of the training, a good three hours of an eight-hour day, is devoted to the science of implicit bias and what the research has revealed over the decades. "I'm not making this stuff up," the trainers tell the cops. "I am showing you the research. Decades of work. It's not just you, it is all of us."

Because police officers as a profession are like Sergeant Joe Friday from *Dragnet*—"Just the facts, ma'am"—this is important and powerful and convincing. Cops don't go for the fuzzy-wuzzy. "Just lay the facts out for me and let me make my own decision based on what I make of them." That's how they investigate crime, that's how they look for evidence. So the training philosophy is to give them the evidence and let them come to the conclusions to which it clearly leads.

Officers taking the training are encouraged to read the original research. "You can get most of this stuff online. You don't like the way I explained it," says Laszlo, "you can read it yourself. You are smart. You get it. You understand science, you understand data. Here it is."

There are four types of implicit biases with direct implication for law enforcement. Throughout the process, the trainers continually ask, "What does that mean for you? What does that tell you about your decision-making?"

The first is association bias. Research in this area focuses heavily on whom we as humans associate with being a threat. Throughout culture, throughout history, it is often people with darker skin color. Arabs, African Americans, dark-skinned Latinx—decades of research reveals that the darker the skin, the more people of all skin tones implicitly associate it with menace. This was news to me.

Second is attention bias. Whom do we pay attention to first? Whom do we focus on right away? Who draws our attention in a crowd? When humans focus their attention on one thing only, they miss everything else around them.

A lot of this work is manifest in school settings, where teachers perceive children of color to be troublemakers but are in fact looking at these children before any others and expecting bad behavior. Attention bias is important to root out in police officers, because if you walk into a situation and focus immediately on a particular individual or group of individuals, you might miss the actual perpetrator.

The famous Invisible Gorilla video demonstrates this to stunning effect. The viewer is instructed to count the number of times persons wearing white pass a basketball as they move around a small room. Count the passes from people in white shirts! In concentrating on the ball and the passer, one completely misses the gorilla that walks to the center of the room, beats his chest, and exits stage right. The teaching point being made is, if as a cop your initial focus is too concentrated on one suspect or line of investigation, you may miss something; and if you miss something you are not going to be as effective in your work. Attention bias will make you ineffective—and God knows cops don't want to be ineffective.

Third is confirmation bias, looking for evidence that confirms what we think we already know. Richard Jewell and the 1996 Atlanta Olympic bombings are a case in point. The FBI was highly focused on this guy because they got some bad information and thereafter excluded everyone else from their investigation. What happened? They got the wrong guy.

Trainers then solicit information from the police officers themselves. "Talk to us about how this might impact your daily decision making. Talk to us about situations you have experienced where this could be real." The teaching point here is that making implicit associations about who is a threat versus who is not a threat can be unsafe. Anna Laszlo, for instance, is a petite blond woman given to wearing pearls. None of the officers in the room know that Anna in Her Pearls is a highly trained marksman who could be a wild card if they opposed her in a gunfight.

A detective in a Toronto training session told this story:

The Toronto Police Department had received intelligence that two or three gang members were going to be coming from Montreal to attend Caribana, a large Caribbean carnival held in the busiest retail areas in downtown Toronto, intent on carrying out retaliative shooting against some rival gang members. Caribana was a big deal; streets were closed to automobile traffic and filled with people. The Toronto police also had intelligence about who the gang members were, the kind of cars they would be driving, and the types of weapons to be used. TPD was on high alert.

A radio dispatch said that a car was approaching matching the description of the one anticipated. Surveillance indicated two men were inside who might be the people they were looking for. They pulled the car over.

Warily, the Toronto cops approached the occupants, two men and a woman. "This woman," said the man recounting the incident, "was drop-dead gorgeous. Very pregnant. Like, about ready to deliver a baby. She's sitting in the back seat. We open the trunk, and sure enough—bingo!—guns and drugs. So we know we've got the right guys. We put the two men in custody. They're in handcuffs on the street and people have gathered around and we impound the car, and the woman is hysterical. She's crying, she's hysterical, and she is unbelievably hot. She's saying, 'This is my boy-friend, what are you doing? I don't understand!'" The man telling the story—a very experienced senior detective, he has been on the force for twenty-some years—went over and tried to calm her down.

Citizens were watching now. "She was shaking," he told the class. "She said, 'I don't have any money, I have to go back to Montreal, how am I going to get back?' So I said to her, 'It's okay, your boyfriend is going no-where, we are just taking the car. We will find a way to get you back to Montreal. When they get back to the police station, we will get you back home. It's okay, stop crying.'

"So she did. She stopped shaking, she stopped crying, I calmed her down. Citizens are watching this and I said, 'Come with me.' I was going to put her in the back seat of my car. I tell her, 'I will take you back to the station, we will get you back home tonight. We promise, we will get you back home tonight.'

"So I'm about to put her in the car when I think, 'I better get an ID.' I said, 'I need identification from you. Who are you? Prove to me who you are.' She's got a big bag. You know, one of those big leather bags? She reaches in to get her identification, and what falls out but a gun. A thirty-eight.

"Right?"

In front of the classroom, he looked at Laszlo and said, "You know what? She is right about this implicit association. I almost put that woman in the back of my car. Why? Because she is gorgeous, because she is preg-nant, because she is crying, because I am trying to be Dudley Do-Right"—remember, these were Canadian cops—"and do the right thing, get her back home. I almost put her in the back of the car, and if I put her in the back of the car and she shoots me in the back of the head . . ."

Laszlo told the class, "Your implicit associations can be unsafe. In-effective."

The fourth teaching point: Policing based on biases is unjust. In this module, the trainer leads the class in a discussion of the history of policing minority communities, from slavery and the post-Civil War Reconstruction era to the role police played in Japanese internment during World War II, the Stonewall uprising, the civil rights movement, Selma, and certainly its role in international policing, including the Holocaust, and how our modern immigrant communities perceive law enforcement officers because of the experience they have had in their home countries. Think of the Laotians, Cambodians, anyone coming from a repressive society, the cops are told; they bring with them their perceptions of police that make it difficult for you as police to engage with them.

Trainers spend a fair amount of time talking about police legitimacy in a democratic society. They then focus on getting the cops to think about why they became police officers in the first place.

Ask young cops why they decided to go into law enforcement. It is not to hurt people, it is to make their communities better. Having now learned about the science of implicit bias and how humans can be impacted, and having talked about this concept of policing a democratic society and the importance of police legitimacy, at this point in the curriculum they are probably thinking, *Okay, I have motivation for why I need to do better: policing based on biases can be unsafe for me and the people around me; I can end up being ineffective, and then I am unjust and I have broken my oath of office. I've got to get my act together.* Hopefully at this point that's what they're thinking.

The next, very interactive segment is meant to develop skills for managing their newly acknowledged bias. The conclusion of modern social psychology research is that total elimination is not realistic; you probably won't eliminate all your biases. It's possible, but highly unlikely. However, we as human beings can train ourselves to reduce and manage bias. The trainers present the evidence and identify mechanisms for bias reduction.

The first mechanism is contact theory, the work of Yale psychologist Jack Dovidio, which holds that if you as a human being have contact, either professionally or personally, with people who are different than you, not only will your implicit biases about that person as an individual be reduced, the biases and stereotypes you have of the group that person represents will also be affected.

Think of the transition made in the past twenty years around gay and lesbian people and same-sex marriage. In my parents' generation the response would have been, "What? Who? That's disgusting. I don't know anybody who does that. What are you talking about?" But as time marched on and gay and lesbian individuals became our neighbors and friends—we go to church together, we know them as people—what do human beings do? They say, "You know, Russell is a really great guy. I don't care if he is married to John. They are fine." Implicit bias has been reduced about that individual, and over time, around the group they represent.

A cousin of contact theory is counterstereotyping, which occurs when an individual sees and engages with people who are the antithesis of the widely held assumptions about their group. Black accountants, Latinx opera singers, Jewish basketball players—name the group and the stereotype, flip it 180 degrees. Counterstereotyping is critically important; it is the theoretical framework of high-quality police use-of-force, Shoot/Don't Shoot training.

In the old days, when young cops were taken to the firing range and told to shoot the bad guy when he popped up, the correct target may have been a black silhouette of a person, or sometimes one with a big sombrero and mustache like the widely seen image of Pancho Villa. It wasn't a white accountant with a tie. They may have not known it, but for twenty, thirty, forty years, police training may have been subconsciously priming recruits to view and treat Black and Hispanic men as dangerous and legitimate targets.

Modern high-quality Shoot/Don't Shoot training is now videoed, of course, but more importantly, randomized. The threat holding the gun could just as likely be a little old white lady, could be Anna in her pearls, could be a Black kid, could be you, could be a white guy, could be anybody. It is exactly the randomness of the assailant that reinforces the concept of counter-stereotyping. Anna in her pearls, for example, would be a counterstereotype to somebody who is dangerous and about to kill you.

A third mechanism is perspective taking. Empathy. The imperative to walk around in someone else's shoes, to push yourself to view the world through someone else's life experience and perspective.

For example, in the training the cops are told to imagine how a Holocaust survivor perceives Germans. Anna Laszlo's parents, who emigrated to this country during the Hungarian Revolution, don't particularly care for the Russians, for instance. This is not rocket science, it is just human nature.

Today, in our discussions around race and America's history of racial tensions, why is it a huge surprise that African Americans, young and old, are distrustful around policing? Look at the history.

The final mechanism is called blurring the lines. It involves creating activities for officers and the public during which each can discover the common elements that unite them rather than set them apart.

All the NYPD's implicit bias instructors are either active or former police officers. One in particular, I'll call him Whaley, fit the stereotype: Army butch haircut, thick neck, thick body, pink; just a pink guy. High voice, thick accent. "If you opened the dictionary to 'good ol' Southern boy,'" says Laszlo, "this guy would pop up."

As Whaley tells the story, he was the training lieutenant at the academy for a Southern police department when his chief made an agreement with the International Association of Chiefs of Police to host a group of Iraqi law enforcement officials for two weeks, who as part of their reform efforts in Iraq, were coming to this country to study American policing. The chief told Whaley, "You've got to host these people, and part of hosting is not only are they embedded in the police department for two weeks, but you have to take them home at night and entertain them and have them over for dinner and treat them like you'd want to be treated."

Whaley said, "No fucking way."

Whaley was a decent sort; this seemed out of character. But it turned out that while in the army, one of his sons had been stationed in Iraq, and another was in Baghdad as they spoke. Whaley told his boss, "These people blew up New York. I'm not doing it. I'm not doing it."

His chief forced him to take the assignment—because the chief had that power—and Whaley found himself hosting a group of Iraqi law enforcement officials and taking two of them home to dinner. You can imagine how uncomfortable that was. But, said Whaley, "I spent two weeks with them, and over a period of time, here's what I learned that you need to know: I learned that they were just as worried and sick over their sons being on battle lines as I was. One of them had had a son killed during the war. They wanted to improve their police department to be just like us. At the end of the day," he told the gathered cops, "I realized that there was more that joined us together than separated us."

It sounds kind of squishy, but when a Southern good ol' boy says that to a group of Southern cops, it's hard to deny.

The NYPD training sessions offer two strategies for managing bias. One is to thwart the identification of the stereotype. A very simple litmus test to be used when encountering someone outside one's normal realm of contacts: Ask yourself, "Would I be treating this person this way but for the fact that they are _____ ?" Fill in the blank. Could be better, could be worse. "Would I be treating Anna Laszlo kindly and with respect if she weren't a little skinny blond older lady?" "Would I be treating Jamaal Smith harshly if he weren't a young, tall, Black kid with dreads?" If the answer is "Yes, I am treating this person differently," then you need to regroup, because those are your biases kicking in.

A law enforcement example:

A white woman in a predominantly white neighborhood calls 911 and says there is a car sitting in front of her house, been there for about an hour, with a Black man behind the wheel. She is concerned.

The trainers made up the specific details in this case, but this is a common occurrence. The caller has not identified any criminal activity, only that she's anxious. Given this, the cops will likely say, "There is really no criminal activity here, so what am I going to do? The person has a right to be in a car." Working in small groups, the officers are instructed to provide three courses of action, and to analyze the pros and cons of each.

Option One: See if you can ascertain more information about the man in the car and consider what that tells you. Call the dispatcher back and have the dispatcher call the complainant—the white woman—and say, "What else did you observe? Did you observe a person slumped over?"

Some cops will say, "What if he's just stopped? He's looking at a map, or he's lost and looking for directions, or he is waiting for a friend across the street?" Others will say, "What if he is injured? What if he had a heart attack or a health issue? Don't you think that we should check on him? What if?"

Option Two: Either walk or drive by and see if there is anything wrong. If not, be on your merry way.

Option Three: Approach the man—nicely, courteously—and say, "Excuse me, sir, can I help you? Is there something wrong?" And see what happens.

All three options provoke a robust back-and-forth among the officers. After much discussion the trainer tells them there is really no right or wrong answer in this case scenario; it is ambiguous. If you approach the car, even if you approach the car with all the tact in the world, cops are taught to be aware that this may not be the first time this week, or perhaps even today—and certainly not in his lifetime—that this person of color has been approached by a police officer, no matter how courteously, just because he was sitting in a car.

So what are we trying to do here? We have talked about how training builds on itself, how you reinforce a concept and move forward, that this is how adults learn. Under ideal circumstances they now have empathy for this man. You don't pull him out of his vehicle and taze him. You don't shoot him where he sits.

And what about that caller?

What have police departments taught American citizens, especially since 9/11? "If you see something, say something." And we will come. The cavalry will arrive. So there is sympathy for this woman as well; she thought she saw something and she's doing what she was told. She could be a Karen, if you will, but it's too early to tell for sure. Our training says beware of other people's bias, it can put you in a box. Beware of profiling by proxy.

This is when an officer's analytical, intervention, and communication skills gain heightened importance. Approach people with empathy, and if you have to say to the gentleman in the car, "I am here because we got a call from someone on the street saying they were concerned," do that. Have a conversation, understand that you may be hitting a nerve, understand the effect of your presence, guard against belligerence.

These are skills to develop: reduce your biases, manage your biases, beware of other people's biases.

Skill number four: slow things down.

Research makes very clear that time and distance are a police officer's friend. If you can back away, you allow yourself the opportunity to talk people down from a ledge. This is important for mental health issues—lifesaving to the officer and the individual.

In three timed, seven-minute segments, trainers describe this scenario:

Mr. Aktan lives in a tough Seattle, Washington, neighborhood filled with immigrants from the Caribbean, he among them. There have been robberies. Plainclothes officers patrolling the neighborhood see Mr. Aktan on a porch. He is pacing and looking around.

The trainers stop the narrative. "Okay," they tell the cops in the classroom, "you now have three minutes, what are you going to do about Mr. Aktan? What's going on here?" The officers divide into small groups, talk about it, and report out for discussion.

Most often they report, "There is nothing happening here, right?"

What is Mr. Aktan doing?

"I don't know, maybe he is waiting for the pizza guy to deliver."

"It's dark, so he probably knows that there have been robberies in his neighborhood and that stuff, so maybe he is just walking out to make sure everything is okay."

"It's a nice night, he's just enjoying his porch."

"He's just walking back and forth. Maybe he's waiting for somebody in the house to come out. His girlfriend is in there, they're going out and he's just waiting for her. Women are always late."

It's a fun conversation. They say all kinds of fun stuff there.

Then they answer the question, What are you going to do?

In ten years of running training sessions, Laszlo has never had someone kill Mr. Aktan at this point. They're all going to just sit and wait. They're just going to watch, maybe drive around the neighborhood again. Nothing suspicious is going on here, they are just going to sit around and see what happens—or see if *anything* happens. They're just going to wait.

In section two, the trainer says the cops now decide to get out of the car and approach Mr. Aktan to talk to him. As they are approaching the porch, Mr. Aktan sees them coming and starts backing toward the door.

In the class discussion the cops ask, "Why are they getting out of their car? They are placing themselves in officer-induced jeopardy. What is wrong with these people?!"

The trainer then asks, "Why is Mr. Aktan backing up?"

"Well, he knows about the armed robberies that were committed by a group of white kids. These guys are in plain clothes, they're in jeans and sweats, and they are all white. Maybe he thinks he's going to get robbed."

In section three, the cops facing Mr. Aktan are saying, "Stop, police!" He is fiddling for his keys. "Why isn't Mr. Aktan responding to 'Stop, the police!'?" the trainer asks.

"Well, he could be deaf."

"Maybe he's not American. Maybe he's from one of those Caribbean countries. He doesn't understand English."

Or, "He understands the word 'police,' and if he's an immigrant, in his country the police are not your friends."

Laszlo is pleased with the responses. The program goes out of its way to reinforce its learning techniques and she hears that the cops have absorbed the lesson they had been taught earlier, in module two, concerning immigration and the perception of police and why people might not want to engage with them.

She tells them, "It took you seven minutes real time to get to this point." Actually, including the reports and debriefings and discussion, it's more like forty-five minutes have gone by. "You had time to stop, slow things down in segment one, think about what you were seeing, right? Section two, you wonder about getting out of the car. Section three, you consider reasons Mr. Aktan might not be responding to you. The scenario takes seven minutes. In real life, that was Amadou Diallo. What you experienced took seven seconds from the time they rolled up to the time they shot him. In seven seconds Mr. Diallo was dead."

Amadou Diallo was a Guinean immigrant shot and killed by four plainclothes NYPD officers outside his apartment in the Bronx in 1999.

The entire class says, *"What?!"*

The point is never to permit that to happen again, to train NYPD officers to make the right decisions all the time.

We also recognize that cops don't always have time. As one trainer said, "If it's a gun day, it's a gun day." If a gun is pointed at you, this is not the time to be having a conversation. There are gun days and there are not gun days.

There is a video of a Texas trooper who responds to an elderly man, probably in his seventies, on a car stop. The driver comes out of his vehicle and points a sawed-off shotgun at the trooper at point-blank range. The trooper walks toward the man and yells to him, four times, "Put the gun down, put the gun down . . . !" The driver has his finger on the trigger and is pointing dead center at this cop. The cop says to him, "Put the gun down, put the gun down!" and the man fires.

What was the trooper thinking? Laszlo says, "If somebody was six feet away from you with a firearm pointed at you, and he had his finger on the trigger and you had a weapon, I mean what would you do? I would shoot the guy. It's not the time for conversation. You've got the gun to my head and I ain't talking."

It's important to be realistic with cops. All cops know that not every situation is avoidable. You don't want to kill someone, but if it's not avoidable it's unrealistic to think otherwise.

We don't know what was going on in the trooper's mind. Did he keep yelling "Put the gun down, put the gun down!" because the driver was elderly and maybe the officer made an implicit association that such an elderly man wouldn't pull the trigger? We do not know. We also do not know if, faced with a young Black kid, he would he have said, "Put the gun down" four times before firing. We do not know the answer, but it is a fair question to ask.

Trainers have stopped using the video because it is too difficult to watch. You can hear the trooper gurgling as he dies. But when trainers say, "If it's a gun day . . ." that's what they mean.

The foundation for implicit bias training is science, but courses vary depending upon what is needed to best improve the department. It stands to reason; one would teach a command-level person different skills than one would teach a street cop. There is specialized training for patrol officers, supervisors, midlevel managers, executives; for command level, which is all about strategic planning and organizational changes that need to take place; for community leaders and for civilians in law enforcement agencies. A seven-part strategic planning program for command-level implicit bias training, for instance, covers policy development, recruitment and hiring strategies, accountability, outreach to diverse communities, and measurement, with a booster in which trainers go back to those departments after a period of time to evaluate progress in all elements.

Skill five: Know your agency's policy on bias policing. Most police agencies in the United States have policies that describe when race, ethnicity, and other demographics can be used in law enforcement decision making. To make absolutely certain the officers understand specifically what they are allowed to do, implicit bias trainers dissect the policy of the specific organization that has hired them.

Skill six: Analyze your decisions with a fair and impartial policing lens.

You, as a sergeant, catch a call alleging unfair enforcement around hip-hop bars. The citizenry is complaining that your officers are using aggressive tactics when responding to hip-hop bars and not using the same tactics when responding to country music bars in nearby neighborhoods. So what do you do?

Use your data. Are the local hip-hop bars more dangerous than country music bars? How do you find out? You might check emergency room records at local hospitals to see the range of injuries, if any, resulting from each. You might take a look at the history of other calls to service to this particular set of bars. Are there times of day that are more problematic than others? What does the comparison look like?

With the facts in hand, how do you then approach the community about explaining your enforcement? If your data does, in fact, show a higher number of shootings at these hip-hop bars, and people have been in the hospital at a higher rate, and the calls for service are heavily weighted to one type of bar as opposed to the other, and this is problematic, how do you share and use that data to support any actions that you are taking? Just because the citizenry thinks that you are unfair does not mean that you actually are. Does the aggressive policing really signify unfair treatment or does it reveal a department that is truly focused upon maintaining community safety?

If the facts show that the complainants are correct, that policing surrounding the hip-hop bars has been unequal, more aggressive, and influenced by bias, then you need to communicate that to the citizenry. How do cops most effectively apologize? What actions can be taken to correct the problem?

Then the key question: How to monitor the results. How do you know whether the training has worked?

Posttraining evaluations are undertaken for a variety of reasons. First, to find what approaches are most effective. Second, to find which trainers are doing a good job.

Overwhelmingly, officer response is along these lines of, "Seventeen years on the job and this is probably the best thing I have ever had. Where were you guys in 2005 when I had internal affairs complaints?" Or, and this happens often, "I was forced to go to this training, I didn't want to go, I thought this would be awful. . . . This is actually pretty good."

There is no talk in implicit bias training about the issues, for instance around institutional racism; the talk is about history. But the program is entirely fact based, and history is facts. It is a fact that police officers enforced sundown town laws. It is a fact that cops escorted Japanese people into the internment camps. It is a fact that in Germany, the police were collaborators with the Nazis. Fact. Fact. Fact. Unemotional fact, followed by practical skills based on case scenarios to which cops can relate. There is not a place in the country that hasn't received a 911 call from Gladys, the woman with a Black man sitting in a car in front of her house. *There is a Black person walking down the street. There are two Black kids in Starbucks having a conversation.* Every cop can relate to that, whether in a small town or in a big city. There are now memes—BBQ Becky, Permit Patty, Pool Patrol Paula, and the ubiquitous Karen—about the calls they have to answer.

Implicit bias training is starting to expand into other criminal justice agencies. The Florida Department of Juvenile Justice commissioned a customized training for juvenile detention and probation officers. The Oakland County, Michigan District Attorney's Office asked proactively to bring implicit bias training to prosecutors. One of the advances being worked on is a plan that allows police academies throughout the country to infuse the principles, competencies, and philosophy throughout Academy curriculum as part of the first socialization for the young men and women entering the profession. Whether they are making a traffic stop, handcuffing a suspect, going on a domestic violence call, they will look at it through a new policing lens: "Would I be treating this person this way but for the fact that they are _____?" "Am I doing anything to make myself unsafe, ineffective, and unjust?"

The transformation is far from complete. The questions remain: How do we make that happen? How do we begin this process of socialization in a positive environment? How do we educate our young police officers that this is just the way that we do business in policing? That this is what a good cop is?

At the same time, it must be said, there is no replacement for careful and professional recruitment and selection of police personnel. Police officers must be held to the highest standards. As Robert Peel has written: *The police are the public and the public are the police.* Implicit bias training does not prevent murder. It cannot make an honorable human being out of someone who is not one. It is incumbent upon the police department to staff itself with the members of the public who deserve the position.

Some cops should not be cops. There has been a torrent of examples of bad cops doing bad things, which has led to the national outcry against police officers and policing in general. While granting that horrific individual acts of cruelty and abuse have occurred far more often than is acceptable, I think the passionate hatred of police and policing is over the line. And when the retaliation against police officers gets violent, no matter how historically understandable the righteous rage, that is not only unacceptable but illegal. You can't stone cops and firebomb their squad cars and think, one, that it is acceptable because of past grievances, and two, that you're going to get away with it.

Unlike with other professions in which bad people do terrible things, we have a tendency in our society to paint all police officers with one brush. But there are corporate executives who milk their companies of millions of dollars and engage in stock fraud; this doesn't define every corporate executive as a thief. There are priests who rape children, yet it is accepted that not every clergyperson is a pedophile. There are major league baseball players who cheat to win, but it doesn't mean that every major leaguer is a cheat.

We are in the midst of a flood of publicized policing killings. But there are approximately eight hundred thousand police officers working at eighteen thousand police departments in America. If you believe what you hear in the streets, cops are all violent criminals who will abuse you as soon as look at you. The acronym ACAB—All Cops Are Bastards—has gained currency. Broad-based hatred for police is now a fundamental tenet of some radicals' philosophy. Individuals among them who know cops say, "I'm not actually talking about the people; I know there are nice police officers who walk old ladies across the street. But they are all part of a system that has no redeeming features and must be abolished. And that's what makes them bastards." Calls for defunding and even disbanding the police are based on such accusations, and there is nothing police can say or do to counter such fundamentalist absolutism. No matter that statistics prove them wrong, the community is now doing exactly what we train our officers and officials not to do: stereotyping and lumping all people of one background into the same group. This is a component of the modern tragedy.

CHAPTER 12

Terrorism: Homegrown and Imported

When the airplanes hit the Twin Towers on 9/11/2001, the loss of life was terrible, the need for national protection against the recurrence of such devastating terror was clear, and the prioritization for the funding for local police was dramatically changed.

For the better part of fifteen years thereafter, a significant part of law enforcement funding coming out of Washington was intended to support counterterrorism initiatives. This was due to the awareness that if there were to be another terrorist attack in the United States, the smallest unit of government was likely going to handle it. The theory held that, whether engaging with armed terrorists assaulting a synagogue or a monument or responding to an explosion, whoever arrived first on the scene should be outfitted with matériel and expertise to handle the situation. Heavy-duty equipment and training were therefore needed to facilitate departments from different jurisdictions working together, and their acquisition was an acceptable reason to provide federal funds. Hundreds of millions of dollars went there. For better or worse, this also accounts for the increasing militarization of many local police forces.

When I was LAPD chief, the Rollin' 60s were a set of the Crips, the street gang that had terrorized the citizens of Los Angeles for more than thirty-five years. A set, not a sect. A sect usually refers to a religion; a set is gang talk for a franchise. The Rollin' 60s were formed in the late 1970s as a set of the Crips.

Why "Rollin'"?

Los Angeles street gangs have gone mobile. In the seventies, gang members used to hang out on the street. Street corners were where the action took place, where gangs gathered and did their business. But times change. Now they're all in cars. That's how they commit a lot of their crimes— drive-by shootings, transportation of narcotics—in vehicles. That's how they roll.

Why "60s"?

The numbered blocks in Greater Los Angeles begin at First Street near Dodger Stadium and Chavez Ravine and run south down to 125th Street at Imperial Highway. Over the years, the Sixties, from Sixtieth to Sixty-Ninth Streets in South Los Angeles, have become extremely infested by gangs. There are Rollin' 20s, Rollin' 30s, Rollin' 40s—they're all tough neighborhoods and all tough crews—but among the most violent of Los Angeles street gangs are the Rollin' 60s. They perform mayhem.

Kevin James was in the Rollin' 60s. In the 1990s, James was caught, convicted, sentenced, and sent to California state prison for assault with a deadly weapon. He shot someone. In prison, James professed a religious conversion.

It's not unusual for inmates to align themselves with powerful organizations in prison for protection. There is safety in numbers, and prisoners don't want to get singled out, isolated, and pounced upon by inmates in larger groups. For years, internal prison order has been maintained by the Mexican Mafia, the Black Guerrilla Family, the Aryan Brotherhood. Now, increasingly, there is a growing prison population converting to Islam. The

Nation of Islam, the organization led by Louis Farrakhan, is a prime player in this movement. Whether this is theological enlightenment or physical self-preservation is open to interpretation. No doubt many of these jailhouse conversions are legitimate. We do not know how many are not. (Law enforcement does try to infiltrate these gangs in order to blunt their force. However, prison inmates have First Amendment rights, and the right to express one's religion is very important, which makes the infiltration and monitoring of these new Muslim groups difficult.)

Kevin James converted to Islam.

James was a charismatic man. Big guy. Buffed out, of course, in the way prisoners get when they hit the weights zealously. Shaved head. Tattoos. After several years he became discontented with what was being preached and practiced in prison. While it consistently condemned the U.S. government, and its leaders often spouted virulent anti-Semitism, the Nation of Islam publicly opposed terrorism. Kevin James decided the Nation of Islam wasn't radical enough.

In 1997, Osama bin Laden came on the international radar screen preaching jihad, singling out the United States for attack. That year, at the California Correctional Institution in Tehachapi, James aligned himself with bin Laden's radical philosophy and formed his own sect, calling it Jam'iyyat Ul-Islam Is-Saheeh (JIS), the Assembly of Authentic Islam. He was its imam.

James was an intelligent and literate man and a gifted organizer. He took on several Muslim names, including Shakyh Shahaab Murshid and Abdul-Wahid Ash-Sheena. As leader of JIS, he wrote and distributed what he called its "protocols": All JIS members were required to take an oath of obedience to James personally, to follow his direction without question. They would swear not to disclose the existence of JIS. They would swear to obey the "90-Day Rule," to communicate with James at least once every ninety days. And according to these protocols it was the duty of JIS members to kill "infidels"—nonbelievers, enemies of Islam—including the people in the U.S. government and Jewish and non-Jewish supporters of Israel.

They would commit jihad against the United States. They pledged "loyalty until death by martyrdom."

Through force of proselytization and personality James began to attract a following, and that following began to attract the attention of prison officials. Concerned that JIS espoused such a violent interpretation of the Koran, they scattered its followers to other facilities in hopes of squelching the movement. All this did was send a cadre of radical Muslim recruiters all across the state prison system. In essence, the prison system spread the word. They are still trying to identify all the men James recruited.

One of the inmates recruited by James, then twenty-nine years old, was Levar Haney Washington. The two men met in Folsom prison in Sacramento, where the twenty-five-year-old Washington was doing ten years for assault with a deadly weapon. Washington was even more tatted up than James. He had "Rollin' 60s" tattooed across his forehead, though after his conversion he wore a do-rag to cover it. (Islam forbids tattooing; it is considered mutilation of the body.) Another charismatic guy, Washington gave his oath to James and became a member, taking the names Numair and Abdur Rahman.

Washington was due to be paroled in 2004, and James gave him a mission: Go into the outside world and recruit five people into JIS. Not just anybody; these new recruits were to be from outside the prison system, without felony convictions, people who could buy weapons without raising suspicion among parole agents or law enforcement—people who just wouldn't show up on the radar. James also instructed Washington to acquire two firearms with silencers and appoint one of his recruits to find contacts for explosives or learn to make bombs that could be activated from a distance. When Washington had established his cadre and acquired his ordnance, James would tell them what to do. The time was approaching for jihad.

Washington left prison and was paroled back into Los Angeles. He started attending the Jamat-E-Masijidul Islam mosque in Inglewood, a bordering city, which also bordered on the area in which the Rollin' 60s had their ground zero. At the mosque, Washington wasted no time in forming a prayer group. The first to join him was twenty-one-year-old Gregory Vernon Patterson.

Patterson, who took the name Bilal, came from a middle-class, fairly conservative Catholic background. He took classes at El Camino College in Torrance and Cal State Northridge and still lived at home with his parents. His father, Rodney, was a professor at Los Angeles Harbor College, where his mother, Abbie, was an administrator. Patterson had attended Junipero Serra High School, a Catholic school in Gardena, whose alumni include baseball's Barry Bonds and football's Tom Brady. The school's vice principal called him "an overachieving nerd."

Patterson was a new convert to Islam and was studying the Koran. Washington, who had studied under James, didn't tell him they were going to commit jihad; he talked about learning Islam in a more pure form than the mosque's imam was providing. Patterson was keen to pursue this new passion and the two of them started praying together.

Patterson was already studying one-on-one with Hammad Riaz Samana, also twenty-one, a permanent U.S. resident who had been born in Pakistan and who spoke, read, and wrote Arabic. Samana was a studious and mild-mannered young man whose first language was Urdu. A clerk at a Barnes & Noble, he attended Santa Monica College, played cricket, and ran cross-country. Samana was, in turn, studying with the Jamat-E-Masijidul mosque's imam Hashim Ansari, to memorize the Koran in Arabic in order to recite it verbatim, with proper pronunciation, cadence, and rhythm, during Ramadan. This was orthodoxy by rote; they didn't discuss the meaning of the words. Samana, who had attended the mosque for two years, was about a quarter of the way through.

Washington and Patterson recruited Samana into the prayer group and slowly, over the course of three or four months, Washington converted them both to an extreme fundamentalism. He didn't have much success recruiting others, but Patterson and Samana were convinced. Such were Washington's powers of persuasion that they joined JIS and pledged themselves to James, whom they had never met, as their spiritual leader.

Then the word came down. In a written message smuggled out of prison by a third party, Kevin James outlined his plan: Washington, Patterson, and Samana were to attack the United States and the infidels, the prominent Jewish presence in Los Angeles. The jihad was on. That's all he gave them. He left the details to his crew.

Washington, as crew chief, started delegating missions to Patterson and Samana. One of these missions was to gather money; they'd need funds to pursue their goals. He sent Patterson, who had no felony record, no tattoos, and a tidy, middle-class appearance, into a gun shop, where he ordered an AR-15 assault rifle. In California, there's a ten-day waiting period before you can get a handgun, rifle, or firearm of any kind. You go through a background check. No problem for Patterson. So it was in the works, they were going to get an AR-15. He went out and bought a Mossberg 12-gauge shotgun. Just went to a Big 5 Sporting Goods store and bought it. They needed cell phones, so Patterson went and signed up for a group plan. Three phones came with that, so each of them had a unit. Ten days passed. Authorization went through. Now they had weapons and a communications system.

So Patterson and Samana were driving around Southern California in the spring of 2005 with this shotgun in the trunk of their car. They knew they were going to commit robberies, they just didn't know what kind yet. It was late at night and they saw, well, the only things open late at night are gas stations. So they began taking off gas stations.

At first, Samana drove and Washington and Patterson did the robbing. They cruised until it got late, then pulled in, walked up to the guy behind the register, pointed the Mossberg in his face, took his money—usually around three of four hundred dollars—and drove on down the road.

Over the course of about three months the trio robbed a couple of dozen gas stations along a thirty-mile stretch all through the South Bay and into northern Orange County. They hit Los Angeles, Torrance, Playa del Ray, Bellflower, Pico Rivera, Walnut, Orange, Playa Vista, and Fullerton. Never came close to being caught. This was too easy.

Samana, the student, went online and researched the addresses of army recruiting centers and installations, Los Angeles synagogues, the Israeli Consulate, and El Al Airlines. He researched events scheduled to be held in the Jewish community, and together the three men put together a coordinated plan to attack synagogues on the High Holy Days, on the first night of Yom Kippur, calculated to kill as many Jews as possible. For maximum symbolism and publicity value, the attacks against the army would take place on or around September 11. These plans were detailed for maximum carnage. That was the point: many infidels were going to die. And forget being martyrs; Washington, Patterson, and Samana plotted their getaway so they could attack again and again. Not to be outdone by his coconspirators, Samana went to a park and practiced his marksmanship.

But Patterson and Samana weren't career criminals and they got careless. One night during a robbery in Torrance, Patterson dropped his cell phone. The Torrance Police Department, responding to the robbery call, picked it up. "Guy dropped his cell phone." Usually gang members deal exclusively in disposable phones, and the detectives on the case had no reason to think this would be any different. The phone could have been stolen; though remote, that was a possibility. Still, they conducted the follow-up. It was just normal police work. To their surprise there was a name on the account: Gregory Patterson.

The Torrance Police ran a background check and found Patterson had no criminal record. They got his Department of Motor Vehicles file and found out where he was living. Patterson had moved out of his parents' house and was living with Washington on Twenty-Seventh Street in South LA. Genius that he was—or more likely, upstanding citizen with no background in deceit—Patterson had given that address to the phone company for billing. They got his photograph from his driver's license.

The Torrance Police sat on the house where the phone came back to. They hadn't been there long before they saw Patterson and Washington leave and get into a car. The detectives followed them to a gas station in northern Orange County, where the two committed another robbery. It didn't take much to arrest and take them into custody.

This was a big deal to the Torrance Police. They had snapped a long string of robberies. They had the shotgun, they had the guys, they went back to the Torrance station and began to write their reports. One of the detectives said, "Why don't we get a search warrant and go search this guy's residence."

"Why?" said his partner. "We've got the gun, we've got the money, we've got them. We're on overtime, why should we do that?"

"Well, we might find evidence of other robberies and make the case stronger."

What the hell. They wrote a search warrant, got it, went to Twenty-Seventh Street and served it, and walked in. What they found was a big surprise.

Handwritten documents. Phrases like "Jihad," "War against the United States," "War against the infidels." And among the papers was a sheet with the words "Modes of Attack" across the top. This was a two-page list. On it were the Los Angeles addresses of army recruiting stations, the El Al ticket counter at Los Angeles Airport, the Israeli Consulate, and several synagogues in West Los Angeles. And beside each address were check marks saying the locations had been surveilled, along with scribblings describing the results of that surveillance.

The Torrance cops called a detective from their department who was assigned to the Joint Terrorism Task Force, the FBI multiagency group set up to monitor just such activity. The JTTF responded immediately. They examined the documents and said, "Yeah, this is serious. There's something going on here besides gas station robberies." The LAPD is also part of the JTTF; our force was called in and our intelligence analysts determined, in concurrence with the FBI, that what had been discovered looked indeed like an operational terrorist cell.

Patterson wouldn't say anything. They had him in the Torrance Police Department interrogation room for several hours that night and again the next morning, but despite the fact that he was the one without the criminal record, the one most likely to be shown leniency, he wouldn't roll over on anyone.

Washington, on the other hand, felt no such devotion. He was a convicted felon, a two-time loser, he was facing life in prison. He needed a way out. He asked for a deal but he got none. With no concrete offer from his interrogators, Washington admitted and laid out in full detail a conspiracy to bomb government offices and kill civilians.

Why would he do that?

Most police work is successful because we are not dealing with the most intelligent sector of society. Despite his pledge of martyrdom to James, Washington was ultimately looking out for himself. In his mind, the best way to do that was to come clean and try to lay as much of the criminal activity off on other people. He knew that if he was going to get a deal he would have to be the first one to talk.

So Washington began to talk.

He told the investigators about Samana. Until that moment Samana had been completely unknown to police; this was the first time his name had come up. Samana wrote the Modes of Attack document, Washington said. He quickly gave up Samana's address and physical description. Washington also gave up Kevin James.

At that point the LAPD started rounding up everybody.

They had set up 24/7 surveillance on Samana's home. Their detectives saw a man who looked like Samana leave the house carrying a black plastic bag, cross the street, and toss it in a dumpster, then get into a moving van and start driving east. They tailed him.

A check of the van's license plate led the police to a car rental company. A check of their records revealed that Hammad Samana had indeed rented the van and that his destination was Florida. When Samana crossed state lines they let him go; interviews with his relatives had revealed that he was legitimately moving some furniture down to Florida for a friend and that he was expected back. Plus, during one of his rest stops the detectives placed a tracking device on the truck. Samana didn't know it but he was under surveillance at all times.

The black plastic bags yielded a bonanza: a stack of jihadist literature, more copies of the Modes of Attack, and letters from Kevin James.

Rather than arrest Samana, when he returned from Florida the JTTF invited him in for an interview. Samana was aware that Patterson and Washington were in custody, that's why he was trying to get rid of the material; sooner or later he knew the law would come knocking on his door and he didn't want anything connecting himself to them.

The detectives told him they were conducting an investigation and needed to talk to him about it. He came in.

Why? It is very common for investigators to simply telephone someone they believe has been involved in a crime and ask him to appear. It's an unsettling call to receive but if the suspect thinks the police don't know the full extent of his activities, often he will come in voluntarily. If he doesn't, he knows the police will think he's involved and will look at him even more closely. Short of running, he really doesn't have much choice.

So Samana drove to the FBI office in Westwood, where investigators sat down and started the interrogation. At first he denied any part in the conspiracy. But when the detectives pulled out the Modes of Attack, written in his own hand, it was like flipping a switch. Samana admitted to everything. Agents then examined his computer hard drive and saw the websites he had been accessing. Samana waived his rights and admitted to the whole thing.

In October 2005, Washington, Patterson, Samana, and James were indicted in federal court for crimes including conspiracy to levy war against the United States government through terrorism, conspiracy to kill members of the United States government uniformed services, conspiracy to kill foreign officials, conspiracy to possess and discharge firearms in furtherance of crimes of violence, and aiding and abetting. They were all convicted. For his crimes Washington was sentenced to twenty-two years in prison, Patterson got twelve. Kevin James received a thirty-one-year sentence; Samana got seventy months.

James had contact with many people in the prison system, and we continued to pursue them, slowly vetting the list to see who was still in prison and who had gotten out and could do damage, who had had contact with fundamentalist Islamic organizations that might take terrorist action— and the spiderweb of people with whom each of James's contacts had had contact. It was very likely that there were other Washingtons, Pattersons, and Samanas out there. Homegrown terrorism is like a tumor that is metastasizing. We needed to cut it out.

The Torrance case served as a wake-up call for federal and local law enforcement. We needed—and continue to need—to look not only to Pakistan or Afghanistan or Somalia as sources of terror, but to America as well. Our prisons, our streets. While I was there, the LAPD beefed up its liaison to prison intelligence. Later, the FBI and other agencies increased their awareness as well. This will help America's streets in many ways; as cells are unearthed, not only will major terrorist activities be prevented but our investigations will disrupt others before they become operational.

How? In London, Metropolitan Police Commissioner Sir Ian Blair established six-person community liaison teams in each of the city's wards to gather information from people on a local basis. He tells the story that, after the devastating July 7, 2005, London Tube bombings, one of these officers met a Londoner who had known one of the terrorists. "There were so many men living in one apartment, coming and going at all hours," the man said. "I was surprised when I looked in the dustbin and found eighty bottles of ammonium nitrate." Bomb-making material. This is exactly the intelligence local police can encourage and harvest—in all communities, including Muslim communities. This is one of the reasons why the anti-Muslim campaign is so wrongheaded; aside from the fact that all segments of society should be welcome in America, we need the Muslim community in particular to think of the police as friend, not foe. If the officer had been in place and received and passed that information to Scotland Yard prior to the attack, the terrorist cell would have been discovered and that terrible train bombing would very likely have been prevented.

In Los Angeles, our Terrorism Liaison Officers received information from the LAPD counterterrorism bureau and put that information out to the patrol officers, who worked in the streets and could put it out into the community. In turn, patrol officers gathered information and sent it back through the chain. We created finance sectors, religious sectors, entertainment, utility—all of which met regularly to share information. Through our Tip Line and our street contacts we gathered leads, then pursued them and analyzed the results to determine whether there was reasonable suspicion of criminal activity we could use to disrupt these cells. ("Reasonable suspicion" of a link to terrorist activity is the legal threshold that allows us to begin drilling down into a person's behavior and activities to determine whether there is a criminal predicate, a foundation, for a criminal investigation. It is a threshold not to be abused.)

From 2001 to 2009, we initiated about 250 of these investigations, resulting in 170 arrests for low-level crimes such as credit card fraud, perjury on a driver's license application, marriage fraud, overstaying a visa, petty larceny, that we believed might well have supported terrorist activity. These and similar arrests allowed the police to investigate a suspect's computer, consistently a source of important information.

In this role, we in policing pride ourselves on being a constant disruption to people who mean us harm. We keep them off balance so they are not able to go out and conduct surveillance on potential targets. People who might otherwise have done damage to America have been deported. Had Mohammad Atta, a leader of the 9/11 hijackers, appeared on our detectives' radar screen, we would have used the same techniques. We would likely have found that he was living in a house with another Middle Eastern male and going to flight school. We would have found that he had unusual international travel patterns. His activities would have risen to the level of reasonable suspicion to believe that he was involved in a terrorist conspiracy, we would have pursued all our leads to conclusion, and the horrific events of 9/11 might never have happened. Local policing might have prevented 9/11.

An ancillary benefit of this information gathering is that many crimes that might otherwise have occurred—petty crimes and larger—will be restricted or prevented, resulting in a safer and more secure local community. With more intelligence, police presence will be even more effective.

We prevented a major attack on one of America's largest cities. How did this happen? A local cop found a cell phone and traced it back to a terrorist cell. In its hunt for terrorists in America, the FBI wasn't going to find that phone. Not in a hundred years. If the jihad attack had occurred, if army installations had been blown up, if the recruiting station had been bombed, if people coming out of synagogues after praying on a High Holy Day had been strafed with automatic machine-gun fire—after all that, maybe they would have been able to walk the evidence back to a string of gas stations robberies, much as after 9/11 they traced Mohammad Atta and his crew back to various flight schools. It would have made a great magazine article, an excellent movie script. At that point, however, the awful damage would have been done.

The Intelligence unit of the California Department of Corrections knew about JIS but had no idea it was planning a coordinated terrorist attack. Quite frankly, as a rule they are more concerned with how violent prison organizations are going to disrupt the prison system. This conspiracy was uncovered by good old-fashioned police work.

We got there just in time. As Kevin James had ordered, Washington, Patterson, and Samana were trying to recruit people with bomb-making capability into their cell. They had not found willing partners—yet—but the effort was under way.

Local law enforcement agencies, working together, prevented this terrorism. Torrance Police investigation and legwork, LAPD surveillance assets and intelligence analysis, the JTTF—without their cooperation, those attacks would have taken place. In Los Angeles, we dodged a bullet. Perhaps many bullets. Across America we need to be prepared for much worse.

When I arrived back at the NYPD in 2014, my predecessor Commissioner Ray Kelly's counterterrorism program was vaunted as the best ever. Among his most highly visible initiatives was the forward deployment piece called the Critical Response Vehicle (CRV) program.

The basic concept: The NYPD is divided into seventy-seven precincts, twelve Transit districts, and nine Housing police service areas. If you tell each, "Give me one car," you can cobble together almost 200 cops to be posted, two each, every day, to critical positions in front of critical sites around the city, such as the United Nations; the United States, Israeli, and Iraqi missions; the Chinese and Russian consulates. In case of attack or threat, the cars would be massed and deployed together.

From time to time the department arranged a show of force, a surge, in which dozens of police cars with their lights flashing would stream into high-risk, high-visibility sites such as Times Square or Columbus Circle. These conga-line caravans of police vehicles zooming around the city were physically imposing and great fodder for the media. There were Hercules teams—a roving SWAT team with a canine component and an Intelligence Bureau car—that would roll up with long rifles at high-profile locations. Mostly what this generated was people running up to the cops saying, "What's going on?!" because it looked like something threatening was about to happen. From day to day, you never knew where they were going to turn up.

The theory behind the program held that, because the locations changed daily, anyone doing preoperational surveillance would be kept off-balance. It became a performance—like the changing of the guard at Buckingham Palace. A very impressive, highly ceremonial display of security procedures.

I named John Miller Deputy Commissioner for Intelligence and Counterterrorism, and he was not impressed. The idea of borrowing two cops from every command seemed to him like a disaster waiting to happen. In staffing the CRV, he said, "If I call up a precinct and say, 'Hey, Captain Micallef, I need your two best men and your shiniest car,' who are they really going to send me? The guys who hadn't written a summons in three months and hadn't made an arrest in six months, and the car with the three wheels? Or maybe the guy who was really only interested in the overtime pay? Probably. But even if they do send their two best cops and their shiniest car, what are those officers going to know about how to handle the assignment?" Miller had been questioning Chief of Counterterrorism James Waters, who was in charge of the operation, about whether the CRV program was worth a damn.

Then *Charlie Hebdo* happened. The French newspaper had run drawings of a nude Prophet Muhammad—depictions of the Prophet are banned by Islam, and these were run clearly as a provocation—and in 2015 two Islamist gunmen forced their way inside its Paris headquarters and shot and killed twelve people. Miller watched videos of the attack over and over. The gunmen walked in and first shot an armed off-duty plainclothes police officer who was guarding the office while his partner was out getting them coffee. They then massacred the people gathered in a conference room for an editorial meeting, used one to get an access card and killed others on the way in and out. By the time the partner got back, it was over.

And then they did the strangest thing: they didn't run away. The two gunmen stood outside and shouted, "God is great!" and "The Prophet is avenged!" Miller wondered, *Why aren't they making their escape?*

As the Paris police, who had been alerted to a crime in progress, came driving up the street, the gunmen got back in their car. Yelling *"Allahu akbar"* and reloading, one drove while his brother sat out the window and opened fire. On the video, you see the police hurry to throw their car in reverse and then crash into another vehicle at the end of the street. They are completely outgunned and outpositioned. When backup arrives, the terrorists open fire and shoot them down. As one officer lay in the street wounded, a gunman stood over his body and executed him.

As is protocol after any terrorist attack, we put on a New York overlay—took the details and placed them in our city. What would the difference be if that attack were to take place here?

There would be no difference.

If a CRV unit had been guarding one of the six publications that had published the same cartoons, and gunmen had walked in and opened fire with AK-47s, the two officers would have been killed while they were reaching for their weapons. CRV cops had no particular counterterrorism training. They had no body armor appropriate to confront terrorists. They had no special weaponry. What did the cops know about the specific threats? About the individual terrorist units? About the threat as it related to that location? They might have gotten a taste of it in the roll call—"You go over to the Chinese embassy, you go over to the Egyptian embassy. Sit there all day, keep your eyes open." A lot of them were probably on their phones during instructions, checking their Facebook pages.

Miller made a point of visiting these locations. He would knock on the squad-car window with his NYPD ring, startle the officers, and introduce himself. "Hey. Deputy Commissioner Miller. Tell me about the place that you're guarding. What do you know about it and what do you know about the threat that you're protecting against today?"

The cops would drop their smartphones on the floor, knock over the coffee, and then try to come up with some answers—which they usually didn't have. They were all good cops, it was just a flawed program. NYPD's supposed deterrent to terror attacks was a couple of officers sitting in police cars outside high-risk locations, drinking coffee. We had developed a program of scarecrows.

Miller came to me and said, "We need to bite the bullet. We are running a lend-lease program of counterterrorism resources; we borrow the units and give them back, borrow them and give them back. We don't have the same people every day. They get us a car from the 77th Precinct today with two cops, but tomorrow it's two different cops. None of them are getting consistent training or intel." His solution? "I would give up some of the posts that we protect, and I would take fewer cops if I could have the right cops and they belonged to me."

The CRV, the Critical Response Vehicle, was an aptly named program;

it was just a car. With cops in it. But counterterrorism security was not about the vehicle, it was about the cops inside. We proposed the CRC, the Critical Response Command, which included staffing, equipment, and intensive training. CRC cops would be armed with M4 rifles and heavy vests. They would be trained in active-shooter tactics and counterterrorism tactics, and would be read through every attack around the globe when it happened—What did the bad guys do? How did they do it? How did they succeed? How did they fail? What was the police response? Their brains needed to be on full alert, constantly grinding this intelligence, so even if they had been in the unit a relatively short time they would be thinking and breathing like a counterterrorism professional. We wanted it to become second nature.

I was in discussions with Mayor de Blasio about hiring thirteen hundred more cops and bringing in civilians to free up another five hundred presently doing desk jobs. Obviously, if any commissioner is asked, "Do you want more cops?" they will always answer, "Yes, I want another five thousand." But when we are told, "I want to know exactly where each will be assigned," when we have to justify our number, the issue becomes more involved.

The mayor wanted some answers: What are the new hires going to be doing? Why do we need them? What difference will they make? We broke down the *Charlie Hebdo* scenario and explained that not only were we creating an entirely new, highly competent command, we were in fact delivering seven hundred officers back to their precincts.

We got the bodies and we bought the vehicles.

We staffed the CRC with active NYPD officers. Many were called, few were chosen. They had to qualify on the M4 rifle, be able to function in heavy gear, qualify in pistols, and pass active-shooter training. CRC would be an elite unit, as was entirely necessary.

But the new command was not received with unanimity. "Really?" some asked. "You're going to have five hundred cops who don't write summonses, who don't make arrests, who aren't community officers? This is the least productive form of policing we have ever seen."

Then the Bataclan theater event occurred: first, an attack of multiple suicide bombers on a Paris soccer stadium, then drive-by shootings in city cafés with many people killed and wounded, followed by a full-on attack on a concert venue filled with people that turned into a mass murder and then a hostage situation specifically designed to be a dramatic standoff with the police.

Again we did the New York overlay: Three bombs go off at Citi Field. Deputy Commissioner of Counterterrorism Miller, Intelligence Bureau Chief Thomas Galati, Counterterrorism Chief Waters, Chief of Patrol O'Neill, and I head to Queens because we have suicide bombers attacking the Mets. While we are stuck in the tremendous traffic jam we ourselves have created with our response, an active shooter walks into P.J. Clarke's and opens fire. The next call is shots fired at La Maganette down the street, and then at Webster Hall during a concert where scores of people are gunned down and others are being held hostage. Where is the active-shooter surge capacity with long weapons that will be able to respond to that? Where is CRV? Nowhere.

At the time, Chief O'Neill was building the Strategic Response Group, which was designed to be a citywide task force. High crime in this area? We will inject SRG to augment the precinct. Major event or parade or street fair or Times Square on New Year's Eve? We can send as many as six hundred SRG to cover that event on all ends. Fourth of July fireworks? SRG to supplement the troops. A citywide flying squad. We equipped them with long guns, heavy vests, and active-shooter training as well. Now among CRC, which would protect everything we thought would or could or should be a terrorist target—not the CRV anymore, but officers with the proper equipment, training, and mindset—and SRG running through the streets doing Level One mobilization, missing-person searches, and shooting scenes; and the Emergency Services Unit, our go-to SWAT team, our Navy SEALs, the cops who were rescue oriented, SWAT trained, and heavy-weapons ready, who knew how to go after bad guys in any situation—among all these we had sixteen hundred trained and equipped tactical people out in the streets and briefed into the threat on a regular basis. New York City was covered.

Charlie Hebdo started us on the path to preparedness; the Bataclan theater put the seal on it. If anyone in politics or policing thought the SRG or CRC was a bad idea, a waste of resources, or just too much for a civilized society, they had to know that these attacks last between four and eight minutes. And if you don't have a response that is fast enough to intervene, you will fail.

An emergency command has two important tasks: Stop the killing and stop the dying. Stop the killing means having the ability to meet force head-on with equal or better firepower and superior training. We achieved that. Stop the dying is different.

The largest loss of life in a terrorist attack on U.S. soil since 9/11 was not at a government building or a giant public event, it occurred at 2:30 a.m. in a gay nightclub on Latino Night, off the beaten path in Orlando, Florida. The idea that you can do adequate target protection and prediction and lock things down is wishful thinking. Miller tells his captains and above, "Think about the Orlando attack when you have the night duty in Queens and you're thinking, 'It's three a.m., what could happen? There certainly could not be a terrorist attack, or some great loss of life. Maybe some bad car accident with some drunk.' Think again. Because right now these guys are out there targeting, thinking outside the box. It doesn't mean we shouldn't do our normal targeting preparations, but we need to think beyond that, and we need to have response capability, even at the times when we think it's not supposed to happen. Because they are thinking, 'When do they think it is not supposed to happen?'"

In Al Qaeda's *Inspire* magazine issue number 9 it says, *Wait until they have a big event where all of their resources are committed, and strike on the other end of town. Take hostages and kill them until the police get there. Then stop and wait for the negotiation process and all the press to arrive, and before the police storm in to rescue the hostages, kill the rest of them then.*

Terrorists were—and still are—watching, adjusting, thinking, adjusting again. We needed to increase our capability. The "stop the killing" component meant arriving quickly with the right resources. The "stop the dying" part was complicated.

In an active-shooter situation like the Bataclan theater, Orlando, or the 2017 mass shooting at Fort Lauderdale airport, police enter to hunt the gunmen. There are always reports of multiple gunmen, because individual people see a shooter and describe him or her individually. Sometimes there are multiple gunmen, sometimes not. So cops tend to lock everything down. The ambulance people say, "We don't go in there. There is a shooter on the loose. When the police say it's safe, we will enter."

That won't work anymore. If these attacks run between two and a half and eight minutes—averaging somewhere between four and five—all the killing usually takes place almost immediately, but the search to clear the building can take two and a half hours. That is when people are bleeding out. So we went back to the people we are not ever supposed to talk to— the fire department and Joe Pfeifer, their chief of counterterrorism and emergency preparedness—and said, "Joe, how do we do this?" He said, "Rescue Task Force."

We gathered a group of trained and committed emergency medical technicians and paramedics, requisitioned them the same body armor and helmets issued to our officers, and most crucially, provided force protection. With up to the eleven hundred trained SRG and CRC officers with long weapons and helmets, we would secure and hold the entrance to the building, then secure and hold the first-floor hallway. Get up to the second floor while hunting the gunmen, and secure and hold that. Then we would move in the medics with our tactical units and allow them to start triage: "This guy is dead," "She's dead," "This guy is viable, this guy can walk, let's get him up and take him out of here! Let's get this one on a stretcher. Let's get this!"

We staged elaborate active-shooter drills with little notice, bringing in fire department personnel and EMS people who had signed up for Rescue Task Force duty. We held one at Grand Central Station—took over the whole place in the middle of the night, shot it up with a wide variety of Simunitions, bloodstains. It wasn't long before we were operational. We now have SRG in all five boroughs.

Commissioner Kelly had developed the intelligence bureau from what was basically an executive protection group into a force designed, honed, and built by thirty-year CIA veteran David Cohen. Cohen had re-created a combination of the FBI and the CIA within the NYPD that included undercovers, networks of informants in complex conspiracy cases and plots, and foreign posts all over the world. It had stunning capabilities.

In addition, there was the counterterrorism bureau, which encompassed everything from an important quartermaster section that bought and distributed the correct equipment to outfit a police department in the age of terrorism, to an event-planning arm with what Miller always called the counterterrorism overlay—planning for crowds and traffic and safety, but now also taking into consideration possible suicide bombers and drones and all the modern disturbances that had never before been active elements. Its seven hundred members included the FBI's Joint Terrorism Task Force, hazmat people, and assorted other programs that networked outside resources. A deputy commissioner presided over each.

The problem was, intelligence-counterterrorism was a monolithic operation under which two deputy commissioners and two three-star chiefs handled a collective thousand people.

And the program was in a pitched battle with its partners. The Port Authority's antiterrorism program was ostracized and there were extraordinary tensions with the FBI, state police, and New York Fire Department. Kelly's style held that there is one NYPD, we are the 800-pound gorilla, we make the decisions, we are in charge, and we will call the tune. Basically, "There is a new sheriff in town, and all of you can go fuck yourself until I tell you to stop fucking yourself."

Had I been in charge after 9/11, with smoke coming out of the holes where skyscrapers once stood and three thousand dead, I would have looked around and said, "This is a new kind of challenge and I'm going to need friends. I'm going to need the Port Authority, I'm going to need the state police, I'm going to need the fire department, I am especially going to need the FBI." I came in, appointed John Miller as Deputy Commissioner for Counterterrorism, and said, "Fix all that now!" We weren't fighting anybody, we weren't at war with anybody, we knew our friends and we needed them.

Miller's investigation of the NYPD counterterrorism unit revealed a flawed system. Deployment of both a Deputy Commissioner of Counterterrorism and Deputy Commissioner of Intelligence was creating unnecessary conflict and competition. Counterterrorism controlled a hundred detectives on the JTTF working at the FBI, while Intelligence had seven hundred detectives working with informants and undercovers in the world of terrorism out on the streets. Each deputy commissioner fought with the other for resources and wanted to make new cases and be the first to get his news to the police commissioner. "This is the reason that Washington doesn't work," Miller told me. "Sixteen agencies want to get their things to the White House before the other guy does, instead of operating together and saying, 'What does it mean?'"

Miller suggested having two chiefs report to one deputy commissioner, who can then feed their information up to the police commissioner "and make him proud of both of them." Instead of divide and conquer, we would unite and collaborate. I agreed and put Miller in charge. It took a lot less time to put those relationships back together than it had to break them apart, and everyone was relieved to know we were all friends and partners again. Sometimes it's the tiny things that make a difference.

During Miller's first week on the job there was a big interagency disagreement. When a man from New York had gone to join ISIS, the NYPD had put the FBI onto him, expecting to be kept in the loop. However, the federal agency wasn't sharing its findings, which ruffled a lot of feathers. Rather than having everyone retreat to their respective corners, Miller called representatives into a conference room at the FBI's New York office and said, "Get all your bosses, everyone relevant to this discussion, in the room. I'm going to bring mine." The people in this intelligence community may have been vaguely aware that the new deputy commissioner used to work in the FBI, and as a TV reporter had developed relationships of trust with figures such as Mafia don John Gotti and Osama bin Laden. Now that he was with the NYPD they didn't know quite what to expect, but seeing as how they were at odds with the department over so much, they were ready to fight.

As the discussion started about who had what and what should be shared, Miller said, "It's a new day. Whatever the old battles were about, whatever grudges were created and carried forth, we are going to wipe that slate clean. We need you, you need us.

"Look," he told them, "let me explain something to you while we're all here. Commissioner Bratton has been very clear: we are partners in this. Let me tell you what he doesn't care about: He doesn't care about who gets credit, he doesn't care about who holds the press conference, he doesn't care about whose name is on the release, he doesn't care about whose building we do it in front of or whose seal is on it. He doesn't care about who is in charge or who is helping out. What he cares about is, are we protecting New York from terrorism? Is the job getting done? Are we getting along with our partners? Everything else is secondary, or doesn't matter at all."

The room was silent. They were trying to process what they'd heard. *This guy is yelling at us, but he's telling us that we are friends again.* Miller was trying to clear the runway, to make the point that you can get an awful lot done if you are not worried about who gets credit.

Prior to 9/11, the relationship between the FBI and the NYPD had been a model for the nation. Post-attack, at a time when cooperation should have been at its height, it all went to hell. The organizations were constantly leaking bad things about each other, which actually had the effect of undermining cases. The FBI had tried to make it work, even sending an agent to the city whose sole mandate was to fix the relationship. But once Kelly's department realized that was his goal, they knew they could take advantage of him and made it worse. This had to change. And it did. After we tore out the bad pages it was all an open book: you show me yours, I will show you mine.

We made it social as well as professional, hosting dinners and events in order to promote amity. And every three or four months, to ensure the partnerships, we would gather, go around the table, and talk about the direction we were all heading. This boilerplate had existed before my return, but sometimes Kelly came, sometimes he didn't. The message being, "This is my town, and you all work for me." I didn't feel the need to make that point.

For decades the relationship between the NYPD and FDNY was fraught; they had been fighting over jurisdiction since the 1970s. The NYPD Emergency Service Unit, our SWAT and rescue team, was mandated to handle building collapses, stuck elevators, jumpers on bridges, people trapped in auto wrecks. After a terrible 1970 blaze at One New York Plaza, new fire codes were put in effect for high-rises and new construction. Because since that time every new building over six stories high had sprinkler and alarm systems as well as smoke detection and various other safety features—and also because the buildings themselves were now fireproof, instead of being old wooden structures—there were fewer fires, and even fewer serious fires. The fire department lost a lot of business. When a city fiscal crisis caused many firehouses around the city to close, the FDNY started moving in on the car crashes, rescues, building collapses, and other emergencies that had traditionally been ours. The two agencies were estranged and competitive.

Miller had been my counterterrorism chief in Los Angeles, and during our first week there a big threat arose and we were told, "We're going to have to brief the mayor on this. And the fire department." Miller said, "The fire department? We brief the fire department on this? So we *talk* to the fire department?"

"Yeah, all the time."

"How long has this been going on?"

"Since, like, the eighteen hundreds."

"And why do we talk to them?"

"Because if this threat actually happened, they would have to show up on site and rescue people, pick up the dead. They need to understand what it is we're looking at."

"Wow, we talk to the firefighters! Why do we like them again?"

"Because when we get hurt, they come get us."

"In New York," Miller explained, "when we get hurt, we throw you back in the back of a police car and rush you to the hospital. We don't want any firefighters touching us!"

Super Bowl XLVIII was on the horizon, and while the game was going to be played at the Meadowlands in New Jersey, most of the major events surrounding it were going to be held in Manhattan. All the players, coaches, and league officials stayed in the city. They weren't staying in the Meadowlands, so we had to account for buses and routes and escorts and coned lanes. Super Bowl Boulevard—site of the NFL's promotional whirlwind of concerts, TV broadcasts, a field goal–kicking competition complete with goalposts, a snow slide on Broadway below Forty-Second Street, and fan-friendly activities—would run for thirteen unprotected blocks from Herald Square through Times Square.

For New Year's Eve you can put up pens and metal detectors, but for a fortnight in the center of Manhattan, you can't control access. This was prime terrorist territory. What better way to attack the infidel than to create lethal mayhem at the epicenter of its culture? Our mandate was to control access, and where there wasn't access, control behavior. We had to prepare Times Square for an active shooter, a suicide bomber, drones, all modern threats.

The FBI was doing a media story about the range of counterterrorism packages they were putting together. In other years the NYPD would have done its own competing story, since it was department policy that we were the real agency, not the feds. But I said, "Why don't we go over to the FBI and we will do the interview together."

"You mean have the FBI come over here," I was asked, "right?"

"No, we will go over there."

We walked down that buzzing boulevard, across the street, into the FBI, where I stood side by side with the assistant director of the New York Office, George Venizelos, before the FBI seal, with ours and other agencies' all on the same wall. FBI representatives said, "They're doing the interview together? And he came over here?" NYPD insiders wondered, "Why did he go over there instead of making them come over *here*?" Because that's the way that we do it now, we are all friends. They will come to our place next time.

The Super Bowl was our test run with our partners the FBI, the New Jersey state police, and the Department of Homeland Security. Times Square, which we always have extremely well covered, would be even more packed with people than normal. We had radiation detection, not just in the air but on the ground; people walking around with pagers that would start to chirp if they detected a problem. Our BioWatch sensors scanned the air for substances like anthrax and others that grow organically and would not be detected as radiation or gas. (The health department had to change those filters two or three times a day and send them to a lab to see if anything toxic was growing.) Our network of countersniper teams on high ground could detect, isolate, and neutralize a shooter from above. Emergency service units on the ground would serve as counterassault teams in case of an active shooter down below.

We couldn't afford to wait until a shooting started, so we had a network halo of plainclothes people—not just people who look like plainclothes cops, but others with special behavioral detection training who blended into the crowd, wearing football jerseys and various looks designed to fit in.

We had New Year's Eve experience controlling the Times Square environment and keeping out backpacks and packages when necessary, but this was a four-day lollapalooza Super Bowl event, so not only did we need to control access and environment, we had to read it closely all the time and be prepared to react almost instantly if a threat appeared. We were aware of a dozen subjects of ongoing authorized investigations, which is true at any time. We reviewed our ability to know the location of those people at any given moment, because if one or more started to drift toward Times Square, that would heighten our need to keep an eye on them.

Then there were the FBI investigations, which were separate from ours but which our detectives on the JTTF were monitoring. If these individuals became associated with one another and started to show up in the area at the same time, outside of their normal routines, that would have ticked up our interest. We also had to protect the events that were happening outside of Times Square, at other places in the metropolitan area. We were always vigilant concerning the mass-transit system, which is particularly vulnerable and has been persistently targeted around the world, as we have seen in Madrid and London. We had to do a giant counterterrorism overlay just for New York's daily transit system. There were many moving pieces with many partners.

Threats would arrive and have to be run down quickly, but in the end we had no incidents—either because there had been no terrorist actions planned or would-be terrorists had cased the scene and found us prepared for them. Our partners walked away from the event knowing that this was a different NYPD.

As the need to collaborate arrived in subsequent cases, this cooperation bore fruit.

I n April 2014, not long after I had returned to take command of the NYPD for a second time, Asia Siddiqui and Noelle Velentzas were developing into terrorists. One had come to our attention after a tip about another of her acquaintances. American citizens and Queens roommates devouring ISIS and Al Qaeda propaganda online, they had begun talking about targeting police for assassination. We knew this because they were discussing it with an undercover officer, who on authority of subpoena was audio recording everything.

They tasked the undercover to use a college or work computer—some machine not tied to either of the two—to download the Al Qaeda *Inspire* magazine article "Make a Bomb in the Kitchen of Your Mom." *Bomb Making for Dummies*, but a bomb that would work. In it were simple instructions for bomb making using a pressure cooker. Velentzas had been obsessed with pressure cookers since the Boston Marathon attack that killed three people and injured several hundred others.

Each had a defined role; one was the organizer and scientist who would keep the plot on track and design and construct the device, the other the person who would detonate it. "You got the beef," Velentzas said to Siddiqui, "I got the knowledge." They involved the undercover to limit their own exposure, thinking they themselves might have been on our radar. And they were right.

Siddiqui and Velentzas decided the target should be the military or police, arms of the U.S. government that in their minds were harming Muslim people abroad. When they saw television coverage of the sea of cops at the funerals for officers Rafael Ramos and Wenjian Liu, they decided to wait until the next police funeral, place a bomb, blow it up, and kill in quantity.

Their consumption of ISIS and Al Qaeda material became even more voracious—Anwar al-Awlaki, Sheik bin Laden, Ayman al-Zawahiri—and they began to move the plot forward. They wanted to build the same bomb that had been used at the Boston Marathon bombing, the same bomb that José Pimentel had been building in his apartment in Washington Heights, in a case before I returned to the NYPD. Apparently, in the terrorist world, everybody likes that Al Qaeda recipe.

We were faced at that moment with a decision: Were we going to supply these two people, who have now discussed targets, with enough ammunition to convict themselves?

NYPD, FBI, and JTTF had an extensive library of tapes, we had the undercover officer's testimony. NYPD and FBI together had the federal investigation. The FBI said, They are talking about having propane tanks, they are talking about getting the bomb-making recipe; we are going to start to lose the controlling features here and we are burning up a lot of surveillance and people on this. We have a conspiracy, let's take this down.

We arrested them at home. They both pled guilty in federal court. Siddiqui was sentenced to fifteen years in prison and Velentzas was awaiting sentencing during the COVID-19 pandemic.

How do we track the bomb-making pipeline? One would think the police and federal agencies would be extremely vigilant in this regard. We are. As part of our Nexus program we contact private purveyors of a bomb's chemical precursors and say, "This is what a suspicious sale looks like. Track these for us." Not long ago that was sufficient for a start.

Now, however, we are in a different age. If you log on to Amazon.com and fill your shopping cart with bomb-making staples like a remote-control toy car, a quantity of 9-volt batteries, battery holders and connectors with open wires on the end, one pressure cooker, and three pounds of black powder, before you click Proceed to Checkout you will be shown an array of products—"Customers who bought these items also bought"—including a Westclox timer, electric match, a host of accessories. The idea that retailers are poised on the edge to notify authorities to suspicious buying trends is nonsense. There is no reporting. It is an algorithm, the information never touches a person. And retailers don't set the algorithm to send an alarm to the authorities, because they are worried about sales. They have been asked to establish such a system—often—but claim "privacy of our buyers" or "complicated process," and we get nowhere. This needs fixing. We live in an imperfect world.

A valuable source told the Joint Terrorism Task Force and the FBI that three Uzbeks living in New York were preparing to travel to join ISIS. They didn't like their landlord, however, and before they left they decided to behead him. Then they would get on a plane and go fight for ISIS. The JTTF relocated the landlord—"You are going to go on vacation, go to a motel, but we can't really tell you why. We're just going to take you out of the building for a couple of days."

We had to arrest the men on the way to departure, because in these cases we need to eliminate the blowhard defense—"That was a thing I was saying to impress my friend, I was never really going to go. I bought the tickets, but I was going to change them . . ." We needed them to demonstrate the intention to leave.

The three were intercepted in the jetway to the plane. "FBI, JTTF. You're under arrest. NYPD. You're coming with us." And they fought, ended up rolling around on the ground. One of our deputy inspectors was injured. This is a pattern in these cases; people prepared to kill and die for the ISIS or Al Qaeda cause will fight hand-to-hand to the death. Harming the enemy is the essence of what they do.

Evidence was mounting that the entreaty to "Join the caliphate, come here" was working on people in New York. Our concern was the back end of the propaganda, the message "If you can't figure out how to get here, fight for us where you are." And in spring 2015, with the cases of Noelle Velentzas and Asia Siddiqui and the three Uzbeks, we started to see the emergence of people who say, "Well, I can't get over there, but I can do something here." "Make a bomb in the kitchen of your mom"—is that too hard? "How to run people down with a truck"—I have a truck. "How to stab people with a knife in the mall"—I've got better than a knife. "How to shoot up a government building."

We found ourselves in the middle of a cadence and pace of plots and cases that we had never seen before. Not in New York, not in LA, not in Washington, D.C. ISIS had cracked the propaganda model.

Al Qaeda had never figured that out. Al Qaeda's recruiting flaw was that it was all about them. In their videos, it was bin Laden saying, "This is what I think and this is what we should do, and this is what is right, this is what God says." With Zawahiri it was less theological, just forty-five minutes of him pointing a finger at the screen, talking about politics and instructing people to kill.

The leading jihadist recruiter was Anwar al-Awlaki, a man who spoke perfect, unaccented English and understood the American psyche. He grew up in New Mexico, California, Washington, D.C.—and he was seductive. He would tell his viewers, "Today's video is about how to be a better Muslim. How to practice, how to pray." Tomorrow's video would be about how to be a better father, how to guide your children on the proper path. The next day he would talk about how to take care of yourself, how to exercise, eat halal food, follow the instructions. John Miller says, "I was looking for the Anwar al-Awlaki videos about *kill kill kill*, but by the ninth video I was well on the way to becoming a better person!"

Anwar al-Awlaki wasn't about *me*, it was about *you*—I am working on you. Then the videos would take a turn. *Now that I have explained to you how to be a better Muslim, how to take better care of yourself, how to treat your family—this is what is required of someone who adheres to the religion at a time when the religion is under attack. You have to step up. You have to go fight. You have to turn to violence.* It was very powerful. In 2008–2009, there were approximately a dozen plots against the United States from people in different cities trying to detonate truck bombs and car bombs and pressure-cooker bombs. Of that dozen, nine sat down and told us, "I was inspired by the videos and the audio recordings of Anwar al-Awlaki."

Al-Awlaki had found charisma, but he hadn't found messaging. He made a personal connection through YouTube with his viewers, and Al Qaeda realized that.

But al-Awlaki didn't want to be a public affairs representative, he wanted an operational command. So when he got out of jail in Yemen, they sent him into the hinterlands to be Al Qaeda of the Arabian Peninsula.

Al-Awlaki developed the underwear bomb with Ibrahim al-Asiri, the chief bomb maker for Al Qaeda of the Arabian Peninsula. Al-Asiri had tested the bomb on his own brother by having him visit the Saudi minister of the interior and blow him up in his house on what was supposed to be the holiday of forgiveness. The minister lived.

He recruited Umar Farouk Abdulmutallab, who came from Nigeria to

Yemen, and groomed him into being a suicide bomber. So you had a very creative bomb maker and a committed young man, who on Christmas Day 2009 took a flight to Detroit, cranked off his bomb, and burned his balls off. (The bomb malfunctioned.) Ibrahim al-Asiri doesn't make any bad bombs; they had field-tested it in the desert a number of times, and it worked fine. Without telling future bombers how to do it right, conditions, temperature, sweat, and other elements affected the detonation system, which failed to do its job.

ISIS, on the other hand, presented slick Madison Avenue–style material that showed the fighters of the caliphate doing battle against the Syrians and the Americans. Their approach was personal and emotional: *This is the caliphate. This is what we have been waiting a thousand years for. This is where we have planted the black flag, this is where Islam the religion now becomes home. It will spring forth through the region and then through the world from this spot. And if that requires the battle of all days, the end of the world, a clash of civilizations—you can be a part of it. You can be one of the people who brought this religion to glory.*

For a generation of people who had grown up in an environment where it was normal on Facebook and then Instagram to broadcast what you had for lunch and a picture of the dish, and then tweet out every aspect of your vacation or your day at school—a generation that had grown up living out loud, and for no particular reason—you have a terrorist group that was not a shadowy organization being controlled by a man in a cave, but one that had actually taken ground. Planted a flag. Created an infantry and said, "Come and join this fight and you will be a part of history." ISIS was on Twitter and Facebook, they were on YouTube, and they were a terrorist group that lived in the same modes their potential recruits grew up in. They communicated on multiple platforms and showed the fighters and the caliphate growing and expanding.

ISIS painted a picture of three things:

Valor. Join us and you are a hero.

Belonging. You will belong to something bigger than yourself; you won't be a kid going to City College on a student visa.

Empowerment. If you get killed, you are going to paradise. If you don't get killed, your valor will have become heroism on a scale that makes you a historic figure. You are Saladin, the sultan of the next millennium.

That is a powerful elixir by any measure. More powerful if the person on the receiving end feels not only that they don't have valor, but that they are insignificant. Not only that they don't belong, but that they are ostracized. Not only that they lack empowerment, but they are powerless.

When we saw these films and propaganda pieces coming out for mass audiences on the internet, we recognized the difficulties to come. The internet isn't television, where you fast-forward through the commercials. It is a buyers' market; your search brings material you are searching for. ISIS knew that by the time a viewer hit play, they had an interested customer.

The Uzbeks had associates; we were aware of the presence of other travelers whom we could not waylay. We knew they were going to be trained, that they were going to fight; we know they were going to acquire battlefield capabilities, maybe bomb-making experience. We knew they had the potential to come back.

So as we were seeing a potential threat in people from the United States joining a terrorist group, we were also seeing a potential second wave that could return here as hardened terrorists. We began to grapple with these issues.

In May of that year, once we took down the Asia Siddiqui case, we were confronted with Junaid Hussain. Hussain was part of an electronic caliphate, an ISIS cyber group and global radical Muslim community whose mission was to recruit and motivate active converts worldwide into violent action. Junaid Hussain, Neil Prakash, Omar al-Britani, and Mohammed Emwazi—who gained international attention as "Jihadi John," one of the so-called Beatles who beheaded western captives—changed the whole game. They used the internet as a tool of terror.

Hussain was a factor on Twitter. The JTTF and their international partners and other intelligence agencies were all pointing to him. His Twitter handle changed often, but we followed him there and to other platforms, where he went dark. Even so, we got onto him and were following his communications.

Hussain told his followers, in sum and substance, "Gone are the days where you had to travel to a training camp to learn these capabilities. It is all available online now. If you are interested in advancing the caliphate, contact me directly." When followers did contact him and said, "Brother, I am interested, I want to go fight," Hussain would say, "Meet me on my Kik account. Meet me on my Snapchat"—encrypted platforms designed so messages are read and then evaporate, which we could not monitor. We are aware of 109 encrypted messages that flew between Hussain and Alton Simpson and another convert as they drove from Phoenix, Arizona, to Garland, Texas, and then opened fire with various weapons—including an AK-47 with thousands of rounds of ammunition—on the First Annual Muhammad Art Exhibit, produced by a woman from New York City who is known for that kind of provocation. (Again, depictions of the Prophet are banned by Islam.) Both men were killed by a traffic officer who happened to be standing under a nearby shade tree and shot them with his Glock .45 duty pistol. Which is the difference between Texas and New York. Texas is the only place where ISIS can be outgunned at an art show.

That event registered. Terrorists were being recruited on Twitter.

Monitoring Hussain's account, JTTF detectives found he was talking with a young man in Queens, Munther Omar Saleh. By all accounts, Saleh was a normal kid who worked at a supermarket owned by his parents, across the street from their home. Hussain turned Saleh and assigned him to find the woman who organized the Garland art exhibit, chop her head off, and get it on video. When that job was slow to take shape, Junaid Hussain started to lose patience. Rather than have Saleh perform a beheading, in May he assigned him to bomb the Fourth of July. Hussain gave Saleh the Boston Marathon recipe, "Build a Bomb in the Home of Your Mom," and discussed potential targets, like the Statue of Liberty.

Saleh recruited another teenager to help him and was in contact with a Fareed Mummuni from Staten Island.

With Saleh reassigned, Hussain then contacted Usaamah Rahim in Boston, told him to put together a team, and sent him the home address of the Manhattan woman he wanted beheaded. That video was to be posted online, with credit to be claimed by the Islamic State. At the same time, Hussain contacted a Sammy Topaz in New Jersey, and talked to him about another plot.

At this point, beginning in April 2015 and going into July, we had the two women who were planning a bombing for Anwar al-Awlaki, Al Qaeda, and ISIS; the three Uzbek travelers; the Garland shooters; and now in the works a Fourth of July bombing, an Upper East Side kidnapping and beheading, and a plot with a target undetermined coming from New Jersey. We had several people who had never met one another, who had no association with one another, being brought together by the ISIS network in a series of encrypted online platforms. We were juggling these plots involving people who had never been to a training camp and never met their handler, who had been radicalized online and had been contacted personally. This was not the Lackawanna Six; ISIS wasn't recruiting people and getting them over to a campus in the Middle East, training them and sending them back to America; it was mass-marketing terrorism to hundreds of thousands or millions of people, then taking the ones who came forward saying, "Put me in, Coach," giving them specific instructions and turning them loose. And they were doing it all online. This was a new and very troubling development.

JTTF surveillance on Omar Saleh and his friend was very tight. After running around, trying to lose them, they finally confronted one of the officers, who called for backup. When put on the ground the two were found to be carrying big knives and were arrested for possession of the weapons. Terrorism charges followed. We had surveillance teams on Sammy Topaz in New Jersey. The Boston JTTF had surveillance teams on Usaamah Rahim and his associate David Wright, and found they were communicating with another man named Nick Rovinski, in Providence, Rhode Island.

All these wheels were turning and we were like the Dutch boy, trying to plug the holes in the dike. But there were too many holes and we were running out of fingers. Usually in these kinds of cases you try to introduce someone into the conspirators' community as a member of the plot, at which point you get access to controlling features: if you supply a bomb, it is not a bomb that is going to go off; if you supply a gun, it is not going to fire a bullet; if you supply a plot, it is not going to succeed because you know about it. We didn't have that. We didn't have people on the inside. We were trailing the plot from behind, because we were not running it.

After we took down Saleh and his friend, we knew that information would bleed out when Fareed Mummuni in Staten Island realized that Saleh was no longer answering his correspondence, or saw in the paper that he had been arrested. We got a JTTF search warrant, and FBI SWAT went to Mummuni's house in Staten Island to search for evidence that might define the target or identify the plot, perhaps evidence of preparation for the pressure-cooker bombs. We were extricating his mother and sister when Mummuni came down the stairs, reached around his mother and stabbed a SWAT agent. The blade pierced the agent's protective vest but not the agent.

That was a favor. Now Mummuni was under arrest for assault on a federal officer. We could supersede that later with plotting to attack the United States on the behalf of a foreign designated terrorist organization, but he was going in.

We executed the search warrant and found a backpack with a machete on the front seat of the car. Mummuni later told us in statements that he was instructed by Junaid Hussain to be armed at all times because if the feds came to get him, if he couldn't complete his actual plot he must be prepared to strike, which is exactly what he did. FBI Newark wrapped up Sammy Topaz as part of the plot.

Miller came to my office on a daily basis, sometimes twice daily, with up-to-the-moment details, and we were feeling pretty good. But at 5:45 on a June morning, Miller's phone rang. Counterterrorism Chief Waters, says, "Hey, Usaamah Rahim, the guy in Boston?"

"Yeah? The guy that is supposed to come down now and kidnap the woman and do the beheadings?"

"Right. He just picked up the phone and said, 'It's too complicated, and I can't wait, and it's gonna take too long, I'm going to go out and kill a cop right now.'"

"Like, *right* now?"

"Right now."

"Are we on him?"

"We are on him. He hasn't left the house yet."

The surveillance team had him from his house to a big mall drugstore, where Boston JTTF agents moved in. Like the Uzbeks and Mummuni, Rahim confronted them, this time with a knife. The Boston cops ended up shooting and killing him. David Wright and Nick Rovinski were both arrested and made statements.

Neil Prakash was captured and went on trial in Turkey. In his opening statement at the arraignment he told the judge, "I am sorry for the trouble I have caused the world." Junaid Hussain was killed in a drone strike on a car in a Raqqa, Syria, gas station in August 2015. He was twenty-one years old.

It had been a good idea to reset the partnerships. When the plots started coming like out of a tennis ball machine set too fast and the FBI ran out of surveillance teams, they said, "We've got too many bad guys and too few surveillance teams."

"Give us targets," we told them. "We'll use our surveillance teams."

After a successfully safe Super Bowl, with the Counterterrorism and Intelligence bureaus under one deputy commissioner, and the resources flowing back and forth as needed between FBI, NYPD, Intelligence, JTTF; with former tensions gone and enemies converted to allies, Miller began calling around about the Fourth of July.

"All right," he said. "All our bad guys are rolled up—that we know about. We are dealing with 2.6 million people who come to see this. We have the most significant counterterrorism overlay that has ever been applied to a Fourth of July crowd, on the idea that there may be a plot or plotters that we don't know about from the same place or from somewhere else. Bag checks, wanding, response teams; people under surveillance; all the high-profile targets are being watched. The giant package."

Securing all this were FBI Special Agent in Charge of Counterterrorism Bill Sweeney; his boss, FBI Assistant Director Diego Rodriguez; the head of the Secret Service, Bobby Sica; and Homeland Security Special Agent in Charge Angel Melendez.

Miller asked everyone, "Where you going to be?"

"I'm going to be working, I'm going to be on my command post, monitoring everything."

"I'm going to be working, but I'm going to be over in the office, just off the command post. If something happens, they can come and get me."

"I'm going to be working, but we will be at our headquarters."

Miller had a better idea. "If something happens," he said, "I want all of these people in the same room."

So, we invited them all to go out into New York Harbor on our big seventy-foot police launch. "You have all your people at your command post," Miller said, "including your assistant special agents in charge; and very competent people are actually going to run this thing. Let's all go out on the boat. We will all be together, we will have every form of emergency communication, and we will be in the one place where there won't be an attack—the middle of the water."

We would site the joint operations center at police headquarters, One Police Plaza. Would consolidating all the security apparatus in one place be safe? Of course. You can't blow up One Police Plaza, good luck with that. We could take the entire management of local and federal law enforcement together on one platform and move it right into the dock in lower Manhattan. Two vans would be standing by for a dozen or more people to jump into for the dozen or so blocks to our joint operations center, and we would have NYPD, command center, FBI, Secret Service, Homeland Security, ATF, and other intelligence agencies with three letters, in a command-and-control center, all in one place. The assistant director of the FBI, the head of counterterrorism, the specialists in charge of the Secret Service and the Department of Homeland Security investigations. It was a meeting of the mobs commission, but with badges.

We went out on the boat, we enjoyed the fireworks, and on that Fourth of July, the only things that blew up were the things that were supposed to blow up—in the sky.

Of course, when we woke up on the morning of July 5, it wasn't as if the decks had been cleared. There is still the world of active terrorism.

NYPD Counterterrorism found a man wearing an ISIS baseball hat running violent pictures and content on his Facebook page. Their intelligence found a way to get a source into him. The man began talking about traveling to join ISIS, and if that was not possible, creating mayhem here.

At the same time, we had a case going against Sajmir Alimehmeti, a twenty-two-year-old Albanian living in the Bronx, who had attempted more than once to travel to join ISIS. We surveilled his online purchases and found he was buying large, tactical, serrated beheading knives—the Marine combat fighting knife, as seen in the beheading videos that were spreading across the internet; they come in Canadian and American models and had become popular in some circles—as well as pepper spray, zip ties, and handcuffs.

Alimehmeti's passport had been revoked after his first attempt to join

ISIS, and he was trying to get it reinstated. Watching these orders, we became very concerned that while it was doubtful he would make his trip—he was not going to be able to get on a plane with pepper spray, zip ties, handcuffs, and giant knives—he seemed to be gearing up for action in our area. As with Velentzas, we were able to insert an undercover. Jointly, the Intelligence Bureau and JTTF began providing high-end surveillance resources and electronic monitoring. Using the diversity of the NYPD, where we have people from 142 countries speaking 159 languages, we were able to find effective officers in the undercover program and put them on the case as well. We took out both terrorists.

We don't trip over these cases. Each is the result of painstaking investigations between the Intelligence Bureau and the JTTF that result in concerted action.

For instance, a bomb threat was called into Harlem Prep, a charter high school in the Bronx. In some cities cops would search the school, clear it, and say, "We're done." Our intelligence bureau traced the call to a sixteen-year-old female Harlem Prep student. An interview found that she had been sexually abused by a teacher. We referred the case to the NYPD sex crimes unit, which found another student who confirmed the abuse and also reported that the same teacher had been paying students fifty dollars apiece to remove explosive powder from fireworks and empty it into containers. Sex Crimes relayed this information back to Counterterrorism. The JTTF was alerted. They got a search warrant, hit his place, and found far more than expected.

Twin brothers Tyler and Christian Toro were busted with thirty-two pounds of explosives and a magnesium strip—key bomb-making ingredients—a jar of gasoline-Styrofoam mix that can be used to create homemade napalm, a box containing twenty pounds of iron oxide, five pounds of aluminum powder, five pounds of potassium nitrate, a box of firecrackers, a bag of dozens of metal spheres of varying sizes, and a yellow backpack containing a purple notecard that read, UNDER THE FULL MOON THE SMALL ONES WILL KNOW TERROR.

Looking to the future, we have an intelligence system that doesn't work anymore.

The Intelligence Bureau includes three components: intelligence, interdiction, and prevention. Can we position ourselves to find out about a planned terrorist attack? Can we get in the middle of it? Can we stop it? The Counterterrorism Bureau includes prevention, preparedness, response. Prevention is where they cross over. We have to stop these things before they happen.

Counterterrorism preparedness: Are we ready for a chemical attack? Do we have the equipment, the know-how, the people? Are we prepared to respond to the active shooter? The NYPD now has sixteen hundred people. Are they ready to go?

There are three brands of active terrorist:

Directed. The Bataclan theater gunmen. Trained in the camps, sent with a manager, told to strike.

Enabled. The Junaid Hussain devotee. Motivated, encouraged to act, provided with targeting and requirements.

Inspired. The lone wolf. They never meet Junaid Hussain, they've never been to a training camp, they just drink the Kool-Aid online and decide to self-initiate. They are not going out to meet anyone, they are not looking online for help, they are not asking their friends to join the plot. They own a conspiracy that exists only between their mind and the glow of that screen.

Ahmad Khan Rahimi detonated a bomb on Twenty-Third Street in Manhattan. He appears never to have been in touch with any particular terrorist group or training camp. His diary and notes showed he was a voracious consumer of radical Islamist propaganda. He was shot and arrested in New Jersey by Linden police after a running gun battle in the streets of Linden, during which he wounded one officer (the bullet was stopped by a vest) within fifty hours of his bomb going off.

Ahmad Khan Rahimi was a puzzle. We couldn't document any contact between Rahimi and any terrorist group, but he had traveled to Afghanistan and stayed for months. When he was questioned upon his return he told U.S. Customs and Border Protection agents that he went to Afghanistan to visit his wife and children and returned to the U.S. to go back to work so he could send money home to them. We never knew if Rahimi made contact with Al Qaeda, or went to a camp in Afghanistan. We do know that sometime, he learned to make a number of different bombs, with different explosives and different containers. He had pressure-cooker bombs and pipe bombs, and he learned that somewhere.

Sayfullo Saipov ran down nineteen people, killing eight, on the West Side Highway. He had over seventy ISIS videos on his phone and watched all of them numerous times. He was a pure product of the propaganda. He was shot and arrested at the scene by the NYPD.

Akayed Ullah blew himself up under the Port Authority Bus Terminal. He had watched *Flames of War II*, a remake of the ISIS film *Flames of War*, and seen a Christmas poster showing Santa Claus with a bag full of dynamite standing in Times Square. He watched a news story in which someone was asked, "I saw the Santa Claus ISIS thing, do you feel safe?" and had answered *Yeah, I feel safe*. Ullah thought, *Why should that guy feel safe? Why should anybody feel safe here? I'm looking at what they're trying to do to Muslims overseas in Syria. It is my job to strike.* His bomb was a partial dud, and he was arrested at the scene by NYPD detectives.

People ask: How do you prevent a person from walking into the middle of Grand Central and blowing the place up? Could it happen there? Yes, it could happen there, because it could happen anywhere. Is New York the best-protected city? Yes, it is. Has it devoted more resources to intelligence and prevention than any other city? Yes, it has. Has it spent more money than any other city on its police department? Yes. But can I tell you it can't happen there? I can't say that. We keep learning this over and over again.

We can increase the odds of our stopping everything we can or could stop, by being vigilant and acting in accordance with well-laid plans. We can increase the probability that our response is going to minimize injury and death by devoting resources and providing nonstop training. That is what we are doing. But anyone who tells you they can prevent every terrorist attack in an open and free society doesn't know this world.

I retired from the NYPD at the close of business on Friday, September 16, 2016. Jimmy O'Neill was sworn in as my successor in a small, private ceremony at police headquarters that evening. The larger public event would be held several days later. His first official day would be Monday. On Saturday evening, a pressure-cooker bomb filled with shrapnel exploded on West Twenty-Third Street in Chelsea. The entire department went into high gear to find the bomber. A few hours later a second bomb was discovered four blocks away. Jimmy faced cameras and questions, and handled the tense situation with grace and professionalism. That night, with the attack still unresolved, the new commissioner asked John Miller, "Do you have any suspects?"

"Sir," John told him, "it just went off. I mean, we're putting it together . . ."

"Well, I have one," O'Neill said.

Pretty quick, thought Miller. "Who's that?" he asked.

"Bill Bratton. He did this to me. Three years without a successful terrorist attack, and I get one on my first day. It's not even my first day!"

Miller sympathized. "Yeah," he said, "we did see a shadowy figure walking away from all these cameras that did look like him, but I know it's not him."

"How do you know?" asked Jimmy.

"Because Bratton would never walk away from a camera."

CHAPTER 13

Defunding Defending: The Future of American Policing

s there systemic racism in America? Of course there is. The country was built on slavery—as I have said, America's original sin. From the start, its economy depended on slave labor; its Constitution legalized and enshrined the practice. The Civil War, America's most terrible internal struggle, was fought over it. The country's moral center has been called into question because of how we have treated one another, and often Americans have been found wanting. The economic and cultural fallout has continued for almost four hundred years. Policing, at its worst moments, supported it. Education, housing, health care, peace of mind—all have been denied to people of color over the course of American history, and we are fortunate now to be living in a time when that fact is no longer doubted. Or, at least, is in less dispute than at any time I can remember.

Is there systemic racism in American policing? My answer is "Yes, but."

Some try to label the NYPD as a racist organization, yet the department is majority minority and highly and increasingly committed to diversity. There is a mistaken and widely held assumption that the NYPD's practice of stop, question, and frisk was and is intentionally racially discriminatory. This is incorrect. The majority of stops were made in high-crime areas around the city, often in response to calls from the community to the police. Did the police overuse it? Certainly. Did SQF disproportionately impact minorities? It certainly did. But why?

Where is crime occurring? We put cops on the dots. Where are the dots? In New York, crime is high in about eight of the city's seventy-seven precincts, largely in Black and brown neighborhoods. The disproportionate impact cannot be denied, but the disproportionate percentage of people doing the shooting and committing the crimes are Black and brown.

Who is being affected? The victims are disproportionately Black and brown people. The police department is fully aware that the bulk of the crime citizens call upon us to confront, the bulk of the 311 calls, the bulk of the disorder in New York City occurs in Black and Latino neighborhoods, way out of proportion to what is happening in white neighborhoods. We pursue all criminals. We do not pursue criminals of color because they are of color, we pursue them because they are criminals.

One of the reasons there were so many stops in the 1990s, when SQF was instituted, is that there was so much crime: 2,243 murders a year, 5,000 people shot. By summer 2019, crime was at historic lows, including murders, shootings, and all the FBI's seven major crimes. This is not hyperbole, it is fact. At the same time, the NYPD had achieved a policing anomaly: it had reduced crime to nearly the bottom of what people thought was possible, but did it while simultaneously reducing the number of arrests and the number of criminal summonses issued. Police uses of force in its encounters with the public were down, complaints against the police officers were down, and the department had initiated the most ambitious neighborhood-policing philosophy ever tried by any major city, an intimate style of policing in which Build the Block meetings were held at people's personal homes, with community stakeholders and representatives of the department getting together at the ground level. Every indicator was going in the right direction.

By 2019, reported stops were down 93 percent from 2011. Arrests and criminal summonses fell by 46.6 percent and 79.7 percent, respectively, by the end of that year. One hundred forty-eight thousand fewer people of color were arrested than in 2013. With the smaller enforcement footprint came deep cuts in crime—in a city of eight million, murders fell below three hundred in a year for the first time since 1951, and shootings below eight hundred, as well as a 33.4 percent drop in robberies and 38.4 percent drop in burglaries.

New York City easily sustained its ranking as the city with the lowest overall index crime rate among the 20 largest cities in the nation. It also made significant progress against shootings. Although shootings rose by 22 incidents in 2019, they were down by 327 incidents, or 30 percent, across the first six years of the de Blasio administration. The hallmark of my and my successor Jimmy O'Neill's terms as commissioner has been significant decreases in crime in the context of greatly reduced enforcement, especially in communities of color. In the broadest sense, this is what the NYPD has meant by precision policing, the judicious use of police power in support of focused crime reduction goals.

And then, something happened that is still not widely understood or appreciated. A small group of advocates, political activists, and others joined together under the umbrella of Criminal Justice Reform and convinced the State Legislature to stick into a budget bill a series of laws that were going to fix this unfortunate situation. Well, they fixed it all right.

I predicted confidently for twenty-five years that, because of CompStat and progressive neighborhood-oriented policing, crime would never again go up in New York City; we had dropped the crime rate so low, and through the advent of precision policing and continuing advances in policing theory and practice, had the ability to identify emerging patterns and trends so quickly that we could put cops on the dots and prevent its expansion. I was very confident.

Boy, was I wrong. I did not take into account the ill-conceived and ill-instituted efforts of the legislature in Albany and the City Council to fix problems without consulting with the police, the judges, or the prosecutors, whose business it is to handle them. Under the mantle of bail reform, discovery reform, and criminal justice reform, they dismantled a system that while not perfect, was improving.

When I was a kid there was a toy called the Magic Slate. It was a piece of cardboard with carbon-backed sticker paper on its front. You could write anything you wanted on it—words, drawings, musical notes, tic-tac-toe—and there it was in black-and-white. When you were done, you lifted the sheet and everything disappeared—the page was once again blank. It was Etch-a-Sketch, only simpler. Policing is now going through just such an Etch-a-Sketch moment.

The criminal justice reform movement was well intentioned. Its goal was to reverse what it defined as systemic racism that resulted in a policy of mass incarceration of people of color. It is fair to say the court system has, throughout American history, not treated all citizens as equal in the eyes of the law, and making it more equitable is a justified and worthy goal. There is no reason for anyone to languish in jail because of lack of funds. The history of evidence discovery, often misused by prosecutors, has tended to hinder defense and keep people incarcerated longer than necessary. And the right to a speedy trial is fundamental to American jurisprudence. I applaud the intent of lawmakers to address this inequality. However, in attempting to ameliorate these injustices, lawmakers and activists did not serve the community well and passed a series of laws that went many bridges too far. It appears to me that righteous indignation overpowered reasoned consideration.

The first mistake was to write these laws without consulting with all the agencies that would be affected. This was a set of laws written by and for the defense bar and signed into law without the input or expertise of police or prosecutors or judges as to their real-world results. In light of previously unconsidered facts, the NYPD begged the State Legislature and others to reconsider these laws before they took effect. We could have told them these were not sound ideas, that they had unintended consequences that ought to be addressed before putting the entire package into law. They ignored our requests.

Take, for example, discovery reform. A bill was intended "to overhaul New York's antiquated discovery process by which prosecutors could withhold basic evidence until the day the trial begins." It required that "both prosecutors and defendants share all information in their possession well in advance of trial. Defendants will also be allowed the opportunity to review whatever evidence is in the prosecution's possession prior to pleading guilty to a crime. Prosecutors will be required to provide the defense with discoverable information and materials within 15 days of arraignment." In an effort to protect victims and witnesses from intimidation and coercion, and to "ensure the . . . sanctity of the judicial process," prosecutors could petition for a protective order, "shielding identifying information when necessary," though no guarantees were made that this order would be granted.

The cost in time and money to the city and state of providing the information in that timeframe was gargantuan. More than its cost, the law made the city less safe.

Let's take a benign example. Say there is a shooting. No one is actually hit, there is no victim; someone is just having target practice against a wall. A neighbor sees it from her window. She knows who fired the shots; he lives nearby. The neighbor calls 911 and leaves an anonymous tip. However, because of technology the police now have her telephone number. They trace the call and learn her name.

The cops are nearby, they pick up the armed shooter, make a report, and arrest him on a felony weapons charge. Not long thereafter the prosecutor shows up at the caller's door and says, "Listen, we found the gun, but we can't prove that the guy discharged it. We need your testimony." The prosecutor would have to tell the anonymous caller that there is a good chance the shooter will learn her identity.

The caller doesn't want to be on the bad side of a man with a gun; she just doesn't want shots fired in her backyard. If she even decides to testify—not at all a given—what does she say as a witness? "I don't remember. I can't tell you if he actually fired any shots. I know I called and said that, but it might have just been firecrackers. I think it was just firecrackers. You know what? It was just firecrackers."

Why would she lie? Because the shooter is a bad guy, he doesn't want to be ID'd by anyone for anything, and it's entirely possible that he might shoot the caller—or her friends, or her family—to make absolutely certain the risk has been eliminated. Life can become difficult for someone who is labeled a snitch. In some neighborhoods the No Snitching ethic is subscribed to pretty hard. The *New York Post* ran this story in August 2019:

"Dying pal of Nipsey Hussle tells cops, 'Fuck you' when asked to ID shooter. A mortally wounded gang banger hated cops so much, he defiantly refused to identify his killer—instead telling officers, 'Fuck you, son!' with one of his last breaths, law-enforcement sources told the *Post*. [The dying man's] refusal to aid police came amid five fatal shootings over less than 24 hours in the Big Apple—and underscored the hurdles cops face as they try to keep the city safe amid an uptick in shootings."

So what do you think defendants in more extreme yet commonplace cases are going to do to witnesses or complainants they believe violated that ethic? Is it a surprise that the crime rate rose precipitously when the law was put into practice?

Bail reform, the elimination of cash bail for low-level misdemeanors or nonviolent felonies, was created to decrease the time in custody of people with few funds, a move that supporters have said will help address racial disparities and overcrowding of jails. It had the unintended consequence of returning remarkable numbers of suspected felons to the streets in a matter of hours. The "Bail Reform Law" or "Criminal Justice Reform Bill" contained not just "bail reform" and "discovery reform," but also legislated away an officer's ability to make certain arrests. Under these new laws, a cop who responds to a shoplifting call may be arresting the same guy for the tenth time, but shoplifting arrests can no longer be put "through the system" and have to be issued a Desk Appearance Ticket. Whether to make an arrest or issue a DAT used to be, in many cases, at the officer's discretion. Now, that discretion has been eliminated and the regular shoplifter knows that stealing gets only a disappearance ticket, so it must not be serious. More important, it removes the main deterrent of even the possibility of spending a night in jail. A lot of the incentive *not* to commit a crime has been removed.

Because the law took the power to hold people before trial away from judges, almost everyone arrested—aside from those facing murder or attempted murder charges—would not see a jail cell before conviction; they would be arraigned and put back on the street. Drug dealers got DATs. A career criminal released with fifteen priors was arrested on a subway platform for attempted forcible rape—in progress. The man arrested for inciting to riot when he called on people to loot the Queens Center Mall was already out on a gun charge. He was released on the inciting to riot charge, and when he was later charged—with video evidence—with looting a Lower East Side liquor store, he was released again. It is not just about enforcement. It is about consequences.

Right now, approximately 40 percent of the people being arrested for gun crimes in New York are released on their own recognizance. In Brooklyn, home to most of the city's gang-related shootings, the figure is actually 80 percent. That does not count the number of cases in which the DA declines prosecution or "defers" prosecution awaiting DNA tests on the gun. New York State law requires a set of mandatory minimum sentences, running from one to four years, for possession of a gun in the city. Right now, out of over 2,200 people charged with gun offenses, only 11 percent are listed as "in custody." That means between letting almost 40 percent of them walk out of court at arraignment with no bail at all, and with 50 percent making bail, only 11 percent are in. Or, put another way, 89 percent of the people we arrest with loaded guns in the middle of a wave of shootings are walking the streets. How is that going to reduce shootings?

The corner grocery store, the local supermarket, the bodega are fixtures in a community. They provide both a service and tangible proof that the neighborhood is functioning. With bail eliminated and the immediate consequences of an arrest off the table, shoplifting skyrocketed. Criminals caught on. Supermarket owners became increasingly frustrated by shoplifters who just came in and took what they wanted, seemingly fearless of the police being called or any legal consequence. This is a growing pattern seen at bodegas, supermarkets, at Duane Reades and Walgreens, where people (homeless, mentally ill, regular criminals) just load up on what they want and leave. What's more, if a person takes a tube of toothpaste and runs out the door, that is a larceny. But if he comes in every day and takes stuff, and the owner intervenes, shoves him away, that is not a larceny, it is a robbery by force—still a non-bail-eligible offense, which means he can come in and do it every morning and be released from court to do it again in the afternoon. Criminals know this. The people who are suffering are the community members walking around on the street. With a simple, well-intentioned law, the legislature contributed to the destruction of confidence and order in the city's neighborhoods.

The mayor and City Council, at the height of the coronavirus pandemic, decreased the population of Rikers Island, the city's largest jail, by three thousand inmates, but did not sufficiently budget for their reinsertion into society. What happened? People convicted of domestic violence went home and did it again. Sex offenders resumed their activities. Recidivists went back at it. And the NYPD was tasked with arresting them . . . again. At the same time, the state of New York was releasing hundreds of convicted felons from state prisons back into communities that were not prepared to receive them.

The results have been disastrous. The number of New York's victims is increasing—these are real people with real lives and real families—and the vast majority of those victims are people of color. All this during a discussion of how police should be doing less.

It's a confusing time for New Yorkers. Now even *The New York Times*'s real estate section is running articles touting eight suburban communities and basically advising New Yorkers on how to flee the city. The mayor doesn't seem bothered by the idea of letting the rich and the middle class leave. In a rhetorical flourish, he seems to encourage stripping the public school system of middle-class students. This seems to me remarkably shortsighted. Aside from the value of those young minds, it is exactly those families whose income, through the tax base, supports the city's public schools. There do not appear to be plans to make up the shortfall.

George Floyd's murder—and it was 100 percent a murder—was one of the worst things I have ever seen done to a person by a police officer. At the beginning of the coronavirus pandemic, when most of the nation was shut indoors, fearful, alone, in need of human contact, and reexamining the actual functioning of society, it seemed to encapsulate all that was wrong with the way America was being ruled and the people who were ruling it. It showed a bad cop doing a terrible thing.

I am by nature an optimist, but this threw me. I spent a significant part of the year not knowing how to defend my profession and the thing to which I have dedicated career and life against those who would insist that it is something that it is not.

And yet I found a silver lining. The terrible death of George Floyd brought the awareness of systemic racism to the surface. A month earlier, you would have been hard-pressed to find more than one senator or network anchor or elected official willing to say it out loud, let alone go on camera and admit to its existence. A day later the idea was in the streets.

Streets that cops had to police.

The event was horrific and galvanizing. Protests erupted the next night, and quickly became violent. The pent-up fury of communities of color combined with the indignation of progressives motivated by frustration at the nonstop political provocations of Donald Trump and his government were joined in their physical activism by several anarchist groups whose goal was to smash the state. This live spirit produced a powerful and mobilized force.

They were in turn joined by groups of people of little means who saw this as an opportunity to smash and grab. Black Lives Matter was the leader of this movement, but it had many moving parts and grew organically in many cities around the country.

Cops were their immediate target. A bad cop had tortured and killed a Black man with depraved indifference. He put his knee on George Floyd's neck, heard him whimper piteously, heard the crowd, heard his fellow officers, and continued on his path to the man's death. It was shameful, and the boldness of the killing seemed, in some minds, to epitomize the attitude and actions of police in general. The fact that there is no epidemic of police indifferently murdering Black men did not matter; even one was too many. Police-officer-as-wanton-killer was a widely held image, seemingly confirmed by a series of cell-phone videos from around the country. No amount of facts disproving that assertion was going to change anyone's mind. The rage against cops was fierce.

In New York, a dozen young men jogged down Eighth Street after smashing plate-glass windows at a nearby Starbucks and the Gap on Broadway, shouting "Break everything! Break everything!" and laughing. Another gang hired Ubers to take them to Chelsea, where they could break into clothing stores. Loot in hand, they stopped to rob an all-night fruit vendor of his day's cash earnings . . . with a toddler in tow. This wasn't revolutionary ardor, they weren't smashing the state, and I do not believe this was four hundred years of oppression bubbling to the surface. This was opportunists trying to take advantage of a chaotic situation and come home with something to convert into cash. This was crime, and it's up to the police to put an end to it. We don't need the looters to be given free rein, or to get a pass from the court system so they can come back the next night and do the same thing. Which they did. But the idea that they represented any significant portion of the protesters was false as well, and was peddled to demonize and increase hostility against them. Partisans were stockpiling their arguments.

A major thrust of the Black Lives Matter movement, in concert with the white people who were doing similar organizing alongside it, was the idea of getting rid of the police as it now exists. The thought continuum: There should be no racism in society; there should be no racism in police departments; police departments are racist, therefore demolish the police, abolish the police. The phrase that stuck was *Defund the Police*. In New York that didn't take long to devolve into *Fuck the Police*. The catcall of choice was "NYPD Suck My Dick!" That came out of the crowd with a distinctly visceral disrespect, and "NYPD SMD" was spray-painted on the plywood that replaced street-level store windows up and down Broadway the morning after the first demonstrations and lootings.

Like Black Lives Matter, Defund the Police is a political hashtag that means different things to different people. Some want to abolish the police altogether; others want to take money out of police budgets and give it to social-service agencies to be used for community needs and activities, particularly focused on minorities. Still others want to, as they put it, *redesign* or *reimagine* policing. All are centered around the idea of taking from law enforcement organizations many of the responsibilities and associated funding that have become flash points—dealing with the mentally ill, the homeless, the addicted—and putting them in other hands.

But there's a reason those responsibilities have fallen to the police over the years: society in general, and the state in particular, decided it did not have the willpower or the funds to run programs that would handle them successfully. Mental institutions closed; shelters became unwelcoming and unsafe; addiction services became underprioritized and overwhelmed. So who ended up as the dumping ground for the homeless in the 1970s? The police. The drug addicts of the '70s and '80s? The police. Who is having to deal with the issues of today? The police. Police departments around the country would be pleased to pass along many of these responsibilities and focus on more traditional policing concerns, but they cannot do that until some other fully capable entity is prepared to step into the breach.

Replacing the police as government caregivers is a great concept; its advocates just have it backward. We saw how small-government representatives sucked funding out of most social programs since the Kennedy administration. Neutered them, starved them, and then tried to eliminate them. And we saw that the only one standing at the bottom of all society's safety nets, when people fall through the holes because they are frayed and worn down or purposely ripped open, is the cop. And the country got very comfortable with that.

Shall we invest money in developing more care for emotionally disturbed people? Shall we increase hospital beds and institutions for the mentally ill? Shall we adjust the insurance laws so their needs actually get covered? Or should we just say, "Ahh, screw it. The cops will handle it"? Society had made that choice already, now they were rethinking it. Should we deal with the homeless with treatment and housing? Or should we tell the cops to tell them, "Keep moving it along"? Again, we've done that before; that's how the cops became the enemy of the homeless. Should we deal with drug addiction and rehab and programs on a national basis, or should we just say to the cops, "Try to arrest your way through this and make it better"?

You can't defund the police before you make those investments. You can't withdraw police services until you have sustained and secured those services in other ways. You can't take the money from the cops and throw it to failed agencies that don't know what they're doing. You have to make those investments, and then over time, as these specifically trained organizations get into gear and respond successfully to the responsibilities being given, the police can relinquish their role and defund themselves. The NYPD goes on an emotionally disturbed person call *every 4 minutes*, 24 hours a day, 7 days a week, 365 days a year. If it was not the department's responsibility, think of all the time that would be available to reduce disorder and prevent crime.

The money must be reinvested first, and then one day police departments across America should be able to wake up and say, "Wow, we don't need that many cops. We don't have that many calls, we don't have as big a drug problem, we don't have a serious homeless problem, we are not affected as seriously by mentally ill people who are neither being cared for in a hospital nor supported on the outside." At that point the departments themselves can say, "You know, we've got lots of cops who don't have that much to do. You can have a few thousand of them back."

But we are not there; we're nowhere near. And we can't possibly get there by taking a billion dollars out of the police budget, as has been proposed for the NYPD, including 60 percent of overtime funding, which is the department's go-to tool during a crime wave.

It seems to me that a formidable portion of the effort to defund the police, abolish the police, fuck the police is just punitive. People are angry and hateful and spiteful. It doesn't make sense, it's not well thought out. You can't defund an institution to punish it and think that this action is going to make it better. Under normal circumstances, you have to pour more money into an institution with needs, not less. So "Defund the Police" has never made sense to me. "Defund the police and send the money elsewhere" is at least rational, but that money isn't being sent anywhere else, and the government and/or private agencies in line for those funds didn't become any smarter or more efficient in the meantime. Those agencies must be rebuilt. Meanwhile, we are going to see exactly what we're seeing, which is the police doing the job that every other agency has failed to do.

If you defund the police and tell them to stop doing those jobs—to disengage from the homeless, to walk by the mentally ill—the streets will not be pretty. As funds are being withdrawn and no replacements are being put in place, nothing is working. In June 2020, the 60 percent cut in overtime pay resulted in thousands of New York City cops being taken off the streets. The crime rate, particularly shootings, went through the roof. NYPD commissioner Dermot Shea equates it to turning off the hoses while a fire in a building is raging. He asks, "What did you expect would happen?"

#DefundThePolice was a catchy hashtag driving policy. However, policy needs to be based on facts, figures, and an understanding of the issues. Defund, redesign, reimagine, abolish the police all had their moments.

The worst idea is that somehow America should simply abolish the police, yet you can hear that call emanating from any number of protest podiums. There is an active opposition to the entire concept of policing that is using this upheaval as a shovel at a grave, saying, "We can abolish this!" What could they be thinking?!

Anytime police are absent, society degenerates. When the powerful but sociopathic decide they are going to take what's not theirs, who is best trained and able to prevent bad actors from preying upon the community? Cops. With no cops in the streets, lawlessness prevails. Robbery, rape, casual violence, horrendous murder rates. Who's going to stop them? Social workers? Self-appointed citizen vigilantes? Who are those people and who sets their agenda? It's not pretty, armed anarchy. So, please, that is not going to happen. Forget about abolishing the police.

Black Lives Matter led the demonstrations after George Floyd's death. In New York, the demonstrators took to the streets. More than a few threw rocks and bottles at officers and firebombed police cars. The police mentality at these demonstrations is complicated, because the cops are highly aware that the thousands of people in attendance, yelling and chanting, are protesting against both their institution and them personally. And yet there's work to be done. The streets belong to the people, but it's the cop's job to keep them safe.

There is a lot of anger on the street, and recently—beginning well before the murder of George Floyd—officers have begun encountering a new phenomenon: the impact of social media increasing resistance to the police.

Police often endure hostility during a street encounter, generally and particularly from younger people. The anger confronting them is consistent and visceral, and a mass of cell-phone cameras appears. The subjects of law enforcement find themselves in a new position; not only are their friends watching, but the whole scene is going to be on Facebook or You-Tube. On a personal level, if they don't resist, in their crowd they're some kind of pansy. Plus, they've got a big audience, and some are thinking, *Well, I've got a crowd, I've got a bunch of cameras, if I push hard enough the cops will back down and I will get away.* So, factoring in the anger, what used to be simple arrest situations now have to be recalculated by police officers, who have to figure out whether this particular confrontation is going to be worth the struggle.

Often cops are responding to information received via 911. It is not unheard of, and not infrequent, that people will jazz up that call to get the police to arrive more quickly. *"He's got a gun, he's got a knife!"* So the cop's tension level is already elevated. Some cops press forward, and the scene can get ugly as the assignment gets done. Some back off, which makes performing their job more difficult the next time. So everybody is angry at each other.

And of course there are cases of terrible police malfeasance. To say their names: Tamir Rice, Daniel Prude, William Green, Elijah McClain, Breonna Taylor. There are more. These are horrors and tragedies that demand to be corrected. The facts in each are different, but sadly they are lumped together in one giant but overstated allegation of institutional police brutality.

Even in the midst of demonstrations against them, cops have a job to do: escort demonstrators, in accordance with their legal permits, from point A to point B; try to maintain the flow of traffic, not always an attainable goal when there are large numbers of people. And if the crowd decides to block traffic, after issuing a warning, officers can decide, "All right, are we going to give up this street or this bridge, or are we going to make arrests?"

That is where police face some challenges. I would be lying if I said that months of antipolice demonstrations did not affect morale. On a more practical level, when cops roll up on some condition in the street—a large, late-night BBQ where gang members are present and there is likely to be a shooting, or a dice game that is likely to result in either a robbery or a shooting (the number of shootings connected to dice games is remarkable), or both—you now see a different dynamic. When cops engage in quality-of-life enforcement they are very likely to be challenged. People often surround them and start yelling, and if officers make an arrest, with the ever-present cell-phone cameras going, more and more people feel the right or the need to resist arrest. One of the new laws holds that if during an arrest a police officer compresses a suspect's diaphragm—intentionally or unintentionally—the cop may end up being the criminal, so you can see why they may be less likely to get involved in preventing the very actions that may result in violence later that same night. That is a shame on many levels.

Do the cops step back or slow down? The NYPD is a diverse, hard-working, dedicated police department. It is made up of Blacks, whites, Hispanics, Asians. It's a police agency that looks in some measure like the city it polices. More and more young and minority officers live in the city, so no—it's not that the cops don't care, or that they are not invested, or that they don't put their lives on the line each day to prove their allegiance to the law. But as elected officials in Albany and the city pass increasing numbers of laws giving latitude to people charged with breaking the law and less and less to those charged with enforcing it, it is no wonder these officers may in some cases be more hesitant to get involved in enforcing violations.

There is a widely held belief that "qualified immunity" means that a cop can do just about anything and not worry about getting sued for it. That's why some people want to enact legislation that would take "qualified immunity" away.

First, here is what "qualified immunity" is not: it is not a statute, but rather a legal doctrine based on years of case law developed largely through the federal courts. Qualified immunity gives many public officials, including police officers, a certain "cover" for actions taken in good faith while performing their official duties. Every case is different, but the two basic tenets of qualified immunity are that the action the officer was taking was "clearly defined in law," and second, under the circumstances in the moment the officer took that action, it was "objectively reasonable," or more simply put, the police officer did not believe—all things considered in the moment—that it was grossly negligent and the wrong thing to do.

Let me give you an example:

There is a high-speed chase on a freeway. The sheriff is chasing two people in a stolen car. We've passed the first test; stopping a stolen car is "clearly defined in law."

A mile ahead, a state trooper throws a spike strip off an overpass just as the stolen car is approaching. But now the stolen car is going a hundred miles an hour. The tires blow, the car skids, rolls over, hits a concrete abutment, bursts into flames, and the driver of the stolen car and his passenger die. The passenger's family sues the sheriff and the state police and names the officers individually in the lawsuit. Do they have immunity?

Maybe. That's why it's "qualified." After all the facts are known at trial, the judge and the jury would ask, *Were their actions "clearly defined in law?"* and *Were they "reasonably objective"?*

The ability of the officers to chase or stop a stolen car is "clearly defined in law." That's the easy part. What about throwing the spike strips to disable the fleeing car? Was that "reasonably objective"?

The state trooper might argue that he had used spike strips successfully in other pursuits before. He might add that he used them consistent with his training. He might add that while he knew it was a car chase, he had no way of knowing if the car approaching was going sixty miles an hour or a hundred. While the outcome was bad, the trooper would argue he was "reasonably objective" in his decisions, given his training, the limited time and information he had, and his prior experience. That trooper and the sheriff might well be covered by "qualified immunity" in that case.

Think about it. If every police officer, in a job that sometimes requires making split-second decisions with high stakes—sometimes life-and-death situations—also had to calculate whether or not they would be sued, held personally liable, maybe lose their savings or home, many cops would hesitate to take action when it was needed most. Despite what some may think, a police officer making life-and-death decisions usually makes the decision that is meant to save a life, and in most cases it is the right call.

Society and the courts have conferred qualified immunity because they understand that sometimes, even with the best of intentions, things will go wrong. If a police officer is acting on behalf of the people, empowered by the people, and yes, risking his or her life for the people, that officer should have a little cover from the same society that has asked them to take these risks.

Here is the irony: Cops have qualified immunity for split-second decisions. Prosecutors and judges enjoy "absolute immunity"; that means, no matter what the circumstances, it is all but impossible for them to be held personally liable. And remember, the decisions of DAs and judges are weighty and important, but those people also have plenty of time to consider them. Yet the only people in the criminal justice system whom the "advocates" seek to strip of these protections are the police, the people who often have the least time to make a tough call and who face the greatest dangers.

For Congress to pass a law that strips police officers of the limited protections they have would be a disservice to both the police and the public. I want my cops to be brave. I want my cops to be risk takers, and yes, I want them to be risk managers. But I *don't* want them to be armchair litigators when they need to be clearheaded and focused officers during a dangerous situation in which they can save a life. That's not when they should be trying to calculate who might sue them and for how much. We owe them that much.

To allay public suspicion and ensure honorable work by officers, within the past year reforms have been enacted in the disciplinary system. Departments are now obligated, notwithstanding ongoing criminal investigations, to investigate in a timely manner whether violations by officers have occurred. The key element here is timeliness. There will be no more Pantaleo five-year waits.

Departments around the country are becoming proactive in determining which of their officers might be at risk of stepping over the line. Over the years, the City of New York paid out tens of millions of dollars in lawsuits and settlements as a result of officer malfeasance, and it is in the interest of both the city's coffers and its people to keep the incidents that incurred these expenses to a minimum. After rising steadily from 2010 to 2013, during my and my successor Jimmy O'Neill's time as commissioner, new lawsuits against the cops, notice of claims against New York City over the actions of cops, and recently, payouts over such suits, have declined dramatically. From 2014 to 2018, CCRB complaints, particularly involving excessive use of force, declined steadily.

As a result of a federal monitorship, in the past year the NYPD has instituted Early Intervention, a nondisciplinary risk management program derived from best practices included in early consent decrees and that in the case of LAPD's consent decree was known as an Early Warning System.

Early Intervention's core concept is that there are specific indicators that can be used to identify potentially at-risk officers, and when a designated threshold is crossed, the department will take a hard 360-degree look at those officers, make a determination as to whether intervention is warranted, and if so, determine what might, as Deputy Commissioner for Risk Management Jeff Schlanger says, "put them back on the righteous path."

Early indicators that might trip the wire and identify an officer at risk include: complaints lodged against him or her with the CCRB, civil lawsuits against the officer, declinations by district attorneys' offices of prosecutions of arrests by that officer, failure of the city to indemnify or defend an officer in a lawsuit, a finding of adverse credibility from a district attorney or the court, and at a pretrial suppression hearing, successful suppression of an identification or evidence as derived from an officer's testimony. There may be problems between cops as well, not only with the public.

Departments are reluctant to give up on cops. Certainly no officer will be sent back out into the field if the department is in any way unsure of their fitness to do the job; we prefer to reeducate and retrain, while monitoring progress. For instance, if an officer has three CCRB complaints or crossed other lines of demarcation, Early Intervention's senior executive committee would review the rest of their department history. It would seek input from the cop's commanding officer and determine whether an intervention would be of benefit. If one is in order, they would outline the parameters, choosing from among all available options.

Interventions range from additional instruction and training to mentoring to enhanced supervision, including through body-worn camera viewing. The officer is brought to the Risk Management Bureau for a mentoring session and told *Here's why you're here. Here's what we expect the benefit to be. Here's the risk for you if it doesn't work.* Success is expected, but the results of Early Intervention can lead to a modified assignment or transfer to a position in which they will not interact with the public, or in some situations a referral for disciplinary investigation, which could, in an extreme case, lead to termination.

I have a lot of respect for District Attorney Cy Vance and the work the NYPD does with the Manhattan district attorney's office. But let's measure what he has said against the facts. Vance wrote:

> In recent years, as our city's annual murder totals reached an all-time low, my office challenged Broken Windows orthodoxy by declining to prosecute low-level offenses such as marijuana possession, fare evasion and unlicensed vending that exacerbated the multi-generational harm caused by mass incarceration while serving little to no public safety purpose. As a result of these policy changes, we cut prosecutions by 58 percent over the past decade, while violent crime plummeted.

While it is great that his office has to do 58 percent less work, it is not great if you go to a precinct community council meeting where the residents are complaining about people smoking and selling weed in the lobby, or the violence we see associated with marijuana-related robberies or shootings or turf battles. People in those neighborhoods don't understand how the DA would be permitted not to enforce the laws that prohibit the very crimes they are complaining about.

Here's how a cop views Broken Windows enforcement. She doesn't need to troll for lawbreakers; they are on the streets in abundance. "I see an actual violation. I don't have to find the marijuana in his pocket, he is smoking it in front of me. He is drinking beer from an open container. He is urinating in the street." Pejoratively, among the cops on the street, this is called beer-and-piss enforcement. "When we got our beer-and-piss we've got a legitimate stop. We don't have to articulate what we saw, what we thought, what we felt, what we imagined. We can say, 'I saw the violation. He was peeing in the street, he was drinking beer, he was smoking weed. So I stopped him to introduce the concept of giving him a summons. To do that I had to get him to identify himself. Once he identified himself, I could now run him for a warrant, I could find out that he was wanted for two robberies and lock him up for those two robberies and use the summons as the basis for my stop.'"

The purest form of Broken Windows uses the minor enforcement to unearth the violent criminals who were already walking around the street breaking the law in other ways, in between their more serious violent acts. That was far different from SQF, but in the legislative mind they were lumped together. The idea that by suddenly stopping quality-of-life enforcement because the DA decided unilaterally that this somehow helps to end "mass incarceration" ignores the fact that no one *ever* was sentenced to jail time, or held on bail, for possession of a small amount of marijuana or for jumping a turnstile or being an unlicensed vendor. That is simply factually untrue.

The first thing we did to reduce subway crime twenty-five years ago was to get lawbreakers as they entered the system. When we arrested people for fare evasion, we found many had weapons, knives, guns, or were wanted for violent crimes or robberies in the subways. Since the district attorney stopped prosecuting the crime of jumping the turnstile, New York experienced two logical results: first, and most important, violent crimes on the transit system went up; second, many more people simply stopped paying the fare because they knew there was no consequence. That cost an already strapped MTA increasing amounts of money and was not fair to the law-abiding rider who paid to get on the system.

Broken Windows policing was an effective tool in the mid-nineties, when violent crime was at all-time highs. It worked. Today's precision policing—created from the lessons learned from the misuse of SQF—focuses very narrowly on the gangs, crews, and/or individual actors who drive the violence in individual neighborhoods. Who are the shot callers, the shooters, the armed robbers? Cops use that intelligence and *all* the laws available to focus on those drivers of violence to make that neighborhood safer. When district attorneys and/or judges decided they were going to eliminate entire sets of laws from that tool kit, and the State Legislature decided to change laws to make it harder for police to do their jobs but easier for criminals to do theirs, we saw a correlation: crime jumped up after we had it down to historic lows.

The district attorneys in both Manhattan and the Bronx have said, in effect, "We are not prosecuting gambling arrests anymore. If you arrest people on the street for shooting dice, we are not pursuing those cases or taking them seriously. It is not the job of the police to stop people from having fun." In a bizarre twist, if cops make a dice arrest, they can be fined by the prosecution.

Here is the problem. Cops routinely get to the site of a shooting and find dice on the ground. There are shell casings and there are dice. They pick up one cup and find a 9mm shell casing, pick up the next cup and it's a pair of dice. A recurring scenario: there was a dice game, somebody was winning and somebody was losing; someone claimed cheating and someone pulled out a gun. There was a big shooting. New York is living its own version of the song "Stagger Lee."

Here is the solution: If you sweep away the dice games in their early stages, you reduce the possibility of a later shooting or the fight that ensues when five guys show up to rob everyone. Gambling is illegal, the arrests would be justified, and the neighborhood would not only be safer for them, it would thank the cops who made them.

By eliminating the low-level arrests brought in under Broken Windows enforcement, the cops, at the behest of the DAs, are actually encouraging the crimes that have historically followed. Times have changed; it's increasingly difficult to find someone who minds people smoking marijuana. But cops and community members know that the people out there smoking weed and drinking forties are going to end up being in that shooting later that night. What did you think was going to happen?

Criminal justice reform failed miserably. After this fix was enacted, shootings went up, homicides went up, crime in the street went up, disorder went up, and New York was caught in the grinding wheels of a movement that says that if police do less, somehow the world will be a better place.

And yet we are at the beginning of an unsettling trend. Across the country a host of new prosecutors are being elected, all talking about their goals for criminal justice reform and saying explicitly that they want fewer people in jail. And while some of what they strive for has merit, there are legislatures and city councils around the country that acted precipitously, now sitting in the middle of the street with a hubcap in their mouth like the dog that caught the car, saying, "What the hell am I supposed to do now?"

The underpinnings of the demonstrations following the death of George Floyd grew from the specific to the general. Protests were not simply that one Black man had been senselessly killed by police, but that senseless killings of Black men by police are widespread and systemic. Organized protesters set about creating a national protest movement, all entirely within their rights as citizens. Policing those protests, meanwhile, remained local. And while departments from city to city watched and learned from one another's efforts, there was no centralized policing organization dispensing strategy and tactics. Within the protest movement, however, police departments found a broadening network of combatants.

In the past few years, we have encountered a brand-new phenomenon that flies in the face of the great American tradition of civil disobedience. When Dr. Martin Luther King Jr. marched, he would often sit down and accept arrest. It was civil disobedience. And for disobedience, it was indeed civil. Recently, what police have never seen before is 100 percent resistance of arrest. The idea, once a person has been taken into custody, is to effect a "de-arrest." The concept started during the protests in Hong Kong and uses a technique taken from the combat theories of martial artist Bruce Lee that they call "Be Like Water."

Most of these situations involve de-arresting people who have committed some aggressive act that will attract police attention—throwing a bottle, a rock, a brick, a Molotov cocktail—after which a cop catches and grabs them. The person tries to get away, and while he is resisting, the crowd surges in and hugs him, trying to pull him back. As the officer struggles to retain control, you have what appears to be the police beating on two people who seem to be hugging each other. Meanwhile members of the crowd around them put both hands in the air and say loudly, *"Peaceful protest, peaceful protest!"* When backup cops try to assist the officer, they have to wade through protesters, who stand their ground. Shoving is inevitable. Now you have people with their hands in the air saying "Peaceful protest" being shoved to the ground. When the reporter from *The New York Times* arrives to describe the scene, she writes what she sees; rather than describing the arrest of a violent rock-thrower or arsonist, she is likely to say, "In a sea of peaceful protesters, the police brutally bludgeoned a man. . . ."

The activists understand exactly what they are doing. Cameras and reporters do not often catch the original act; their attention is attracted by the de-arrest process, which is engineered to make the police look brutal. In their internal communications on their own message boards on the web, they have created tutorials and rated the success of their actions by how violent they got the cops to look. They have shirts and graphics and video examples of what is defined as a good de-arrest, with techniques running the gamut from hugging a comrade to hitting police with a hard object to doing a flying kick into a cop's chest. To them, failure is when the cops could not be caught in acts that appear brutal. They have trained to do this, they have practiced, and they create these viral moments to great effect. You have to hand it to them; they've thought it out, planned it, executed it, and they have succeeded.

Which doesn't mean that in the course of protests there weren't ugly moments during which cops passed their breaking point. But by and large, the provocations were willful and effective.

Deputy Commissioner for Intelligence and Counterterrorism John Miller met with Attorney General William Barr. The Trump administration was trying very hard to show that the wave of protests in the summer of 2020 was nationally led and controlled by the radical antifascist leftwing movement, antifa. They had the idea that there was a Godfather-like figure, the head of all protests, who was controlling, coordinating, and funding the whole operation. This was simply not true. Anarchists are anarchists. First they unite in a cause against the police. Then, once they get three groups together, they start fighting with one another, because they can't agree on anything. Miller was shocked and amused to find that in New York there was an actual organization called the Metropolitan Anarchist Coordinating Council, which was in and of itself an oxymoron. How can you be an anarchist with a coordinating council? "We want to create anarchy, but the first thing that we need to do is be organized."

This is what the police are up against: disorganized organizations.

During the first days of the George Floyd protests in New York, distinct and disparate groups came together. The anarchists showed up and started protesting, tagging buildings and cars with graffiti, breaking windows, tussling with the police. The larger groups took time to get in place, but by the third or fourth day, Black Lives Matter protesters arrived, from all walks of life.

The marches fell into an informal order. The anarchists were up front, followed by legitimate BLM protesters, and behind them the looters. The looters weren't really protesters, but they started marching with the groups, carrying signs, contributing to the noise before, as the sun went down and the hours got later, breaking into a coordinated looting operation. They may have agreed with the protest in spirit, but their anger certainly had little to do with politics and everything to do with feelings.

What may have seemed from the outside like a monolith—particularly to the hostile and uninitiated who were being primed to see all dissent as un-American—was actually nothing of the sort. It began to fray when Black groups and the more established socialist democratic white groups started to reject anarchist violence, saying it was distracting from the message and hijacking the movement. The anarchists, in turn, said, "These people aren't committed enough." When the schism between the Black leadership and the anarchists caused both to temporarily quit the field, cops noticed that suddenly most of the marchers could be characterized as angry white kids with really good teeth. The looters ran wild for two whole nights, but after the NYPD regrouped and made four hundred arrests, they knocked it off for a while and went off to sell or redistribute their pilferage.

In the springtime, when demonstrators "liberated" a portion of park near City Hall and renamed it Abolition Park, rather than send the entire protest community into the streets each night, the city let them keep it. The park attracted white anarchists and homeless people, who arrived when word spread that they could sleep outside. Tents were erected and three meals a day were donated by restaurants and well-to-do donors. Activists at first used NYPD barricades to create a police line, and then rearranged them to close off the area they controlled. They established checkpoints at which they questioned everyone who was walking through, asking who they were and why they were there before deciding whether they could come in. Essentially, Abolition Park became a public area taken over by a group that was basically doing stop, question, and frisk at every gate. If they didn't like you, they didn't let you in; if you went in anyway, they followed you around and harassed you. People started getting pushed around and beaten up. Belongings were stolen. Then they added their own security force, run by a big, tall guy with a cowboy hat and a hammer who called himself the Sheriff. Between their surveillance, their checkpoints, their questioning and profiling of innocent people, it took them about ten days to actually become what they abhorred.

The street medics are a volunteer collective of professionals and amateurs who provide medical advice and assistance to demonstrators across the country. Some are doctors, some nurses, most seem simply to be interested citizens who want to do their part. They carry first-aid bags, and if somebody gets hit in the head or maced or worse, they treat them on the scene. The street medics moved in and set up shop.

Not long thereafter, they left. I find their statement, posted within the park and within the movement, very telling. It said,

> There will no longer be an organized street medic presence at City Hall. We are following Black leadership by shifting our attention to mutual aid and community care. We will be establishing an off-site, mobile/pop-up facility to serve the City Hall Encampment, the local houseless community, and our comrades harmed by the carceral system. While planning for this next step we will continue to provide support and communication to any remaining medical providers.
>
> We are no longer able to maintain our presence at City Hall because of a lack of safety and consent. While street medics routinely operate in dangerous conditions, medics

at City Hall have been repeatedly assaulted physically, emotionally, and sexually. Patients have also been attacked while
under our care.

While we cannot accept the abusive conditions at City
Hall, we are proud to have been part of the abolitionist space
and worked alongside those caring for the people. We look
forward to serving our comrades and community in our new
capacity.

They had begun with a utopian vision of a society without police. In less
than two weeks they recognized they needed a security force, and the first
thing it did was become abusive. Policing is complicated. Its administration is not for everybody.

How do we cut through the rhetoric and politics and return to a place
where we're giving fair and good policing to New York City and America
as a whole? Will policing come around to change? Of course. Over the past
fifty years I have seen its growth and the profession's increasing willingness
to adapt to new conditions.

After having fallen into civic disrepair, New York City reemerged in the
1990s because the police made it safe again. And for twenty-five years it
was the city's safety that allowed New York to be clean and prosperous, to
encourage businesses to arrive and grow and expand, to welcome the economic and social boom of national and international tourism, to provide
jobs and investment and social benefits for the working, middle, and
wealthy classes all. The NYPD consistently earned credit for creating and
maintaining this era of good feeling. With the advent of criminal justice
reform, that went away and crime and disorder once again exploded. Sadly,
at some point I came to feel that, despite the efforts of so many highly
talented, wise, sensitive, and positive thinkers with whom I have worked,

all of our gains have been erased. I fight that uncomfortable thought every day and I refuse to allow it to take hold.

I am all in favor of reimagining the police mission with a look toward the future. None of it is cost-free, of course. It will take money and resolve to turn the country around. Defunding defending—taking money away from the fundamental function of law enforcement at a time when there are so many critical and identifiable needs—is a truly bad idea.

How do we fix this?

It took twenty-five years of carefully adjusting the criminal justice process to make New York the safest big city in America. It took less than a year to break that. How do we fix this? The same way we broke it: quickly. None of these reform laws were without value, but each needed some critical, in most cases small, adjustments. We can do that when the legislature or the people who elect them decide we want fewer victims and that right now we are having too many.

First, I would emphasize the importance of the police. We are an essential element of democracy and because of our centrality and policing's checkered racial history we need to pay strong attention to our system of accountability and control. The processes of selection, training, and evaluation must be improved throughout the country. Increased diversity should be a stated goal. We are no longer a monolith. I encourage all candidates to enter and bring their perspectives to the profession.

In the age of heightened technology, I would mandate the development of a "color-blind" algorithm system that would determine whether releasing a suspect was safe based on their arrest history, on whether they had committed crimes while on release from previous arrests, on whether those crimes were violent, and if so how many. I would encourage the creation of a scoring system that would tell us that we are releasing someone into the public who has statistically proven that he presents a real danger to his fellow citizens and neighbors. And in those cases where people were deemed a danger to the community, I would expedite their trials.

I would return discretion to the officers as to when to issue a DAT summons or make an arrest.

I would lobby to reengineer the bail law to give judges the discretion to hold suspects they determine are dangerous to the public. No more double-shift rapists. New York is the only state in which judges do not have that power.

I would have the prosecutors resume prosecuting the crimes that the neighborhoods are complaining about.

I would lobby for a law that says if a person is resisting arrest and an officer restrains them in a manner that has been sanctioned by the police department as safe, and in which he or she has been trained, the officer is not subject to arrest.

I would continue and improve neighborhood policing. It is working. To weave new ideas into the existing police force I would institute in-service training for those who have been on the job longer than the new ideas have been in practice. All officers would rotate through a neighborhood policing program sometime in their career to make it personal. The worst way for cops to meet people is on a call; the community members are already in crisis and the encounters are likely to be filled with tension. Plus it is likely to be brief and perhaps too tightly focused, because the police business model demands a quick resolution of whatever problem is presented in order to get on to the next one. The best way to create any relationship is under nonstressful circumstances. Investment in neighborhood policing promotes that change.

Police are supposed to handle crime. But as the country becomes aware of the disparate and heightened effects of the coronavirus on communities of color as opposed to white communities, in many circles racism is being considered a public-health emergency. Perhaps there is a progressive way forward that may present an opportunity to combine community safety with community health, with neighborhood policing as a catalyst. Police will to have to coordinate and cross over with issues of health because those are increasingly the problems they are being called upon to respond to.

Because one size does not fit all—you don't respond to a heroin addict in the same fashion that you respond to someone on meth—I would increase de-escalation training, the training of officers to recognize the varying symptoms among out-of-control drug users, the different types of drugs, and how to respond to them. We gave New York cops instruction over and above what they were receiving in the Academy because the rest of government, health, and hospitals couldn't deal with the problems and always called us.

Too few have been asked to do too much with too little for too long. And it has finally caught up with us. I would divest the police of such social-service responsibilities as dealing with the homeless, the mentally ill, the addicted—but only when excellent programs have been designed and are in place at agencies specifically empowered and able to fulfill them. That will cost a lot of municipal money, but if it solves a problem that has expanded crime and exploded disorder, it will have been well worth the investment.

But what is the actual goal? Even if there existed a parallel response system with mental-health capacity, in the field and responsive twenty-four hours a day, seven days a week . . . Even if you built these fantasy Neighborhood Nice teams in which ordinary citizens go and gently ask the neighbor who is causing a huge noise disturbance, or has a raging party, to stop . . . The Nice team is not carrying a gun and is not introducing use of force into the equation. In real life, those scenes are not going to go very well for very long. Those are going to be situations that end really badly. At which point the cops will show up.

And yet those situations—knocking on the door, telling the loud party that it needs to stop—aren't the kind that result in a police officer using force and ending up in national headlines. So what are we trying to avoid? What are we really winning if we spend large amounts of money to build parallel systems?

Distrust of the police is epidemic. One means of dissipating it would be the expanded distribution and use of body cameras. Keep them on. A body camera mysteriously out of service during a problematic police encounter only deepens racial suspicions. Because cell phones generally capture the disputed response, not the original action, and because officers can be counted on to do their job, body-cam footage is more often than not exculpatory, so early release of those videos would provide context that would likely abate the level of tension, not increase it. Increased transparency at a time of heightened controversy is becoming more and more important.

I see this crisis as an opportunity to bring all sides together to find common ground, not in the midst of chaotic street demonstrations, but in the calm of an academic setting. I would encourage the convening of an executive session at a major university, bringing in the best minds in the country to a series of seminars resulting in the creation of a modern Policing Commission—an expansion of what President Obama was trying to do with his 21st-Century Policing model before the world took a turn for the worse. This would provide the impetus for a new president, in one of his first acts, to rethink and reimagine the profession and define policing as one of the most important elements in America. What better forum?

Although the country is now going through a social and racial upheaval, I am pleased to say I believe we are not far from achieving our goals. What seems to have been lost in the anger and rhetoric is the fact that as recently as 2019, the NYPD had reduced crime in New York City to its lowest point since the Dodgers played in Brooklyn. New York did it, and so can America. The country's daily safety is in the profession's hands, and with the collaboration between cops and community in programs like neighborhood policing, predictive policing, precision policing, and with judicious leadership, a willingness to root out both bias and the biased, and a refusal to tolerate either brutality or aggression, we can recognize each other's humanity—we can see each other.

Epilogue

We began thinking about and working on this book in 2016, when I was in the last months of my second tenure as New York City's police commissioner. To publish in spring 2021 meant that writing was essentially completed in late 2020. Since then, the policing profession and public safety in America have been through many storms. We predicted a number of them, because, as I often say, "What's old is new again," and when we reread the book in preparation for its paperback release we were gratified to see that fifty years of experience paid off in predictions and prescriptions that are as valid now, as we write in winter 2021, as they were in autumn 2020—or in any years of my half-century career.

But there were also changes we felt we had to address, particularly with regard to spiking homicides and gun crime, a concerning increase in domestic unrest, the Capitol insurrection of January 6, 2021, and unprecedented attacks on the very need for and legitimacy of this thing that has and will keep us safe: good policing. It is with all this in mind that we offer this epilogue for the 2022 paperback edition.

It began like almost any other attack on a defended position: The attackers wanted what was inside. The defenders had an idea that something might be coming but not enough good intelligence about what, exactly—nor sufficient preparations to face it.

The attackers gathered to hear exhortations about the righteousness of their cause. "If you don't fight . . . you're not going to have a country anymore," their leader told them. They armed themselves and were directed to march to the perceived site of their grievances, and then threw an initial wave against the stronghold, and then another and another.

This wasn't Bunker Hill, or Little Round Top, or the ammo dump at Long Binh during the Tet Offensive. It was January 6, 2021, and it was an insurrectionist attack on the United States Capitol in the midst of a symbolic but legally crucial stage in our country's 224-year tradition of peaceful transfers of power. The attackers weren't redcoats or rebs or NVA and Viet Cong, they were a summoned collection of conspiracy theorists, malcontents, knuckleheads, ne'er-do-wells, and others from all walks of life, including soldiers and cops. The stakes were simultaneously radically lower than those other examples and, if possible, just as high. This wasn't wartime, by any stretch of the imagination, but there was a body count.

I think our union, and the institutions that uphold it, were at risk that day. Cops saved them.

It's worth remembering that initially, pundits and press insisted that the police were in on it, that cops had abdicated their defensive duties or even purposefully opened the gates. In shock, the media looked around for someone to blame and pointed at the officers. It took days for video to come out, showing heroic acts like that of Capitol Police Officer Eugene Goodman, leading the mob away from the people he was sworn to protect, or bravery and suffering like that of Metropolitan Police Officers Daniel Hodges and Michael Fanone.

The attack on the Capitol caused a lot of people to remember what cops do. In its very first words, the Constitution of the United States speaks of establishing justice, ensuring domestic tranquility, providing for the common defense, promoting the general welfare, and securing the blessings of liberty—and good policing contributes to them all. That was made manifest on January 6. Unfortunately, a level of aggression and potential sedition was made manifest, too—despite the denials of many people who participated, others who traffic in opinions, and some members of Congress. It "was not an isolated event," FBI Director Christopher Wray told the Senate in March. "The problem of domestic terrorism has been metastasizing across the country for a long time now and it's not going away anytime soon."

This was demonstrated dramatically on January 6. There was an insurrection against the government of the United States! It came close to upsetting our democracy. Fortunately, the United States held, but those events shook our foundation and demanded a 9/11-style investigation. I am strongly disappointed that it did not occur; I would have been pleased to have served in it.

I often say that cops count and police matter. But for the actions of the Capitol and Metropolitan police that day, we would have lost our democracy. There was a deliberate, concerted effort on the part of the sitting president of the United States and his minions to reverse the election and prevent the inauguration of a duly elected president. It is clear that, going forward, we're going to have to watch very closely that this doesn't happen again.

What is the role of police in defending society in that moment? Critical. Essential. Police must be centrists. They can't be politicized. It was highly concerning to see the government try to politicize several federal agencies. On the local level, whether working for a Republican, Democratic, or Independent mayor or governor, it is vital for law enforcement to resist being pulled too closely into their orbit. Don't drink the Kool-Aid! One of my successors as New York City police commissioner fell in line behind Rudy Giuliani, who himself clearly took a huge gulp when he tried to turn the 2020 election for Trump.

Watching large numbers of insurrectionists streaming out of the Capitol Building following its invasion—streaming out of a crime scene!—television viewers could be forgiven for wondering where all the cops were and why they weren't restraining these people with zip ties, putting them on the ground, and preparing them to face responsibility for their actions.

We certainly had restrained turnstile jumpers in the New York subway, and this was obviously a much more serious breach.

The problem, as I saw it, was that the two principal responding agencies, the Metropolitan Police and the Capitol Police, were spread too thin. The violators outnumbered the cops, and effecting an individual arrest ties up two officers, if not more. The cops could have spent all day arresting people, and probably would have loved to arrest the men and women who had spent the afternoon attacking and assaulting them, but the most important objective was to empty the place and finalize the process of certifying the election. *Let's clear the building so we can get this vote done.*

Clearing a building is not unlike dispelling a riot; arrests actually distract from the task at hand. To effect arrests you need apprehension teams; you need to get those teams to the arrest site while maintaining sufficient personnel to continue all necessary force protection and force projection efforts.

Say it's a melee on a Friday night at a bar closing in any town in America. Everyone is leaving and suddenly a massive fight breaks out with fifteen or twenty people involved and only five or six cops on the corner to handle it. The police objective in that case is to make the brawlers stop fighting and disperse. Whoever is on the street, bloodied and injured, is going to the hospital. If the cops can grab one or two who are witnessed dishing out more than they are taking, great, but that is not the goal. Really what they are doing is clearing the place.

My sense was that, for the Metropolitan Police, their goal was to get there and clear that building. I have heard nothing about planning procedures for mass arrests. There is a lack of clarity on nabbing anyone. I don't know that a processing center was ever set up. Certainly not by the Capitol Police; they were just basically going to defend the perimeter. The Metropolitan Police probably had protocols for arrest, as they would for any demonstration, but the crime scene was on the Capitol grounds, and there are intricate jurisdiction issues there. So who knows.

But this is part of the frustration. These are unanswered questions that a 9/11-style National Commission investigation would pursue. We have the House of Representatives' Select Committee to Investigate the January 6th Attack on the United States Capitol, formed to look into the events before, during, and after the insurrection. But because of the limitations on its powers and the lack of participation on the part of many of those who have the most information about the events, that committee is unlikely to produce a 9/11-style report.

At about the same time as the attack on the Capitol, national data began to show a surge in violent crime that caused people to remember the main reason Sir Robert Peel told us we have police: to prevent crime and disorder. It's far too early to expect much academic insight into this crime surge, which began in many cities during the COVID lockdowns and took off after the murder of George Floyd. Graphs of shootings in New York City show 2020's numbers skyrocketing as May turned into June, and the year ended with a total number nearly double that of 2017, or 2018, or 2019. A decade's progress lost in a year.

Right now it appears that, in New York, 2021 is in the realm of 2020's numbers, so perhaps it's not getting worse, but that's cold comfort to those experiencing the shootings. That is also not the case in many other large cities in America. As 2021 came to a close, the majority of America's major cities were experiencing dramatic increases in shootings and murders; some of them historic highs. This increase, in both percentage and numbers, has never happened before in the history of the republic.

Some on the left stubbornly claim that crime is not actually up. This view relies on measuring "crime" as the aggregate of the seven major crimes tracked by the FBI's unified crime reporting: murder, rape, robbery, aggravated assault, burglary, grand larceny, and grand larceny auto. Numerically, grand larceny comprises the vast majority of the overall crime rate. Pretty much any American city could see its homicide rate triple, or even quadruple, but if it also experienced a 5 percent decrease in larceny, its overall crime rate would go down. COVID kept millions of people inside, and as a result larceny declined. So many observers on the left say "overall crime is down," which in late 2021 is true but, once again, cold comfort for those experiencing violence.

Some have also pooh-poohed the current situation by pointing out that today's crime is nowhere near as bad as at the height of the crime wave, circa 1990. This is also true, but one could say the same thing about COVID versus the 1918 flu. As of September 2021, the number of deaths from each pandemic was about the same, approximately 650,000, but America's population today is nearly 332 million versus 103 million in 1918. That's cold comfort to those experiencing the virus.

Some on the right hyperventilate about the largest violent-crime increases by percent in decades. This is disingenuous. Pre-pandemic violent crime was generally so low, compared to 1990, that even small numerical increases create large percentage repercussions. New York City saw 2,245 murders in 1990, compared to 468 in 2020. Nevertheless, the 2020 total is up from the modern-era low of 289 in 2018, and it's the highest murder total since 2012. That's a shocking jump. The increases are real.

So what is causing this?

The long answer is that there are a host of possible contributors to the homicide-and-gunfire increase. Obviously, we have just experienced—and may experience again—an unprecedented global pandemic. Jobs and schools were radically disrupted. Huge numbers of offenders were released into America's streets from prisons and jails, and new court cases all but ground to a halt, sending legitimate suspects back to where the crimes occurred.

In many places, however, the crime increase preceded the pandemic. As I have discussed, the closing of mental institutions throughout America created a social and economic disaster the repercussions of which the country is still dealing with fifty years later because we don't have any place to put the former patients. The mental illness issue compounds crime, disorder, and homelessness, and impacts so many aspects of society. And although the pandemic was a global event, no other first-world nations have seen increases like ours. So what else might it be?

Frankly, while progress and improvement are constantly necessary, the criminal justice reform pendulum has swung too far too fast. Across the country, newly elected progressive prosecutors have consistently deemphasized prosecution and established alternative justice programs.

During the COVID pandemic, the court system was basically emptied. With courts not in session and prisons cleared out because of concerns over widespread contagion, there was a crying need for the cops to control streets that were more crowded than ever with known felons who faced fewer restraints. Fifty to sixty percent of the New York City jail and prison population has significant mental health issues and drug addictions, so the thousands of men and women let out of Rikers were already a disturbed population, now back out on the streets.

What about alternative justice programs?

There is hope in some circles that alternative justice mechanisms, sometimes referred to as restorative justice, are the future of criminal justice, but that may be quite a bit premature. Many communities have them, but they are by no means widely in place. And they are hit-or-miss. For the most part, such mechanisms mean cops or prosecutors divert low-level cases away from the courts and into community justice centers. Trained mediators at these centers work with perpetrators and victims so that perpetrators can better understand the impact of their acts and victims can get resolution and restitution. In many instances, this can be very effective and very powerful, particularly with first-time offenders. Victims frequently want apologies and an acknowledgment that they've been harmed more than they want criminal-justice outcomes.

But there is an elasticity to alternative justice, and I believe it may be reaching its snapping point. Two of the biggest concerns for any community considering alternative justice have to do with which defendants get referred and whether there are consequences. Recidivists—people who have proven immune to alternative justice, who after being released from incarceration commit crimes time and time again, and who pose a danger to others—and felons accused of low-level crimes are not good candidates for AJ, as it's called. And it must be clear and consistent that whenever a defendant fails out of AJ, courts have to take him or her for adjudication and go the distance. It takes some doing to fail out of the alternative justice process, but even when it happens the courts will sometimes say, "The cops sent you to AJ preemptively; you have failed out, but now that you've come back to us, we're going to dismiss it anyway." In other words, perpetrators learn *I do the crime, I get caught, but all I've got to do then is nod my way through AJ. I don't really learn anything. If I pass I'm back on the street, and if I flunk out the court won't take me anyway, so I'm back on the street either way.* That's not acceptable, and it parallels a general sense that the kindness behind our desire for less intrusive, less punitive criminal justice is being interpreted by criminals as weakness.

Criminal Justice Reform?

The Criminal Justice Reform movement is in the ascendance. Laws are being passed with the intent of decreasing incarceration rates and lessening the impact of arrest and prison records on people's lives, often people of color. The goals are laudable. Unfortunately, during the writing and enactment of these laws, representatives of the judiciary and law enforcement have not routinely been consulted. The results have been catastrophic.

What we are seeing around the country is clearly the result of the well-intended but ill-conceived criminal justice and bail reform movements. Legislatures—often without consultation with police, judges, and district attorneys, who have informed perspective on these matters—have passed sweeping bail reform, and in the case of New York State, drastically limited judges' ability to jail and incapacitate violent recidivists. Legislatures, court cases, and settlements have continued to constrict law-enforcement authorities with respect to quality-of-life issues and low-level crimes. Increasingly in America we have fostered a sense of lawlessness and put police in a position where they cannot enforce the law.

In New York this is compounded by the raising of the age of criminal responsibility from sixteen to eighteen years. Now defendants under the age of eighteen are tried in Family Court, where prosecutors do not have full access to their previous records and therefore can't make fully informed arguments regarding serious crimes. A finding of guilty in Family Court is a disposition, not even a conviction, and is routinely sealed. In the name of a desired decrease in incarceration, people who have committed crimes are being returned to the streets of the communities they terrorize.

In California there is most notably a total disregard for the law as it relates to shoplifting. Gangs of people are going into stores, emptying shelves, and then leaving. Clerks and even security guards are instructed not to interfere with the criminals because no thefts below the $950 threshold are arrestable. Take that in: If a cop is called to a 7-Eleven or Walgreens in San Francisco because someone has stolen under $950 worth of goods, she must write a citation to appear in court at a later date; that theft is not even an arrestable offense. Basically she must let them go. Anyone in San Francisco can pick up $949.99 worth of goods, get a citation, and keep on moving. We're never going to see them again. Police are handicapped in their ability to deal with theft of less than $950 both in terms of the ability to arrest and also whether progressive district attorneys will prosecute. So we have created a criminal justice system with no teeth.

Increasingly, state laws are being passed allowing individuals to carry concealed weapons into commercial establishments such as restaurants, movie theaters, bars, and amusement parks, with very limited restrictions. I predict in the months and years ahead we're going to see a great deal of difficulty controlling behavior involving firearms as a result. People are now being authorized, and in some instances encouraged, to carry those weapons with them everywhere. There is a growing momentum in this country of lawlessness and potential vigilantism. Ready access to firearms—we believe there are approximately four hundred million in the US—will increase the peril.

Another significant contributor has been police withdrawal. There are a lot of components to this. In some places, staffing is drastically diminished, either because localities defunded or because officers retired or resigned at accelerated rates.

The movement to defund the police has led to widespread negative consequences. At first these consequences were unseen, but now as the results of the various defunding initiatives have begun to swamp vulnerable communities, they are becoming clearer. Fortunately, the tide seems to be turning. Not quickly enough, as far as I'm concerned.

Which is the lunacy of the Defund the Police movement. We are literally undermining the system of—and this has become a dirty term—law and order. Because it includes no deterrent, the main thrust of the criminal justice reform movement seems to have the effect of encouraging lawless behavior. We are seeing the rise of abnormal behavior that in many effects is encouraged by laws that no longer either are enforced or penalized. The new Manhattan district attorney is making it clear that he is not going to put anybody in jail for a whole series of crimes, including some I think of as serious offenses, particularly when repeated. If a shoplifter or turnstile jumper understands that he's never going to jail, he'll just keep committing the same crime.

For its part, the NYPD has been effectively demoralized to the point that they will not effectuate assertive policing—not aggressive policing, but assertive policing. (There's a difference.) *Why should I risk arresting a shoplifter if I have to throw them to the ground, a person who will aggressively resist my stopping him, and wind up being sued because I* inadvertently *put my arm around his neck and be arrested for using an illegal chokehold?*

There is a confluence of actions happening at the same time that undermine the ability of the police to enforce the law. We are shaping police departments that in many respects are discouraged from responding. The public will be furious, and rightly so. *I've got a problem and the cops don't show up. They* tell *me they're not going to show up!!* And who are they going to blame? The cops. The police profession is in its toughest position in fifty years.

In Burlington, Vermont, a city of 45,000, in June 2020, after a concerted defund effort, the city council slashed the authorized size of its police force from 105 to 74. With fewer and fewer officers available for patrol, acting chief Jon Murad had to create a priority response plan. He divided calls for assistance into three categories: priority one, priority two, and priority three. Depending on how many officers are available, the plan performs law-enforcement triage. Priority one calls have to do with people's safety, such as assaults, domestic violence, robberies, DUIs, or a motor vehicle crash with an injury or fatality, and they will always get as rapid a response as possible. Priority two calls are more situational, such as burglaries and disturbances and mental health issues—a rapid response will depend upon whether the crimes are in progress or whether someone's safety is impinged. Priority three calls are basically quality-of-life crimes—larcenies from a building, noise complaints, public intoxication, public urination. When staffing is low, these priority three calls get answered irregularly, if at all. Instead, the Burlington police "stack" priority three calls, meaning that only after calls involving physical safety are addressed do cops get dispatched to the others. "That late report of a burglary—they got burgled last night, now it's Tuesday morning—you guys go handle that." Along with the priority response plan, Murad also created new "community support liaison" social worker positions to address mental health issues and homelessness, and he increased the number of unarmed civilian "community service" positions to answer quality-of-life complaints, but calls from the public are still stacked about 15 percent of the time.

With fewer cops, Burlington, to its city council's surprise but not mine, saw violent crime rise. Annual gunfire incidents went from two to a dozen; aggravated assaults increased 25 percent.

The essential equation is: defund the police and crime rises by multiples. The reverse is also true: More cops, less crime.

This was not the result expected by those in Burlington who had put defunding into effect. After more than a year of turmoil, during which cops left in large numbers, the city council made efforts to restaff and even offered new cash incentives to undo what they had done, but the cops felt unsupported and unappreciated. As patrol numbers got thinner, so did services, although Murad's plan has maintained response so far. Austin, Texas, lost 17 percent total headcount and unilaterally stopped responding to their equivalent of priority-three calls. They just wouldn't go anymore, at all. Burlington was down 32 percent total headcount, 43 percent on the road, but tried as much as possible to keep services available.

The austerity policies that Burlington and Austin put into place, which advocates saw as re-envisioning police and realigning budget, but which cops saw as a punitive path toward abolition, contributed to the growing lack of confidence and trust in the police. By making the police less effective without actually building any alternatives, advocates left victims hanging. Why call the police when they're not coming? Even as police departments were trying to increase trust, other governmental entities were creating conditions that worked in the opposite direction—without creating new systems to address the gap.

In some places, there are new local laws or policies that hobble police, like prohibitions against foot pursuits in Chicago, limitations on reasonable suspicion investigations in Washington State, and the recently overturned "diaphragm law" in New York that criminalized the lawful use of force. And in all places, members of the profession feel unsupported. To a certain extent, it's as irrelevant to a local cop that this or that progressive reform happened far away and doesn't directly affect her as it is to a local activist that Minneapolis is nowhere near his town and no one in his local department has ever perpetrated anything like the murder of George Floyd. Every cop in the country experienced anti-police protests, negative media attention, fair-weather politicians, and withered public support.

From the cops' perspective, every new development seems designed to incentivize them not to engage when they should. The list is long:

- the constant threat of being the next viral video or the next scapegoat

- fewer and fewer prosecutions or consequences for criminals, which renders tickets, citations, and arrests (and the work that goes into them) less and less meaningful

- bail reform and de-incarceration putting perpetrators right back on the street

- rioters afforded greater freedom to destroy than the police are afforded powers to protect

- knee-jerk rules banning foot pursuits and ill-conceived laws prohibiting safe physical-control techniques

- arbitrary political decisions to reallocate, diminish, or remove police funding

- assertions that cops' skills are insufficient to handle things cops have long been the only ones handling and that they handle properly and well 99.9 percent of the time

- calls for police transformation that exclude the police, as well as judges, district attorneys, and other law-enforcement elements, either by barring them from participating in reform efforts or by ignoring their expertise when they offer to help shape new directions

- accusations of racism, systemic racism, and irremediable bias

- attacks on qualified immunity, and the attendant risk of being sued

- capricious and uninformed oversight by people with no experience in the field and no basis of knowledge, and the attendant risk of being disciplined or fired

- new laws limiting longtime legitimate police powers, and the attendant risk of being criminally tried.

A compounding issue is vaccine mandates. I am perplexed by the resistance among many officers to what I strongly believe is a lifesaving requirement. I just wish they would stop resisting.

I support mandatory vaccination. Cops object to it widely. I just don't understand that. In a profession in which contact with individuals of unknown health is constant, why would anyone want to risk their own health and that of their family, friends, and neighbors? Cops will run into a burning building to save a partner; they will take a bullet for them but won't take a vaccine that would protect them from getting or passing along a terrifyingly deadly disease, even though they're sitting in the same car, at close quarters, for eight hours a day. The government mandates many things—polio vaccines, driver's licenses, fishing licenses, height requirements to get on amusement park rides—with no public objection. Cops don't want mandated vaccines. Why not? I don't have the faintest idea.

Talking to cops, they can't even explain it. Is it because they just don't want to be told what to do? Actually, cops are among the people least resistant to being told what to do; they are in a profession where sergeants, lieutenants, and captains tell them what to do all the time. But cops are also, by and large, relatively independent characters. One reason so many become cops is that they are independent thinkers. I think it comes down to the sense that the very parties telling them that vaccination is the right and best thing to do are also the parties that have historically spoken down to them, haven't made the effort to understand them, and the cops feel don't listen to them anyway. It is not a rational objection, but it is strongly personal. They are clearly not acting in their own best interests. In fact, in

2021 by far the largest number of police deaths was caused by COVID. Ninety-three percent more police lives were lost to COVID than to violent acts against them.

The issue of religious objections to the mandates is, I believe, going to get kicked up to the Supreme Court. New York City saw a jump in the number of religious exemptions being applied for, and the city rejected a lot of them. *You are a Seventh-day Adventist? How long have you been with the church, seven days? You saw the light when vaccines were mandated?*

And yet none of this means that good police departments don't want to identify avenues for improvement and reform. Around the country, departments are embracing new ways of working. There's the Police Executive Research Forum (PERF)'s Integrating Communications, Assessment, and Tactics (ICAT), which helps slow down and de-escalate situations that don't involve firearms but may have a mental health component. There's Crisis Intervention Team (CIT) training concerning mental health, some of which involves departments exploring co-deploying officers with social workers, like programs in Colorado and Oregon. There are new use-of-force policies, increasingly adopted at the state level, that require de-escalation, deceleration, duties of care, duties to intervene, and duties to report.

What can be done in the face of this demoralization and crime increase? There are paths to improved public safety, but they take resources. My experience, echoed by academics like Peter Moskos at John Jay College and Cory Haberman at the University of Cincinnati, says a part of the solution is precision policing. The relative success the NYPD is currently seeing with regard to tamping down the murder spike and freezing the increase in shootings stems in part from the fact that the rhetoric in the 2021 New York City mayoral election turned to crime, but it has more to do with the fact that Police Commissioner Dermot Shea took the opportunity to double down with federal partners on gang takedowns. (He had to use the feds because DAs in Manhattan, Brooklyn, and the Bronx won't prosecute.) Gang takedowns are effective examples of the focused crime-and-disorder enforcement part of precision policing.

All this reform won't matter if we don't have cops. And this brings us to the biggest challenge of all: the retention and recruitment time bomb that had been ticking since the summer of 2014 and exploded in 2020.

Cops are idealists. They take the job because they believe in possibility—the possibility of safe communities, of neighbors who can go about their lives unafraid, of the wayward brought back to the fold. They believe both in the need for consequences for bad acts and in the possibility of wrongdoers being redeemed. More than anything, cops believe in the possibility of preventing crime and disorder.

This may sound romantic, but I believe in the possibility of redemption. That's the essence of Broken Windows policing; we go after minor transgressions before they become major. People who might have been on the path to criminality do not continue on that path. We change behavior. That's the heart and soul of where I come from, and the twenty-five-year decrease in crime in New York City is proof that it works.

But that sense of possibility can coagulate into cynicism. Shift after shift, cops routinely see awful things—car crashes, injured victims, dead bodies—and absorb them on behalf of others. Less routinely, but not rarely, they see evil—abused children, rape, murder—and they absorb that, too. And atop it all, they see many of the possibilities in which they believe being thwarted. This was especially true in 2020. Across the country, communities are slowly drifting back to violence, people who are arrested face fewer and fewer consequences, and there is fear in the air.

Violent language has increasingly taken over American public life. Rhetoric has hardened and now strongly affects how people act in the street, how people treat each other. At an Idaho town hall hosted by a right-wing activist recently, one of his supporters got up and said, "When do we get to use the guns? That's not a joke, I mean literally, where's the line? How many elections are they going to steal before we kill these people?" Someday soon, at a school board meeting or a rally, some American citizen is going to pick up a weapon and shoot somebody. In fact, it has already happened. Ask Kyle Rittenhouse. And it will be up to the cops to protect the community when it does.

Words matter. This is not new in America; our history is replete with anger. In newspapers and public discourse during the run-up to the Civil War, people said pretty vile stuff. The difference today is that men and women are not basing their opinions on what they read in newspapers or see on the evening newscast or hear live during a partisan oration. Hate speech is assisted tremendously by social media. It is coming at us from everywhere, and it's what cops are up against. Violent talk is not being held unacceptable; it is being encouraged. Right now, politics rewards it, and the police are having to pick up the pieces.

Police exist to prevent crime and disorder. They represent the best interests of the communities they serve. And yet now increasingly there are no holds barred when talking to a police officer; the disrespect and invective directed at cops has exploded exponentially. And ironically, pretty much the only ones in society who are expected to bite their tongue are cops. They are rightly expected to behave in a civil manner, and for the most part they do.

Functional communities need to find common ground on which all can stand. That common ground has now shrunk to the size of a postage stamp. The United States Senate likes to describe itself as the world's greatest deliberative body, but they don't deliberate anymore; there's little interest in coming to the center and making accommodations for the common good. Senators just get in their respective camps and abuse each other; the opposing side is defined not as people with different ideas, but effectively as the enemy. The Republican Party in particular eviscerates anyone who steps out of line. Thirteen Republican senators voted for an infrastructure bill that would benefit not only their constituents but every community in America, and they were almost run out of the party. It is a disappointment and growing concern, as we move further into the twenty-first century, that aided and abetted by unchecked social media both parties are increasingly unwilling to come to the center. We really are two separate nations now. The violent differences make new and unforeseen demands on the profession of policing.

Twenty-first-century technology has played a significant role in fueling the controversies that have increased public resistance to law enforcement, particularly in minority communities. Resistance to police technology informs a significant part of the racial justice movement. Artificial intelligence, drones, facial recognition, and robotics are not trusted by communities that are already ambivalent about the police. ShotSpotter, for instance, is a highly effective law enforcement tool that some activists want to do away with.

ShotSpotter is a sophisticated electronic gunshot detection system in use in several cities around the country. (Full disclosure: I so strongly believe in ShotSpotter's efficacy that I have joined its board of directors and am advocating for its expansion.) When a shot is detected anywhere in the five boroughs of New York City, for example, notification is sent to the NYPD Operations Division, which sends the information to Division Radio, which puts it over the air so cops can respond and also creates a 911 call. (Believe it or not, many times guns are fired and nobody calls 911. Sometimes people who get shot are not completely forthright with the cops who arrive to investigate.)

The effect is substantial. The ShotSpotter information allows the department to respond—sometimes to people who have been wounded, sometimes to crime scenes, sometimes to disturbances—and aids immeasurably in conducting an investigation. It enables police officers to pinpoint locations where people were fired on, so we can go and collect ballistic evidence on the street in an effort to solve the crime.

Given that up to 80 percent of shots fired in various cities are never called in to the police because people just don't feel the police are going to come, ShotSpotter has proven to be a highly successful means of understanding how much crime and disorder is going on in a given neighborhood.

And yet recently in Chicago, an aldermen wanted to do away with the program. Why? Because he felt ShotSpotter brings additional cops into

Black neighborhoods to terrorize the Black community. His feeling is widespread.

But why would the cops be on alert in Black neighborhoods? Because evidence and collected data indicate that's where shots are being fired. A system that was established explicitly to aid communities in trouble has been totally flipped on its head.

The undermining of technology is being used as a wedge against police. This technology revulsion is fueled in significant part by the idea that it's being used against minorities. *Well, we don't want to report these shots because it just brings the police in to stop and frisk every Black kid in the neighborhood.* But it's not that cops are being redirected from one precinct to another. Cops aren't "coming into" Black neighborhoods; they're already there. I repeat: *Cops are already there!* They are stationed there every day in decentralized precincts, and since the advent of neighborhood policing, in decentralized sectors within precincts. ShotSpotter will help them police more effectively.

What is the good news? Is there a way out?

Sadly, I don't see one coming anytime soon. It's going to require a drastic change in laws, and a drastic change in support for police enforcing those laws. And it will take the entire country wrestling with the encompassing issue of race. Because the reality is that a significant amount of serious crime is committed by the Black population against the Black population. According to the data compiled by the FBI's unified crime reporting, in the year 2020 45.8 percent of the murders in America were perpetrated by Black people, with Black people comprising 55.8 percent of the victims. But Black people make up 13 percent of the US population. This is the third rail of American criminology, about which you still can't speak. But when you look at the sheer amount of crime still being committed in the Black community, it begs for response, help, attention, and resolution. Theirs is without question a community completely worthy and deserving of protection, but there is no national desire to recognize race as a central issue, or even talk about it. It is a conversation no one wants to have.

I do. Broken Windows, CompStat, community policing, precision policing. All the ideas and programs that paid off so handsomely for New York, Boston, and Los Angeles when instituted properly and practiced with care and attention—they will work because they show the community the respect of taking its safety seriously.

America is going to have to make a decision. Do we want to continue defining down the normalcy of bad behavior? Which, by our laws, we have been doing. Due to criminal justice reform, in both New York and Chicago people who have committed egregious crimes, including assault and robbery, have been released on either bail or monitoring, and have then committed murders. There having been no substantial consequence for the initial act of criminality, it can be said that this misguided view of criminal justice has allowed the next ones to occur. Will we, by our practices, encourage people to disobey the law because there is no penalty for doing so? Or will we protect our communities in the lawful and respectful ways they deserve?

In the chapter on race, we talked about fear as the foundation of our discord. Americans today fear so many things—fear of the pandemic, fear of crime, fear of unrest. After the assault on the Capitol, we fear insurrection. We watch antifa clash with the Proud Boys and we fear a twenty-first-century Harpers Ferry or Bloody Kansas. Some people fear racial injustice, some people fear racial unrest, and some people secretly, and often not-so-secretly, fear racial equality.

Because of the ascendance of the criminal justice reform movement, crime was already on the rise before COVID began ravaging America and the world. COVID exacerbated and accelerated the problems when it shut down the criminal justice system. There were no trials. They were letting people out of prison in droves, and what were many of these formerly incarcerated people doing? Committing more crimes. Out-of-control criminal justice reform, the removal of police powers, rampant disrespect for law enforcement and the law itself—a confluence of negatives has surged into a tsunami of crime that is in some ways comparable to the buildup that ultimately erupted into global climate change. All the signs point to a continuing increase in crime and disorder unless we start getting serious about taking control. As with climate change, we've seen it coming; everyone can see it and feel it, and yet at the same time we have a large group of people who don't believe. As with climate change, there are deniers, there are supporters, we are fighting over it and we are seeing larger and more dangerous storms affecting increasingly large numbers of people.

The dramatic increase in murders and shootings over the past several years is not isolated to one area of the United States. The shoplifting issues, the rampant looting disorder, the violence at political rallies and school board meetings, the ginned up disbelief in the tallying of votes in the 2020 presidential election all point to a widespread, and I would say intentionally created decrease in respect for the law. The public trust in all forms of government is declining, and as with climate change we better recognize that this process is accelerating.

There was even an increase in highway speeding. The speed record for the Cannonball—which is a real transcontinental road race, not just a Burt Reynolds/Dom DeLuise movie—was re-set four times in March and April 2020 because no one was on the road to get in the way: not cops, not traffic, hardly anyone at all. So people hollowed out their cars and installed extra gas tanks; they and their friends basically threw in a bunch of junk food and drove as far as they could, as fast as they could. They clipped about five hours off the record. And it was just because these folks said, "Oh, I'll take advantage of this." Not unlike criminals.

W here do we go from here? I wish I had that answer. We are in the midst of a growing storm, but we have the ability to steer out of it before the seas grow wilder.

There is no common ground on law enforcement; there are two parties locked in combat, and everyone is coming out of their corners, swinging away. The old maxim about cops—they hate only two things: change and the way things are? It holds here. The cops are in some ways threatened by the progressive changes being discussed and implemented because, whatever the flaws, they think the new laws handcuff them instead of the criminals, and put them increasingly in harm's way. They also have seen what happens when change occurs overnight and without their input. Their role is to prevent and reduce crime, and they are feeling vindicated by its recent terrible rise. Vindicated but not happy about it, because it makes their job more dangerous. Line-of-duty shooting deaths of police were up 25 percent nationally in 2021, while the National Fraternal Order of Police reports that ambush-style attacks, in which police officers were shot without any warning or opportunity to defend themselves, increased 139 percent—and that was only in the first ten months of the year.

On the other side are people who hate the way things are—the bias, the inequality, the systemic racism—and are advocating for sweeping change. They make solid points, because things must change; being aware of racial and social inequities, we can't keep policing exactly as we've always done. But at the same time, if change is pursued heedlessly, we've seen the result.

What is needed is common ground. Because things do have to change. I was convinced that so much good work had been done over the course of my career that we would never go back to the bad old days. For twenty-five years crime had plunged and I was convinced we had the programs and the will to keep it down forever. I told whoever would listen, "It's never going to go back to the way it was."

I spoke too soon. We are by no means there yet—we are not at 2,245 murders per annum in New York City, as we were in 1990. But things got much worse much faster than anyone thought. It took twenty years to build to that number, but only two years—going into and coming out of COVID—to jump-start the ascent again.

Was there a crime year in the modern era that matched this acceleration? Not in terms of percentage. The New York City murder increase in 2020 was 46.7 percent; the next closest jumps are 1968, at 32.2 percent, and 1971, at 31.2 percent. Steady increases from 1960 to 1969 amounted to 167 percent, but that was over a ten-year period. Murder doubled again from 1970 to 1990, over twenty years.

Nationally, murder was up 29.4 percent in 2020. That's a higher annual percentage increase than in any year since at least 1940. The numerical increase was also the greatest in the past eighty years.

When your job is to come when others call because they're afraid, you exist in an environment of fear. And fear is contagious. But confidence is contagious too. And cops—who come when others call, who overcome fear—can be turned into patient zero for confidence, if we help them do it.

We need to reinvigorate trust. If we can do that, we can bring more people into the profession—new people, with an openness to new ideas, even as they have the same capacity for compassion and the same ability to take dynamic action when it's necessary. Can the trust be repaired? I believe it can, if we maintain a belief that there's something we're working toward, something better.

It has to go both ways—the cops can't be the only ones asked to give and grow, reform and change. We have to find some way to undo or reframe those developments that have disincentivized cops from engaging with the conditions we need them to tackle. We need to encourage officers to hold on while we ease back on the drastic changes made in a moment of national passion. We need them to keep suiting up, because cops count and police matter. The longer they hold, the more time they buy for everyone to join them in Peel's "historic tradition that the police are the public and that the public are the police." The world is not compatible with the naiveté of police abolitionists or police absolutists, but it isn't the dark place the cynics say, either. Most of us can come together on this and make things better. Police can regain the trust of their communities, and communities can regain the trust of their police. I believe in that possibility. Borrowing from Sweet Alice, I believe we can learn to *see* each other, really see each other.

ACKNOWLEDGMENTS

Cops are great storytellers, and I am probably the worst storytelling cop in law enforcement history. We are very grateful to the following for their time and gracious assistance, recollections, and insights in the creation of this book:

Richard Aborn, Bill Andrews, Lou Anemone, Charlie Beck, Fred Booker, David Bratton, Cynthia Brown, Laura Bruno, Lawrence Byrne, David Cagno, Zach Carter, Rick Caruso, Gerry Chaleff, Andre Clansy, Mayor Bill de Blasio, Joe Domanick, Dean Esserman, Ed Flynn, Mitch Garber, Bruce Gyory, Mayor James Hahn, Edna Wells Handy, "Sweet" Alice Harris, Susan Herman, Mike Hillmann, Michael Jacobson, Anna Laszlo, Mark Leap, John Linder, Greg Longworth, Sean Malinowski, Tom Maloney, Rafael Mangual, the Manhattan Institute, Michel Moore, Jimmy O'Neill, Bob O'Toole, Cathy Perez, Connie Rice, Jeff Schlanger, Dermot Shea, Al Sweeney, Tim Swift, JT Thomas, Lawrence Tolliver and his barbershop, Tim Trainor, Ben Tucker, Zachary Tumin, Bob Wasserman, Chuck Wexler, Gene Whyte, and Athena Yerganian.

We also want to thank our editors, Scott Moyers and Mia Council, agent David Black, copyeditor Jane Cavolina and production editor Jennifer Tait, marketer Danielle Plafsky, publicist Gail Brussel, vetting attorney Karen Mayer, and transcriber Ian Wehrle.

Special thanks to:

Jon Murad, a Harvard-educated cop's cop with a steel-trap memory for police history and a great way with words. The best adviser any commissioner could ever hope for.

George Kelling, cocreator of Broken Windows policing. George was my theoretical rock. He participated in this book with great knowledge and grace while battling cancer. Sadly, he passed away before its completion. We walked the talk together, and together we helped to change the American police profession for the better.

Scott Glick, Detective, NYPD. His assistance compiling the photo files for this book and coordinating my social media sites has been invaluable.

My cowriter, the wordsmith Peter Knobler. Peter captured my voice. He cowrote my autobiography, *Turnaround*. In our younger years we were on opposite sides of every barricade. We now find ourselves sharing them. Our collaboration was a mutually satisfying learning experience.

My incredible wife, Rikki Klieman, whose repeated personal and professional sacrifices made so much of this journey so memorable and satisfying. No man could have a better partner and love of his life.

John Miller, ace reporter, writer, raconteur, LAPD deputy chief, FBI assistant director, and my friend, sidekick, and adviser. As NYPD Deputy Commissioner for Intelligence and Counterterrorism, he keeps New York safe from terrorism.

INDEX